FOREIGN POLICY WITHOUT ILLUSION

How Foreign Policy-Making Works and Fails to Work in the United States

Howard J. Wiarda

UNIVERSITY OF MASSACHUSETTS, AMHERST

SCOTT, FORESMAN/LITTLE, BROWN HIGHER EDUCATION
A Division of Scott, Foresman and Company

Glenview, Illinois   London, England

Acknowledgments

Tables and figures from *American Public Opinion and U.S. Foreign Policy 1987*, by John E. Reilly, ed. (Figure 4.1, 4.2 and tables 4.1 through 4.12). Copyright © 1987 by Chicago Council on Foreign Relations. Reprinted with permission of the Chicago Council on Foreign Relations.

Table 5.1 from *Television's Window on the World*, by James F. Larson. Copyright © 1984 by Ablex Publishing Corp. Reprinted with permission of Ablex Publishing Corporation, Norwood, NJ.

Table 10.1 from *Vital Statistics of Congress, 1987-88*, by Norman Ornstein. Copyright © by Congressional Quarterly Inc. Reprinted with permission of Congressional Quarterly, Inc.

Figure 11.2 from The United States Government Manual, 1985-86, 1985.

Library of Congress Cataloging-in-Publication Data

Wiarda, Howard J.
    Foreign policy without illusion: how foreign policy-making works
and fails to work in the United States / Howard J. Wiarda.
        p. cm.
    Includes bibliographical references.
    ISBN 0-673-39762-9
    1. United States—Foreign relations—1945- 2. United States—
Foreign relations administration. I. Title.
JX1417.W53 1990   90-31219
327.73—dc20   CIP

1 2 3 4 5 6-MPC-94 93 92 91 90 89

Contents

¶ CHAPTER TEN   Congress and Foreign Policy   197

CHAPTER ELEVEN   Bureaucratic Politics I: State,
                           Defense, CIA   227

Preface

American foreign policy runs the risk of falling into sad disarray. The possibilities for fragmentation and incoherence or creeping paralysis, immobilization, and even sclerosis are strongly present. Many Americans are unaware of the profound and deep-rooted social and political forces that have led to our present, precarious position and of the gravity of the crisis. They think that a small reform here or a modest adjustment there will be sufficient to fix the problem, or that a change of administrations or presidents will do it. But the argument of *Foreign Policy Without Illusion* is that reform will not be easy, since the looming ills of our foreign policy are closely related to the kind of society America has become. As America has become more politicized, partisan, ideological, and often divided in recent decades, so has American foreign policy. It is unlikely that foreign policy will change much until American society and culture change. And, as that is unlikely to happen soon, our conflict over foreign policy and the threat of an incoherent or paralyzed policy-making process are likely to be with us for a long time. Although on some issues and in some areas our policy is actually quite good, it is clear that we are struggling, and the possibilities for a logjam are menacing.

American public opinion is now clearly more divided over foreign-policy issues than it was before Vietnam, making the achievement of a consensus on any complex issue very difficult. Interest groups have multiplied and increased in strength to the point of making the country very tough to govern, and some of these groups have privatized whole areas of foreign policy for themselves. The media are no longer neutral reporters of foreign-policy issues but are themselves protagonists (and sometimes highly biased ones) in the process. The Washington-based think tanks, organized along ideological lines, the warring among powerful new and old lobbies, and the intense politicization of foreign policy add further elements of conflict. Congress and the White House are often at loggerheads, each trying to gain partisan advantages from the other's mistakes. Competition among foreign-affairs bureaucracies—the State Department, the Defense Department, the Central Intelligence Agency, and the National Security Council—is frequently intense, and the involvement in foreign policy of a whole host of new bureaucracies—the Treasury (trade and international debt issues), Justice (drugs and immigration issues), Interior, Commerce, Labor, and Agriculture Departments—has made policy-making even more difficult.

What can be done—if anything—about easing some of these difficulties? And how is it that even with all these problems we still manage, more than occasionally, to carry out a foreign policy that is more or less coherent, more or less rational, and more or less sensible? These questions lie at the heart of this book.

Foreign Policy Without Illusion tries to come to grips with the processes of American foreign policy and why policy often goes astray or ends up adrift. It seeks to comprehend what has happened to us as a nation and as a people that explains why our foreign policy is so controversial and often in trouble. It presents American foreign policy, and particularly the processes of American foreign policy-making, as it actually is, not as we wish it to be—in short, "without illusion." It is a "tough" book in this regard, and raises some very difficult and disturbing questions. It offers no quick-and-easy solutions; there are none, and the sooner we recognize that, the better off we will be. But, at the same time, the book also recognizes our successes and that the system does work—albeit often slowly and painfully.

Three important influences have gone into the writing of this book. First, for many years I lived abroad, studying politics and social change in both developing and developed nations—a field of specialization called comparative politics—because I am interested in how different countries work or fail to work. I assumed (and still, deep down, do assume) that the knowledge and understanding I tried to convey in my studies and books might have a long-term, positive impact on U.S. policy toward the areas about which I wrote.

Then came a long stint in Washington with the American Enterprise Institute for Public Policy Research (AEI), one of the country's major think tanks, which provided a marvelous opportunity to observe foreign policy-making firsthand and to participate in the process. It gave me access to the White House, the National Security Council, the Congress, State, Defense, CIA, and a host of other agencies. Because AEI was thought at home and abroad to be a prime source of the administration's policy ideas, I was frequently courted by lobbyists, foreign governments, and opposition politicians. In this book I have tried to capture some of this spirit, some of what it feels like to have access and to be a semi-insider in Washington.

Third, over the course of my years in Washington I retooled as a scholar and became a specialist in foreign policy as well as in comparative politics. The longer I stayed in Washington, the more I became convinced that U.S. foreign policy is not driven so much by what happens in Europe, the Middle East, Africa, El Salvador, Nicaragua, or other countries and areas where I had spent research time, but rather by what happens in the United

States. What counts is not always the actual situation in Asia, the Soviet Union, or Central America, but what Americans *believe* is happening there—the metaphors we use to interpret events in other countries, and how these events "play" in terms of our own domestic politics. In Central America for example, one side in our domestic debate feared "another Vietnam" was in the making, while the other celebrated that, in acting forcefully, we were overcoming our "Vietnam complexes." Neither of these two metaphors had much to do with what was actually happening in Central America; instead, they had to do mainly with *our own* hangups as a nation, *our* conceptions of the issues, and the domestic political debate. Meanwhile, both a Republican president and a Democratic Congress played partisan politics with Central American issues.

Knowledge of what is happening in foreign countries is still important, of course—crucially so. But, from a Washington perspective, what is happening in other countries constitutes only one side of the equation. At least as important in determining U.S. foreign policy on many issues is what goes on politically in the United States itself. So domestic politics has become foreign policy and vice versa.

This book has been fun to write. It forced me to go back to some of the classic as well as the more recent books on American politics, rediscovering my own country in a sense after decades of studying other countries. More than that, the book draws extensively on my years in Washington, which included participant observation in all the agencies discussed. While it covers all the main topics of a comprehensive foreign-policy text, it tries also to relate the flavor, the spirit, the chaos, the frustration, and the sheer joy of participating in the process. That is why, in addition to familiar topics, it contains discussions of subjects that, to my knowledge, no one has ever covered in a foreign-policy book before: The Washington social circuit; the nature of Washington "friendships" and how these influence foreign policy; the backstabbing and enormous ambitions of many foreign-policy activists in Washington; the role of the media in shaping the foreign-policy agenda; and think tanks and foreign policy.

ACKNOWLEDGMENTS

Over the past decade I have been particularly fortunate to be associated with some of the country's foremost research centers and think tanks. These include the Harvard University Center for International Affairs (CFIA), the American Enterprise Institute, the Foreign Policy Research Institute (FPRI), and my home institution, the University of Massachusetts/Amherst. Many of the ideas explored in this text were first tried out in some lively courses and graduate seminars at George Washington University, at the University of Massachusetts/Amherst, and in many foreign policy forums, seminars, and discussion groups. Among those to be singled out for special thanks at these institutions are Samuel P. Huntington and Raymond Vernon at CFIA; William Baroody, Christopher DeMuth, Evron Kirkpatrick, Jeane Kirkpatrick, Mark Falcoff, and Howard Penniman at AEI; Daniel Pipes and Marvin Wachman at FPRI; Joseph Duffey, Glen Gordon, and the Department of Political Science at the University of Massachusetts; and Maurice East, Hugh Le Blanc, and Cynthia McClintock at George Washington University. I would also like to thank the foreign-policy specialists on the Washington social circuit who are habitués of the think tanks, the Council on Foreign Relations, the Carnegie Endowment, and other *de riguer* locations where foreign policy is hashed out after hours. They have contributed enormously to the storehouse of lore and my understanding of Washington policy-making.

My children are now all old enough to read this book; they helped strengthen the argument to retain the fun and readable passages. Dr. Iêda Siqueira Wiarda has shared our long odyssey abroad, to Washington, and back home to Amherst once again. By her count we have now moved 13 times in a quarter century of married life, but our base has remained Amherst. She has also read the book in its entirety and, as usual, contributed numerous valuable suggestions. But the mistakes, as well as the verbal excesses where my enthusiasm for the topic perhaps overrode the scholar's reluctance to draw broad conclusions, are mine alone.

Howard J. Wiarda

CHAPTER ONE

American Foreign Policy: Crisis and Approaches

❁
❁

American foreign policy runs the risk of falling into chaos. There is so much conflict, confusion, disarray, incoherence, and division built into the American system on such a wide range of foreign policy issues that serious observers are now questioning whether it is possible for this country to carry out a coherent, rational, sensible, and long-term foreign policy. The foreign policy-making process in the United States has become so partisan, so politicized, and with so many strong disagreements over issues and directions that it is sometimes feared we may be reaching a stage of near paralysis. Other terms used to describe our foreign policy situation in recent years are "immobilism," "advanced sclerosis," and "hardening of the arteries."[1]

The congressional elections of 1986 left the country with a situation of divided government: both the House of Representatives and the Senate controlled by the Democratic party and the White House in the hands of a Republican incumbent who continued to enjoy immense popularity.[2] Not only could little be accomplished with respect to policy under these circumstances, but as a nation we soon found ourselves in a condition of intense partisan conflict and confrontation. President Reagan's appointments and policy were stymied as a Democratic Congress sought to embarrass the Republican President (and vice versa), and as the jockeying began for the 1988 elections. The situation of division and paralysis was compounded by the undermining of the President's prestige, popularity, and credibility in the so-called Irangate controversy and by the realization he was, after 1984, a lame duck whose domination of the political agenda would soon come to an end.

In 1988, Republican George Bush was elected president, but the Democrats remained in control of both houses of Congress. Therefore, despite the goodwill that accompanied Bush into office, his legislative agenda faced tough sledding, and there was every likelihood that Congress and the White House would once again be at odds. As these political events unfolded and the conflicts deepened, it became clear that one of the main driving forces in contemporary American politics, including foreign policy, is partisan division. The essential consensus on goals and means that prevailed up to the mid-1960s no longer exists.[3]

It is not just this one cause, however, that accounts for our worries about the potential for foreign policy paralysis and disarray. The United States has actually been experiencing a creeping paralysis in its foreign policy-making process for some time. The recent division between Congress and the executive branch adds one more important ingredient to the stew, but it is by no means the only one. The immobilism that we may now face has been growing for a long period; it reflects the kind of divided, fragmented, more ideological society that we have become. The United States has always had differences over policy, and occasionally stalemate— that is the cost we bear for living in a democratic and pluralistic country. But now the divisions are deeper and more intense, the polarization and fragmentation more pronounced, the sheer numbers of actors and interests greater, the politics and partisanships more severe and, hence, the potential for incoherence and paralysis far larger.

These changes are related to profound structural changes in American society and politics over the last twenty years. The changes are detailed in the next section. Their cumulative effect, however, adds up to a situation in which we may no longer be able to expect a harmonious, consensual, reasonable and long-term foreign policy to emanate from Washington— *regardless* of the issue or area involved and independent of the person occupying the White House. Our foreign policy is often fragmented and in disarray, in short, because our country, our leaders, our ideas, and our institutions are uncertain, sometimes confused, and themselves fragmented and in disarray. Only a president of Mr. Reagan's immense (at the beginning of his term) charisma, skills, and popularity could provide a measure of coherence to this now often unmanageable foreign policy-making system. But his policies proved to be very controversial, they came under strong attack by the political opposition, Reagan proved detached and uninvolved as a leader, his position was eventually undermined, and his successor lacks the political skills and popularity that Reagan enjoyed. Hence, despite President Bush's efforts to steer a middle course, the prognosis must be for continued deep division in the future.

While these conditions are worrisome, they are not necessarily cause for total despair. The fact is, often quietly and on many less controversial issues, the United States still does manage to carry out a coherent and sensible foreign policy. We have taken important steps to improve our relations with quite a number of the developed nations, both allies and adversaries. And, with a few notable exceptions, we are in the process of putting our relations with the less-developed countries on a more rational and normal basis.[4] We have signed a peace treaty with the Soviet Union to reduce nuclear arms and are in the process of negotiating others; we have been working with the Soviets and other parties to dampen some regional conflicts; and we succeeded—for a time at least—in getting our NATO allies to modernize and upgrade their nuclear arsenals. Our position in the world and what we stand for—democracy, human rights, pluralism, freedom—seem to be improving; some would go so far as to say that they have emerged triumphant. Finally, we are beginning to see that our new, more pluralistic, more participatory foreign policy (which some lament because it leads to greater conflict and others applaud because it leads to greater democracy) may not be all bad. First, it will be with us for a long time, and we might as well adjust to it realistically; second, it may produce a foreign policy that is more humane and more in keeping with the views of the American citizens than the elite-directed foreign policy of the past. Hence our need to understand realistically and without illusion, but without hopelessness and despair either, how our foreign policy works and fails to work and the processes involved.

CAUSES OF OUR FOREIGN POLICY MALAISE

The causes of our foreign policy crisis and paralysis are many. Let us briefly review some of these as a way of introducing the main themes of the book. In subsequent chapters we will be returning to each of these main subject areas and discussing them in greater detail.

The General Political Culture

Political culture refers to the basic ideas, values, and beliefs that govern our views about politics. We are now, in terms of these beliefs, a more divided, a more polarized, a more fragmented nation than we were thirty years ago, riven and separated by a myriad of conflicting values, ideologies, and ethnic, partisan, and other loyalties. Among the most important causes of this division were the Vietnam war and Watergate, which undermined our faith in American institutions and (especially the war) destroyed the consensus on foreign policy issues that had once existed. The protest movements, the Nixon Administration, the countercul-ture,[5] and the more confrontational politics of the late 1960s and 1970s added further ingredients. The chaos and confrontations in American cities, the racial tensions, and the sapping of confidence in major American institutions—the military, the presidency, big business, big labor—also played a role in this emerging malaise. In the late 1970s and early 1980s, we had two intensely ideological administrations—those of Jimmy Carter and Ronald Reagan—who polarized public opinion and policy. The downward turn of the American economy and our continuing economic problems further undermined the belief that we were the world's leader in all areas; our self-confidence was sapped.

Other broad cultural and societal changes were also at work. The egoism and self-centeredness of the "me generation" tended to make our politics and foreign policy more unidimensional and nonconsensual. The increasing secularization of American society, and with it the rise of what was called situational ethics, meant that virtually anything could—and frequently did—go. The alienation of our intellectual elites—in the universities, the publishing houses, the press, the churches—from America and American institutions tended to produce a negative view of the country and a blame-America-first mentality, as if all the problems in the world were our fault. Of course, some of our recent presidents, by their actions, provided the fuel for these negative sentiments to spread. In addition, American politics and political discourse have become more ideological, more partisan, more nasty, more sharply divided, and more vocal. We live in an era, it seems, when all institutions are fair game and under attack; we should not expect our foreign policy to be exempt from this tendency.

Public Opinion

Public opinion in the United States is at one and the same time fickle, jumping from issue to issue on a daily or weekly basis; poorly informed about foreign policy issues; and contradictory.[6] One week the hot issue is South Africa, the next the Middle East, then the Soviet Union, China, NATO, or Central America—each commanding our foreign policy attention for a brief span before we move on to other issues. At the same time public opinion is often uninformed, woefully ignorant of geography, and unable to discern whom the United States supports or opposes in various parts of the world. The public's views on Central America underline the contradictory nature of public opinion. Polls show that 80 to 85 percent of the American public wants no more "second Cubas"—no more Marxist-Leninist regimes allied to and operating as military bases for the Soviet Union. But exactly the same percentage wants no more foreign aid, no CIA involvement, and no commitment of American ground forces in Central America. For American policymakers, the dilemma in these figures is clear: the policy goal is set (no second Cubas) but none of the instruments (foreign aid, CIA involvement, or American troops) can be employed to achieve that goal. How one carries out a successful foreign policy in Central America given such contradictory views from the public is not clear, either to policymakers or to the rest of us.

Or take the way pollsters see American public opinion as being divided. About one-third of the American public is isolationist (favors a strong America but wants no part of foreign entanglements), about one-third is liberal-internationalist (favors human rights over other considerations of American interests, North-South dialogue, and coopera-tive relations with the Soviets), and about one-third is conservative-internationalist (favors a strong defense and is suspicious of the Soviet Union). This means that a liberal president who comes to power will right from the start have to face the likely opposition of two-thirds of the electorate (the isolationists and the conservative-internationalists). A conservative president will likewise probably face the opposition of two-thirds of the electorate (the isolationists, who will support his defense proposals but not his foreign aid and other programs, and the liberal-internationalists, whose agenda will be different). How any president, liberal or conservative, can carry out an effective foreign policy when two-thirds of the country is almost guaranteed to be opposed to some parts of his program is unknown.

"Elite" opinion (the media, publishing, academia, and so forth) is at least as deeply divided, and in the last two decades (since Vietnam and Watergate) it has become increasingly negative. Elite opinion often tends to blame the United States (not the Soviet Union or others) for most of the world's ills and was as hostile to Democratic President Carter as to Republican President Reagan. These negative attitudes on the part of these important opinion-leaders have sown a sense of profound distrust of all American actions and policies and have added a new dimension to our foreign policy paralysis.

Domestic Political Considerations

The discipline of political science has not contributed overwhelming amounts of scientific certainty to our knowledge, but in one area—congressional voting behavior—its contribution is quite clear: When all other factors (party, religion, ethnicity, gender, district, etc.) are held constant, the one factor that explains congressional votes and White House decisions the best is the desire to be reelected.[7]

On all sides foreign policy has been politicized. At the White House, very little is done (despite the protestations of all of our presidents to the contrary) without weighing the media impact and its consequences for the president's reelection possibilities. "How it will play in Peoria" is not just *a* consideration but often *the* dominant motivation behind a presidential decision. More recently, the White House has been preoccupied with providing the correct public relations "spin" on events to the sacrifice, one fears, of the substance.

Members of Congress are at least as public-relations oriented. They have become masters of the thirty-second comment or "sound bite" designed to get them on the evening news. To facilitate these appearances, Congress now has its own television studio on Capitol Hill. Those speeches whose snippets we see on TV making the congressman look serious and concerned are often just that: thirty-second snippets, hardly demonstrating profound thought, written by his staff, and meant to make the congressman

"Congratulations, Dave! I don't think I've read a more beautifully evasive and subtly misleading public statement in all my years in government."
Drawing by Stevenson; © 1987 *The New Yorker Magazine*, Inc.

sound profound but in actuality containing just the one snappy line that gets the congressman on the "tube" in his home district and maybe even, if the staff is good, on the national networks.

In all this posturing, it is domestic political considerations that are being served rather than serious, long-term foreign policy goals. When President Reagan gave his important speech on Central America in 1983, the real message of the speech was contained in the last two paragraphs and was directed at the Congress: If you vote against my policies and El Salvador falls to communism, we in the White House will blame you, Mr. Congressman, when you next run for reelection, as the one who "lost" El Salvador. That is a message that congressmen (who much prefer to stay in Washington than return to wherever they come from) understand. So the House voted just enough aid to put the president into the El Salvador quagmire up to his chin and, in effect, said: "OK, Mr. President, here's your aid but now it's *your* war to win or lose, and if you lose we will not hesitate to blame *you* as the man who 'lost' El Salvador." Thus far El Salvador does not seem to have been "lost" either way, but the point is the intensely partisan and political nature of the debate, which has everything to do with American domestic politics and very little to do with poor, strife-torn El Salvador.

Interest Groups

Three major questions are taken up under this heading. First is the privatization (long preceding the exploits of Colonel Oliver North in the Irangate controversy) of American foreign policy. To what degree have large private interests (big labor, big business, big agriculture) assumed and taken over some of the key functions of American foreign policy? Some aspects of American foreign economic policy, for example, rely heavily on private business and business associations for staffing and implementation. Meanwhile, the AFL-CIO runs a large share of American labor policy abroad. Do these activities really serve the public interest or chiefly the private interests of the groups involved? Do such private groups carry out these activities competently? The evidence raises substantial doubts. And is there accountability and oversight? The answer is very little. Since no politician wants to tangle with either big business or big labor, effective accountability or oversight is practically nonexistent. Meanwhile, as shall be seen in Chapter 6, some very questionable activities have been going on.[8]

Second is the sheer proliferation of these groups. Some 50,000 interest associations now act as lobbies in Washington, D.C., double the number from fifteen years ago. Are we therefore at a stage of pluralism run amok, with so many interest groups having a veto over policy that the country has become quasi-paralyzed? Is the success of these interest groups sapping strength from American political institutions and making the country all but ungovernable?[9]

The third problem is the proliferation of new single-interest lobbies that are able to hamstring foreign policy on many issues. Here we have in mind the religious lobbies (the Bishops' Conference, the National Conference of Churches, the Moral Majority), the human rights lobbies, the associations of doctors or actors or scientists on all sides of the political fence who have taken highly political positions often outside their areas of expertise, the Committees in Solidarity with the People of ... [fill in the country], as well as the new right-wing groups. No one quarrels with the right of these groups to organize and express their views vigorously. They present several problems, however: (1) these groups often know very little about the subjects on which they make strong pronouncements; (2) they tend to have a tunnel vision, focusing on their single issue to the exclusion of all other considerations and a more balanced view; (3) they tend not to be evenhanded (focusing on human rights abuses in rightist regimes like Chile or South Africa, for example, but seldom on at least equally bad abuses in Cuba or Ethiopia); and (4) they take advantage of their religious or show business connections to gain special access even though their views may not be representative of their own constituents. Not only do these groups often exert veto power over policy, but they have added enormously to the number of interests that must be satisfied (now virtually an impossible task) if a successful foreign policy is to be pursued.

The United States now has a new kind of participatory and *national* foreign policy in which groups from Berkeley to Harvard Square and all points in between are represented. While this has undoubtedly made American foreign policy more democratic, it threatens to make it more unmanageable and difficult to carry out, which many suspect is the actual political agenda of some of the leaders of such groups—to purposely and consciously paralyze American foreign policy.[10] There can be no doubt that such participatory foreign policy will be with us for a long time, and is likely to become more pronounced as more groups get into the act. Broadened participation by students, nuns, preachers, ethnics, businesspeople, mothers, children, accountants, lawyers, and other new classes of foreign policy participants will undoubtedly require a different kind of consensus building than foreign policy decision makers are used to dealing with. Or it may lead to such unbounded pluralism and chaos that, in effect, we have no foreign policy.

The White House

The White House in recent years has not provided the guidance, leadership, and direction in foreign policy that the country sorely needs. If indeed the country is more deeply divided and fragmented than before over foreign policy issues, then the presidency remains the sole source of coherence and unity and must serve as the focal point of decision making, the hub of the system. But for various reasons we have not had that kind of needed presidential leadership in foreign policy, allowing the system to fragment even farther.

Of our modern presidents, only Eisenhower, Nixon, and now Bush have had any independent experience and knowledge in foreign affairs. None of the others have ever lived abroad, studied abroad, or had any experience requiring them to live in foreign countries for any length of time or to empathize with a culture other than their own. The American way of choosing leaders (local dogcatchers, school boards, councils; then mayors or county executives; then congressmen or state officials; finally the try for the presendency) has no requirement whatsoever of experience in foreign affairs. Indeed most politicians say that living abroad for any period is detrimental to a political career, and there is an ingrained suspicion among Americans of anyone who has spent too much time out of his or her own country.

Nor have presidential staffs been consistently up to the job of filling in the gaps left by presidential foreign policy inexperience. The staffs often tend to be preoccupied with domestic political considerations and, like the president, inexperienced in foreign affairs. At low levels, the staff too often consists of persons who carried the luggage during the last election campaign and were rewarded for their energy and loyalty with a White House job. At higher levels, too, the staff sometimes consists of more glorified "luggage carriers"—persons who know how to answer a telephone, provide the right political and public relations twist to a story, and run a media campaign but who are appallingly lacking in knowledge of foreign countries or regions. This country has such an abundance of smart, able, and knowledgeable people that it is shocking that so few manage to make it as far as the White House, which is after all the epitome of American ambitions and power. The reasons for this abysmal situation is that it is loyalty to the president and political considerations above all others that determine appointments at this level and not necessarily considerations of merit and talent.

The same charge can often be made against the National Security Council, the one agency in the White House that is supposed to be knowledgeable about and give coherence to our foreign policy. Once again, however, even at the NSC it is politics and loyalty to the administration in power that may be the main criteria, not always or necessarily talent or knowledge. NSC appointees are seldom selected from the most knowledgeable people in the country but on the basis of political connections, service in the election campaign, and "knowing someone who knows someone." The result frequently is appointees inexperienced in critical areas, with no knowledge of the language of the areas in which they are supposedly specialists. In one celebrated case, a person responsible for the critical Soviet affairs slot at the NSC had never been to the Soviet Union.

Now if the president were knowledgeable and adept at foreign policy, it would be enough for the NSC to merely coordinate the flow of papers and run errands. But in some recent administrations we have had the untenable combination of inexperienced appointees at the NSC *and* presidents who knew very little about the outside world. These themes will be discussed in more detail in Chapter 14.

The New Role of Congress

Since Vietnam, Congress has become more assertive in foreign policy. It not only *oversees* foreign policy—its proper constitutional role—but it is now also involved in the formulation and actual *making* of foreign policy.[11] The question that concerns us here is whether a body of 535 very diverse and highly individualistic members (435 in the House, 100 in the Senate), whose knowledge of foreign affairs is often limited, can carry out an effective foreign policy. The short answer is an emphatic no, as some of the more thoughtful members of Congress will themselves admit. The real issue, therefore, is not whether Congress on its own can carry out an effective foreign policy but how it can have an effective role and what precisely that role should be.

The causes of this new congressional activism are many: the incredible growth of congressional staffs that enables each member of Congress to have his own corps of foreign policy advisers; the decline of the seniority system and party discipline that allows members to speak and act more independently; Vietnam, Reagan, and the distrust of presidential leadership; the proliferation of subcommittees that permits every congressman to chair something; and national television news shows that broadcast congressional opinions no matter how outlandish or irresponsible.

The War Powers Act, passed in 1973 over Nixon's veto and still the subject of major differences and uncertainty about its precise meaning, gives the Congress extraordinary power to limit American foreign policy initiatives by requiring congressional approval of the commitment of American ground forces after sixty days. The requirement of certification of human rights progress in difficult countries like El Salvador has involved enormous amounts of NSC and State Department staff time; has proved tremendously divisive, involving lying (the Washington term is *dissembling*) on all sides; and may even—surprisingly—have improved the human rights situation in Central America. In addition, senators on the right and left routinely hold up for months administration nominations to high-ranking positions over some ideological, political, or pork barrel consideration. In these efforts, it becomes clear, some (usually only a few) congressmen are not out to constructively criticize and improve policy but to actively sabotage that policy or an entire administration.

Members of Congress now routinely carry out their own foreign policies. Representative Stephen Solarz (D-NY) for a time went off to the Philippines on an almost weekly basis to negotiate the departure of President Ferdinand Marcos; Senator Christopher Dodd (D-CT) frequently involves himself in Central American negotiations; Senator Jesse Helms (R-NC) pressures the State Department to stop treating former dictator Pinochet of Chile like a pariah; while members of the congressional Black Caucus fly off to South Africa on "fact-finding" missions. This is not to say that these congressional activities are necessarily bad—some are even good—but rather to emphasize the new congressional assertiveness in foreign policy and the proliferation in the number of participants.

The situation clearly goes far beyond the checks and balances between executive and legislative branches that the Founding Fathers intended. With Congress and the White House often at loggerheads and some members of Congress pursuing their own foreign policies, the result is a spreading chaos and paralysis in foreign policy-making. This proliferation of foreign policy actors is also troubling and confusing to our international friends because they can't be certain who is in charge of American foreign policy.

Meanwhile, at one end of Pennsylvania Avenue, presidents frequently promise far more than they can deliver, refuse to recognize limits to foreign policy objectives and finances, present overblown statements of national prospects and goals, and pursue strategies that would have the United States serve simultaneously as policeman and missionary to the world. At the other end of the Avenue, members of Congress posture chiefly for television and the electorate at home, seek to embarrass a president of the other party, try to squeeze partisan advantage out of every issue, tie up legislation and foreign policy nominations and refuse to budge on them, thus preventing a rational and coherent foreign policy from being carried out.

Bureaucratic Politics

It is the bane of our allies that American administrations speak with several voices on foreign policy. The State Department, Defense Department, Central Intelligence Agency, White House, National Security Agency and, more recently, the Treasury Department (international debt, trade, and other economic issues), the Justice Department (drugs, immigration), and the Department of Energy (oil supplies) are often bureaucratic rivals in the foreign policy-making arena out of which different views and perspectives spring. These departments and agencies are often competing with each other for foreign policy influence rather than all contributing to a single, coherent foreign policy.

The administration of President Jimmy Carter was widely criticized for having an incoherent, confused, and self-contradictory foreign policy. The Reagan Administration was determined to change all that and enforced greater ideological unity and consistency in foreign policy appointments than any previous administration. But soon the bureaucratic, factional, and organizational rivalries (State *vs.* Defense, Reaganites *vs.* moderates, ideologues *vs.* pragmatists) surfaced there as well. Seasoned foreign policy observers began saying they had never seen such a high degree of foreign policy fragmentation, not even under Carter.

A large degree of political and bureaucratic rivalry is built into the American political system, including now its foreign policy-making. The question is not whether such competition among bureaucratic agencies can be eliminated (it cannot) but whether it can be managed moderately well and kept from producing such overt conflicts that our foreign policy is paralyzed. It seems likely, however, given the proliferation of agencies and departments with responsibilities in the international arena and the desire of bureaucrats who run them for travel and the high adventure that foreign affairs entail, that the situation of bureaucratic politics and rivalries will likely get worse, not better.

The Media

The media—whose practitioners are no longer just neutral reporters but "interpreters" and even advocates of policy—have been playing an increasing role in foreign policy. The causes of this new media involvement are many: the star quality of television reporting, and appearances by outside guests; the widespread coverage of Vietnam and Watergate, which helped lead to distrust of all American institutions; new styles of aggressive investigative reporting; the power and prestige associated with the media, especially television; even the lure of money and the opportunity for self-aggrandizement on the part of television anchors and reporters. On the one hand, the media (alone among American institutions) are protected by the First Amendment whose interpretation is often so broad that it elevates the media almost literally to a fourth branch of government. On the other hand, the media are businesses, and very profitable ones at that, with enormous built-in potential for conflict of interest.

Three factors have a particular impact on foreign policy: media bias, irresponsibly exercised influence, and ethnocentrism. The elite media, as will be seen in more detail in Chapter 5, are overwhelmingly liberal, in ratios of four or five to one, and inevitably this bias creeps into the stories to be covered and the way they are covered.[12] Irresponsibility is frequently seen in the media's overdramatization and overpersonalization of the issues, its preference for blood and conflict, and its tendency to present polarized viewpoints rather than those in the responsible center—thus adding to our foreign policy fragmentation. Ethnocentrism, which is hardly confined to the media, implies a lack of in-depth understanding on the part of many reporters of the foreign trouble spots to which they are assigned, often on short notice. Rather than comprehending these nations in the nation's own terms, values, and language, too often the reporters rely on their own values and preferences (usually shaped by their undergraduate training or political beliefs) to interpret what is going on.

Media coverage of foreign affairs has improved greatly in the last twenty years, but it still has a long way to go to be fair, factual, and balanced. Meanwhile, the media have not been just reporting the disarray, incoherence, and fragmentation that all too often characterized American foreign policy but have been themselves agents, catalysts, and even instigators of some of these divisions.

At the same time, while it is valid to emphasize these criticisms of the media, it also needs to be said that all recent presidents, as well as other politicians, have sought to use the media for their own purposes, restrict its coverage, and shape the news that the media report. Therefore, both sides of this equation require our attention: the biases and other faults of the media as well as the government's efforts to influence the media.

The Think Tanks

The Washington-based think tanks, which are research institutions producing many of the books and position papers on which policy-making is based, may similarly be both reflections and agencies of the growing dissension over foreign policy. Chapter 8 is devoted to the role these new institutions play in foreign policy-making.

In *Our Own Worst Enemy: The Unmaking of American Foreign Policy,*[13] I.M. Destler, Leslie Gelb, and Anthony Lake have an intriguing thesis that the decline in influence over the last two decades of the older New York-based Council on Foreign Relations has been paralleled by the rise of the Washington think tanks. The Council used to provide many of our foreign policy elite (and the Council's influence has been enhanced in the Bush Administration), but now the recruits into high-level foreign policy positions are coming increasingly from the "tanks." These authors suggest further that the bipartisan consensus that the Council was a primary agency in shaping in the 1940s and 1950s has been replaced by divisions and partisanship among the rival research institutions in Washington along political and ideological lines.

Doubtless the argument may be overstated. Probably more consensus and commonality exist among the major think tanks than the ideological labels sometimes applied to them would imply. But there is no doubt that: (1) major influence in foreign policy-making has shifted from New York to Washington; (2) it has shifted away from the Council toward the think tanks; (3) it has shifted from an older elite of bankers and Wall Street lawyers—foreign policy generalists—to a new elite of younger academics and policy advocates; (4) it has shifted from a more middle-of-the-road and nonpartisan basis to a more intensely political and ideological one; and (5) with the shift has come a foreign policy that is more ideological, more political, and more erratic, swinging violently (like a clock pendulum) from one administration to the next.

OVERCOMING PARALYSIS

The dangers of a fragmented, incoherent, quasi-paralyzed American foreign policy are real and are beginning to be reflected in the literature. This literature describes a nation whose foreign policy is often in disarray, polarized, and unable to respond adequately to the issues that confront it. Certainly all the elements analyzed here—the general political culture, divided public opinion, domestic political considerations, divided and divisive interest groups, inexperienced presidents and staffs in the White House, an intensely politicized Congress, a media that is no longer neutral, more ideological think tanks, and doubtless other factors beside—have helped contribute to the immobilism we now see and which could easily become worse in the future.

At least as interesting as our partial sclerosis and sometimes *immobilism*—important though these are—is how we still manage, sometimes more than occasionally, to conduct a rational foreign policy at all, given the incoherence and confusion that we see all around us. In fact, the foreign policy accomplishments of recent years are many and profound, and it is important that they be acknowledged: the INF treaty, better Soviet relations, a strong Europe and Japan, resolution of some Third World conflicts, and so on. Rather than drown in gloom and doom, we need to arrive at a balanced view of both our accomplishments and our limits in the foreign policy area. Very often the accomplishments are obscured in a sea of faultfinding and nit-picking that is itself a product of our new divisiveness. Meanwhile, the world does go on and not altogether badly.

At the most general level, credit must go to the new bipartisan foreign policy emphasis on democracy and human rights, the increased strategic preparedness and stronger defense, the stronger economy of the 1980s, the talks and eventual progress of arms limitations, the renewed confidence and faith in ourselves and our system that has occurred over the last several years, and the greater emphasis on working out differences. Now it is the Soviet Union and its satellites and proxies that are most often on the defensive or in difficulty, and no longer the United States.[14]

With regard to individual countries and areas, our foreign policy has similarly registered some notable gains. China policy has mainly stayed sensible and largely on an even keel, without the disruptions and disarray characteristic of policy in other areas.[15] Relations with Europe go through ups and downs and are presently subject to renegotiation over NATO, American troop levels, and the burden-sharing of our common defense; however, we still share with Europe a sense of being a part of a common, Western, democratic civilization, and our relations are normal and mature. There will continue to be differences with Japan principally over economic policy, but such differences do not mean we cannot have good relations with Japan. In Latin America also, despite the controversy that frequently swirls around El Salvador and Nicaragua, our efforts to aid democratization have secured bipartisan support; and our relations with most of the area have begun to be put on the same normal, mature basis that we have long maintained with Western Europe.[16]

The "real news,"[17] therefore, is not that we are sometimes stalemated and often ineffective and incoherent in our foreign policies but that policy does nonetheless move forward with some real accomplishments to show for it.

CONCLUSION

Ultimately American foreign policy is a reflection of American society itself. The fact is that since the 1960s we have become a more divided nation, somewhat less sure of ourselves, and more partisan and ideological, all of which is mirrored in our foreign policy. For these reasons, building domestic support on almost any foreign policy issue is more complex than it used to be. The old foreign policy consensus that prevailed through the 1950s is largely gone, replaced by a myriad of special interests, partisan posturing, and highly vocal and often politically motivated spokespersons. But after all, during a time when all established verities and institutions (home, family, religion) are under attack, foreign policy could hardly expect to escape unscathed. The paralysis and fragmentation that have sometimes resulted, and that are now institutionalized within the body politic, go way beyond the traditional checks and balances of the men who wrote the American Constitution and beyond the sometimes "untidy" foreign policy we have experienced in the past.

We have reached in this country in some areas of our foreign policy-making a condition that has been called *morbific politics*.[18] Morbific politics refers to a situation in which the number of interest groups has become so many, the divisions between them so deep, and the attachment to any central core of agreed-upon values so weak that the system tends to fragment and not function effectively. Each group in society (students, clerics, actors, doctors, trade unionists) no longer has one organized interest to represent its views but many, almost all of them highly partisan, political, and ideological, determined to advance its pet view at the cost sometimes of the unity and integrity of the nation as a whole. This tendency toward fragmentation and polarization goes far beyond traditional checks and balances, pluralism, and the tempering of policy that all administrations require to keep them in line and that most of us think of as among the best features of American democracy. In some respects it is similar to the deeply fragmented nation of Argentina, a "conflict society" whose divisions are quite a bit deeper than our own but whose chaotic, disintegrative politics we should not want to emulate.[19]

In our present divided and politicized condition, we need to keep in mind this possibility of becoming "another Argentina." Our tendency is increasingly and too often toward impotency, ineffectiveness, and incapacitation; our foreign policy-making system cannot work effectively under such circumstances. Foreign policy criticism, which ought to be fair and constructive, now goes considerably beyond that. In some quarters, the aim seems to be to undermine and subvert American policy rather than correct it. When our president is compared to Adolf Hitler, when the United States is referred to as "the most evil country on earth," when some

groups use violence or deny free speech as a way of silencing government spokespersons, or when mistruths are purposely used to undermine American policy, then it is clear that our foreign policy discussion
has moved beyond the pale of rational discussion. It is doubtful that
as a country with global responsibilities we can continue to be
savagely criticized, to have our policy paralyzed, and to limp along in
this way.

It requires a president of extraordinary political skills and popularity
to overcome the system's now powerful trends toward partisanship and
immobility. This is not a partisan statement but surely one must
acknowledge President Reagan's considerable talents in these regards,
particularly during his first term. He was masterful at dealing with a divided
Congress, achieved a remarkable legislative agenda, was a marvelous
communicator to the public (whatever one thought of the contents),
handled a skeptical or hostile media with aplomb, and adroitly managed to
separate his strong rhetoric (mainly for domestic political purposes) from
his quite moderate actions. When he put the full prestige of his presidency
behind a certain policy initiative (as in his dealings with the Soviet Union,
and sometimes in Central America), he was able at times to coax and cajole
the system out of its tendency toward immobility and toward effective
action. Indeed Reagan's successes in these areas tended to obscure the
trends toward immobilism that have gone forward inexorably beneath the
surface and that under a less-skilled president would have produced even
greater paralysis.

That is why the unraveling that occurred as a result of the capture of
the Senate by the Democrats in 1986 and the revelation of the secretive
American policy toward Iran, known as Irangate or the Iran-Contra scandal
(involving an effort to sell weapons to Iran in return for hostages, and to
use the profits clandestinely to resupply the Nicaraguan resistance
forces—and the domestic reverberations of these events) was so worrisome. At this point the one force that tended to hold the foreign
policy-making system together and give it coherence—the President and
his still great popularity—was also undermined. The decline of the
President's popularity and political position produced a situation in which
incoherence and unraveling increased, immobilism and paralysis spread,
and members of the Congress and other groups sought to step into the
vacuum by claiming power for themselves. The foreign policy problems
diminished somewhat in Reagan's last year, and he left office with his
popularity intact and with several major foreign policy accomplishments.
But President Bush lacks Reagan's popularity and charisma, is not a strong

or forceful personality, and has thin popular support, so we will have to see if Bush's brand of soft-spoken pragmatism can hold the system together or if his administration too will be plagued by paralysis.

What can be done about these disturbing tendencies toward immobilism? Probably not much. We can urge that the decibel level in the partisan debate be turned down somewhat; we can request less exaggeration and verbal overkill from our spokespersons; we can try to rebuild the domestic consensus (a very difficult process); we can provide better foreign policy training for journalists, congressional staff, and others; we can be more sensitive to the special pleading of various partisan groups; we can work for greater efficiency and competence in executive branch decision making; we can work for greater cooperation between Congress and the White House; and we can continue to plead for greater good sense, prudence, rationality, moderation, pragmatism, and restraint both in foreign policy and in foreign policy discussions. These are useful but still fairly modest expectations.

The problem is that the fragmentation, paralysis, and incoherence that mark our foreign policy are to a large extent a reflection of the more divided, fragmented, egocentric, and politicized society that we have become. It is unlikely therefore that American society will soon or easily change for the better. The problem is not just in our foreign policy; it is in ourselves and in the kind of nation we are. There are some signs of national change—more hope, more vigor, more confidence, greater prudence and centrism—but they are still weak and incomplete. Indeed with a system of divided government, with political campaigning continuing virtually nonstop (the political lineups for 1992 and 1996 are already taking shape), with little time to fashion a rational and coherent policy in the intervals between elections, the prospects are that the disarray and paralysis in foreign policy-making that now seems so deeply ingrained in the American political system will continue into the indefinite future. Things, as the old saying goes, may get worse before they get very much better.

In this chapter we have reviewed some of the major ingredients in our foreign policy crisis that have led to fragmentation and an inability to act or carry out policy decisively. In the next chapter we will try to put these developments in a larger perspective by exploring the models and intellectual frameworks that scholars and policymakers use to understand foreign policy-making. To the usual models employed in the field we will add some new ones that help account for today's altered domestic circumstances: a personal self-aggrandizement model and a partisan or political process model.

Notes

1. An earlier version of this chapter was published by the author as "The Paralysis of Policy: Current Dilemmas of U.S. Foreign Policy-Making." *World Affairs* 149(Summer 1986):15–20.

2. Glen Gordon, *The Legislative Process and Divided Government* (Amherst: Bureau of Government Research. University of Massachusetts, 1966).

3. Robert Pranger, "Participatory Politics and Foreign Policy Coherence" (Paper presented at the Public Policy Week Forum on American Foreign and Defense Policy in the Next Decade: Opportunities and Constraints, American Enterprise Institute, Washington, D.C., December 3–4, 1986).

4. Howard J. Wiarda, *Finding Our Way? Toward Maturity in U.S.-Latin American Relations* (Washington, D.C.: University Press of America, 1987).

5. Paul Hollander, *The Adversary Culture* (New Brunswick, N.J.: Transaction Press, 1987).

6. John A. Reilly, ed. *American Public Opinion and U.S. Foreign Policy 1987* (Chicago: Chicago Council on Foreign Relations, 1987).

7. David Mayhew, *Congress: The Electoral Connection* (New Haven: Yale University Press, 1974).

8. Grant McConnell, *Private Power and American Democracy* (New York: Vintage, 1966).

9. Samuel P. Huntington, "The Democratic Distemper," in *The American Commonwealth,* ed. Nathan Glazer and Irving Kristol. (New York: Basic Books, 1976).

10. Alan Garfinkle, *The Politics of the Nuclear Freeze* (Philadelphia: Foreign Policy Research Institute, 1984).

11. Thomas M. Frank and Edward Weisband, *Foreign Policy by Congress* (New York: Oxford University Press, 1979).

12. S. Robert Lichter, Stanley Rothman, and Linda S. Lichter, *The Media Elite: America's New Powerbrokers* (Bethesda, Md.: Adler and Adler, 1986).

13. I. M. Destler, Leslie H. Gelb, and Anthony Lake, *Our Own Worst Enemy: The Unmaking of American Foreign Policy* (New York: Simon and Schuster, 1984).

14. This is the subject of a new study by the author and Vladimir Tismaneanu, *Vulnerabilities of Communist Regimes* (Philadelphia: Foreign Policy Research Institute, Forthcoming).

15. David M. Lampton, "China Policy: Interests and Process." *World Affairs* 148(Winter 1985–86):139–42.

16. This is the theme of Wiarda, *Finding Our Way?*

17. After the title and theme of Ben Wattenberg's book, *The Good News Is the Bad News Is Wrong* (New York: Simon and Schuster, 1984).

18. David Truman, *The Governmental Process* (New York: Knopf, 1953).

19. Kalman H. Silvert, *The Conflict Society: Reaction and Revolution in Latin America* (New Orleans: American Universities Field Staff Reports, 1966); also Howard J. Wiarda, "The Latin Americanization of the United States." *The New Scholar* 7(1979):51–85.

Suggested Readings

Destler, I. M., Leslie H. Gelb, and Anthony Lake. *Our Own Worst Enemy: The Unmaking of American Foreign Policy* (New York: Simon and Schuster, 1984).

Dougherty, James E., and Robert L. Pfaltzgraff, Jr. *American Foreign Policy: FDR to Reagan.* New York: Harper and Row, 1986.

Dull, James. *The Politics of American Foreign Policy.* Englewood Cliffs, N.J.: Prentice Hall, 1985.

Frank, Thomas M. and Edward Weisband. *Foreign Policy by Congress* (New York: Oxford University Press, 1979).

Garfinkle, Alan. *The Politics of the Nuclear Freeze* (Philadelphia: Foreign Policy Research Institute, 1984).

Gordon, Glen. *The Legislative Process and Divided Government* (Amherst: Bureau of Government Research. University of Massachusetts, 1966).

Hartmann, Frederick H., and Robert L. Wendzel. *To Preserve the Republic: United States Foreign Policy.* New York: Macmillan, 1985.

Hollander, Paul. *The Adversary Culture* (New Brunswick, N.J.: Transaction Press, 1987).

Huntington, Samuel P. "The Democratic Distemper," in *The American Commonwealth,* ed. Nathan Glazer and Irving Kristol. (New York: Basic Books, 1976).

Lovell, John P. *The Challenge of American Foreign Policy.* New York: Macmillan, 1985.

McConnell, Grant. *Private Power and American Democracy* (New York: Vintage, 1966).

McCormick, James M. *American Foreign Policy and American Values.* Itasca, Ill.: Peacock, 1985.

Nathan, James A., and James K. Oliver. *Foreign Policy-Making and the American Political System,* 2nd ed. Boston: Little, Brown, 1986.

Quester, George H. *American Foreign Policy: The Lost Consensus.* New York: Praeger, 1982.

Reilly, John A., ed. *American Public Opinion and U.S. Foreign Policy 1987* (Chicago: Chicago Council on Foreign Relations, 1987).

Spanier, John, and Eric M. Uslaner. *American Foreign Policy-Making and the Democratic Dilemmas,* 4th ed. New York: Holt, Rinehart & Winston, 1985.

Truman, David. *The Governmental Process* (New York: Knopf, 1953).

Wiarda, Howard J. *Finding Our Way? Toward Maturity in U.S.-Latin American Relations* (Washington, D.C.: University Press of America, 1987).

Wiarda, Howard J. "The Paralysis of Policy: Current Dilemmas of U.S. Foreign Policy-Making," *World Affairs* 149 (Summer 1986):15-20; reprinted in amplified form in Howard J. Wiarda, *Finding Our Way?* Chap. 11. Washington, D.C.: University Press of America, 1987.

CHAPTER TWO

Models of American Foreign Policy-Making

❂
❂

Most Americans have a quite simple notion of the way foreign policy-making works. We assume that nation-states make decisions on the basis of the best information possible, carefully weigh the pros and cons of various possible alternative policies, rationally choose the one that best advances the national interests, and then proceed to implement the chosen strategy. In that way, it seems accurate to say, as our television commentators frequently do, that "Washington did this" or "Washington did that," or that the position of Moscow on this issue is such and such. Such an understanding of policy-making—the "rational actor model"— suggests a unity, a coherence, a rationality, and a singularity to policy-making that we already know from Chapter 1 does not exist.

Later scholars introduced newer complexities to our understanding of foreign policy-making. These were referred to as the bureaucratic and organizational models of decision-making.[1] We came to recognize that policy-making was not so neat, unified, and coherent as described above but involved other factors as well. Among these were the fact that different foreign policy-making bureaucracies within the United States government—the State Department, Defense Department, Central Intelligence Agency, National Security Council—often had different viewpoints and interests that they sought to advance, and that these interests were not always subsumed under a single *national* interest. Hence the term "bureaucratic politics" came into existence to describe these often intense interdepartmental rivalries.

At the same time we discovered that these same foreign policy bureaucracies had regular organizational procedures and plans (standard operating procedures, or SOPs) that they ordinarily followed, and that such SOPs were part of a routine bureaucratic way of doing things. For example, during the Cuban missile crisis of 1962, in which the United States confronted the Soviet Union over the issue of Soviet missiles installed in Cuba, we learned that the U.S. Navy had its own way of proceeding with a blockade of Cuba and of intercepting the missile-carrying Soviet ships—a quite dangerous way, it turned out—regardless of the explicit directions of President Kennedy. Kennedy wished the Navy to proceed one way, but the Navy insisted on doing it its own way. Kennedy was furious; meanwhile the world teetered on the brink of a full-scale, United States–Soviet confrontation. Hence we need to talk about an organizational model of foreign policy alongside the bureaucratic one.

More recently it has been suggested that we need to add some additional models to aid our understanding of the foreign policy-making process. These would include, as suggested indirectly in Chapter 1, a domestic politics model, a media model, a self-aggrandizement model, and perhaps others. A domestic politics model is necessary because so much of our foreign policy discussion is politically motivated, with many of the decisions dependent on cutting political deals that often have nothing to do with the particular issue at hand. A media model is treated in Chapter 5. The self-aggrandizement model is introduced because so much of our foreign policy-making now seems to be based on politicians' egoistic, self-serving, and self-advancement motives.[2]

By combining these models—rational actor, bureaucratic, organizational, political process, self-aggrandizement, perhaps others—we have a more complete and accurate picture of American foreign policy-making than any one of these interpretations can provide by itself.

MODELS AND INTERPRETATIONS— WHY USEFUL?

It should be clear when we used the term "model" in the preceding paragraphs that we are not implying either approval or disapproval. Model is a neutral term; it is an intellectual construct used to sort out, organize, and simplify more complex processes. It helps us understand and give some coherence to events that otherwise would be so disorganized that they would not make sense.

At the same time it should be understood that a model is not an exact mirror of reality. A good and useful model simplifies reality, breaks it up into diverse and manageable components to enable us to better understand it. But reality is always more complex than any single or even several models can fully capture. A model is a very helpful device to use in social science (including foreign policy) analysis, but it is not to be confused with the even more complicated kaleidoscope that is reality itself.

What, then, is the utility of employing such models in our analysis of foreign policy-making? Among the reasons are the following:

1. Models help us to organize, highlight, and give coherence to events.
2. Models help put events in a larger context, enabling us to see the bigger picture, provide perspective.
3. Models force us to think more clearly about complicated events.
4. Models are heuristic devices; that is, they *teach* us things and enable us to see patterns.
5. Models help simplify complex events, enabling us to understand them more clearly.

Models should also be seen as pragmatic instruments. To the extent that they are useful and helpful, as outlined above, let us use them to help order our thinking. But models should not be worshipped or reified. New events or facts may alter our interpretations, forcing us to change or revise our models or scrap them altogether. Models are not sacrosanct. We employ them where they are useful; but we should not hesitate to replace them when they have outlived their utility. In either case, the overall usefulness of such models in one form or another should be recognized.

THE RATIONAL ACTOR MODEL

The rational actor model, as its name implies, is based on a notion of the foreign policy decision-making process that is orderly, coherent, and *rational*. It assumes that nation-states have geostrategic and national interests that can be identified and advanced by a rational, singular, and unified foreign policy. It assumes that states, in pursuing their national self-interest, speak with one voice and that they have a single and definable foreign policy position. The rational actor model suggests foreign policy decision making can be isolated from the political process and based on cooly calculated considerations of the national interest. The process is neat, organized, and proceeds according to the canons of logic, merit, and rational argumentation. Such a rational, logical, decision-making process may have existed some time ago, but the model seems to have less relevance today.

Typically the rational actor model presumes a choice among carefully weighed and considered policy alternatives. In our generally idealized version of how American policy-making works, we assume that these policy alternatives are fairly set forth and that the arguments for and against each one are carefully evaluated by the Department of State, sent to the NSC, which clears them with the Department of Defense and other agencies, and then forwards them to the president for his final decision. Once that decision is made, then presumably the entire United States government dedicates itself to implementation.

To illustrate, let us look at United States policy toward Nicaragua. Here we have a revolutionary Marxist regime, one that is increasingly Marxist-Leninist at its leadership levels, allied to Cuba and the Soviet Union, on record as vowing to spread its revolution to other nations, and worrying United States officials that it may allow its national territory to be used as a military base for the deployment of weapons, the subversion of its neighbors, and other activities directed against the United States. What should the United States do?

The rational actor model suggests a careful weighing of the alternative policy responses and the pros and cons of each. We could:

1. Do nothing. Practice "benign neglect." But one day we might be confronted with the reality of a full-fledged Soviet base in Nicaragua and Marxist-Leninist revolutions in other countries that are "close to home."

2. Negotiate with the Sandinistas. But, as committed revolutionaries, they may not wish to negotiate on the issues the United States views as critical: internal democracy, expelling Cubans and Soviets, reducing armaments, restoring genuine freedom and pluralism.

3. Break diplomatic relations. This may be too mild and would likely accomplish little.

4. Impose a full economic blockade. This is a tough sanction and should be seriously considered, but it is by no means watertight.

5. Find and finance a mercenary army that would either topple the Sandinista regime or prove so costly to fight that it would ruin the revolution by draining its resources. But this could antagonize the Congress as well as other groups in American society.

6. Send in the United States Marines to get rid of the Sandinista regime. But that would seem to imply "another Vietnam."

In the typical rational actor memo outlining these scenarios and their consequences, the first and last options are usually throwaways. They represent extreme positions that no one really wants to carry out. And the fact is, the United States never seriously considered either option 1 or option 6. Hence the middle options, in this case 2 through 5, are the only ones that were seriously considered. It should be noted that clever memo writers know how to structure the options so that their own preferences come out in the middle, knowing that a middle position is what most presidents or secretaries of state will probably choose.

In the Nicaragua case, option 3 (break diplomatic relations) and 4 (economic blockade) were rejected, although the United States did make an effort to try to squeeze the regime economically. It opted mainly for option 5, applying maximum pressure to the Sandinista regime through a (initially) CIA-financed Contra army. But it determined also to hold open option 2 in case at some point, after the other pressures had been applied, the Sandinistas did still wish to negotiate. While the Reagan strategy was to give *most* emphasis to option 5, the position of the liberal Democrats in Congress (Reagan's chief opposition) was to concentrate on option 2, although some Democrats also wanted to break diplomatic relations and, in 1984, Democratic presidential candidate Walter Mondale came out in favor of option 4. Hence the policy debate in the United States was largely between options 2 and 5, with some expressing preference for options 3 and 4 and others looking for varying combinations of these.

Similar option papers (as they are called at State and the NSC) have been fashioned for other difficult policy issues. The choice among such options is usually thought of as the rational actor model. But note how quickly (in the Nicaragua case and others) what began as a set of policy options for the president quickly became a matter of intense domestic political debate.

It is interesting to note that the rational actor model continues to operate. That is, the State Department continues to formulate position papers with several policy options from which to choose; so does the NSC, and the National Security Advisor continues to present such options to the president for his decisions. So this model of a rational, coherent, carefully considered decision-making process cannot be dismissed entirely. The real question, however, is not whether such option papers continue to be written but whether the assumptions of the rational actor model of unitary action and of instrumental and substantive rationality in the process still hold.

The rational actor model is no longer the only basis for policy-making. All too frequently the orderly processes implied in this model are simply overwhelmed by other forces. These include bureaucratic and personal infighting, interest-group struggles, political and partisan considerations, media leaks of the key options resulting in spirited public debate of them, motivations springing from the desire for political self-advancement, and all the rest. This is not necessarily to imply criticism of the rational actor model. But it is to say that other pressures are simultaneously at work that frequently force the careful, rational considerations of this first model into the background.

This conclusion has major implications. First, it suggests that foreign policy-making has more complexities than can be accommodated in the neat, organized patterns of the rational actor model. A variety of other influences, pressures, and models must be included in our calculations of how foreign policy is decided. And second, it should alert us to be skeptical of many of the foreign policy pronouncements we see in the media or hear from friends or even teachers. Blanket statements that "the Reagan administration did this" or "the Carter administration did that" should spur us to inquire further: *which* official in the administration, speaking for what bureaucracy or interests, at what point in time, with what private ax to grind, or for what partisan purpose. Once we know all these things, then, and only then, will we be in a position to discuss seriously and in depth all the subtleties of policy.

For some purposes, as the analysis of Graham Allison makes clear,[3] foreign policy *can* be explained as the result of action taken by a unitary, rational decision maker. But this model is not a complete or sufficient explanation. For government also consists of a conglomerate of large, loosely related bureaucratic organizations that play major roles in foreign policy. To some extent, elected and chosen government leaders sit formally atop this structure. But government leaders tend to perceive foreign policy issues in terms of the information provided to them through these larger bureaucracies which have a permanence that elected leaders do not. These bureaucracies also have organizational procedures for the way they do things.

Each organization has responsibility, presumably, for certain facets of policy. State handles diplomacy, Defense handles military matters, the CIA handles intelligence, and so on. But in reality these functions often overlap. In addition, each organization also operates quasi-independently in its own area of specialization, often with only the most minimum guidance from the president or other elected officials. In this way policy often reflects the input of several bureaucratic organizations whose practices and procedures are only partially directed by elected representatives. Government leaders can often influence but not entirely control, let alone dominate, such organizations and their habitual practices.

Those who live within the Washington, D.C., beltway and who believe that they know the answers to all these policy questions may tend to overstress the subtleties and differences, to see the trees but not the forest. Sometimes they are so preoccupied with the comings and goings of rival groups and officials, which faction is rising or falling in power, that they fail to see the big picture. An equally mistaken view, however, is to see only the forest, only the big picture, to speak of whole *administrations* rather than their separate parts and factions. This perception often leads foreign policy observers to fail to understand the subtleties, the divisions, the changes, and the opportunities for maneuver and change that are present in the shifting power and personal relations within any administration.

THE BUREAUCRATIC MODEL

The foreign policy bureaucracies in Washington, D.C.—State, Defense, CIA, NSC, and now, increasingly, Treasury, Labor, Commerce, and Justice—are not just well-oiled cogs in a smooth running rational actor machine. Rather they are institutions with lives, practices, and interests of their own. They frequently see the world from different perspectives and have different points of view. They must all compete for the same scarce budgetary dollars and to get their viewpoints across. Moreover, within some of these large bureaucracies—Defense is the best example—are various subbureaucracies that may, and frequently do, compete with each other for glory, weapons systems, and a larger share of the Defense Department budget. Here we are particularly referring to the rivalries between the services: Army, Navy, Air Force, and Marines.

The White House and the National Security Council are supposed to coordinate and harmonize these differences among the rival foreign affairs bureaucracies. But frequently they are preoccupied with other matters—a president's reelection campaign, say, or just his public image—and do not devote sufficient time to the business of coordination. Or the person holding the NSC position on South Africa, for example, may be so young or inexperienced or lacking in stature that he cannot possibly bring powerful agencies like the Defense Department into line. At the same time, the interests of these departments may be so divergent on various issues that no amount of coordination, whether by cajoling or other methods, is going to work. Short of firing his frequently-at-odds (over competing bureaucratic positions) Secretary of State or his Secretary of Defense, which no president really wants to do, or of entirely remaking the Defense Department (not a realistic possibility), some bureaucratic rivalries will *never* be resolved. Foreign policy must live with these limitations and try to cope with them since a resolution of the problem seems impossible and, under our system of checks and balances, may not even be desirable.

Under President Carter, the bureaucratic rivalries between the State Department and the NSC, between State and Defense, between the United Nations mission in New York and the State Department in Washington, between the Treasury and State on economic issues, and sometimes between the NSC and the CIA were so intense that American foreign policy was in shambles. President Reagan tried to rectify this situation by recruiting only foreign policy advisers who shared his vision. These precautions did not prevent the bureaucratic interests from reasserting themselves, however, because *real* bureaucratic *interests* were involved, not just competing individuals with particular views. Within a few months of Reagan's inauguration, the competition among the foreign policy bureaucracies was as intense as ever.

The bureaucratic politics of foreign policy-making is treated in more detail in Chapters 12 and 13; here let us simply note a few examples to illustrate the points made. During the Vietnam war, the State Department was often skeptical of our role there while the Defense Department was initially more gung ho. Later, however, it was Secretary of Defense Clark Clifford who concluded that the war was unwinnable and that the United

States should begin looking for a face-saving way out. The military was burned professionally and its prestige and honor impugned by the Vietnam experience. Hence, in the early 1980s, when Secretary of State Haig began to talk about a military solution in Central America and "going to the source" (presumably Cuba) of Central America's problems, the Reagan administration discovered—to its surprise—that it was the Defense Department that *least* wanted to get involved in that region. From Defense's point of view, there was insufficient public support for Reagan's policy there, the goals were not entirely clear, and the United States military would likely get bogged down again in some indeterminate and protracted guerrilla struggle. American public opinion would become disillusioned, the military would be discredited, and then we really would have (from the Defense Department's perspective) another Vietnam on our hands, which we did not have up to that point.

In Lebanon, too, the State Department wanted American troops in that troubled country as a way of providing a semblance of order to bolster the beleaguered Lebanese president and to serve as a vague "presence." But from the beginning the Pentagon was skeptical of such an unclear mission and of the strategically indefensible position it was obliged to take up. When 241 slumbering marines were killed when their Beirut barracks was blown up, it appeared that Defense had been right all along and the troops were soon withdrawn.

In the mid-1970s, in another instance of bureaucratic competition in the foreign policy area, the American "energy czar" James Schlesinger was at odds with the State Department over policy toward oil-rich Mexico. More recently, differences have arisen between the State Department and the Drug Enforcement Agency (DEA) over the handling of drug traffickers. The DEA wants to arrest all drug traffickers (even if that includes the president, cabinet members, and armed forces chiefs of quite a few Latin American countries), while State has as part of its mission to maintain amicable relations with these same countries. The State and Treasury departments are frequently at odds over foreign economic policy. These differences are supposed to be resolved by the in-country American ambassador, who nominally is in charge of his entire mission team. Often, however, the DEA, CIA, Defense, and other missions abroad report directly to their superiors in Washington without going through the ambassador. Therefore, added to the lack of foreign policy coordination in Washington is often a lack of coordination in the field as well.

These bureaucratic rivalries are often portrayed in the media as rivalries between individuals (Secretary of State Cyrus Vance versus National Security Advisor Zbigniew Brzezinski under Carter or Secretary of State George Shultz versus Scretary of Defense Casper Weinberger under Reagan) because the media likes to personalize these conflicts and in that way simplify them. But these are not individual rivalries; they are *bureaucratic* rivalries and need to be understood as such, for they will continue regardless of the person occupying the position. Hence to our rational actor model we need to add a bureaucratic politics model to help make our analyses more complete.

THE ORGANIZATIONAL MODEL

Not only do foreign policy bureaucracies have perspectives and interests of their own, but they also have their own *procedures* for doing things. These are the normal, everyday, routine procedures that any organization develops over time in conducting its activities. The problem is that different foreign policy-making agencies may have different organizational procedures, or work at a different pace.

We have already mentioned the case of the Cuban missile crisis. President Kennedy and his White House advisers wanted a certain kind of blockade of Cuba. The Navy, however, had its own way of proceeding with a blockade and, despite the fulminations and even expletives of the President, would not change its procedures. The State Department has its separate way of functioning, and so do the CIA, NSC, and all the rest. These procedures and organizational norms may not always mesh, or even work in conjunction. Some agencies—for example, the Defense Department under Secretary Robert McNamara—are highly organized and keyed to fast reaction; others, by the very nature of their work—for example, diplomacy as practiced by the State Department—must necessarily be slow.

The Defense Department, for instance, has within its file cabinets (now computerized) contingency plans for the invasion and/or occupation of most of the countries in the world. If a crisis occurs in Burundi that is serious enough to warrant strong American military action, the Pentagon files have a set of plans to invade and occupy Burundi. The files contain information on flight plans, local airports, road conditions, key installations, and so on. In the case of the United States occupation of Grenada in 1983, however, it was discovered that a large share of the information on file was inaccurate or woefully out of date.

But let us take a case that will illustrate the importance of the organizational model. In 1965, a revolution was launched in the Caribbean country of the Dominican Republic that some within the Lyndon Johnson administration feared might lead to a Communist takeover. At first the United States assumed that the Dominican military could handle the insurrection. When, however, the regular armed forces were defeated and began to disintegrate under the onslaught of an aroused populace, it appeared that the revolutionaries might win. At this point the Johnson administration started to get nervous, and the President decided to send American troops. The Defense Department pressed the button marked

Dominican Republic and out came the file that showed that the only good airport in the country at which the American transport planes could land was the San Isidro Air Force Base. What the contingency plan did not show was that the San Isidro Base was under the control of one faction in the civil war and that our landing there would immediately be seen as bolstering that faction. In addition, the Pentagon machinery is so efficient in this kind of exercise that within minutes the transport planes were en route, the Atlantic Fleet was steaming toward the Dominican Republic, troop-carrying helicopters were in the air, and the amphibious landing craft were headed toward shore with United States occupation forces abroad. By morning American troops were in the country. Meanwhile the Department of State, which by the nature of things proceeds more slowly, was still trying to figure out the exact nature of the revolution, whether it was in fact under Communist control, who was who, and so forth. While these deliberations were still going on, the American ambassador awoke the next morning to discover United States paratroopers camped on his lawn.

Here we have a case in which the organizational procedures of the Defense Department were simply quicker and more efficient than the procedures of the State Department. Too quick, some State Department officials grumbled. Here they were with a full-scale military occupation on their hands before adequate assessment had been made of the nature of the revolution and its likely outcome. Moreover, the Pentagon's contingency plan had not taken account of political factors—that is, that landing at what everyone agreed was the best airport would inevitably bias the perception of whose side the United States was on, and would probably determine the revolution's outcome. The Defense Department was simply following its SOPs (Standard Operating Procedures), but in this case the SOPs were hardly neutral. Defense proved its "efficiency," but here efficiency outran careful planning, analysis, and assessment.

As this analysis suggests, many crucial aspects of foreign policy implementation are based on organizational routines and practices rather than rational choices or even bureaucratic rivalries. These routines or standard operating procedures are increasingly important as government becomes larger, more specialized, and more dependent on having rules and regulations to govern the internal behavior of the organization. That is why the organizational model has come to play a larger and larger role in foreign policy explanations.

THE SELF-AGGRANDIZEMENT MODEL

The self-aggrandizement model represents a quite cynical way of looking at American foreign policy-making. It suggests that congressmen and appointed officials alike are in the foreign policy "game" not necessarily to serve the public interest, as the usual campaign rhetoric suggests, but to garner prestige, power, personal career advancement, and sometimes plain old money. If the public interest also gets served in this process, it happens as a by-product of serving these other me-oriented goals. At a minimum, congressmen and policy-makers only carry out policy if it *simultaneously* can be viewed as helping themselves and helping the country.

A rich literature exists on what has been called "psychopathology and politics." This literature suggests that politicians and high government officials are only rarely the selfless, public-spirited defenders of the public interest that their own language and many of our elementary civics texts suggest. Rather, politicians tend to make their political career goals their first priority and to serve the public interest only as these private goals are also served. Listen to the analysis of Harold Lasswell, one of the century's great political scientists and a pioneer in the psychopathology and politics school:

> Political man is a deceptive creature. He imposes his private motives on public objects, but he does so in a manner that few can see through.[4]

Lasswell is quite cynical—many would say realistic—about politicians. He calls them "actors in disguise" because they always say they are serving the public when in fact they are merely serving their own self-interests. Politicians, according to Lasswell, engage in "ritualistic displacements of motives." That is, they are chiefly interested in advancing their own personal and political careers, but they can't say that publicly so they talk about serving the "public interest" or the "good of all." Says Lasswell: "Political prejudice, preferences, and creeds are often formulated in highly rational form but they are grown in highly irrational ways." In short, politicians seek to advance their own private careers and agendas but they cover this over with less self-serving language.

This tendency toward self-aggrandizement and self-centeredness under the guise of serving the public interest became even more pronounced in the 1970s. Then, as political party discipline and seniority declined in the Congress, and as Vietnam, Watergate, and a host of other domestic problems sapped the strength and legitimacy of our main institutions, the dominant orientation in public affairs as elsewhere became to "look out for number one."[5] The attitude is difficult to measure exactly, but few doubt that as a nation we (and that includes our politicians) have become more self-centered, more inward and self-concerned, with a greater emphasis on serving selfish personal and career goals rather than the broader and more selfless national interest. Such egoism and self-centeredness are now as prominent in political affairs as they are in the worlds of finance, entertainment, and other areas.

Some years ago, political scientist Edward Banfield made a distinction between what he called "private-regarding" attitudes toward public policy and "public-regarding" attitudes.[6] Private-regarding politicians are concerned primarily with advancing themselves, their families, or their clan or patronage groups. Public-regarding politicians, in contrast, are concerned primarily in serving the public interest. A private-regarding attitude, in Banfield's analysis, was characteristic of political leadership in the more traditional or less-developed areas while a public-regarding attitude was supposedly characteristic of the more developed countries. But in recent years, the United States has also become, to some degree, a private-regarding nation, with our emphasis on self and serving the private as distinct from the public weal, while emphasis on genuinely public service—for all the individual cases of truly selfless service that we may know about—is definitely on the decline.

Hence when we hear elected officials complain about how poorly paid they are and how salaries of public officials should be kept competitive with those in the private sector, we should probably be quite skeptical. Most public officials are paid very well, the perks and power associated with high office are very attractive, and few ranking politicians would be able to find a comparable place in the private sector even if they were interested. But they are not; virtually all the congressmen and public officials at the federal level love their jobs, love their influence and position, love the elite club atmosphere of the Senate or State Department, love the power, money, opportunities, and political "groupies" that hang on their every word. So we should not feel too sorry for such officials; more than that we need to come to grips with these self-centered motives as a powerful explanatory force in understanding some of the newer dimensions of American foreign policy-making.

Such an explanation, however, should not be carried too far. We should not elevate a useful but still partial explanation into an all-encompassing one. On the one hand, there should be no doubt that the self-aggrandizement motives discussed here (money, power, prestige, career and personal advancement) have become increasingly important in the last two decades. On the other hand, the amount of solid, empirical data about such explanatory factors is still limited, and the state of the art of our understanding about the relations between psychopathology and politics is not as certain as we would like it to be.[7] While we should take these selfish and self-centered motivations into account in our analysis of the factors behind foreign policy-making (and other kinds of policy-making), we should not give these factors such a great importance that they become the only or even the most important ones.

THE POLITICAL PROCESS MODEL

An explanation with surer footings is the political process model. We have so far looked at the rational actor model, the bureaucratic politics model, the organizational behavior model, and what we irreverently called the self-aggrandizement models. Later in the book we will look at the media model and still other approaches. Doubtless all these explanations have some utility in understanding foreign policy-making, but the one that presently seems to have more utility than most is the political process model.

The political process model, in foreign policy analyst as well as practitioner Roger Hilsman's words, views foreign policy as emerging from the political interactions of, quite literally, thousands of groups and actors.[8] Some of these actors have more power than others, and their relative power will vary over time and from issue to issue. Some groups are strong on Central America policy, others on Middle East policy, and others on South Africa policy. They may also have different ideas about policy goals and how to achieve them.

These actors and power centers try to build coalitions of like-minded groups so they can be more effective in influencing decisions. They involve themselves in the hurly-burly of politics: they try to get their position across, they manipulate, argue for their own views, try to persuade congressmen and others and, when necessary, apply what political muscle they can muster. These groups may get all of what they want, some of what they want, or none of what they want. They may decide to compromise and continue the political struggle. But the end result of all these political machinations is very often a policy that is not entirely logical or internally consistent but which represents the mishmash that results from these conflicting interests and from trying to give a little bit to everyone and never completely satisfying anyone. But then that is how politics in America works.

The political process model is based on the assessment that foreign policy, like domestic policy, is shaped by powerful actors and forces in the political system more generally and cannot be separated from these. Foreign policy is, in short, a reflection of domestic politics.[9] The days when "politics stops at the water's edge," an expression attributed to Senator Arthur Vandenberg of Michigan and, in an earlier time, chairman of the Senate Foreign Relations Committee, are over. By that statement Vandenberg meant that it was all right to play politics with domestic issues, but on critical, life-and-death foreign policy issues on which the fate of the nation and all its citizens might hang, political considerations should be eliminated, the nation should speak with one voice and one voice only, and divisive, partisan posturing should be eschewed.

Those days are gone forever. Politics and partisanship now *routinely* dominate our foreign policy discussions. Interest groups and special interest lobbies now routinely try to mobilize public opinion and make propaganda in foreign policy areas as they long have over domestic policy issues. Once public opinion is mobilized, the media seeks to set the agenda, and the think tanks take up the cause. Congressmen of one party seek to embarrass a president of the other; meanwhile the White House postures over foreign policy issues the same way it does over domestic policy issues. Foreign policy now *is* domestic politics to a degree unheard of in the past. When former Speaker of the House Thomas ("Tip") O'Neil says "all politics is local," the implication is that foreign policy issues are as much subject to partisanship, debate, and political deals as is domestic policy.

Our foreign policy has been politicized and made the stuff of domestic, political and partisan considerations. Both political parties have had a hand in this politicization process, and so have both Congress and the White House. As in domestic politics, foreign policy positions are often considered "cards" to be traded for some other political advantage; just like on domestic issues. Some politicians try to "make it" to the top and advance their political careers (the self-aggrandizement model) by loudly and publicly disagreeing with the president over foreign policy issues. Votes on foreign policy issues are similarly *routinely* traded for favors in other areas: a defense department installation in a congressman's home district, federal assistance for the local tobacco or wheat growers, a dam or a major public works project, or a subsequent vote on an entirely unrelated issue. For example, in seeking to secure the required votes to get the Panama Canal Treaty through Congress, President Carter had to make lavish promises (completely unrelated to the Treaty) to several key congressmen. Without these deals, the treaty would not have been approved. All this may be lamentable from a "rational" foreign policy point of view, but that is how the system works. We cannot and will not change that system easily. That is why this volume is titled *Foreign Policy Without Illusion.*

The political process approach is, in our view, a very important and useful approach in explaining American foreign policy-making. Not only does it closely correspond to the observed realities—the increased politicization and partisanship of foreign policy decisions—but it also provides a broader and more all-encompassing model than any of the alternatives offered thus far. This is not to minimize the importance of the rational actor, the bureaucratic, the organizational, or the personal aggrandizement models, but to emphasize that the political process model is broad enough to include many of the other factors here analyzed. It includes, for example, the competition between rival bureaucracies, the organizational peculiarities previously discussed, the decision-making process of the State Department and other agencies, as well as the personal career-enhancement goals outlined in the self-aggrandizement model. The political process model is thus both a useful and an independent approach to analyzing foreign policy-making, made particularly attractive because of its ability to incorporate at least some features of the other approaches here put forth.

CONCLUSION

A variety of approaches may be usefully employed in studying American foreign policy-making. None provides a full and complete explanation by itself. At the same time, however, all of the approaches here analyzed have some useful insights to offer.

We should beware, in foreign policy as elsewhere, of all-encompassing, single-cause explanations. Those who advance and argue for such single-cause explanations, or seek to elevate one model, however useful, into a position of being the only one permitted or utilized, usually have some ideological or methodological ax to grind. At the same time, an approach that emphasizes too many models or vantage points tends to lose us in the complexities of its explanations. That is not the purpose of using models to study foreign policy decision-making either.

We need an approach that is multifaceted enough to account for the complexities involved but that is simple enough not to lose sight of the main forest for all the trees. The several explanations and the approach set forth here seek to strike a balance between these two extremes.

Each of the models analyzed here—and that are woven into the successive chapters that follow—provides some insight into the workings of the foreign policy-making machinery. At the same time, no one of them offers a sufficient or complete explanation by itself. The trick is to be eclectic while at the same time seeing the patterns that exist. For example, we need to understand when and where the bureaucratic politics model applies while recognizing that it is only a partial explanation of the foreign policy process. Other models need to be woven together to complement the bureaucratic model and shed light on the factors which that model does not illuminate.

These models, in short, need to be seen as complementary to each other rather than as rivals. Where the organizational model is useful, let us certainly use it while also recognizing that it most likely needs to be supplemented with other approaches. The decision about what model or models to use should be pragmatic rather than ideological. If one model enlightens one aspect of an issue, then we will use it; but if we see that other models are also helpful, then we will use them as well. Our approach will be to weave these several models together, to use elements of each where appropriate, to look for complementarity between them, and to borrow eclectically from each.

At the same time, we need to recognize that not all explanations are equal and that the relative balance between them may change over time. At present, the rational actor model seems to be in decline as a way of explaining how foreign policy decisions get made while the political process model is ascendant. Not only does the political process model offer a broader explanation and encompass some important ingredients in foreign policy-making but, as political factors have in fact become more important in our foreign policy-making, so the political process model has taken on increasing importance as an explanatory device.

Let us then proceed with our analysis of foreign policy-making, keeping these models and approaches in mind as we do so. We begin with an analysis of the American political culture and public opinion, and their influences on foreign policy.

Notes

1. Graham Allison, *Essence of Decision: Explaining the Cuban Missile Crisis* (Boston: Little Brown, 1971): Roger Hilsman, *The Politics of Policy-Making in Defense and Foreign Policy: Conceptual Models and Bureaucratic Politics* (Englewood Cliffs, N.J.: Prentice-Hall, 1987).
2. Howard J. Wiarda, "Power and Policy-Making in Washington, D.C., in the Latin America Area: Impressions and Reflections" (Paper presented at the Center for International Affairs, Harvard University, Cambridge, Mass., 1985).
3. Allison, *Essence of Decision.*
4. Harold Lasswell, *Psychopathology and Politics* (Chicago: University of Chicago Press, 1977): 8, 153.
5. Robert Ringer, *Looking Out For Number One* (Beverly Hills, Calif.: Los Angeles Book Corp., 1977).
6. Edward Banfield, *The Moral Basis of a Backward Society* (Glencoe, Ill.: The Free Press, 1958).
7. See, for example, Doris Kearns, *Lyndon Johnson and the American Dream* (New York: Harper and Row, 1976).
8. Hilsman, *Politics of Policy-Making.*
9. Don C. Piper and Ronald J. Tercheck, eds. *Interaction: Foreign Policy and Public Policy* (Washington, D.C.: American Enterprise Institute for Public Policy Research, 1983).

Suggested Readings

Allison, Graham. *Essence of Decision: Explaining the Cuban Missile Crisis* (Boston: Little Brown, 1971): Roger Hilsman, *The Politics of Policy-Making in Defense and Foreign Policy: Conceptual Models and Bureaucratic Politics* (Englewood Cliffs, N.J.: Prentice-Hall, 1987).

Art, Robert. "Bureaucratic Politics and American Foreign Policy: A Critique," *Policy Studies* (1973).

Halperin, Morton. *Bureaucratic Politics and Foreign Policy.* Washington, D.C.: The Brookings Institution, 1974.

Hermann, Charles F., Charles W. Kegley, Jr., and James N. Rosenau, eds. *New Directions in the Study of Foreign Policy.* Boston: Allen and Unwin, 1987.

Krasner, Stephen D. "Are Bureaucracies Important? (Or Allison Wonderland)." *Foreign Policy* 17(Summer 1971).

Neustadt, Richard. *Alliance Politics.* New York: Columbia University Press, 1970.

Piper, Don C. and Ronald J. Tercheck, eds. *Interaction: Foreign Policy and Public Policy* (Washington, D.C.: American Enterprise Institute for Public Policy Research, 1983).

Wiarda, Howard J. "Power and Policy-Making in Washington, D.C., in the Latin America Area: Impressions and Reflections" (Paper presented at the Center for International Affairs, Harvard University, Cambridge, Mass., 1985).

CHAPTER THREE

American Political Culture and Foreign Policy

❂
❂

The United States is a funny, peculiar, distinct nation in many re-spects—including those that pertain to foreign policy. All nations are, of course, unique, with their own histories, cultures, ways of doing things, and geostrategic positions that in turn help shape their behavior. But because we are a superpower, because we are a "beacon on a hill," a model for other nations; because our history has been so distinctive and because our attitudes and practice of foreign policy are often so much at variance with those practiced by the rest of the world, the United States and its unique attitudes and methods of foreign policy merit special attention.

We have already, in the preceding paragraph, provided the definition of political culture with which we need to begin this chapter. Political culture refers to the ideas, beliefs, attitudes, and behavioral patterns that help undergird a nation's political system. Political culture is to be distin-guished from the older, (and discredited) "national character" studies ("Italians do this," "Americans are that," and so forth) that involve unac-ceptable stereotyping. Political culture is more precise and empirical: it can be measured by means of public opinion surveys; it stresses *patterns* of behavior rather than stereotypes (not all Americans, therefore, are pre-sumed to fit the general pattern); and it is more rigorous and systematic. In this chapter we will be concerned not with the entire American political culture in all its manifold complexities but only with those aspects that relate to and influence American foreign policy-making.

FUNNELS, CIRCLES, AND THE PLAN OF THE BOOK

Before beginning the discussion of political culture and its influence on American foreign policy, let us review for a moment the plan and logic of this book and why we have organized the chapters in the order found here. Having finished the Introduction and the chapter on models of foreign policy-making, this is a good point to preview what comes next and why. There is in fact a logic and principle to the sequence of chapters.

Scholars of foreign policy frequently use two visual images, or metaphors, to describe the effects of different pressures and groups on foreign policy-making. Either image can profitably be used to better understand foreign policy-making; these should, therefore, be looked on as aides to learning or as teaching and organizational devices, and not as magical formulas. The two images we employ here are a "funnel of causality" and a series of concentric circles.[1]

The funnel image, as the name implies, is rather like a funnel used in a chemistry laboratory or for putting radiator fluid in a car (see Figure 3.1). The funnel is wide at the top and narrow toward the bottom. At the widest end of the funnel are located the broadest and most general influences on foreign policy: political culture, public opinion, the mass media. At the next level (and with fewer numbers) are the intermediary groups: political parties, interest groups, think tanks. These organizations help channel the often diverse and inchoate foreign policy opinions of the mass public into organized positions. Then come the Congress as well as the bureaucratic agencies and influences: State, Defense, CIA, and so forth. Finally, at the narrowest part of the funnel, are the actual foreign policy decision makers—the president, the National Security Council, the White House staff,

Figure 3.1
Funnel of Foreign Policy Causation

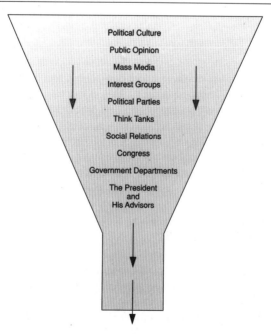

and key advisers who help convert all these influences into concrete policy. Such decisions then flow out of the lower end of the funnel as American policy.

Another image frequently used to illustrate the same points is that of concentric circles (see Figure 3.2). In the outer ring are, again, as in the funnel metaphor, the most general influences on foreign policy: political culture, public opinion, mass media. The next circle contains the political parties, interest groups, and think tanks that help articulate foreign policy. The third level contains the Congress and the foreign affairs bureaucracies. And at the decision-making center of all this activity is the president and his key advisers.

Neither of these images is to be taken literally. Rather they both serve as pictures of how the foreign policy *system* works. It proceeds from very general and broad influences on policy-making to very specific decision making at the White House level. The images illustrate the intermediary or "transmission belt" functions performed by such agencies as the political parties, interest groups, and think tanks. And, in going from the general to the particular, from broad-based explanations of and influences on policy-making to narrower and more concrete ones, funnel and concentric circle images also provide the organizational principle of this book. That is why we proceed from the influence of such a broad-brush explanation as

Figure 3.2
Concentric Circles of Foreign Policy Influences

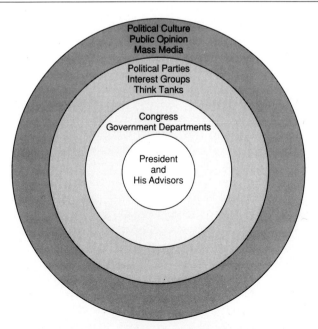

political culture in this chapter and public opinion in the next to some very specific and concrete explanations as we approach the epicenter of decision making in the White House.

That is the logic and principle of organization of policy-making in a pluralist democracy; it is also the principle on which the organization of this book is based.

THE UNIQUE AMERICAN EXPERIENCE

The United States has not long had a serious foreign policy or even serious foreign policy interests. Foreign policy is a relatively new responsibility (mainly in the twentieth century and, some would say, only since World War II) for the United States, and we are not, by the accounts of most objective observers, very good at it. We tend to be naive and inexperienced in foreign affairs, constantly confusing and mixing up our moral and ethical preoccupations with the necessities of a hardheaded defense of the national interest, and there are peculiarly American traits that may make us respected, even lovable, in some respects but that do not always serve our foreign policy needs. For example, Americans are, generally, a kind-hearted, helpful, open, and trusting people, so much so that we discuss all our weaknesses (and secrets) in front of strangers and we are often trusting and helpful even to those who want only to take advantage of us. In fact, we have a hard time believing there are people in the world who could or would take advantage of such well-meaning people as we. The rest of the world thinks Americans are crazy (but also endearing) in these respects, but how can we carry out a serious foreign policy on such a naive and do-gooder basis? Can we somehow retain those traits that we all value as Americans and at the same time conduct an effective foreign policy? More and more analysts are no longer sure of the answer. They see very serious problems arising from trying to pursue both idealism and a hardheaded defense of the national interest at the same time.

America's problems in carrying out a serious and coherent foreign policy have their origins deep in the historical past. This is not a book about diplomatic history, and we do not intend here to review the entire United States record. Rather, our purpose is to interpret and select from that history the most salient features that have had—and continue to have—an effect on our foreign policy and help explain it.

To begin, America is a product of geography. Our foreign policy has been strongly shaped by our location. On our eastern flank we are protected (before the onset of intercontinental ballistic missiles) from Europe by five or six thousand miles of ocean and thus have avoided until World War I any entanglements in Europe's numerous and debilitating conflicts. On our western flank, we are protected by an even broader expanse of water and the absence, until recently, of any serious strategic threat from that side. The emergence of China, Japan, and the Soviet Union as an Asian as well as European power has changed all that.

To the north, we have that long, peaceful border (the longest nonmilitarized border in the world) with fellow English-speaking (for the most part) Canada—and everyone knows, of course, that English-speaking countries are more trustworthy than any of the other kinds. That leaves only our southern flank exposed, and there we have a large number of mostly small, weak, seemingly endemically unstable Latin American countries. While these nations have never posed a serious direct threat to us, we have always worried that the very weakness and instability of the countries of Central America and the Caribbean will enable some foreign power to establish a base there from which to attack or do damage to United States interests. Spain, France, and Great Britain were viewed as the main challenges in the past, then Germany during the two world wars, and obviously the Soviet Union now. It is no accident that American military interventions and occupations, when they have occurred, have almost all taken place in Central America and the Caribbean.

Geographic isolation has kept us out of most European conflicts, kept us immune (until recently) from big power rivalries, and enabled us to avoid ever having to fight a major international war on our own territory. It helps explain why we are such newcomers to the "game," responsibilities, and sometimes downright nasty strategies of big-power international politics. And it explains our sense of isolation from such conflicts, our reluctance oftentimes to get involved in policing actions that may be in our best interest to perform. And it explains that peculiarly American notion that force and diplomacy are to be employed only in times of all-out war, and that the rest of the time we can and should remain aloof from international politics, the use of force, or power politics.

A second major conditioning factor historically has been the sheer wealth and self-sufficiency of America. We are a nation that is richly endowed. We are the world's most productive nation agriculturally. For a long time we were self-sufficient in petroleum. We have abundant coal and iron ore in juxtaposition for the smelting of steel. We have gently flowing and navigable rivers, abundant forests, inland waterways, some of the richest land on earth, and a wealth of other mineral and vegetable products.

All this wealth and abundance has meant we have never—historically—had to be dependent on, or interrelate with, the rest of the world. Indeed, because of these riches, we have always behaved as though we could get along perfectly well without the rest of the world. That helps explain why, compared with persons from other countries, so few Americans speak any foreign languages and why they are often so ignorant of other countries and cultures. America's sheer affluence and self-sufficiency have led us to conclude that we could go it alone in the world, thumb our noses at entangling foreign conflicts, build protectionist barriers, and retreat into a self-contained existence.

Such isolationist sentiment was virtually universal in nineteenth-century America. It began to change around the time of World War I, and definitively changed during and in the aftermath of World War II, when the United States emerged as the world's foremost superpower with global interests and responsibilities. Even today, however, surveys show that the American public remains about one-third isolationist, wanting to go it alone in the world and to throw up protectionist walls to keep out foreign products—as if that were realistic and still possible in today's modern, interdependent world. In 1988, Representative (and presidential candidate) Richard Gephardt (D-MO) sought to tap this strong strain of populist, protectionist, and isolationist sentiment by standing for stronger trade barriers against foreign-made products.

America was also founded, thirdly, on a basis that was Christian, largely Protestant, and with strong Puritan and Calvinist beliefs. This history, too, has shaped our foreign policy attitudes and posture. Only later did the colonies—and the nation—become genuinely pluralist and more secular. This early history and religious basis help explain America's preoccupation with doing good in the world, its missionary spirit to bring the benefits of American civilization to less-favored lands, its inability to treat nations and regions with different cultures and religions on an equal plane. It explains our efforts to export democracy and human rights, to serve as a moral beacon in the world, to try to act ethically in an essentially anarchic world. It further helps explain our sense of guilt, remorse, even "original sin" when we fail to do good in the world or commit atrocities, as occurred in certain instances in Vietnam. Just as Puritan preacher Cotton Mather, when he had a toothache, wondered what sin he had committed with his teeth, so many Americans today worry that they must atone for their past "sins" in the Third World and are often agonized with guilt over past interventions or aggressive actions.

The conditions of geographic security, self-sufficiency, and isolationism help explain the early history of American foreign policy or, more accurately, the absence of one. During the earliest period of our history, the thirteen colonies essentially had no foreign policy, nor had they any need of one. They were protected by geography, distance, and the navy of the colonial master, Great Britain, from European conflicts as well as from the marauding pirates and imperial rivalries that characterized the British, French, and Spanish colonies in the Caribbean. New England merchantmen traded with Africa and the Caribbean, but as colonies they could not have—nor did they much have a need of—any kind of military force or foreign policy.

Nor did independence much change matters, at least initially. George Washington warned against getting involved in those "entangling alliances" of the European powers, and for a long time (1789–1916) we largely heeded his advice. Thomas Jefferson sent the American "fleet" (what there was of one) to the Barbary Coast to beat up on the pirates operating there, but that was just a brief police action. In 1823, President James Monroe issued the famous doctrine that bears his name, but at the time the United States lacked the military muscle to back up Monroe's moral injunctions to keep Europe out of the Western Hemisphere. In fact, the United States did not develop a serious military and naval force until the end of the nineteenth century.

Our foremost concentration as a new nation during the past century was on internal, continental development, not foreign expansionism or international military ventures. Our settlers first spilled over the Appalachian Mountains into the upper south (Kentucky, Tennessee) and midwest. In the Louisiana Purchase, the United States acquired the Mississippi basin and the lands to the northwest. From the 1820s through the Civil War and beyond, the doctrine of "manifest destiny" carried us west, all the way to the Pacific. Indeed it was manifest destiny that largely involved us in the few wars that we fought during this century: the war for Texas independence in 1836, the war with Mexico in 1846, and the war with Spain in 1898. Manifest destiny was by then thought to lead us south into the Caribbean and Central America and no longer just westerly toward the Pacific.

By this last conflict in 1898, in fact, the United States *had* become a significant world power—but not before. Our preoccupation in the nineteenth century was not with foreign affairs but with settling, filling up, and developing the vast American interior. America was the land of opportunity, a golden land, where farms could be acquired cheap if not free, and the preoccupation was getting rich, or at least starting anew and getting ahead. In our internal preoccupations, we had no time, no inclination, no enthusiasm (to say nothing of no military) for foreign affairs.

With massive immigration into the United States in the 1880s and afterwards came a new interest in international affairs. The immigrants came from many lands and carried with them an abiding interest in the countries of their origins. They helped draw the United States closer to Europe and hence to European affairs and even conflicts. Although ethnic loyalties were often submerged under overwhelming Americanization, the immigrants—and their descendants—retained an interest in their homelands. The waves of new immigrants added a greater diversity to America, made it more pluralist in both political and religious ways, and provided the seeds for future ethnic-related differences over foreign policy issues.

At the same time, following the Civil War, the United States began to emerge as a major manufacturing and industrial power, and began simultaneously to develop the military might to go with its newfound economic strength. We developed a navy and began to flex our military might. As a result of defeating Spain in 1898 we acquired Puerto Rico and the Philippines, established a protectorate over Cuba, and became the major military and political presence (replacing Great Britain) in the Caribbean and Central America.

It is important to emphasize that these were not viewed as conquests by the United States. Rather they were in keeping with a long history by which the United States justified (and doubtless actually believed) its military conquests by the use of moral, even religious, principle. That is another abiding characteristic of American foreign policy that bears emphasis. There is no doubt that the United States thinks of itself as a special nation, a Zion, a beacon on a hill, a country blessed by God's will and with a moral and religious mission in the world. This urge, this ethos, reaches deep into our colonial and Calvinist past.

No one doubts, for instance, that when the Texans fought to achieve independence from Mexico, and then ten years later when the United States defeated Mexico in war and deprived Mexico of almost half its national territory, that we were acting in accord with moral law, with God's design for the universe, and in accord with ethical principles. Manifest destiny was similarly presented in quasi-religious terms, as corresponding to God's will. President McKinley is reported to have prayed and received God's blessing before he took the Philippines; the entire Spanish-American War, in fact, was viewed as a moral crusade to save Cuba and other Caribbean nations from the "evils"of an "inquisitorial nation" (Spain) and from the clutches of the "papal legions."

This moralistic, missionary strain is very powerful in America. It means that we can seldom act on the international level simply because our national interests demand it; rather our policies need to be justified by resort to some higher end and purpose. Our policies must be morally and ethically good and noble. That helps explain Jimmy Carter's crusade for human rights and Ronald Reagan's attempt to justify his Central American policies on the basis of support for democracy.

Some foreign policy analysts criticize and lament this need always to justify our actions in moralistic terms, and there is no doubt life would be simpler for us (in a foreign policy sense, of course) if we just acted from a purely national-interest point of view, as virtually all other nations in this essentially lawless international environment do. But most analysts, including such a hardheaded spokesman for a policy of *realpolitik* as Henry Kissinger, have now concluded that in the United States it is not possible to have a successful American foreign policy based on purely national-interest considerations. A moral component (democracy, human rights) must be built in. The trick, of course, is to come up with a foreign policy that is both morally good and also serves our national interests. But sometimes, as in Vietnam or Central America (as we explain in more detail later in the book), that is not possible, or convincing, or the two prove contradictory. That is when we as a nation (and our foreign policy) often get in trouble.

The United States entered World War I for a moral reason—"to make the world safe for democracy," as President Woodrow Wilson put it—as well as to defend the national interest. But the isolationist urge was still strong. Having entered the war and achieved its objectives (as it had against Spain in 1898), the United States then immediately retreated again into its isolationist shell. For that reason we refused to join the League of Nations (the forerunner of the United Nations) and, in the 1920s and 1930s, refused to exercise the military, diplomatic, and policing functions now commensurate with our power and needed to keep the peace. The United States once again concentrated on domestic affairs, refusing to take adequate cognizance of the rising German/Nazi threat in Europe or Japanese expansion in Asia and the Pacific.

World War II was the key turning point. The United States entered the war with the familiar assumptions (that we were doing good in the world by defeating fascism as well as defending the national interests) and thought that, as in the past, once the war was over we could go back to the familiar task of getting ahead. But this time things were different. The United States emerged from the war as the world's leading, and virtually only, industrial and military power. Everyone else—France, Britain, Germany, Japan, even the Soviet Union, which would soon emerge as our chief rival—had been exhausted and devastated by the war. The United States was thrust into the position of playing a leading role in the world whether we wanted to or not (we did want to, but often quite reluctantly). The shift was not abrupt or dramatic. During the year or two of good feeling that followed the war, we again disbanded our armed forces and returned to our peacetime pursuits. But with the Soviet takeovers and continued presence of Red armies in Eastern Europe; Soviet aggressions and efforts to destabilize existing regimes in Greece, Turkey, and Iran; the Communist triumph in the Chinese Civil War; Communist North Korea's war of aggression against the South; and, overall, the onset of the cold war, the United States had to reenter the global arena.

The United States took up an international policing role with grave reservations. We wanted to expand our influence but we also wished to concentrate on getting ahead at home. Isolationist sentiment remained strong immediately after World War II, but by the early 1950s (the later Truman and early Eisenhower years), only about one-third of the electorate supported isolationist policies. Among internationalists, who now numbered upwards of two-thirds of the electorate, there was remarkable consensus on what the basic goals of American policy should be. These goals were shaped by the events of the 1930s and 1940s leading to World War II and the war years, as well as by the cold war and the emerging rivalry with the Soviet Union. The basic goals on which the internationalist consensus was based included the following:

1. Stand firmly for democracy and freedom.
2. Contain communism.
3. Resist aggression and not appease it.

Now these were lofty and noble goals. They powerfully shaped an entire generation and more of post–World War II American policy-makers. Doubtless most Americans still believe in these goals today. They served as the basis for the Marshall Plan to aid Western Europe, for American opposition to Communist incursions in various parts of the world, for resistance to North Korean aggression, and for John F. Kennedy's Alliance for Progress. The consensus on these goals was widespread among the American electorate, it transcended political party lines, and it served as the basis for a generally successful postwar American foreign policy.

But the war in Vietnam destroyed this consensus, and may have also destroyed the possibilities for an effective American foreign policy. By the late 1960s, that war had led to protest movements in the streets, had deeply divided the American public, had produced by the 1970s our first-ever defeat in war and the bitter recriminations that followed, and had resulted in a severe questioning of the very basis of our foreign policy assumptions that led us into the war in the first place. Was it really democracy and freedom that we were standing for in Vietnam? Numerous acts on our part seemed to point to a negative answer to that question. Were we really containing communism, or were we only standing against Vietnamese nationalism and a desire for social justice? Were we really resisting aggression by the North Vietnamese or were we intruding in a conflict more in the nature of a civil war among divided and perpetually quarreling South Vietnamese elements?

It is almost impossible to overstate the devastating effects the Vietnam war had on American foreign policy-making. Not only was the public divided by the war, but so was the foreign policy-making elite. As a result of the war, we lost our nerve, our willingness to get involved in international disputes, even our direction as a nation. During the later Nixon, Ford, and Carter years, we turned inward, often tried to avoid foreign entanglements, deemphasized our defense and preparedness requirements, and stood idly by as the Soviet Union surpassed us in many military areas. There was a lot of finger pointing, of looking for scapegoats, of passing around blame for the debacle we had suffered. Meanwhile, race riots spread in our cities, the economy went into a tailspin, our political system cracked and creaked with the Watergate revelations of presidential (Nixon) indiscretions and a cover-up, the then president (Carter) talked of a national "malaise," and economically the United States lost its overwhelming preeminent place in the world. We began to speak of lowered expectations and living standards, and of our incapacity any longer to serve as policeman of the world.

Some of these trends were reversed under President Reagan, but many of the underlying problems remained. The 1980s saw renewed vigor in the economy, new hopefulness among Americans, a renewed defense buildup, and a willingness to act—even aggressively at times—in defense of our interests. But many in the Congress and in the public distrusted the President's motives and his capacity to conduct foreign affairs. Reagan received two overwhelming electoral mandates in 1980 and 1984 and remained personally popular throughout his term, but foreign policy—in Central America, in dealing with the Soviets, in the Middle East—remained tremendously controversial. Serious foreign policy analysts began to question, after the Carter and Reagan experiences, whether the United States was able to carry out a serious, mature, long-term, and rational foreign policy. These problems continued to plague the new administration of George Bush as it took office in January 1989, and was immediately confronted with a myriad of problems that again seemed almost to defy solution.

AMERICAN FOREIGN POLICY BEHAVIOR

If we consider this in many ways unique American historical and cultural experience, we can extrapolate from it a number of behavior patterns that enable us to see why ours is often a distinctive kind of foreign policy.

1. Isolationism. With secure borders on all sides and immense resources and domestic wealth—both agricultural and mineral—the United States has never felt it needed a strong and coherent foreign policy. We have historically believed, and about one-third of us *still* believe (as we see in the next chapter) that all that is necessary is for America to stay strong, throw up barriers (military as well as economic protectionist) all around, and go it alone in the world regardless of friends, neighbors, allies (to say nothing of adversaries), alliances and, most recently, complex economic interdependence. Nevertheless, the isolationist urge remains strong; even among nonisolationists the desire to lash out at our sometimes recalcitrant allies (to say nothing of our foes), or at developing nations that not only don't thank us for our aid but criticize us in international forums besides, is powerful.

2. Superiority. By virtually all accounts, America has been a successful civilization. Our political system is stable and democratic, our renewed economy is still the envy of the world, and our culture, from rock music to blue jeans and Coca Cola, to say nothing of freedom and liberty, is emulated everywhere. But these very accomplishments have sometimes tended to make America arrogant and condescending, especially in dealing with foreign nations. We tend to assume that our ways and institutions are always the best and that we can bring the benefits of our ways to other countries and peoples—sometimes whether they want them or not. In a parallel fashion, our social science models tend to assume that ours are the most "developed" and "modern" of institutions, and that everyone else is, or ought to be, developing toward a system that looks just like ours.

Most Americans tend to believe that our institutions are in fact pretty good ones, particularly when compared not with an abstract ideal but with those of other countries. Furthermore, most Americans believe that it is the right, duty, and obligation of the United States to serve as an example to others, even to bring our institutions to less-favored lands. We really do see ourselves as a beacon on a hill, a model. Most Americans are not cultural relativists; they believe that some ideas and institutions are more productive, more efficient, perform better, are more worthwhile, and more ethical than others.[2] The difficulty comes, however, when we seek to export these institutions abroad where the culture may be entirely different and the capacity to absorb American ways lacking. There are in fact worthwhile and productive things that the United States can do to bring its most-admired institutions, such as democracy, freedom, and human rights, to other nations; but at the same time care, caution, and a great deal of patience and restraint (not among America's most talked-about traits) are also necessary.

3. Impatience. The United States is not a notably patient country. We want to get things done, resolved, over with. We are impatient with the slowness of diplomacy and the difficulties of achieving quick results from our policies. Reflecting our isolationist history, we want to plunge into the world only long enough to accomplish our objectives and then we prefer to pull back again from our responsibilities as a world power. That was our history during World Wars I and II and in many respects, it remains our preference today: go in, but only reluctantly; get the job done quickly; and then revert immediately to "normal" (in the real world of relations among nations, of course, these have not been normal at all) peacetime pursuits. We want "quick 'n' easy" solutions to our problems, as in the American intervention in Grenada in 1983 (intervene quickly, accomplish our objectives, and pull out in two weeks), and not protracted struggles, as in Vietnam or currently in Central America. We want instant solutions to what are difficult and long-term problems.

4. Peace as normal, conflict as abnormal. The one hundred years between 1815 and 1914, during which the United States grew up as a nation, were probably the most peaceful in all world history. There were few European wars and no general world conflagrations into which the United States was dragged. Because of this history, Americans came to think of peace as the world's normal state of affairs and conflict and war as abnormal. That explains why, when we have entered wars and vanquished our foes, we have immediately gone back to the "normalcy" of peacetime activities; it also helps explain our ambivalence about the use of force and our reluctance to engage in power politics. It is hard for us as a nation to think of conflict as the normal state of affairs of most of the world's peoples and nations.

Nor are we at all equipped, for these same reasons, to come to grips with violence and terrorism. Because these features have generally been absent from our own lives and history, we think their occurrence must represent some abnormality or pathology. As Americans, we are ill-prepared to think of violence, coups, bloodshed, and terrorism as expected, everyday, recurring, and normal in most countries of the world and in the relations between nations. That is one key reason why we cannot cope very well with terrorism as the normal technique of politics that it is in many countries of the world. Learning what terrorism is and how it is used is, of course, the first step in combatting it. Our purpose in raising this issue is certainly not to condone violence and terrorism, but only to suggest that these activities are regular, recurrent phenomena in many parts of the globe, and that as a nation we are poorly equipped to understand this.

5. A missionary tradition. The United States, as we have seen, has always had a moralistic or missionary tradition to its foreign policy. No serious historian doubts that President Polk believed he was acting morally when he took from Mexico half of its national territory; and who could doubt that President McKinley was sincere when he prayed before taking the Philippines. President Wilson similarly entered World War I "to make the world safe for democracy"; he also sent United States Marines to occupy half a dozen Caribbean and Central American countries to bring democracy to "our little brown and black brothers" (note, again, the patronizing, superior, missionary attitudes). We entered World War II presumably to defeat fascism, and we have resisted Soviet aggression on the grounds of opposing "godless communism." John F. Kennedy launched the Alliance for Progress, Jimmy Carter began a crusade for global human rights, and Ronald Reagan made the expansion of democracy the centerpiece of his foreign policy.

This moralistic and missionary aspect to American foreign policy has long been criticized by the *realist* school of foreign policy analysts who want the United States, like other nations, to defend its *interests* and not go off on moral crusades. But because of this powerful streak of idealism in American foreign policy, it is really not possible for *this country* to separate idealistic from national interests. We needed to oppose fascism, not just the threat posed by an expansionist Germany; we need to stand fast against communism, not just contain an aggressive Soviet Russia. Kennedy's Alliance for Progress clearly had a strategic purpose (to prevent more Cubas in the Caribbean) as well as an idealistic one; Reagan's democracy initiative was similarly aimed at establishing a democratic regime in Nicaragua that would be in accord with American interests instead of a Marxist one that clearly was not. If Nicaragua's Sandinista leaders had awakened one fine morning and sent their Cuban and Soviet advisers home, renounced their Marxism, vowed not to aid guerrilla forces in neighboring countries, and petitioned to reestablish close ties with the United States, it is plain our concern for "democracy" in Nicaragua would be greatly reduced—not eliminated, because we are really idealistic about this, but certainly ameliorated.

The United States cannot have a successful foreign policy without having a strong moralistic and idealistic component to it. Nor can we have a successful foreign policy (as under Carter) in which the idealistic component is the only or the dominant one. For Americans are a practical people (see below) as well as an idealistic one. Rather, the best strategy is to have a foreign policy in which the realistic or national-interest motivations and the idealist components are combined. Or where idealism can be used to justify a hardheaded and realistic approach—for example, in standing for human rights and political pluralism in the Soviet Union or China. Or where we stand for realism (a strong posture against Germany's further expansionism during World War II) and idealism (anti-Fascism) at the same time. Now, such a posture is good when it can be arranged, but it can sometimes get us in trouble. A monolithic policy of moralistic opposition to all forms of communism may prevent us from playing the "China card" of separating and setting at odds the world's two most powerful Communist countries. And a policy favoring democracy may at times prevent us from assisting some Third World authoritarian regime that alone (no democratic alternative) stands against a Marxist-Leninist takeover, when it clearly would be in our national interest, although obviously not our moral principles, to do so. Thus, while a moralistic foreign policy causes problems at times, it is also the case that the United States cannot have a successful foreign policy unless it has a strong moral component to it.

6. Practicality. It is a curious paradox that while Americans have a strong idealistic streak, they also want to see practical results. Their idealism is not blind but must show a positive outcome. A human rights component in our foreign policy must result in improved relations with various countries and our standing in the world—or it will be rejected. The United States supports democracy in Central America, but the Central Americans also have to do their part. Americans can be very generous with their foreign aid, as in the case of food relief for Ethiopia. But once they begin to understand that such aid is being held up for political purposes by the host government, or is being wasted or, even worse, that the aid that we give *gratis* and at some sacrifice is being sold or hoarded by corrupt officials, then that generosity can dry up very quickly.

7. Ethnocentrism. Because the United States has been such a successful country, by comparative standards, its people have come to believe that all of its institutions are also the best and that we can and should export them to other countries. This goes for a host of American institutions. For example, we think that liberal American democracy and its institutions— free press, independent Congress, independent judiciary, strong local government, checks and balances, and so on—can be easily transferred to less-developed countries if only they can be educated and taught to see the wisdom of our ways. Americans believe that through a well-meaning agrarian reform program, rural El Salvador can be made to look like rural Wisconsin, with medium-sized family farms and a well-educated and civ- ically conscious rural population of yeoman farmers who are also participatory democrats. Because it has been so productive in our country, we think we can transfer an essentially market-based and free-enterprise economy to other countries where a strong state that controls and organ- izes the economy, sets prices, wages, and production quotas has always been the norm.

Because of the particularities of the American experience, we also believe that change must be gradual and evolutionary, not radical and revolutionary. Liberal democratic political institutions and free and open market mechanisms, we believe, are the best way to do this. Moreover, as was the case in our own society, we believe that economic development, social modernization (rising literacy, etc.), and political development (generally understood as democratization) can and do go hand in hand. Because of our own past history, we are optimistic that American institu- tions can solve all problems, and we fully expect that what works domesti- cally will also work internationally.

The problems with these ideas are many. American democracy is not easily transferable, if it can be done at all, to countries and societies where the culture and norms are quite different from our own. Statist economies are not very efficient, but they do provide lots of jobs and patronage functions, and to change them may produce instability. Social, economic, and political development are all good, but they do not always go hand in hand; indeed we have learned that rapid social mobilization may well lead to the destabilization of decent democratic regimes rather than contribut- ing to them. Programs that we favor from a moral or ethical viewpoint, such as agrarian reform, may produce results other than those anticipated, such as lower productivity, which leads peasants to be even worse off. Or we discover that what works in the United States may not work in somebody else's country.

Let us be clear about what we are trying to say. Most Americans believe, with Winston Churchill, that "democracy is the worst form of govern- ment—except for all others." That is, we really believe that our form of government is the best, not only for us but for others as well. The question is whether or not it can be successfully exported, and what are the costs (as well as benefits) of our trying to do so. Similarly with economics: the evidence is by now overwhelming that economies that allow a larger measure of freedom and openness tend to be more productive.[3] But the patronage functions of many statist regimes are also important to keep in mind, for in our zeal to reduce statism and introduce free markets, we may also be reducing the number of public sector jobs in Third World countries, thereby destabilizing inadvertently the very countries we are trying to help. Hence while we obviously treasure our own institutions and believe that other countries would also be better off if they adopted American ways, we need to be careful, restrained, and prudent in implementing such policies lest our good intentions produce consequences that are in fact quite disastrous.

8. Ahistoricism. The United States suffers from a form of historical amnesia. We pay little attention to the past and, therefore, learn little from it. Everything in America, from its vast plains, wide-open spaces, and endless opportunities, historically, to begin anew, is seen as fresh and tractable. Lacking a long historical tradition like the countries of Western Europe, without a feudal past, America assumes that experience is not worth remembering or consulting. As a nation, we are present- and future-oriented, not past-oriented.

The lessons we learn from the past, if we learn them at all, are confusing and contradictory, again because we lack a longer historical sense and the patience and serenity that go with it. We thought we had learned in the 1930s that appeasement is bad and that we must resist aggression, but those lessons did not work very well when stretched to include a non-Western, Third World country like Vietnam, which did not read the same history books we did. Pundits often talk nowadays of the "lessons of Vietnam," as if those lessons were clear and beyond dispute. The Reagan administration stated that we were now overcoming our "Vietnam complexes," whatever those might be. Not only do we not pay much attention to historical experience as a guide for today, but when we do, the metaphors we use (like Vietnam, which is no longer in a sense a real place but only an abstraction, a metaphor) mean different things to different groups.

9. Other traits. Americans are a *pragmatic* people. We value common sense, the wisdom of the man in the street, public opinion. But public opinion in this country, as we will see in the next chapter, is woefully uninformed on foreign policy issues and cannot serve as an adequate basis for policy. The oversimplifications that common sense and man-in-the-street wisdom give rise to reduce our foreign policy debate to the level of bumper stickers ("Ban the Bomb," "U.S. Out of El Salvador," "Ollie North Is an American Hero," "No More Nukes"), as if such slogans really solve anything.

Americans tend toward *optimism.* Ours is a can-do nation, one with all the right answers, that believes we can solve all problems. But in the international arena, such derring-do is frequently dangerous. Most of our international problems—un-American though it is to say that—cannot be *solved*. At most, usually, we can learn to live with them, learn to cope, to manage them, to accommodate them, to hope they'll go away, maybe even to reduce or ameliorate some of them a little bit. But solve them, unlikely.

George Marshall, a very shrewd American secretary of state and author of the Marshall Plan, recognized this when he was asked to explain the basis of American foreign policy. "Well," said Marshall, "we play for time and hope for the best." That of course is not a very lofty and glorious basis for American foreign policy. But it is a prudent and, above all, realistic basis for policy. In fact, the more one thinks about it, the more attractive, sensible, and workable it becomes—especially when compared with some of the other alternatives that have been put forth.

POLITICAL CULTURE AND FOREIGN POLICY

Compared with other nations, the American historical experience has been unique, helping to shape a package of attitudinal and behavioral traits (political culture) that are peculiarly a part of the American heritage. We can neither wish these peculiarities away nor change them overnight, although over a long period political cultures can be and are modified. Decade by decade (it takes that long or longer), the United States has gone through some "sea changes" of opinion, a process that has been accelerated by television, which brings war and revolution into our living rooms on an almost nightly basis. But some of these characteristics are unlikely to change much, at least not within our lifetimes.

The Vietnam war was a key turning point in affecting our political culture and our foreign policy. Up to that time there had been a basic consensus on American foreign policy, namely, containing communism, resisting aggression, standing for freedom and democracy. Americans had had disagreements before over specific issues and policies, but the basic American consensus had held. Vietnam changed all that. It led not only to violent disagreements about the war but to a basic questioning of fundamental American foreign policy principles. American unity and the foreign policy consensus were shattered by the war. We had less faith in American institutions and the legitimacy of these institutions, less confidence in ourselves, doubt and self-questioning that had not existed before. American political culture was now divided and fragmented. Of course Vietnam was not the only cause: the race riots of the 1960s, the decline of our cities, the loss of our competitive edge economically, Watergate and the corrupting of our political institutions, our military decline relative to the Soviet

Union, changes in morals and social relations—*all* helped to erode our former faith and consensus and led to something new, something that we are not quite sure about yet.

In fact, Vietnam and its aftermath led to a considerable democratization of American foreign policy. Policy, as we see in more detail later on, was no longer made by elites in the cloistered hallways of the Council on Foreign Relations or the Department of State but in the streets, in the churches, in town meetings, in university forums, and in other locations where citizens gather. The democratization of American foreign policy has effected a fundamental change in the nature of our political culture and our policy-making. It has made foreign policy-making much more participatory and less elitist but also far less informed and far more fragmented, paralyzed, divided, and difficult to carry out. Hence, while we may on the one hand applaud the greater democratization that has taken place, we must also recognize on the other that we may not be able to carry out a successful foreign policy in such a charged and divided context. We return to this theme later in the book.

How, then, does political culture affect foreign policy? For one thing, it shapes public attitudes and opinion about the issues, it affects the media and its coverage, and it influences the views held by pressure groups. But political culture also affects the mind-set of our leaders and decision makers, indicating to them what to pay attention to and what not, providing them with categories and frames of reference, offering them solutions as well as setting limits on action. Political culture relates to our beliefs and belief systems and also to how such beliefs may change; it relates to our prejudices and ways of looking at the world. Therefore political culture is an important force in shaping our views of foreign countries and leaders, in helping or hindering our ability to understand or empathize (put ourselves in their shoes) with them, and in determining whether or not we can achieve an enlightened foreign policy.

But political culture, while better than the old national character studies, is still a rather amorphous explanation. Different analysts will sometimes have different understandings and interpretations of it. Even statistical analyses of political culture based on opinion surveys can yield quite different results, depending on how the questions are phrased and asked. Political culture still exists at a rather low level of foreign policy theory. It is not very sophisticated as yet as an explanatory tool, and it is too impressionistic. It operates, as we said at the beginning of this chapter, at the broadest and most general end of our funnel of explanation, at the outer edge of our series of explanatory concentric circles. Let us proceed now to sharpen the focus a bit, to go to the next layer in the funnels or circles, by focusing on public opinion.

Notes

1. The "funnel of causality" image was first used to describe the influences on American voting behavior. See Angus Campbell, et al., *The American Voter* (New York: Wiley, 1960). The concentric circles image is used, among other places, in John Spanier and Eric Uslaner, *American Foreign Policy Since World War II,* 11th ed. (Washington, D.C.: Congressional Quarterly, 1988), and earlier editions.
2. Allan Bloom, *The Closing of the American Mind: How Higher Education Has Failed Democracy and Impoverished the Souls of Today's Students* (New York: Simon & Schuster, 1987). But see also Howard J. Wiarda, *Ethnocentrism in Foreign Policy: Can We Understand the Third World?* (Washington, D.C.: American Enterprise Institute for Public Policy Research, 1985).
3. Peter L. Berger, *The Capitalist Revolution: Fifty Propositions About Prosperity, Equality, and Liberty* (New York: Basic Books, 1986), and *The Relations Between Democracy, Development, and Security: Implications for Policy* (New York: Global Economic Action Institute, 1988).

Suggested Readings

Almond, Gabriel. *The American People and Foreign Policy.* New York: Praeger, 1965.
————, and Sidney Verba. *The Civic Culture: Political Attitudes and Democracy in Five Nations.* Princeton, N.J.: Princeton University Press, 1973.
Goldstein, Martin E. *America's Foreign Policy: Drift or Decision.* Wilmington, Del.: Scholarly Resources, 1984.
Hartmann, Frederick H., and Robert L. Wendzel. *To Preserve the Republic: United States Foreign Policy.* New York: Macmillan, 1985.
Hartz, Louis. *The Liberal Tradition in America.* New York: Harcourt, Brace, 1955.
Hermann, Margaret, G., in *Why Nations Act*; edited by Maurice East, Barbara Salmore, and Charles Herman, 49–68. Beverly Hills, Calif.: Sage Publications, 1978.
Hofstadter, Richard. *The Paranoid Style in American Politics.* New York: Vintage Books, 1967.
Holsti, Ole R., and James N. Rosenau. "A Leadership Divided: The Foreign Policy Beliefs of American Leaders, 1976–1980," in *Perspectives on American Foreign Policy*; edited by Charles W. Kegley, Jr., and Eugene R. Wittkopf. New York: St. Martin's Press, 1983.
Hunt, Michael. *Ideology and U.S. Foreign Policy.* New Haven: Yale University Press, 1987.
Kennan, George F. "Moralism-Legalism," in *Major Problems in American Foreign Policy.* Vol. 2, *Since 1914;* edited by Thomas G. Patterson. Lexington, Mass.: D.C. Heath, 1984.

Kolko, Gabriel. *The Roots of American Foreign Policy.* Boston: Beacon Press, 1969.

McCormick, James M. *American Foreign Policy and American Values.* Itasca, Ill.: Peacock Publishers, 1985.

Mead, Margaret. *And Keep Your Powder Dry.* New York: Morrow, 1942.

Mills, C. Wright. *The Power Elite.* New York: Oxford University Press, 1956.

Nathan, James A., and James K. Oliver. *Foreign Policy Making and the American Political System.* Boston: Little, Brown, 1987.

Packenham, Robert A. *Liberal America and the Third World.* Princeton, N.J.: Princeton University Press, 1973.

Perkins, Dexter. *The American Approach to Foreign Policy.* Cambridge, Mass.: Harvard University Press, 1961.

Potter, David. *People of Plenty.* Chicago: University of Chicago Press, 1954.

Spanier, John. *American Foreign Policy Since World War II,* 9th ed. New York: Holt, Rinehart & Winston, 1983.

De Tocqueville, Alexis. *Democracy in America;* translated by George Lawrence; edited by J. P. Mayer. Garden City, N.Y.: Anchor Books, 1969.

Verba, Sidney. "Conclusion: Comparative Political Culture," in *Political Culture and Political Development;* edited by Lucian Pye and Sidney Verba. Princeton, N.J.: Princeton University Press, 1965, pp. 512–60.

Wiarda, Howard J. *Ethnocentrism in American Foreign Policy: Can We Understand the Third World?* Washington, D.C.: American Enterprise Institute for Public Policy Research, 1985.

CHAPTER FOUR

Public Opinion

Political culture is sometimes a rather vague and subjective concept; it involves the history, attitudes, ideas, background, and somewhat amorphous *feelings* that Americans have or bring to foreign policy issues. In contrast, public opinion is more precise and organized; it refers to the views of Americans as expressed in actual opinion surveys. Public opinion is more specific and more concrete; public opinion surveys force people to respond, to give answers, to express preferences, to choose between policy alternatives. Public opinion is the organized, expressed, and manifest voice of American political culture and attitudes, and therefore comes one step closer to the center of our concentric circles of influence.

There is no doubt that public opinion frequently has an influence on the highest levels of American foreign policy decision making, despite the protests of most presidents and congressmen that they act only in the public interest and according to what's good for the country. We should generally disbelieve our leaders when they say things like that. Not only does public opinion often directly influence policy but it also sets constraints, or boundaries, on what our president may do or not do. Public opinion may be channeled directly into White House decision making (the modern president usually has a full-time pollster attached to his office) or it may be filtered through the media, Congress, interest groups, political parties, or other intermediary organization. That also means that public opinion can be manipulated for political or other purposes. By whatever route, however, there is no doubt that public opinion now is a major influence on American foreign policy.

The trouble is that public opinion in the United States, since Vietnam, has, like so many other institutions studied in this book, become deeply divided and fragmented. Public opinion is also inchoate, unformed, and very often uninformed. It is frequently confused and contradictory. All of these features raise serious questions about the viability of democratic assumptions and institutions, specifically about how we can have informed public discussion of the issues if in fact the public is as woefully ignorant of them, as the polls seem to suggest. Questions must also be raised about whether it is possible to have a serious, enlightened, coherent, informed, and rational foreign policy in the United States of America.

POLLS AND POLLING

The first thing to say about public opinion surveys, commonly known as polling, is that we should be very careful and even suspicious of them. Many polls are extremely biased and inaccurate. The questions asked may be loaded, the pollsters are often unprofessional, and the number of persons interviewed may be too small to provide a truly representative sample. These are the most common flaws in polling. Other problems include respondents who tell pollsters what they think the pollsters what to hear, or who give exaggerated or false answers; of pollsters who guide or lead respondents to the answers; and samples that are unrepresentative because only those with special axes to grind will take the time to respond (this is especially the case with mailed questionnaires).

Hence we should be cautious with the use of polls, and skeptical of their results. The fact is, there are bad polls and good polls, and we need to be able to tell the difference. Among the most inaccurate are phone-in polls, since usually only those with a strong vested interest in the question will take the time to call in. Much the same criticism applies to newspaper polls (usually at the local level) in which the reporter talks to a small group of men and women on the street, or in which the newspaper invites readers to send in their views on a subject and then counts the letters. These are *not* accurate representations of public opinion.

"Put me down for 'No Comment' on that one . . . I really haven't read enough polls on the subject to form an opinion!"
Stayskal © 1980 Chicago Tribune

Somewhat better, but by no means free from errors, are the polls commissioned by some major newspapers such as the *Washington Post* or the *New York Times,* or by the national television networks. These polls are often done by professional pollsters, but because the cost of a poll increases as the number of respondents increases, the samples are usually too small to be scientific; moreover, they are often based on notoriously inaccurate telephone polling. And, of course, a lot depends on how the question is asked and whether the language is leading or misleading. Hence when a TV anchor comes on the evening news and announces such-and-such poll results "with a margin of error of plus or minus 5 percent," we should not necessarily take his/her word for it. While these kinds of polls are far better than the first group, unless we know more about them than the anchors say over the air—for instance, the size of the sample, how the questions are worded, when they are asked, and so on—we should expect a margin of error at least double the 5 percent figure usually given.

The best opinion surveys are those conducted by such reputable and professional pollsters as Roper, Gallup, the Survey Research Center of the University of Michigan, or the National Opinion Research Center. The good polls are not only professionally conducted but they are also professionally designed and drafted by more neutral agencies such as the Council on Foreign Relations or a good, nonpartisan university research center. In these settings, the survey questions are carefully drawn up to be free from bias or leading statements. When surveys are done in this way, they tend to be more reliable, although a healthy measure of skepticism and a desire to know more about the survey than is usually stated publicly are always appropriate.

What criteria, then, should be met by a poll? The following elements would seem to be essential:

1. **Heterogeneity of the sample.** The poll must be an accurate cross section of the total population being questioned.
2. **Size of the sample.** In such a pluralist and heterogeneous nation as the United States, the sample must be sufficiently large to be genuinely representative. At minimum, this probably requires at least 2,000 respondents.
3. **Neutrality of the pollster.** The pollster should not have a telling impact on the responses of those questioned in the study.
4. **Fair, unbiased questions.** The questions must be phrased in such a way as to be neutral and not misleading or prejudicial.

How do we get these results? There are several necessary ingredients, including: (1) adequate planning, including research into the target group and questions, and conducting a sample survey well in advance;

(2) adequate resources, both financial and professional; and (3) pollsters who are well trained and without any particular prejudice either toward the issue being explored or the subjects of the study. When these suggestions are followed, the results can be extremely useful: A well-conducted poll provides an accurate "pulse of the nation"; it provides vast amounts of new information; it can often simplify complex relationships into simple statistics; and it can tell us much about how presidents and others make foreign policy decisions.

PUBLIC OPINION AND DEMOCRATIC THEORY

One additional introductory point needs to be brought up before we proceed to the actual discussion of public opinion, and that involves the relationship of public opinion to democracy and to the theory of democracy.

American democracy is based on the assumption of a reasonably knowledgeable, educated, literate public capable of making informed judgments about public affairs. All of our political theory, going back to Madison, Jefferson, and the Founding Fathers, is based on that assumption. Our educational system, which seeks to educate the mass public as well as university-trained elites, is based on that assumption. Our image of the independent yeoman farmer making educated judgments about his self-interests, of town meetings and local government, of federalism and checks and balances, indeed of our entire culture and political ethos—all are based on this assumption. An educated, informed, participatory citizenry that makes responsible choices and exercises responsible oversight of elected officials lies at the heart of our assumptions about democracy.

The trouble is, we now know that it doesn't work that way. In presidential elections, only about half the eligible population votes; in state and local elections, the percentage is far lower; and on local initiatives or in party primaries, a vote of 7 or 8 percent of the eligible electorate is often enough to carry an issue or candidate to victory. The idea of a participatory, democratic political system needs to be reexamined given that so few citizens actually do vote or participate.

The situation may be even worse with regard to public opinion. Democratic theory is, again, based on an *informed* citizenry making wise public policy judgments. But we know from the survey data that most Americans are not well informed on foreign countries or the problems at issue. The misinformation or sheer lack of information is not limited to the subtleties of policy but involves some basic fundamentals. In Central America, for example, a *majority* of Americans could not identify whose side the United States was on in El Salvador (for the government, against the rebels) or in Nicaragua (against the government, for the rebels). Even more disgraceful (so disgraceful we prefer not to even mention the figures) is the number of Americans who could not state on which sides of the country the Atlantic and Pacific oceans are located. Suffice it to say that Americans, including oftentimes educated Americans, show an appalling, atrocious lack of knowledge about foreign leaders, foreign cultures, foreign geography, foreign languages, and foreign affairs.

The survey data on this issue are both consistent over time and very disturbing for the practice of democracy. About 30 percent of the American public lacks even rudimentary information about foreign policy issues. These people never read a newspaper or news magazine and seldom watch the evening news. They cannot identify foreign countries, foreign leaders, or the issues with which United States foreign policy must grapple. They have "no knowledge" about foreign affairs. Another 45 percent are termed *attentive*. These persons read at least the newspaper headlines (before turning to sports or the comics) and watch the television news irregularly. They know the issues at a headline or bumper-sticker level but have no deeper understanding of them. If these two categories are put together, it means that three-quarters of the American public is very poorly informed on foreign policy issues. This lack of knowledge makes it difficult to be optimistic about America's conduct of foreign policy or sanguine about the future of democracy.

Another 25 percent are termed *informed*. That means they read a daily paper, often read *Time* or *Newsweek,* and regularly watch the national evening news. One can question whether this is sufficient to be called informed, but maybe we should not quarrel too much about that point. Then there are 1 to 2 percent of the population who may be termed *opinion leaders*. They not only watch the news and, maybe, the *MacNeil/ Lehrer News Hour* or Ted Koppel's *Nightline,* and read the newspaper, but some may also be letter writers to their local papers, call-ins on the local talk shows, election campaign workers, persons who contact their congressmen, and so forth. Combining these last two categories still adds up to only a quarter of the population. And it is hard to talk about an informed electorate or "participatory democracy"if only one-fourth of the population is sufficiently informed to be participants.

Not only is this lack of knowledge dangerous from a foreign policy point of view, but it raises fundamental questions about the strength and viability of democracy. If Americans are really as poorly informed as the polls seem to indicate, then how can they make sound judgments? How can democracy be participatory if significantly more than half of the public does not participate? How can informed democratic decisions be made if the basis of knowledge and information for such decisions is so weak? How is it possible—or is it possible at all?—to democratize foreign policy decision making if the level of knowledge on foreign affairs is so slim? Given these conditions, is it desirable or even workable to have, as we have had since Vietnam, a more democratized system of decision making? In short, not only do we have a very weak basis in the United States for an informed and enlightened foreign policy, but we need also to ask—and it is a major theme running through this book—whether it is possible to have democracy as a basis for policy if some of democracy's fundamental postulates, such as informed citizen participation, are so tenuous.

THE EVOLUTION OF PUBLIC OPINION

Until World War II, isolationism had been stronger than international-ism in American public opinion. We wanted to avoid foreign conflicts, develop our own country, and maintain our independence behind strong natural as well as military barriers. But World War II brought us perma-nently into the global arena, really for the first time.

After the war, and for a remarkable twenty-odd years thereafter, a solid consensus existed on foreign policy goals. Obviously there were some disputes, but these disagreements came within a framework of fundamen-tal consensus. As we saw in the last chapter, the consensus was based on the principles of resisting aggression, containing communism, and standing for freedom and democracy. There were different emphases sometimes about how best to achieve these goals, but the goals themselves were set and widely agreed to. The United States was the dominant power in the world, and the polls consistently showed that the American public ac-cepted this role. A solid majority favored a strong United States activism in world affairs, favored containment, and favored foreign and military aid—but not military intervention. This fundamental consensus was forged during the Truman presidency, lasted through eight years of Eisenhower, and survived in slightly altered form into the presidencies of Kennedy and Johnson. It came to an end, if one were to pick a single date, with the 1968 Tet offensive in Vietnam.

Vietnam destroyed the foreign policy consensus that had been main-tained during the preceding twenty years. No longer would the United States be in fundamental agreement on the basic bedrocks of policy. The Vietnam war was not only a terribly wrenching experience domestically for the United States, but the war and the protests it sparked also undermined something even more fundamental: the great consensus that had long existed on foreign policy. Hence if the first two post–World War II decades, 1948–1968, could be thought of as the era of American foreign policy consensus, the period of 1968–1973 should be considered the era of the breakdown of that consensus. And, recall, this was also the era in the United States of racial conflict, burning cities, Watergate, political erosion, and economic troubles. Not only foreign policy but the entire fabric of society seemed to be unraveling—or so many thought.

During the next period, 1974–1981, which corresponded to the presidencies of Ford and Carter, the United States tended to look inward. Public opinion favored a certain American withdrawal from the earlier activist role in world affairs. Support for foreign aid diminished almost to zero. The doctrine of containment, the basis of the policy that had served the United States well since World War II, was no longer popular. Public opinion demanded that the United States reduce its international commitments, cease to serve as police officer (and firefighter) for the world, and above all avoid involvement in murky Third World struggles like that in Vietnam. Popular support for international initiatives declined markedly. There was reduced public support for military expenditures and, hence, a decline during this period in military preparedness. As a consequence of America's withdrawal from the world, the Soviet Union scored major gains, especially in the Third World, and during this same period surpassed the United States in certain military areas. The United States lost much of its leadership position in the world.

The fourth post–World War II period, which we will date from 1980 to the present, may be termed an era of new, but still sometimes directionless, internationalism. To a certain extent, the United States had put Vietnam behind it. There was renewed support in the polls for increased military spending. Ronald Reagan was elected president in 1980 and reelected in 1984 by overwhelming margins on a platform of renewal, strength, a prospering economy, and "standing tall" in the world. There was overwhelming public support for the president's *"quick 'n' easy"* invasion of Grenada in 1983.

Yet these sentiments remained ambivalent. The public wanted no part of "another Vietnam" in Central America and was strongly opposed to sending American troops there. The pressures exerted by the "peace" and nuclear freeze movements pushed even so conservative and Communist-hating ("the evil empire") a president as Reagan into signing a nuclear arms reduction treaty with the Soviet Union. Things had certainly changed since Vietnam. Reagan had restored some greater self-confidence and strength to the economy and to the nation, but even this popular president failed to restore the foreign policy consensus that had existed before Vietnam. On numerous foreign policy issues ranging from USA-USSR relations to Central America the country remained deeply divided. Reagan had failed to provide the clear and agreed-upon foreign policy vision that the country needed; it remains to be seen whether President Bush will be able to do so.

CURRENT DIVISIONS IN FOREIGN POLICY ATTITUDES

Public opinion in the United States is not only poorly informed but also deeply divided on its basic assumptions. These deep philosophical differences make it very difficult to forge a working majority in favor of any specific foreign policy issue let alone a deeper and lasting consensus.

Since the end of the Vietnam war (again that watershed), there have been three basic divisions in public opinion on foreign policy issues. Each group commands about one-third of the electorate—figures that have remained remarkably consistent over this fifteen-year period.[1]

The first group may be called the *isolationists*. They want little to do with the outside world. They want the United States to shuck off its allies, who do not consistently support us anyway, and go it alone in the world. The isolationists would have us concentrate exclusively on East-West relations with the Soviet Union, eschewing North-South relations and ending all foreign aid to the Third World unless the Soviet Union is involved there too—as it is in Nicaragua. The isolationists stand for a strong, fortress like America that throws up ramparts and protectionist barriers to keep out foreign influences and products. It is hard to conceive in this day and age, when modern communications and jet travel have shrunk the globe and when the United States is so politically and even more economically interdependent with so many nations, that the isolationist position could still be strong. But it regularly receives the support of from 30 to 35 percent of the population.

Internationalist sentiment commands about two-thirds of the electorate but is almost equally divided into two warring groups, which may be termed the *cold war internationalists* and the *post–cold war internationalists*. The cold war internationalists, like the isolationists, want a strong America, militarily and economically; but they also want the United States to be involved in the world, to be engaged, to take vigorous action. They recognize the growing international interdependence of the world economy and are prepared to operate within it, but from a position of strength. The cold war internationalists believe the Soviet Union is our principal enemy, that it needs to be contained, and that the United States needs its NATO and other allies to deal with the Soviet Union on a global basis. Cold war internationalists recognize the importance of the Third World, but they see it mainly as a battleground to halt Soviet expansion. The cold war internationalist position represents the older, historic (pre-Vietnam) position in American foreign policy; it found reexpression in the presidency of Ronald Reagan; and within the Democratic party it is represented by Senators Charles Robb of Virginia, Sam Nunn of Georgia, and Albert Gore of Tennessee. This position also commands 30 to 35 percent of the electorate.

The third position, also numbering upwards of one-third of the electorate, is the post–cold war internationalists. Because of the growing *detente* with the Soviet Union, these people believe the cold war is as good as over. Hence the United States should concentrate on North-South issues (foreign aid, basic human needs, economic redistribution) rather than East-West ones. They want our foreign policy agenda to be human rights and democracy, not Soviet containment. And, of course, since the cold war is "over," the United States no longer needs to worry about Marxist-Leninist regimes in Afghanistan or Nicaragua and can reduce its defense budget and its military preparedness. The post–cold war internationalist position was strongly shaped by United States intervention in Vietnam and insists that the United States not get involved in other Vietnams. It wants to concentrate on moral and ethical issues rather than military or strategic ones. It believes in turning "swords into plowshares," is opposed to American activities directed against the Sandinistas in Nicaragua, favors a nuclear freeze, and was appalled by the American invasion of Grenada. The post–cold war internationalist position was personified in the presidency of Jimmy Carter, especially in its first two years, and finds expression in the left wing of the Democratic party.

While these divisions in American public opinion are very interesting in themselves, here we wish to show how they serve to paralyze American foreign policy. Now virtually any president who comes to power can count on a nearly automatic, two-thirds majority being *against* almost anything he tries to do. The result of the situation described above is that it is very easy to get a majority against anything but almost impossible to get a majority for anything. No wonder it is so hard to have an effective foreign policy in this country.

Let us take the Jimmy Carter agenda, for example: human rights, North-South relations, turning the other cheek to the Soviet Union, and others. That agenda is going to be opposed strongly by both the isolationists who want no part of such internationalist initiatives, and by the cold war internationalists who will be opposed to each of these particular policies. Or take the case of Ronald Reagan: the president attracted support from both isolationists and cold war internationalists (his natural constituency) for both his defense buildup and his brief invasion of Grenada. But because both isolationists and the post–cold war internationalists were opposed, he could not get support for his military *cum* socioeconomic program in Central America (the Kissinger Commission plan), or his policies in Africa and the Middle East, or his international economic policies. Once again, because of the divisions in American public opinion, the president faced a nearly automatic two-thirds majority against him on virtually every foreign policy initiative he tried. George Bush, more of a centrist that either of his two predecessors, will nevertheless face the same difficulties of forging a working majority for his foreign policy initiatives.

Any president, therefore, must walk a tightrope, counting on the one-third of the electorate that is his natural constituency to back him up and negotiating for sufficient support among the two-thirds who will oppose most of his policies to get at least a few of them through. The room for maneuvering is very narrow, and the president can easily, on almost any issue, find himself without the majority needed. These splits in the electorate between Isolationists, Cold War Internationalists, and Post–Cold War Internationalists—each with about one-third of the electorate—show why it is so difficult to build a working coalition for his policies and to achieve a consensus. Such divisions and negative feelings demonstrate why it is so difficult for *any* president in this country to conduct a reasoned, coherent, long-term foreign policy of any kind.

CONTRADICTIONS IN PUBLIC OPINION

American public opinion is not only divided and often negative but it is also frequently contradictory. The goals are often clear but policymakers are denied the means to achieve them. Or, Americans are unwilling to choose—as they must oftentimes—among policies that represent not good or evil but lesser evils. Or they fail to see that the goals they have in mind cannot be accomplished without a price, that there are bound to be trade-offs in all foreign policy decisions. Let us illustrate these themes by reference to the situation in Central America.

Most Americans do not pay much attention to Latin America, and ordinarily would prefer not to think very much about it. But on one thing they are quite clear: they want no "second Cubas" in the Caribbean. By that they mean no more Marxist-Leninist regimes allied with the Soviet Union and allowing the Soviets to use their territory as a base of military and subversive operations or possibly as a launching pad for Soviet missiles—as in Cuba in 1962. Over the years, by overwhelming majorities of from 80 to 85 percent, Americans have repeatedly indicated that they want no second Cubas in the Caribbean.

The trouble comes when we start to think about how to achieve the agreed upon goal of "no second Cubas." First, 83 to 84 percent of Americans are opposed to foreign aid—*all* forms of foreign aid—so the option of preventing a second Cuba through socioeconomic aid seems to be ruled out. There will never be enough socioeconomic aid to eliminate poverty and thus to prevent the emergence of revolutionary Marxist-Leninist regimes. Second, about 83 percent of the public is opposed to CIA machinations in the area—such as mining Nicaragua's harbors—so that option seems unviable. Third, a slightly higher percentage, 86 percent is opposed to sending American combat forces into Central America. We may be able to send trainers and National Guard forces but no actual fighting forces. And fourth, despite strenuous Reagan administration efforts, most Americans—about 56 to 58 percent—are opposed to aid to the Contras.

What, then, is a president to do? The goal is clear—no second Cubas—but the president is denied any of the instruments to assure that from happening: no foreign aid, no CIA involvement, no American troops, no Contra aid. How can one carry out an effective policy when none of the means to do so are permitted?

The answer is, obviously, you *can't*. You can't send ground forces, so you send a handful (40-50) of advisers. You can't get much foreign aid from the Congress, so you set up a presidential commission headed by Henry Kissinger and manage to eke out a little bit of it. You can't use the CIA, so you turn to Oliver North and run your operations out of the back rooms of the White House—and then you get the Iran-Contra or guns-for-hostages scandal. You try for years to get funding for the Contras; when you finally succeed, the funding is so little that it makes little impact, and eventually the Congress cuts off even that.

The lessons of these constraints that public opinion places on policy are rather somber. The first is that while the public may have a quite clear goal in mind, it is unwilling to give the president any of the means (no aid, no CIA, no combat forces, no Contra aid) to effectively carry it out—nor does the public even realize the contradictions in its position. Second, the public seems to have no understanding of cost-benefit analysis and the trade-offs that are required: that if it doesn't want to send foreign aid, or send troops, or allow the CIA to do things covertly, then it had better be prepared as an alternative to aid the Contras. That is, if you don't want to send "American boys" to Central America, then the alternative is to assist the Nicaraguan resistance so that *it* can do the job. The third lesson has to do with lesser evils. It looks to most informed foreign policy analysts that there are no "good" solutions in dealing with Nicaragua, only choices among "lesser evils." In this case, looking at the percentages, it would seem that Contra aid is the least objectionable of the several alternatives presented. That is of course the route that President Reagan went. But in early 1988, the Congress voted to cut off funding for the Contras, leaving the president to conduct his foreign policy with no leverage whatsoever. The result was that American policy in the area floundered during the last year of Reagan's presidency and that President Bush was obliged to shift policy directions and accept the fact of a "second Cuba" in the Caribbean.

This analysis should not be considered a brief for the Contras, which is not our position. But it is to say that in foreign policy one often has to choose, not between good and evil, but between lesser evils. Our choices may not be happy ones, but they need to be made nonetheless. In dealing with Nicaragua, however, American public opinion left the president with no levers at all, even while insisting that he nevertheless keep Marxist-

Leninist regimes allied with the Soviet Union from establishing themselves in the area.

How can we carry out a serious foreign policy in the face of these contradictions that public opinion imposes on policy? The answer is we can't, or at least we can't very well. It is not easy to be a president or foreign policy decision maker in these post-Vietnam times when public opinion is at once ill-informed, fickle, deeply divided, contradictory, and unwilling to make the hard choices that must be made.

ATTITUDES ON THE ISSUES

Most Americans are not very interested in foreign policy. This lack of interest probably goes a long way toward explaining why most Americans are not very well informed on foreign policy. When asked in which type of news they are most interested,[2] only between one-quarter and one-third (depending on the year) express an interest in news about other countries. These percentages on foreign policy are the lowest on the chart (see Fig. 4.1). When the news is about United States' relations with other countries, however, the percentage jumps to nearly one-half.

Figure 4.1
The Public:
Percent Interested in Various Types of News: 1974, 1978, 1982, 1986

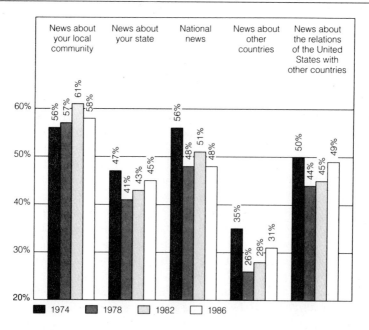

Foreign policy issues are not accorded a very high priority by the American public. If one looks at Table 4.1, it is clear that economic issues (unemployment, inflation) or social issues (drugs, crime, poverty) are generally thought to be more important than foreign policy issues. Only war/peace/defense, lumped together in one category, is given very high priority as a foreign policy issue—and then only by one-fourth of the population. Even relations with the Soviet Union (which still, despite the recent changes, has the power to destroy us) and other Communist

Table 4.1   Most Important Problems *"What do you feel are the two or three biggest problems facing the country today?"*

	Public			Leaders		
	1986	*1982*	*1978*	*1986*	*1982*	*1978*
ECONOMY						
Unemployment	26%	64%	19%	7%	53%	25%
Inflation	8	35	67	2	19	85
Taxes	6	6	18	2	3	6
Energy	1	3	11	1	2	23
Other	17	22	n.a.	32	58	n.a.
GOVERNMENT						
Excessive spending	12	5	9	57	12	13
Other	10	13	17	8	10	22
SOCIAL PROBLEMS AND POLICY						
Crime	10	16	9	4	3	2
Welfare	2	3	8	2	1	3
Drug abuse	27	3	1	8	1	1
Immorality	7	6	2	4	5	3
Poverty	10	2	3	6	2	3
Education	5	2	4	6	4	3
Other	30	19	21	18	14	32
FOREIGN POLICY						
Foreign economic problems	7	4	4	33	10	10
Regional problems	4	2	1	5	2	4
War/peace/defense	25	18	8	44	37	27
Relations with USSR and other Communist countries	7	2	2	16	12	8
Terrorism	5	n.a.	n.a.	2	n.a.	n.a.
Other	13	10	9	12	17	18

1. There is a very slight change in the wording of this question since 1978, when we asked respondents to name "the two or three biggest problems facing the country today that you would like to see the federal government do something about." Because the role of the federal government in the solution of national problems itself became perceived as a political problem since the 1980 elections, we decided the comparability with prior surveys would be enhanced if we dropped the qualifying phrase "that you would like to see the federal government do something about."

2. The sum of percentages exceeds 100% because of multiple responses.

*Less than ½

*n.a. = not asked

Source: Chicago Council on Foreign Relations.

countries are viewed as a major problem by only 7 percent of the electorate. But note that on all of these issues, the views of opinion leaders give
higher priority to foreign policy issues than do those of the general public.

If we ask the public about its desire to have the United States play an
active role in world affairs, some interesting patterns emerge. Table 4.2
traces these patterns over a forty-year period. Note how the percentage of
those who want the United States to play an active world role has stayed
quite consistently at around two-thirds, while those who want the United
States to stay out of world affairs has consistently been between one-fourth
and one-third. That corresponds to the internationalist versus isolationist
split analyzed earlier. Note also the decrease in internationalist sentiment
(59 percent in 1978 and 54 percent in 1982) in the aftermath of the Vietnam
war. Although not shown on this particular chart, it should be recalled that
before Vietnam the two-thirds that was internationalist provided a consensus for American policy that enabled our leaders to act decisively. But after
Vietnam, although internationalist sentiment was still in the high 50 percent range, the internationalists had split into the two warring camps (cold
war internationalists and post–cold war internationalists) that made a
coherent and consensus-based foreign policy all but impossible to forge.
One final element in this table deserves mention, and that is how much
stronger (97 or 98 percent to 1) internationalist sentiment and wanting the
United States to play an active role in world war affairs is among leaders
than among the general public.

Tables 4.3 and 4.4 examine the perceptions of foreign policy problems
as well as the goals of United States policy. Note how high the percentage
is in Table 4.3 for the possibility of war and an arms race with the Soviet
Union. In that same table, terrorism has now emerged as a major foreign
policy issue. But note also how low ranked are the major areas with which
the United States has important relations and critical policy differences,
such as Latin America, the Middle East, South Africa, Europe, and Asia. More

Table 4.2   Desires for an Active U.S. Role in World Affairs *(Percentage saying
U.S. should take an active part in world affairs)*

	Public		Leaders	
	Active Part	*Stay Out*	*Active Part*	*Stay Out*
1986	65%	27%	98%	1%
1982	54	35	98	1
1978	59	29	97	1
1974	66	24	n.a.	n.a.
1973	66	31	n.a.	n.a.
1956	71	25	n.a.	n.a.
1952	68	23	n.a.	n.a.
1948	70	24	n.a.	n.a.

*n.a. = not asked

Source: Chicago Council on Foreign Relations.

recent polls show that drugs are becoming one of our most important foreign policy problems.

It is a truism of American politics that elections are decided on economic, not foreign policy, issues—except, of course, in times of actual war. Table 4.4 illustrates that even when asked to rank American foreign policy goals, the public gives the highest ratings to the goals with domestic

Table 4.3 Perceptions of Foreign Policy Problems. *(Percentages of the total number of "biggest problem" responses.)*

	Public			Leaders		
	1986	*1982*	*1978*	*1986*	*1982*	*1978*
War, arms race with USSR	31%	29%	20%	36%	39%	29%
Terrorism	13	0	0	5	0	0
General foreign policy	15	23	22	15	18	18
U.S. economy	13	13	17	13	9	13
Latin America	7	3	4	12	8	3
Middle East	5	13	13	6	15	18
South Africa	3	1	2	5	1	6
Europe	2	5	1	3	6	2
Asia	0	1	2	1	2	8
Miscellaneous and don't know	11	12	19	4	2	3
Total responses	100	100	100	100	100	100

Source: Chicago Council on Foreign Relations

Table 4.4 Foreign Policy Goals for the United States, 1986 *(Percent "very important")*

	Public	Leaders
Protecting the jobs of American workers	78%	43%
Securing adequate supplies of energy	69	72
Worldwide arms control	69	83
Combatting world hunger	63	60
Reducing U.S. trade deficit with foreign countries	62	n.a.
Containing communism	57	43
Defending U.S. allies' security	56	78
Matching Soviet military power	53	59
Strengthening the United Nations	46	22
Protecting the interests of American business abroad	43	32
Promoting and defending human rights in other countries	42	44
Helping to improve the standard of living of less developed nations	37	46
Protecting weaker nations against foreign aggression	32	29
Helping to bring a democratic form of government to other nations	30	29

*n.a. = not asked

Source: Chicago Council on Foreign Relations

reverberations—protecting the jobs of American workers and securing adequate supplies of energy. Containing communism ranks sixth on the list, while such "moral" goals as promoting human rights, helping developing nations, and promoting democracy abroad rank considerably further down, with only about 30 to 40 percent of the public supporting those goals. In the 1988 primary elections, Congressman Richard Gephardt tried to use the issue of protecting American jobs to propel himself into the White House, and went a long way on the strength of this preoccupation before finally succumbing.

Tables 4.5 and 4.6 examine public attitudes toward America's vital interests around the world and the feelings ("thermometer ratings") Americans have for various countries. It is interesting that in Table 4.5 our two English-speaking allies, Great Britain and Canada, rank so high. Japan (despite our differences over trade issues), the Federal Republic of (West)

Table 4.5   Attitude Toward America's Vital Interests Around the World—The Public. *"Many people believe the United States has a vital interest in certain areas of the world and not in other areas. That is, certain countries of the world are important to the U.S. for political, economic or security reasons. I am going to read a list of countries. For each, tell me whether you feel the U.S. does or does not have a vital interest in that country."*

| | Does Have Vital Interest | | | |
| | 1986 | | 1982 | |
	Public	*Leaders*	*Public*	*Leaders*
Great Britain	83%	94%	80%	97%
Canada	78	96	82	95
Japan	78	98	82	97
Federal Republic of Germany	77	98	76	98
Saudi Arabia	77	88	77	93
Israel	76	86	75	92
Mexico	74	96	74	98
The Philippines	73	81	n.a.	n.a.
Egypt	61	n.a.	66	90
People's Republic of China	61	89	64	87
Nicaragua	60	63	n.a.	n.a.
South Africa	54	63	38	54
South Korea	58	80	43	66
France	56	82	58	84
Taiwan	53	48	51	44
Iran	50	n.a.	51	60
Syria	48	n.a.	36	46
Brazil	45	63	45	80
Italy	41	n.a.	35	79
India	36	55	30	57
Poland	35	n.a.	43	47
Nigeria	31	n.a.	32	53

*n.a. = not asked

Source: Chicago Council on Foreign Relations.

Germany, Saudi Arabia, Israel, and Mexico also rank high. But it appears that in most of the rest of Asia, Africa, the Middle East, and Latin America, the public does not see the United States as having strong vital interests. Opinion leaders, once again, rather consistently assign higher importance to almost all of these other countries and areas than does the public.

When Americans are asked how warmly they feel toward different countries (Table 4.6), Canada and Great Britain again top the list, with West Germany, Japan, Mexico, Israel, the Philippines, France, and Italy all closely bunched together to form a second tier. The third group (Brazil, Poland, People's Republic of China, Taiwan, South Korea, Saudi Arabia, Egypt, India, South Africa, Nigeria, and Nicaragua) are interesting mainly because of their diversity. In descending order of frigidity, the Soviet Union and Iran rank at the bottom of the list. More recently, under Gorbachev, the Soviet Union has been rising but Iran is still at the bottom.

Table 4.6   Thermometer Ratings for Countries—The Public *"Next I'd like you to rate the same countries on this feeling thermometer. If you feel neutral toward a country, give it a temperature of 50 degrees. If you have a warm feeling toward a country, give it a temperature higher than 50 degrees. If you have a cool feeling toward a country, give it a temperature lower than 50 degrees."*

	Mean Temperature (degrees)		
	1986	*1982*	*1978*
Canada	77	74	72
Great Britain	73	68	67
Federal Republic of Germany	62	59	57
Japan	61	53	56
Mexico	59	60	58
Israel	59	55	61
The Philippines	59	n.a.	n.a.
France	58	60	62
Italy	58	55	56
Brazil	54	54	52
Poland	53	52	50
People's Republic of China	53	47	44
Taiwan	52	49	51
South Korea	50	44	48
Saudi Arabia	50	52	48
Egypt	49	52	53
India	48	48	49
South Africa	47	45	46
Nigeria	46	44	47
Nicaragua	46	n.a.	n.a.
Syria	34	42	n.a.
Soviet Union	31	26	34
Iran	22	28	50

*n.a. = not asked

Source: Chicago Council on Foreign Relations

From a security/strategic point of view, the Soviet Union is perhaps the most important country with which the United States has relations. As indicated in Table 4.7, most Americans believe the United States and the Soviet Union are about equal in strength—up significantly since the late 1970s, when fully one-third of those interviewed believed the Soviet Union was stronger. In 1986 (pre-*Glasnost*), as Table 4.6 showed, the Soviet Union ranked next to the bottom on the thermometer. However, as Table 4.8 indicates, this did not prevent most of the public from wanting to negotiate an arms control agreement with the Soviets (80 percent), resume cultural exchanges (78 percent), and increase grain sales (57 percent). With these percentages, it is small wonder that even a conservative president like Ronald Reagan in 1987 signed an arms control agreement with the Soviet Union. But Americans seem to be strongly against our sharing technical information with the Soviets about missile attack defenses.

Europe and the North Atlantic Treaty Organization (NATO) have long

Table 4.7   The Perceived Military Balance *"At the present time, which nation do you feel is stronger in terms of military power, the United States or the Soviet Union—or do you think they are about equal militarily?"*

	Public			Leaders	
	1986	*1982*	*1979*	*1986*	*1982*
U.S. stronger	28%	21%	33%	28%	20%
About equal	48	42	26	59	62
USSR stronger	17	29	32	11	15
Don't know	7	8	9	2	3
	100	100	100	100	100

*Gallup survey #135-G

Source: Chicago Council on Foreign Relations.

Table 4.8   Relationships with the Soviet Union (Percentage in Favor of Cooperation) *"Relations between the Soviet Union and the United States have been the subject of disagreement for some time. Please tell me if you would favor or oppose the following types of relationships with the Soviet Union.*

	Public	Leaders
Favor negotiating arms control agreements	80%	95%
Favor resuming cultural and educational exchanges	78	98
Favor increasing grain sales	57	82
Oppose restricting trade	52	73
Oppose prohibiting exchanges of scientists	53	83
Oppose limiting sales of advanced U.S. computers	33	20
Favor sharing technical information about defending against missile attacks.	23	n.a.

*n.a. = not asked

Source: Chicago Council on Foreign Relations

been important to the United States. Although there is much discussion of NATO nowadays, with vocal groups on both sides arguing that the United States should increase its commitment or, alternatively, decrease its commitment or withdraw, most Americans want neither of those options. As Table 4.9 indicates, the vast majority of Americans, including both the public and opinion leaders, want the United States to keep its commitment at roughly present levels.

Especially interesting for today's students are the attitudes of their parents toward the foreign cultures and languages that their sons and daughters might study. As Table 4.10 indicates, Europe is the preferred area of study of an overwhelming majority of the parents, with Asia far behind and the Third World almost at the vanishing point. Probably that is because, for most of the public, Europe is more familiar and probably viewed as "safer." If my own students are at all representative, however, Asia-Pacific and the Third World are becoming the preferred areas of study.

Table 4.9   Attitudes Toward NATO *"Some people feel that NATO, the military organization of Western Europe and the United States, has outlived its usefulness, and that the United States should withdraw militarily from NATO. Others say that NATO has discouraged the Russians from trying a military takeover in Western Europe. Do you feel we should increase our commitment to NATO, keep our commitment what it is now, decrease our commitment but still remain in NATO, or withdraw from NATO entirely?"*

	1986		1982		1978	
	Public	*Leaders*	*Public*	*Leaders*	*Public*	*Leaders*
Increase commitment	8%	8%	9%	7%	9%	21%
Keep commitment						
what it is	62	77	58	79	58	65
Decrease commitment	11	13	11	12	9	12
Withdraw entirely	5	1	4	1	4	1
Not sure	14	1	18	1	20	1

Source: Chicago Council on Foreign Relations.

Table 4.10   Attitude Toward Foreign Cultures—Leaders, 1986 *"If you had a son or daughter and were sending him or her abroad for postgraduate study, where would you most likely urge him or her to go?"*

Geographic Area Preferred for Postgradaute Study

Europe	70%
Asia	15
South America	3
Africa	3
Middle East	3
Don't know	7

Source: Chicago Council on Foreign Relations.

Table 4.11   Attitude Toward Foreign Languages–Leaders, 1986 *"If you had a son or daughter who was required to become fluent in a foreign language, which one of the following would you advise him or her to choose?"*

Foreign Language Chosen	
Spanish	34%
French	22
Japanese	16
Chinese	12
Russian	10
German	3
Don't know	4

Source: Chicago Council on Foreign Relations.

As far as foreign languages are concerned, Spanish is preferred (probably because of the rising importance of Latin America as well as the increasing Hispanic community in the United States itself) followed by French, Japanese, Chinese, and Russian.

Another hot issue for the United States is defense spending and how much of our resources and budget should be devoted to a strong defense. As Figure 4.2 indicates, American public opinion has fluctuated considerably on this issue, reflecting the broader currents and issues in post–World War II American history already discussed. Through the 1950s and the foreign policy consensus then existing, Americans favored a strong defense and the defense spending to guarantee it. Then in the 1960s, sentiment in favor of cutting back defense spending began to increase, reaching a high point in the late 1960s and early 1970s as public sentiment turned against the Vietnam war. By the mid 1970s, in the face of Soviet gains and perceived American weakness, sentiment for expanding defense spending began to increase again. Such public sentiment for a strong defense reached a peak in 1980 and was undoubtedly a major factor in the election of Ronald Reagan, who called for a major military buildup. Thereafter sentiment in favor of cutting back defense spending again began to rise, and in 1986 the percentage favoring defense cuts as opposed to those wanting defense spending increased was almost exactly even. In fact, most Americans favored a middle policy of keeping defense spending pretty much the same—rather like their attitudes toward NATO.

The final foreign policy issue analyzed here is public attitudes toward the use of troops overseas. Most Americans oppose the use of United States troops overseas, yet there are circumstances—very few—in which public opinion would be willing to use force. As Table 4.12 indicates, the only circumstances in which the public would condone America's sending its troops into battle overseas is if the Soviet Union invades Western Europe or

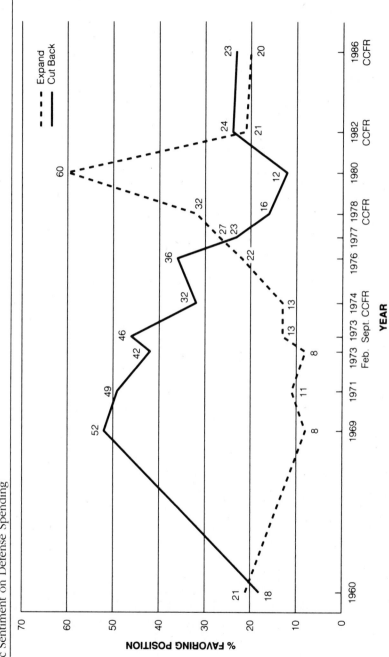

Figure 4.2
Public Sentiment on Defense Spending

Table 4.12 Attitudes on Use of U.S. Troops Overseas: 1986

	U.S. Response:					
	Favor Sending Troops		Oppose Sending Troops		Don't Know	
	Public	*Leaders*	*Public*	*Leaders*	*Public*	*Leaders*
Situation:						
1. Soviets invade Western Europe.	68%	93%	24%	5%	8%	2%
2. Soviets invade Japan.	53	82	36	12	11	6
3. Nicaragua allows Soviets to set up missile base.	45	67	42	27	13	6
4. Arabs cut off oil to U.S.	36	n.a.	51	n.a.	13	n.a.
5. Arabs invade Israel.	33	57	54	38	14	5
6. Soviets invade China.	27	14	61	78	12	8
7. Iran invades Saudi Arabia.	26	n.a.	59	n.a.	15	n.a.
8. El Salvador government is losing to Leftist rebels.	25	n.a.	56	n.a.	19	n.a.
9. Nicaragua invades Honduras to destroy Contra bases.	24	17	60	74	17	9
10. North Korea invades South Korea.	24	64	64	32	12	4
11. China invades Taiwan.	19	n.a.	64	n.a.	17	n.a.

*n.a. = not asked

Source: Chicago Council on Foreign Relations.

Japan. A very slim plurality favors using American troops if the Soviets set up a missile base in Nicaragua, but not if Nicaragua invades neighboring Honduras. These responses suggest that the areas the public thinks worth fighting over are very few indeed. What may be termed the American "security perimeter" or the realm of America's "vital interests" have been very narrowly circumscribed and no longer include, from the public's viewpoint, the military defense of Israel from an Arab invasion, the defense of oil-rich Saudi Arabia should the Iranians invade, the United States defense of Taiwan from Red China, or the military bolstering of El Salvador should Marxist-Leninist guerrillas threaten to take over. Significantly, however, American opinion leaders have a considerably broader perspective of United States defense requirements: these include the defense of Israel against an Arab invasion, the defense of South Korea against North Korea, and opposition to the establishment of a Soviet missile base in Nicaragua. It is interesting also that men are far more willing than women (75 percent versus 62 percent, respectively, if the Soviets invade Western Europe; 63 percent versus 44 percent, respectively, if they invade Japan) to use force.

In summary, the United States has begun to throw off its foreign policy inhibitions, its inward-looking tendencies, and the domestic preoccupations of the post–Vietnam period and now supports a stronger role abroad. But public opinion does not favor the use of American combat troops in very many parts of the world. It supported the defense buildup of the early 1980s, but also favors arms control and various measures of detente with the Soviet Union. The public has a favorable attitude toward Western Europe and Japan but not toward the Third World. Americans remain self-centered and domestically centered, interested in jobs and maintaining access to oil supplies; they are considerably less interested in the "causes" of democracy, human rights, and Third World poverty. The public wants a strong and self-confident America, one that maintains parity with the Soviet Union, but not one that gets into what it sees as Vietnam-like ventures abroad. On all of these issues, American opinion leaders tend to be far more internationalist than is the general public.

ELITE AND MASS ATTITUDES

We have seen in the preceding sections that elite opinion in the United States is both far better informed and far more internationalist than is mass or public opinion. But within that body of informed or "elite" opinion makers, there is one group or a considerable number of its members, that—again, since Vietnam—has turned overwhelmingly hostile and negative toward America, including American foreign policy. Such negative or hostile opinion is particularly strong in the elite media such as the *Washington Post, New York Times*, the major news magazines, the wire services, and the national television networks; among some persons in the major publishing houses; among many academics; in the central offices of some of the main religious denominations; and among artistic and Hollywood types.

These groups are especially powerful in shaping and influencing the attitudes of the public as a whole, so their views are important to consider. Since they are so influential in the main institutions of publishing, television, movies, the universities, and other institutions that disseminate ideas and influence public opinion, their significance is far out of proportion to their numbers. Moreover, because of their influence in these institutions, such elites have the capacity to sometimes hamstring and even undermine American policy.

This element within the elite has been called by some the "blame America first lobby." Wherever there is racism, poverty, injustice, or authoritarianism in the world, this element sees it as America's fault. All the problems and "sins" of the world are seemingly our responsibility— whether South Africa, Chile, the Philippines, United States–Soviet relations, or Central America, it is never the fault of the other countries or their peoples, only ours.

Three points need to be made. First, no one would deny the right of these groups to express their opinions; but given the enormous influence of the institutions in which these naysayers are dominant, one would think a less biased and more evenhanded perspective would be appropriate. At the very least, we need to be aware of the biases involved (more on this in Chapter 5 on the media) and to counterbalance these prejudices with other points of view. Second, many foreign policy observers find it very dangerous for foreign policy to have such an influential body of opinion leaders in the United States so hostile and negative—probably unfairly so—toward their own country. It adds a further element of fragmentation, division, and paralysis to a foreign policy context that already has enough of these ingredients. And third, we probably should understand that this is likely a passing phenomenon. It is a latter-day product of the hostilities and negativeness of the 1960s and 1970s. Once this particular generation, a product of a particular time and set of circumstances, passes from the scene, American elite opinion leaders' attitudes will likely not be so hostile. Until that occurs, however, we will see perpetuated a situation in which a significant share of the intellectual elite are severely estranged from their own country's foreign policy.

INFLUENCE ON POLICY-MAKERS

The impact of public opinion on foreign policy-making is hard to chart and systematize since it changes so rapidly. More and more polls show sometimes different or even contradictory results; public opinion is filtered though more and more conduits (news media, pressure groups, elections, political parties) on its way to decision makers; and opinion on the more controversial issues has become more and more divided and polarized. Once again, the theme of fragmentation has arisen as it affects our foreign policy and our foreign policy-making system.

Following are some ways that public opinion impacts on foreign policy decision making:

1. Public opinion may directly affect the actions taken by a president. All presidents follow the polls closely and, naturally, want to do what is popular and that gets them reelected. Despite their protests to the contrary, presidents *are* influenced by what the polls show.

2. Public opinion narrows the range of possible options available to a president. In the case of Central America, for example, foreign aid, CIA activities, and sending American troops were ruled out, so the president opted for the "lesser evil" of aid to the Contras—but still could not generate sufficient public support to sustain the policy.

3. Public opinion may force a president to take symbolic action even though he may still prefer other options. In response to public opinion, a president may give a speech, set up a task force, or create a commission—all to give the *appearance* of doing something even though in reality little is being done. He may prefer to stall on the issue or he may wish to influence public opinion with new information and arguments, and hence get a new reading on public opinion once the new information has gone back through these channels.

4. Symbolic statements, as hinted at above, are not just symbolic; they also in turn influence public opinion. Influence is not just a one-way street but is complex and symbolic: governments try to influence public opinion and public opinion has an impact on government actions.

5. Congressmen or presidents in close reelection races pay closer attention to public opinion than do politicians whose reelection is considered safe. Similarly, lame ducks (officials whose terms are running out and who are not up for reelection) have greater freedom to choose among options than do politicians who must face the voters again.

DEMOCRACY, DIVISIONS, AND PUBLIC OPINION

The discussion in this chapter does not lead toward great optimism about the role of informed public opinion in a democracy. The public is woefully ill-informed on public policy issues and lacks the knowledge to make sound judgments about many policy options. Three-quarters of the population have no or only limited knowledge of foreign affairs, and one-third is still isolationist, believing unrealistically that in an era of international treaties, economic interdependence, and intercontinental ballistics missiles that the United States can simply throw up the walls and go it alone in the world. The figures lead one to be quite pessimistic both for United States foreign policy and for the fundamental principles of democracy.

Public opinion is not only poorly informed, it is also deeply divided. Vietnam was the turning point. Until then, a broad consensus on foreign policy goals had existed. After Vietnam, opinion became divided and the views were often so strongly held that they have clogged up our foreign policy-making system. Not only is there a division between isolationists and internationalists, but international opinion is itself sharply divided between cold war internationalist and post-cold war internationalists. On top of that comes the highly negative views of significant sectors of the intellectual elite in this country. One begins to wonder, given these deep divisions, how or *if* the United States can still have an effective foreign policy.

And that is precisely the point, as we saw in Chapter 1 and will see again at various points in our analysis. The United States is a country so pluralistic, so divided and fragmented, that our foreign policy is often in disarray. The disarray and incoherence are evident both in public opinion and at decision-making levels. The divisions and fragmentation may be leading to a situation of expanding foreign policy paralysis and sclerosis. We have not yet reached the stage of immobilism, but the possibilities for chaos and discontinuity of the foreign policy system is discouraging and very worrisome. Since the problems are deep, the logjam will not be broken by a single presidential election or by some superficial changes. Years, maybe decades, will be required. That is why so many foreign policy professionals are deeply pessimistic about our capacity in the future to conduct a serious, rational, long-term, and coherent foreign policy.

Notes

1. The analysis here follows that of Ole R. Holsti and James N. Rosenau, *American Leadership in World Affairs.* (Boston: Allen & Unwin, 1984).
2. The analysis in this section is taken from the best of the nationwide surveys of American foreign policy attitudes: see John E. Reilly, ed., *American Public Opinion and U.S. Foreign Policy 1987* (Chicago: Chicago Council on Foreign Relations, 1987).

Suggested Readings

Almond, Gabriel. *The American People and Foreign Policy.* New York: Harcourt, Brace, 1950.

Central America at the Polls. Washington, D.C.: Washington Office on Latin America, 1984.

Cohen, Bernard. *The Public's Impact on Foreign Policy.* Boston: Little, Brown, 1973.

Cottrell, Leonard S., and Sylvania Eberhart. *American Opinion on World Affairs.* Princeton, N.J.: Princeton University Press, 1948.

Cutler, N.E. "Generational Succession as a Source of Foreign Policy Attitudes." *Journal of Peace Research,* no. 1 (1970):33-47.

Dallek, Robert. *American Style of Foreign Policy: Cultural Politics and Foreign Policy.* New York: Knopf, 1983.

Deibel, Terry L. *Presidents, Public Opinion and Power.* New York: Foreign Policy Association, 1987.

Erskine, A. G. "The Cold War: A Report from the Polls." *Public Opinion Quarterly* (Summer 1961).

Foster, H. Schuyler. *Activism Replaces Isolationism.* Washington, D.C.: Foxhall Press, 1983.

Gallup, George, and Saul F. Rae. *The Pulse of Democracy.* New York: Simon & Schuster, 1940.

Galtung, Johan. "Foreign Policy Attitudes as a Function of Social Class Position." *Journal of Peace Research,* no. 1 (1964):206-31.

Gergen, David. "The Hardening Mood Toward Foreign Policy." *Public Opinion* (February/March 1980):12-13.

Ladd, Everett Carll. "Where the Public Stands on Nicaragua." *Public Opinion* (September/October 1987):2 ff.

Levering, Ralph B. *The Public and American Foreign Policy: 1917–1978.* New York: Morrow, 1978.

Lippmann, Walter. *Public Opinion and Foreign Policy in the United States.* London: Unwin Brothers, 1952.

Maggiotto, M. A. and E. R. Wittkopf. "American Public Attitudes Toward Foreign Policy." *International Studies Quarterly* 25 (1981):601-31.

Mueller, John. *War, Presidents, and Public Opinion.* New York: L. Wiley, 1973.

Oldendick, R. W., and B. A. Bardes. "Mass and Elite Foreign Policy Opinions." *Public Opinion Quarterly* (Fall 1982):356-82.

Public Opinion and Foreign Policy: The View from Central America. San Jose, Costa Rica: Institute for Social and Population Studies, 1985.

Reilly, John E. "The American Mood: A Foreign Policy of Self-Interest." *Foreign Policy* (Spring 1979):74-86.

———— "American Opinion: Continuity, Not Reaganism." *Foreign Policy* (Spring 1983):86-104.

———— "America's State of Mind." *Foreign Policy* (Spring 1987):39-56.

Rogers, W. C.; B. Stubler; and D. Koenig. "A Comparison of Informed and General Public Opinion in U.S. Foreign Policy." *Public Opinion Quarterly* (Summer 1967):242-52.

Rosenau, James N. *Public Opinion and Foreign Policy.* New York: Random House, 1961.

Rouner, Mark. *Trouble at Our Doorstep: Public Attitudes and Public Policy on Central America.* Washington, D.C.: The Roosevelt Center for American Policy Studies, 1987.

Schneider, William. "Elite and Public Opinion: The Alliance's New Fissure?" *Public Opinion* (February/March 1983):5-8, 51.

Simon, J. D. "Social Position and American Foreign Policy Attitudes." *Journal of Peace Research* 17, no. 1: 9-28.

Verba, S.; R. Brody; E. Parker; N. Nie; N. Polsby; P. Ekman; and G Black. "Public Opinion and the War in Vietnam." *American Political Science Review* (June 1967):317-33.

Wittkopf, E. R., and M. A. Maggiotto. "Elites and Masses: A Comparative Analysis." *Journal of Politics* 45(1983):303-34.

CHAPTER FIVE

The Mass Media and United States Foreign Policy

❁
❁

The United States, as we saw in Chapter 3, has a unique, distinctive history and political culture—a special set of values to which most Americans adhere. We also examined, in Chapter 4, American public opinion on a variety of foreign policy issues and the role that public opinion plays. We are now ready to ask how this special American political culture and public opinion get translated into actual foreign policy.

The answer is, by diverse means, one of which—perhaps now the main one—is the media. The other means by which our values and opinions are translated into policy influence are through elections and electoral choice, through interest groups, and through political parties. But of all the groups and institutions performing these "transmission belt" functions—that is, conveying the thoughts and ideas of ordinary American policy-makers, as well as policy decisions emanating from the government back to the public—the media has emerged as number one. A variety of public opinion surveys have told us that Americans now receive most of their ideas and views about foreign policy through the media. And among the media, television has replaced newspapers, as the primary source.

The print, and especially the broadcast media, are not only the main source of news but they—especially television—have also become participants in the news. Rather than simply reporting the news in a neutral, nuts-and-bolts fashion, the media have themselves become actors in the drama. The media help set the agenda and parameters of foreign policy discussion, they shape and mold opinion as well as report on it, they often interject their own views and biases into the reporting of the news, and they themselves have sometimes become significant players in the policy-making process.

The questions we must ask now are just how biased are the media, and in what ways; have the media become the arbiters and educators of our tastes in the foreign policy as well as other arenas? Do the media really have the background and the knowledge to justify their practice sometimes of imposing their views of foreign policy on us, and what are the larger implications of the media's playing such a major role in foreign policy?

THE STRUCTURE OF THE MEDIA

The first thing to know about the media is that they are among the few institutions in the United States that are protected by their own constitutional amendment. Freedom of the press is one of the most cherished of America's democratic freedoms. The First Amendment guarantees that the press will be free from government control and that it will be a free, crusading, and frequently critical press. The press has been given a special and privileged role in the American constitutional system, and most Americans favor a strong, free, independent, and even critical press.

But freedom of the press is not an absolute right, and therein lies a series of rubs. Does freedom of the press include the right at times to be an angry, snarling, offensive, and nasty press, free to undermine or disparage cherished American institutions? Does it include the right to examine the garbage of public officials or to spy through their windows, or to camp on the driveways and sidewalks of politicians who are in trouble, watching malignly as they "dangle in the wind," playing out maudlin scenes of tears and ruination?

Does press freedom include the right to invade the privacy of individuals and thus perhaps to trample on rights that are as valid and important as the media's own freedom? Does it include the right to misrepresent the facts of a situation, most often inadvertently but sometimes purposely, so as to present an interpretation closer to the reporter's own views? Does it include the right of nonelected reporters to be rude and offensive to democratically elected officials, as if the reporters had a mandate greater than that provided by the electorate? During a photo session involving the president of the United States and a visiting foreign head of state (a session that had earlier been declared off limits to questions), does it include the right to shout questions at the president on matters that have nothing to do with the visitor's presence or country and which leave the visitor both mystified and insulted?

These are all troubling questions. They raise serious issues about where freedom of the press begins and ends, and where it shades off into conflict with other fundamental rights and freedoms. They also hint at a question that troubles many Americans: in the present era, has the press—especially television—become too powerful but without the accountability, responsibility, and checks and balances that need to go with power if it is not to become abusive?

The second thing to know about the media is that they have become big businesses, among the biggest in America. Their first priority as a business, naturally enough, is and must be to make money. It is not necessarily or primarily to report the news in an objective and straightforward manner. The major objective of the business—any business—is to achieve a large enough profit to attract and satisfy investors, to keep their stockholders happy. The news is only one small facet of the media's overall programming, but even the news must be structured in ways that are oriented toward profit making.

Television, especially, provides information and entertainment to the public in order to give the advertiser a large body of potential customers and to attract advertising fees. Hence there is intense competition among the major television networks for audiences and also for advertising, and the networks' news divisions are an integral part of these financial/advertising/profit calculations. Thus it must be remembered that the television networks, which have become the major sources of political information for most Americans, are not motivated solely by a desire to inform the public but also by a desire to attract the largest possible number of viewers—that is, large audiences that enable them to jack up their advertising rates and also their company revenues. Television must of necessity therefore be primarily "show biz," meant to entertain and only secondarily report the news.

That explains, in part, why television news does such a poor job of informing the American public. Good public affairs programs cannot be shown very often because the majority of the public does not want to watch them and therefore advertising revenues would suffer. The morning shows consist more and more of "entertainment," with little in the way of hard news. Movie stars and glib announcers are sometimes hired who have little knowledge or background as journalists. On the main network evening "half-hour" news programs, once the lucrative advertising time is subtracted, only twenty minutes are left for news. The news itself consists of short "sound bites," often fifteen seconds long, which means the message must be very brief and superficial, at about the intellectual level of a catchy phrase or slogan. Some stories may run for ninety seconds, as if that were sufficient time to be informative; features may run to a "full" two and one-half minutes.

In recent years, there has been a dramatic shift away from the written word as the main source of information and toward television. Surveys have shown that Americans, even those with college degrees, are reading fewer books, and certainly not serious books on international affairs. Television has now replaced newspapers as the main source of information about public affairs. The shift came between 1960 and 1970 as newspaper readership declined and television replaced newspapers as the medium on which the public primarily relies for news. Since the 1960s, the trend has become even more dramatic, with some 80 percent of the public now relying "primarily if not entirely" on television for their news digest. But if the television coverage of the news is often as shallow and superficial as we have suggested, then it is small wonder why so many Americans are so poorly informed about public policy issues. The public's reliance on television for information is undoubtedly a major factor in the absence of in-depth knowledge about foreign policy issues and other countries as described in Chapter 4.

The third thing to know about the structure of the media is that not only are the media businesses but they are increasingly concentrated businesses. More and more of the media are being concentrated in fewer and fewer hands. Previously independent newspapers as well as local radio and television stations are being bought up by large chains. What on Wall Street is called "acquisitions mania" has hit the communications industry as well as others. Even large television networks have been bought up by larger conglomerates. The new owners always vow initially that they will maintain the integrity and independence of the money-losing news bureaus; but eventually financial reality sets in, the budget axes fall on the news division, and coverage usually changes as well. The question we raise here, however, is not just concentration, even monopoly (or oligopoly in the case of the three major networks) in the ownership and control of the media, but control over the editorial content of the news as well.

A fourth aspect to consider, then, is the structure of the news and news reporting and the biases this structure generates. Much could be said on the subject; here we concentrate on only a few issues of direct relevance to a discussion of foreign policy.

First, in the news programs themselves there has been a decided evolution away from "hard news" and toward "soft news"—features, entertainment, sports, "persons of the week," and so forth. Most Americans like these features and, therefore, as profit-making institutions whose profits are tied directly to viewership, the networks have gone more and more in that direction. But viewers should have no illusions that what they are getting is real news. The problem is especially acute for foreign policy coverage, which is expensive, hard to do, attracts little viewer interest (sad to say), and, therefore, receives little attention from the networks.

A second problem is the star quality of network television news. The anchors of the three main networks, all of whom could be called good "face people," receive millions of dollars annually in salaries and perks essentially for reading the news. They are not journalists in any traditional sense; they cannot write particularly well and, therefore, have "ghosts" who prepare their copy for them; and they are people of limited talents or analytical skills. But because they have pleasing faces and attract the viewership necessary for network profitability, they receive these immense salaries and are thought of as important people—indeed among the most influential in America.

Much the same applies to network reporters. Essentially what they do is read a few lines of news. There is no good reason for them to identify themselves by name at the end of their reports: "Lesley Stahl, CBS News, at the White House." This takes away from the precious little time given over to the news item itself, it personalizes the report in unnecessary ways, and it serves mainly to enhance and glamorize the reporter rather than contributing anything to the report itself. Again the emphasis is on glamor—"showbiz"—and not so much on the dissemination of information. Note also that television reporters tend to be handsome and/or glamorous (and to get fired if they are not, or start to look old)–considerations that have little to do with merit, achievement, or news reporting.

A third problem is the heavy reliance of television news on the wire services. Most of the news broadcast on television is not actually based on the reporting of its own reporters but is simply read straight off the teletype machines of the major wire services (Associated Press, United Press International, Reuters). By actual count, 70 to 80 percent of the foreign news stories reported on national television come from that source. The television networks do little actual reporting of international news, and their extensive use of the wire services makes the news secondhand and subject to the whims and biases of the wire services.

The fourth problem is that few newspapers or television networks maintain foreign bureaus, chiefly because overseas bureaus are expensive. The *New York Times* and the *Washington Post,* which have more foreign coverage that any other American newspaper, maintain approximately twenty to fifty news bureaus worldwide. Most newspapers have few or none. For the *Post,* the list is as follows:

1. Tokyo	12. London
2. Rome	13. Africa
3. Jerusalem	14. Mexico
4. Bonn	15. Central America
5. Moscow	16. Caribbean
6. Paris	17. Toronto
7. India	18. Johannesburg
8. South America	19. Manila
9. Cairo	20. Warsaw
10. Bangkok	21. Nairobi
11. Peking	

In most of these bureaus, the *Post* may have only one reporter, or it may rely on a part-time reporter, a "stringer" who simultaneously works for other news organizations. Note that all of the main European capitals are covered, but few capitals in Asia, the Middle East, Africa, or Latin America are. The foreign bureau locations of the major newsmagazines, *Time* and *Newsweek,* roughly parallel those of the *Post.* The fact that the major news organizations have chosen to concentrate their bureaus in Europe rather than the Third World presents a built-in bias in the news that is reported.

Television news has even fewer foreign bureaus than do the larger print media, again because to maintain the equipment and crew of a television unit, which usually consists of three persons, is even more expensive than maintaining a print reporter. Hence the television networks usually have only five or six foreign bureaus: in London, Paris (sometimes only one for all of Europe), Jerusalem, Moscow, Tokyo, and perhaps one for Latin America. The reporters (usually only one) in these bureaus must often cover an entire continent—impossible realistically to do—which helps account for the superficiality of so much of the coverage. Or else the television network, like the newspaper, will hire a "stringer" a person more or less permanently stationed, in, say, Nairobi and who covers the news in his or her area or continent whenever the occasion arises for several news organizations. One understands why (chiefly financial) the news organizations all operate this way, but such a limited number of news bureaus does not assure that the news in many countries is covered adequately, if at all.

The fifth problem, therefore, is a decided bias in which countries are covered and which are not. As Table 5.1 shows, approximately 60 percent of the news coverage on the three major networks is devoted to the United States. Among foreign nations, the Soviet Union receives the most coverage—as it should, seeing that the Soviet Union is the main rival, preoccupation, and threat to the United States in the world. Then comes Israel, a small nation, followed by Great Britain. Vietnam and Iran were important countries in terms of media attention during the years of this survey (1972 to 1981) but have since declined in importance in terms of number of stories. Other countries are farther down on the list; some receive no coverage at all. Does that mean nothing is happening in those countries or nothing important? Not necessarily. In fact, a great deal is always happening abroad everyday in virtually every country, but almost none of that ever gets on our television news broadcasts or into our newspapers.

Table 5.1 illustrates another feature, or bias, about the news, and that is its need for a "local angle." If the story is international, it must have an American connection or it will not get on the evening news. Events may be occurring in various countries, especially in the Third World; but since most American viewers are not much interested in the rest of the world, the story must be crafted to play to an American constituency. That is why Israel ranks so high on the list of countries covered; why stories about Latin America are most likely to focus on human rights, the debt issue, or drugs; and why stories about Japan usually concern trade issues. The reason is that issues like drugs and trade are important issues to *Americans.* Other important events may also be occurring in these countries, but because there is no United States connection they will seldom be covered. That is the sixth problem of news coverage with which we must be concerned.

The seventh problem, a related one, is the type of foreign stories that get on the air. They almost all focus on disasters, calamities, bloodshed, and war. Television coverage of Israel in 1988 gave the impression that all West

Bank Arabs were up in arms and demonstrating in the streets. Likewise coverage of South Africa has focused almost exclusively on black protests without a hint that even in that tortured country, life, including for most blacks, simply goes on in a more or less normal way. Reports from Colombia or Ecuador focus almost exclusively on mudslides, earthquakes, and other natural disasters; from the Middle East, on terrorism; and from Africa, on drought, AIDS, and starvation. American coverage of Mexico, which next to the Soviet Union may be the most important nation in the world from the viewpoint of American foreign policy, has concentrated overwhelmingly on drugs, corruption, earthquakes, and emigration, as though those were the only, or even the most important, stories occurring in that dynamic

Table 5.1   Coverage of 50 Most Frequently Mentioned Nations, 1972–1981. Expressed as a Percentage of Sampled International Stories

	ABC		CBS		NBC	
Nation	*Rank*	*% of Stories*	*Rank*	*% of Stories*	*Rank*	*% of Stories*
United States	1	57.0	1	60.5	1	58.8
USSR	2	16.7	2	17.1	2	16.2
Israel	3	14.3	3	13.4	3	13.6
Britain[a]	4	9.8	4	9.9	5	8.8
South Vietnam[b]	5	9.1	5	8.7	4	9.0
Iran	6	8.7	6	8.5	8	7.4
Egypt	7	7.7	7	7.7	6	8.0
North Vietnam	8	7.5	9	7.1	7	7.8
France	9	6.2	8	7.2	9	6.3
China, People's Republic	10	5.3	10	4.6	10	4.6
Lebanon	11	4.2	12	3.9	17	3.0
West Germany	12	4.1	11	4.4	11	4.0
Japan	13	4.1	14	3.4	15	3.2
Syria	14	3.5	13	3.5	13	3.2
Cuba	15	3.2	15	3.2	14	3.2
Poland	16	3.1	17	2.9	17	3.0
Saudi Arabia	17	2.9	13	3.5	12	3.3
Italy	18	2.8	20	2.3	16	3.1
Kampuchea[c]	18	2.8	16	3.1	18	3.0
Afghanistan	19	2.3	29	1.4	23	1.5
Zimbabwe[d]	20	2.2	21	2.2	25	1.3
South Africa	21	2.2	18	2.7	22	1.7
Northern Ireland	22	2.1	26	1.6	23	1.5
Canada	23	1.8	19	2.6	19	2.3
Iraq	24	1.8	30	1.3	27	1.2
Turkey	25	1.6	27	1.5	27	1.2
Jordan	25	1.6	24	1.8	26	1.3
Switzerland	26	1.4	19	2.6	24	1.4
Libya	26	1.4	25	1.7	26	1.3
Mexico	27	1.4	23	1.9	21	1.8
South Korea	28	1.3	22	1.9	20	2.1
India	29	1.3	31	1.1	28	1.1
Spain	30	1.2	26	1.6	25	1.3

Table 5.1   Coverage of 50 Most Frequently Mentioned Nations, 1972–1981. Expressed as a Percentage of Sampled International Stories - con't

	ABC		CBS		NBC	
Nation	_Rank_	_% of Stories_	_Rank_	_% of Stories_	_Rank_	_% of Stories_
Pakistan	30	1.2	35	0.9	33	0.8
Panama	30	1.2	28	1.4	35	0.7
Cyprus	31	1.1	33	1.0	31	0.9
Greece	31	1.1	30	1.3	25	1.3
The Philippines	32	1.0	36	0.8	34	0.8
Thailand	33	1.0	34	1.0	24	1.4
The Vatican	33	1.0	35	0.9	29	1.1
The Netherlands	34	0.9	37	0.8	35	0.7
Algeria	34	0.9	35	0.9	36	0.7
Angola	34	0.9	35	0.9	34	0.8
Laos	34	0.9	41	0.6	30	1.0
Uganda	34	0.9	35	0.9	32	0.9
Portugal	35	0.8	32	1.1	30	1.0
Austria	36	0.8	40	0.7	37	0.7
Argentina	37	0.8	37	0.8	38	0.6
Nicaragua	38	0.7	40	0.7	37	0.7
Chile	38	0.7	34	1.0	34	0.8
Sweden	38	0.7	33	1.0	38	0.6
East Germany	38	0.7	38	0.8	33	0.8
Taiwan	39	0.6	39	0.7	34	0.8
Belgium	40	0.6	40	0.7	33	0.8
N = (stories)		2377		2391		2286

[a]Excludes Northern Ireland.
[b]After the year 1976, all references to Vietnam were coded as North Vietnam.
[c]Formerly Cambodia.
[d]Formerly Rhodesia.

Note: Rankings are based on the absolute number of stories in which each nation was mentioned. Due to rounding, nations with different ranks may appear to be cited in the same percentage of sampled stories. Nations are listed in the order of their rank on ABC. More than 50 nations are included in the table because of differences across networks. Percentages sum to more than 100 percent because multiple nations may be mentioned in a single news story.

Source: James F. Larson, _Television's Window on the World_ (Norwood, N.J.: Ablex Publishing, 1984).

nation. Stories such as these provide a distorted picture, prejudice our attitudes about foreign nations, sometimes reinforce racial, ethnic, and cultural stereotypes, and in general do a disservice to our foreign policy.

THE POLITICAL AND IDEOLOGICAL BIASES OF THE MEDIA

In addition to the structured biases listed above, which are built into the very organization of the media and the way stories are covered, there are also political and ideological preconceptions held by reporters and their news organizations. The ideological values that reporters hold and the blinders they wear also bias and distort the news we receive. When such biases fall into predictable patterns and become institutionalized within the media, then we have some real problems on our hands in terms of our understandings of foreign realities.

Those dominant within the media recently have tended disproportionately to be products of what is called the "Berkeley generation." That is, they grew up politically in the 1960s and 1970s; witnessed Vietnam, race riots, and then the infamy of Watergate; learned that their government frequently lies to them and is sometimes on the "wrong side" in Third World conflicts; and protested the injustices that they saw around them. These elements tend to be hostile to all institutions, especially those identified with a more conservative, older order; they are suspicious and doubtful even now of whatever the government tells them; and they are aggressive in asserting their rights as journalists to uncover grubby and damaging stories. They are often hostile to government leaders and institutions, oriented toward ferreting out stories regardless of the damage they may sometimes do to persons and careers, and determined to serve the public interest—as they have defined it. In short, many of those who work in the media (the empirical evidence is presented in the following pages) tend to think of themselves as on the left, are hostile to many traditional institutions, and are products of the 1960s counterculture. But whether such views are representative of the rest of America, both the older generation and an emerging new one, is a question we will have to face.

The fact is, such views are not representative of the nation as a whole. They represent a minority view. The "public interest" that the media often claim to represent is usually not that at all, but only a small part of the public. The biases of the media are not just anti-institutional, therefore, but are political and ideological as well. And these biases inevitably influence the coverage that we get, the way stories are covered, which stories are covered, and the editorializing that far too frequently creeps into supposedly straightforward news stories.

The evidence of media bias is now overwhelming and can no longer be denied—especially by the media, which doesn't like to be criticized, can dish it out but frequently cannot take it, and has a strong vested interest in trying to discredit studies critical of it. The evidence consists of both public opinion surveys of media officials and reporters, and also careful monitoring of media content virtually around the clock. In scores of journalism schools, sociology and political science departments, and research centers throughout the country, teams of students and researchers are watching all the networks constantly, doing content analyses of their stories, and systematically marking down every instance of bias or one-sidedness.

Here is what that research reveals.[1] Among a large, representative sample of what is termed the *media elite* (journalists and broadcasters who

work at the most influential media outlets, including the *New York Times,
Washington Post, Wall Street Journal, Time, Newsweek, U.S. News and
World Report,* the Associated Press, United Press, Reuters, and the news
departments of CBS, NBC, ABC, and PBS), 95 percent were found to be
white; 79 percent are male; 68 percent are from the northeast or north
central states; and 75 percent have incomes of more than $40,000. The
media are dominated by a white, male, eastern, liberal establishment.

Moreover, the media elite is biased politically. A majority (54 percent)
of the media elite identify themselves as liberal while only 19 percent say
they are conservative; the rest profess to be independent or neutral. When
journalists rate their fellow journalists, however, even greater differences
emerge: 56 percent say that the people they work with are mainly to the left
of center while only 8 percent identify their colleagues as being to the right
of center. The ratio is about seven-to-one liberal. Comparing the 8 percent
figure for those identified by their colleagues as conservative with the 19
percent figure for those who actually are of that persuasion may mean that
the conservatives keep their political views to themselves more or are
afraid to express them given the dominant liberal orientation of the
newsroom.

These same surveys revealed that, among the media elite, 94 percent
favored Johnson over Goldwater in 1964; 87 percent favored Humphrey
over Nixon in 1968; 81 percent favored McGovern over Nixon in 1972; and
81 percent favored Carter over Ford in 1976. Only one in ten favored
Reagan in 1980 or 1984. Hence by ratios of at least four or five to one, and
sometimes far more, the elite media has been consistently on the liberal or
Democratic side of the political spectrum. The political preferences of the
media elite are clearly not in accord with the views of the American general
public as expressed through the electoral vote.

The media elite's views on a wide range of social and political issues
are consistent with its preferences for presidential candidates. The surveys
show a strong commitment among journalists to expanding the welfare
state, to income redistribution, and to strengthening the hand of government—all views that are contrary to those of the majority of the public. In
foreign affairs, 56 percent of the media elite agree that American economic
exploitation has contributed to Third World poverty, 55 percent would
prohibit the CIA from undermining hostile governments in order to
protect United States interests, and half agree with the New Left notion that
the main goal of our foreign policy is to protect American business
interests. A majority of the media elite shares the counterculture view that
United States foreign policy toward the Third World is exploitive and
immoral, that American society is "alienating," and that it requires a
thorough "overhaul."

Such attitudes are widespread among the media elites and contribute
to the skeptical and often biased reporting that we get. For example, the
press is hostile toward the South African regime while its coverage of the

African National Congress, a Marxist-Leninist-inspired resistance group that sometimes uses terrorism to achieve its goals, is sympathetic. Now the fact is that most Americans are offended by the racial prejudice practiced in South Africa, but that does not mean they no longer favor evenhanded reporting. In Central America, much of the press has been very hostile to United States policy and often sympathetic to the guerrillas whose avowed aim, after all, is to defeat the United States. The kind of biases permeating media coverage of Central America is perhaps illustrated by the *Washington Post's* chief correspondent during the revolution in Nicaragua, whose reporting helped romanticize the Sandinistas and portray them as Robin Hoods: "Most Western journalists are very eager to seek out guerrilla groups, leftist groups, because you assume they must be the good guys." The "bad guys" in this analysis would be not only the dictator Somoza, but the United States as well[2]. The *Post* reporters who covered Central America thus became heroes to the American counterculture. But we must stop and ask: What kind of coverage will we get and how accurate can we expect it to be if the journalists reporting the news are so hostile to the United States and friendly to those who describe themselves as our enemies?

The surveys of the political attitudes and voting preferences of elite media reporters and news executives presented above were carried out in the late 1970s and early 1980s. Since then, a considerable amount of evidence has accumulated to show that the media have moderated their views. These changes have not turned the media elite into Reagan Republicans, but they have led the media to become somewhat less biased and more evenhanded. It appears that the Reagan era (1981 to 1989) did have its effects in at least making conservative views more acceptable, including among the media elite. The result is a media that by the 1990s has become somewhat less biased, less hostile to traditional American institutions, less inclined toward what has been called "advocacy journalism," and more oriented toward presenting the news fairly and without prejudice.

It used to be said that while the media elite were predominantly liberal, the media in the rest of the country were not. But it is doubtful if that is true anymore. Papers like the *Boston Globe,* the *Christian Science Monitor,* the *Minneapolis Tribune,* and even the *Grand Rapids Press* have become increasingly liberal in their perspectives, often so much so that their reporting and editorials are indistinguishable from those of the elite media. The coverage in small-town and rural America still tends to be predominantly local oriented and conservative (except, typically, in college and university communities), but the problem for evenhandedness is that very few Americans live in such communities anymore. In addition, most of these local papers get their foreign news directly from the wire services of the media elite.

It also used to be said that,while the reporters were often liberal, their editors and owners were conservative, therefore the two tended to balance each other out. But that is no longer true either. Owners and management rarely set policy for the media they own anymore, and the policy they do set is just as likely to be liberal as conservative. Among editors or, in the case of television, producers, the persons in these critical positions (who decide what stories to cover, how they should be covered, and what is printed or gets on the air) are now most often as liberal as their reporters. For example, at ABC the news is produced by a former press secretary of ultraliberal presidential candidate George McGovern; at NBC the nightly news is supervised by a former aide to New York Governor Mario Cuomo; and at CBS the political editor is a veteran of the Kennedy, Mondale, and Hart campaigns. It appears that many Democratic party activists but few Republicans, have moved into key positions in the news divisions of all three networks as well as in public broadcasting. It should be clear that no one questions the right of these activists to be where they are; rather, the questions revolve around the biases that thus creep into the news, whether these biases are pervasive throughout the news media, and whether other points of view are given a fair and equal airing.

It is probably accurate to say that too many news stories take the form of vastly oversimplified melodramas, with "good guys" and "bad guys" filtered through the reporter's own views. It is also fair to say that too many stories are marked by a lack of balance—or even the effort to try to achieve balance. And yet, when criticized for an absence of fair-mindedness, the press tends to react defensively, sometimes to whine, to elevate their biases and even occasional boorishness into virtues, and to retreat into pompous self-righteousness. The press then hides its mistakes behind the First Amendment. Any questions of bias, we are told, or misrepresentation, or pack journalism, or how the media conduct their own affairs constitute a "clear and present danger" to the republic and will have a "chilling" effect on the news.[3]

One further element of bias concerns us here, and that involves media coverage of the Third World. Most journalists have not spent a lot of time in the Third World and do not usually think of it as an assignment that will enhance their careers. Moreover, as "international affairs reporters" they may be sent from one hot spot—Central America, South Africa, the Middle East—to another on very short notice, without time to build up the expertise in an area that will enable them to truly understand it, on its own terms, and in its own language. When faced with a new area about which they have little expertise, journalists—probably just like the rest of us— tend to fall back on their own preconceptions or to resurrect intellectual categories learned in some undergraduate course. Thus. in Latin America the "oligarchy," the Church, the army, and the United States embassy become bad guys; while the "people"—the poor, the workers, and the intellectuals—become good guys. Or some variation on these themes.

The result of such oversimplifications and, frequently, inaccuracies is news coverage that is misleading and often false. If the reporters do not know or fully comprehend what is happening in the country they have been sent to cover, they tend to rely on shopworn theories or old cliches that may or may not apply and that inevitably color the kind of coverage provided. The model they use to interpret events is usually the United States itself, or perhaps some romantic classroom comprehension of the British, French, or Russian revolutions. But in the fields of economics, sociology, and political science, we know that the socioeconomic and political experiences of Western Europe and the United States are not likely to be repeated in today's Third World, that the cultural traditions and political conditions are different there, and that we must come to grips with Third World areas on their own terms and not as some pale imitation of the earlier Western experience.

It should be clear to all of us by now that we cannot understand Iran, China, Japan, India, Africa, the Middle East, or even Latin America (which is partially Western but by no means entirely so) using purely Western criteria, or Western criteria alone. We must understand the Third World in its own cultural and social context, a requirement that may take years to develop, and one that reporters visiting a country for two or three days are unable to quickly absorb. That is why media reporting on the developing nations, the Third World, is probably the least satisfactory of all. Lack of comprehension and of empathy (understanding other nations on their own terms) is thus added to the biases that already exist to make reporting on the Third World quite inadequate.

The Third World has responded to these persistent biases and prejudices about them (as corrupt, inefficient, comic-opera) that dominate the news stories by imposing greater controls on news coverage. One may sympathize with the Third World's efforts to get better and more accurate coverage, but de facto censorship of the news media is not the answer. The only hope is better education of the journalists who cover these countries so that they truly understand the nations about which they write rather than simply relying on the simplistic, tired, and usually inaccurate categories they learned as undergraduates.

HOW THE PRESS COVERS FOREIGN AFFAIRS

There is a new style in journalism and news reporting today. It is called investigative reporting, and has both positive and negative aspects associated with it. Investigative reporting means aggressively getting to the bottom of particularly sensitive issues, sometimes regardless of the larger costs; ferreting out sensitive information, even if this at times compromises national security; attacking hypocrisy and established institutions, even if doing so undermines the republic; going after persons in power, even at times to the extent of character assassination; invading the privacy of friendships and families; badgering, misleading, and sometimes even threatening informants; inserting the reporter's own slanted but presumably "higher" values into the coverage of the story; and then hiding behind the First Amendment when attacked for arrogance and obnoxiousness. Investigative reporters have a certain romantic aura about them, but the image has a dark side as well.

The picture that emerges of the modern investigative reporter is often not very complimentary. Not only are the reporter's methods frequently sneaky and vicious but they are also destructive because big foreign policy stakes are often involved. Ever since Woodward and Bernstein's *All the President's Men,* which was a no-holds-barred portrait of the Watergate scandal and the Nixon administration, a new model for the investigative reporter has emerged. In Watergate, not only was a major story uncovered, but the story meant big bucks, promotions, movie rights, career enhancement, and "star" quality for the reporters. That has too often become the goal of investigative reporting, for not only can a juicy story be revealed— whether in Central America, on the West Bank, in South Africa, in the Pentagon or White House, or in Iran-Contra—but the reporter may in the process acquire great wealth, fame, celebrity status, and entree into the very pinnacles of the American system. This is very heady stuff.

At the same time, while remaining aware of the self-serving aspirations of some of the new investigative reporters, we must also acknowledge the service many of them perform. Investigative reporting has unearthed a number of outright scandals, examples of crime and corruption, and incompetence on the part of public officials who deserved to be exposed. The questions we raise are whether this style of investigative reporting is or should be applicable to foreign affairs reporting, where the stakes are higher and more dangerous compared with domestic affairs, and whether the approach of American-style investigative reporting is really appropriate in other countries, where conditions and behavioral norms are far different from those in America.

Another problem is the reporter's knowledge, or the lack thereof. It used to be that foreign affairs correspondents were stationed in one country or region for years. They came to know it well and were sensitive and informed in their reporting. But with the availability of modern jet travel, reporters are now often stationed in New York or Washington and flit to this week's trouble spot—wherever it may be—on a moment's notice. For the news organizations, it is cheaper that way. But as roving journalists, foreign correspondents no longer have the time to acquire expertise in any one particular area or country. That is why their reports are often ill-informed, shallow, and ethnocentric. Often they stay in a country only 2-3 days, until the crisis-of-the-moment has passed, and then they must move on to another crisis somewhere else. Such crisis-hopping does not enable the journalist to build up any degree of expertise in any one part of the world, it leads to shallow reports that are based on simplicities rather than in-depth analyses, and it forces the reporter as indicated earlier to fall back on sophomoric generalizations in the absence of very much deeper knowledge about the country on which he is reporting.

To be fair, some journalists do stay in their foreign affairs posts for several years. Some really get to know the countries to which they are assigned. Some produce very solid reporting, some of which is actually value-free, and some reporters eventually write very substantial books about what they have seen. Hedrick Smith's *The Russians* and Alan Riding's *Distant Neighbors* (about Mexico) are examples of the very best kind of sensitive, empathetic, fact-filled reporting. But these examples are too rare in the journalistic community; unfortunately, the kind of superficial reporting described earlier is far too prevalent.

If a reporter is sent to a "trouble spot" that he knows little about, how does he or she go about reporting the stories? There is a pattern that emerges, presented here with only a little hyperbole. The first day's story is often written on the basis of what was told the reporter by the taxi driver who drives the reporter from the airport to the hotel. But that is a notoriously unreliable source since the taxis are often provided or subsidized by the government, which of course biases the views of the drivers. The second day's report is generally based on what the new arrival has heard over drinks from fellow journalists or from local United States embassy personnel—both of which are secondhand sources and not necessarily well informed. By the third day, when the reporter has begun to get a feel for what is really going on, lined up some independent interviews, and begins to see the crisis at a more complex level, it is time to leave.

When coverage is that brief and superficial, not only is the reporter likely to have limited factual information, but the interpretations offered may misrepresent the situation in the country being reported on as well. Studies have shown that in the absence of much intimate knowledge about the country to which they have been assigned, reporters tend to fall back on an often idealized understanding of American society and to use that as a model to judge all others. Thus when talking about agrarian reform, reporters usually have in mind a model based on the American Midwest; when talking about local government, journalists usually think of the New England town meeting or the reform movements in American cities; and when talking about human rights, reporters use as a model the civil rights struggle in the American South.[4]

Virtually every foreign institution is interpreted through the rose-colored lenses of the reporter's own American background. Civilian-military relations abroad are interpreted through the lens of America's strict separation between military and civilian realms and the careful subordination of the former to the latter, even though such arrangements are not possible in most Third World countries. The model of trade unionism is the collective bargaining system of the United States, even though most other countries practice a much more politicized unionism. "Democracy," "pluralism," and "representation" are interpreted according to the American understanding of those terms rather than in the diverse ways that these are often practiced outside the United States. Peasants and workers abroad are often assumed to be struggling for an American-style pluralism when their real goal may be a monolithic Marxist-Leninist regime. And so it goes. Virtually every institution and movement abroad is interpreted through American eyes by persons whose knowledge is superficial. Such reporting distorts the meaning of many events abroad and perpetuates greater misunderstandings in the United States about the countries with which we must deal.

Such coverage is particularly characteristic of the smaller countries that are off the beaten path, which do not have major international news bureaus lodged in their capital cities, and which therefore do not receive much regular attention. In the big cities where there are established bureaus—Mexico City and Rio de Janeiro in Latin America, Tel Aviv in the Middle East, Nairobi in Africa, Tokyo, Paris, London, Moscow—the coverage is often pretty good; but in the remaining 150 countries of the world, the coverage is often very spotty. Yet it is in precisely these obscure countries that we know and understand the least—El Salvador, Vietnam, Lebanon, Nicaragua, the Philippines, southern Africa—that the major crises in United States foreign policy have come in recent years.

Let us suppose it is not a crisis time, however. If a reporter sets out from the news bureau post in Rio de Janeiro, for example, to make a routine, four-times-yearly visit to the obscure countries in the region that are also a part of the beat—Paraguay, Bolivia, maybe Uruguay—some interesting dynamics are set in motion. Since visits by leading American reporters to these countries are still rare, the local United States embassy as well as local political groups (all with axes to grind) usually have advance word that the reporter is coming. They try to meet with the reporter to get their point of view across and into his or her stories. From this mishmash of information gleaned in a two- or three-day visit, what stories the reporter chooses to write about and what angles he or she gives them are tremendously important because they will appear in the trend-setting *Washington Post* or *New York Times* the next day. Since the story appears in the *Post* or *Times*, it will be an agenda item that day for Washington policy-makers, think tanks, congressmen, and others who, for various reasons, have a particular interest in that country. In the absence of very much other information about the country, what the *Post* or *Times* prints is tremendously important because that is what policy-makers and opinion-leaders read. What these papers say will shape and condition the official and unofficial interpretation of that country for months. For example, there is little doubt that the changes in official United States attitudes toward the birth control program in China occurred as a result of the stories by a *Washington Post* reporter concerning the widespread practice of abortions there. Policy changes such as this indicate why the visit of an American reporter is so important, why the reporter's role is so critical, why what the reporter says is so strategic, and why therefore it is so important for the reporter to do his job well.

There is a further twist to this tale. After the original story about a country appears in the *Post* or *Times*, it is often translated and reprinted in the local newspapers of the country that is the subject of the story. At that stage, politicians and others, who probably planted the story anonymously with the reporter in the first place, can go to their colleagues and say, "See, even the respected *New York Times* now confirms what I have been telling you." There are, in other words, layers upon layers of meaning in foreign reporting, and ways upon ways that reporters can be used to serve someone else's private political agenda.

The individual roving reporter is one thing; the mobs of reporters that descend on some poor, unprepared country in times of crisis are quite another. When Lebanon has a car bombing, when South Africa oppresses blacks, when El Salvador has an election, or when Nicaragua begins peace negotiations, literally hundreds of reporters may appear in the country. A small country like El Salvador cannot handle all these journalists. The reporters commandeer all available rental cars, tie up the entire national telephone system, monopolize hotel space and translators, and all try to interview the same people. It becomes a mob scene, a circus. It is doubtful if our understanding of the country is enhanced by such antics. Within two or three days, however, the reporters all rush off to the next hot spot, and the country reverts to its usual obscurity. But complete inattention by the press is often as disastrous as too much attention, because that allows small problems to fester in obscurity until they become big problems, once again forcing the country back onto American television screens as some new crisis unfolds.

Three additional themes command our attention. The first is the increasing ability of the media to set the agenda of our foreign policy. By its coverage of the changes in the Soviet Union, for example, the media help decide which issues are important, why they are important, who the principal actors are, and what the range of solutions is. But if its coverage of foreign events is often as biased and inadequate as suggested here, is it really appropriate for the media to play that role? Are these the issues that are really important to the Soviets—or only to the American reporters? Recall, also that while the media have influence, they do not have final decision-making power. They can shape and mold public opinion as well as reflect it, but in the United States it is still other, elected officials (or others appointed by them) who actually make the critical decisions in foreign policy. In the same vein, while the press may help set the national agenda, it does not finally decide it. The media may amplify the voices of the groups they highlight, but they do not by themselves determine what the national mood on a given issue will be.[5]

The second theme is the capacity of the media, especially television, to "hype" the news. By this we mean the ability of the media to build up the drama, to focus on personalities, and to polarize issues. The evening news programs and the news-oriented talk shows—*MacNeil/Lehrer News Hour* and *Nightline*—especially like to air two dramatically opposed viewpoints. That lends drama and controversy to the issue, may lead to fireworks, and leaves the host or anchor looking like the only sensible, rational, centrist person around. To give an illustration. Once, at the time of the killing of several nuns and religious laypersons in El Salvador, a colleague received a call from the programmers of one of these evening discussion programs who said, "Mr. so and so, we are having a Maryknoll nun on tonight and we want you to come on and take the opposite point of view." "Does that mean," he asked, "that you want me to be in favor of dead nuns?" (Around that person's research institute, his stance on such matters became known as "the pro-dead-nun position.") Actually, on most foreign policy issues, there is far more consensus in the foreign policy community, between the political parties, or between the Congress and the White House, than the debates and disagreements on national television seem to convey. That is because television wants to hype the drama and to build in more controversy and division than in fact exists. Such drama and controversy may be good television, and the shouting and conflict help attract viewers; but such polarized opinions are not often an accurate reflection of the nation's foreign policy views, which are mainly centrist and not polarized, and they may in fact help confuse and divide the country while also adding to our difficulties of carrying out a sensible policy.

The third theme is the media's actual participation in foreign policy-making, as demonstrated in the following examples. When Walter Cronkite, the former CBS anchor, decided after the Tet offensive that the war in Vietnam was unwinnable, that conversion (which may or may not have been based on an accurate assessment of the facts) probably had as much to do with changing American public opinion and forcing American withdrawal from the war as did all the previous protest demonstrations. Vietnam was of course the first war to be carried "live" into American living rooms and became known as the "television war." The TV coverage—especially of the war's bloody and brutal scenes—undoubtedly helped influence American opinion about the war and in many ways affected American policy, including the ultimate decision to end the war.

On another occasion, CBS got Israeli Prime Minister Menachem Begin on one screen and Egyptian President Anwar Sadat on another facing him, apparently trying to force a showdown between them, with the anchor acting as chief negotiator, presumably to bring "peace to the Middle East." Or, when President Reagan went to Moscow in 1988 to sign the historic

Intermediate Nuclear Forces (INF) treaty with Mikhail Gorbachev, television was so heavily represented that it became a participant in the event, not just an observer, whose agenda included changing the image most Americans have of the Soviet Union. Finally, when Dan Rather in an interview challenged the veracity of Vice-President Bush during the 1988 election campaign, it was clear that television was seeking to precipitate events rather than simply report them.

A concrete manifestation of television's inexorable influence on foreign policy is provided by the question of "friendly tyrants." That is, what should the United States do about authoritarian regimes that are friendly to the United States and resist communism but which also have atrocious human rights records. It is a difficult conundrum for policy-makers, involving hard choices between strategic considerations and human rights concerns. Examples include the Shah's regime in Iran during the 1970s, Marcos in the Philippines, Somoza in Nicaragua, Pinochet in Chile, and the South African regime of apartheid. The dilemma of when and how, or even if, the United States should break its ties with such regimes is a difficult one; but one thing we do know is the effect of television coverage on the issue.

When one of these "friendly tyrants" first gets in trouble and his regime starts to wobble, the first emphasis in the United States is usually on strategic considerations: the country's importance, the need to protect sea lanes, precious minerals, the potential communist threat, or oil supplies. But as soon as American television gets into the act, the focus shifts from strategic considerations to human rights concerns. The reason is not necessarily that biased TV reporters favor human rights over strategic considerations (although they may), but that oil tankers steaming by or jets taking off from the local United States military base can be shown only once: such scenes do not make "good"—that is, dramatic—television. Far more interesting from television's point of view is people being beaten up in the streets or being mowed down by the police. That is good television and, unlike the tankers, can be shown every night in dramatic form. Once the international media coverage shifts from strategic to human rights considerations, United States foreign policy is usually obliged to make a parallel shift, and the days of the "friendly tyrant" are usually numbered.[6]

CONCLUSION

The media in the United States now play a far more important role in foreign policy than previously. Some analysts have begun referring to the media as the "imperial press"—and often as increasingly imperious as well. The media, riding on the protections afforded by the First Amendment, have arrogated to themselves a role that constitutes almost a "fourth branch of government." No longer content to simply report the news, the media now try to shape and set the foreign policy agenda, to hype the news and polarize the issues, and themselves to become participants in foreign policy-making. Reporters now routinely interview other reporters as if they were real experts on the issues, even though we know from sociological studies that most reporters have a limited bachelor's degree educational background and often no special expertise in foreign policy issues or areas. The arrogance, rudeness, and presumptuousness of many reporters have by now produced such public hostility toward the press, and such a general discrediting, that when members of the press are roughed up or put in their place, the audience now cheers the perpetrators and blames the reporters. That is a very scary First Amendment issue which, we are not pleased to report, the press has in considerable measure brought upon itself by its one-sided or inadequate reporting.

We have seen in this chapter that the media are biased. While their biases tend to be on the left, they are liable to attack established institutions of all kinds, President Carter as well as President Reagan, Congress as well as the White House. We have seen how the media have tended to become the arbiters of our tastes in foreign policy as well as in other areas, but without always having the knowledge or experience to justify their playing such a leading role. The media have taken on a far greater importance in influencing foreign policy without that necessarily being accompanied by a greater sense of responsibility or accountability. Probably the press, like most groups, wants it both ways: great power but little responsibility. In a democracy, however, that is not only a dangerous and an arrogant position but also probably an unsustainable one, at least for any length of time. Hence those attitudes have recently begun to change and the media have similarly begun to change.

In terms of the overall themes of this book, it is probably accurate to say that, in addition to their reporting functions, the press has been in on many key issues in the last two decades a further destabilizing, fragmenting, polarizing, undermining, and destructive force, rather than necessarily a constructive one. The media have not just reflected the growing dissensus over American foreign policy and the nation's tendencies toward greater divisions, but they have accelerated the process and been agents of it. The press has added to our distrust of public officials and helped sow distrust and skepticism about America's purposes and institutions—not, we hasten to add, without good reason in quite a few instances. Too often, however, the criticism has been for the purpose of undermining policy or American institutions, frequently in biased and unfair ways, rather than faithfully reporting on the debate.

Are there hopes for any change? Actually there are. The number of journalists who specialize in foreign affairs has become larger than ever. Moreover, in the last decade their sophistication in foreign languages and cultures has increased remarkably, and the number of seminars and special training programs to help educate reporters about foreign policy issues and countries has multiplied manifold. In some areas, the coverage and number and depth of news reports have improved noticeably. While the improvements are significant, nonetheless, the more fundamental issues raised here have yet to be resolved.

One final comment is necessary before we close. In this chapter we have discussed the media's sometimes ill-informed and inappropriate incursions into the foreign policy arena, and the language has at times been quite condemnatory of the press. It must be emphasized, however, that politicians and government officials use and abuse the press at least as often as the reverse. They plant and leak stories, give out false or misleading information, and try to manipulate the press to serve their own personal, policy, or partisan purposes. The result is a kind of "dance" in which the media try to ferret out the news while public officials try often to control it or give it a slant favorable to their point of view.

Such conflict between government officials and the press is not only natural in a democracy based on checks and balances and on a certain degree of adversarial relations between the two, but it is also a good thing. The only question we raise here—and a recurrent one in our analysis—is whether the adversarial nature of this relationship may be getting out of hand, resulting not in a healthy system of checks and balances but in polarization, conflict, and a tearing apart of America's social and political fabric.

Notes

1. See, among others, S. Robert Lichter, Stanley Rothman, and Linda S. Lichter, *The Media Elite: America's New Powerbrokers* (Bethesda, Md.: Adler & Adler, 1986).
2. Joshua Muravchik, *News Coverage of the Sandinista Revolution* (Washington, D.C.: American Enterprise Institute for Public Policy Research, 1988).
3. William A. Rusher, *The Coming Battle for the Media* (New York: Morrow, 1988).
4. Howard J. Wiarda, "The Media and Latin America: Why the Coverage Goes Astray," *The Journalist* (Fall 1985):18–19.
5. See the research work of Martin Blonsky as reported in the *Washington Post* 24 April, 1988, sec. D-1; also his book *Reading America* (New York: Oxford University Press, 1989).
6. Adam Garfinkle and Daniel Pipes, eds., *Friendly Tyrants: A Troubled Legacy* (Philadelphia: Foreign Policy Research Institute, 1989).

Suggested Readings

Arno, Andrew, and Wimal Dissanayake, eds. *The News Media in National and International Conflict* (Boulder: Westview Press, 1984.
Boyer, Peter J. *Who Killed CBS?* New York: Random House, 1988.

Bray, Charles. "The Media and Foreign Policy" *Foreign Policy*, 16 (Fall 1974) 109–25.

Bray, Howard. *The Pillars of the Post* New York: Norton, 1980.

Cohen, Bernard C. "The Influence of Special-Interest Groups and Mass Media on Security Policy in the United States," *Perspectives on American Foreign Policy*, edited by Charles W. Kegley, Jr., and Eugene R. Wittkopf. New York: St. Martin's Press, 1983.

————. *The Press and Foreign Policy* Princeton, N.J.: Princeton University Press, 1963.

Emery, Michael, and Ted Smythe, *Mass Communications* Dubuque, Iowa: William C. Brown, 1986.

Epstein, Edward J. *Between Fact and Fiction* New York: Random House, 1975.

Graber, Doris A. *Mass Media and American Politics* Washington, D.C.: Congressional Quarterly Press, 1989.

Hallin, Dan. *The Uncensored War: The Media and Vietnam* New York: Oxford University Press, 1986.

Joyce, Ed. *Prime Times, Bad Times* New York: Doubleday, 1988.

Larson, James F. *Television's Window on the World* Norwood, N.J.: Ablex Publishing Corporation, 1984.

Lashner, Marilyn A. *The Chilling Effect in T.V. News* New York: Praeger, 1984.

Lichter, S. Robert, et al. *The Media Elite* Bethesda, Md.: Adler and Adler, 1986.

Mollenhoff, Clark. *Investigative Reporting* New York: Macmillan, 1981.

"The News Media: Rights, Responsibilities, and Remedies." Special Report of *The World and I,* February 1988, pp. 18–55.

Ninno, Dan D. *Political Communication and Public Opinion in America* Santa Monica, Calif. Goodyear Publishing, 1978.

Paletz, David L., and Robert M. Entman. *Media - Power - Politics* New York: The Free Press, 1981.

Reel, Adolph F. *The Networks: How They Stole the Show* New York: Charles Scribner's Sons, 1979.

Reston, James. *The Artillery of the Press: Its Influence on American Foreign Policy* New York: Harper & Row, 1967.

Rice, Michael. *Reporting US-European Relations: Four Nations, Four Newspapers* New York: Pergamon Press, 1982.

Rusher, William. *The Coming Battle for the Media* New York: Morrow, 1968.

Sentan, Richard, et al. "The Presidency and the Print Media: Who Controls the News" *Sociological Quarterly* 27 (Spring 1986):91–105.

Shaw, Donald L., and Maxwell E. McCombs. *The Emergence of American Political Issues: The Agenda-Setting Function of the Press* St. Paul: West, 1977.

Stevenson, Robert, ed. *Foreign News and the New World Information Order* Ames: Iowa State Press, 1984.

Weaver, Paul H. "The New Journalism and the Old—Thoughts After Watergate." *Public Interest* 35 (Spring 1974):67–88.

Wiarda, Howard J. *Ethnocentrism in Foreign Policy: Can We Understand the Third World?* Washington, D.C.: American Enterprise Institute for Public Policy Research, 1985.

CHAPTER SIX

Interest Groups and Foreign Policy

✪
✪

Political participation in the United States through organized interest groups dates back to the earliest days of the republic. In fact, the right of representation was one of the main demands of the colonists over two centuries ago in their quarrel with England. In *The Federalist,* James Madison spoke at length about the benefits to democracy of the interplay of countervailing interests, and over the course of the last two hundred years, the United States has become a much more pluralist nation—socially, politically, and religiously—a feature that most Americans think of as one of the glories of American democracy.

In recent years, a dramatic increase has occurred in the number of American interest groups. In fact, so many have moved their offices to the nation's capitol that Washington, D.C., is saturated with about 50,000 interest groups. Not only have their tactics and strategies become more sophisticated than in the past, but these groups have become increasingly active in the foreign policy arena, often integrating themselves directly into the political debate, and sometimes even taking over whole areas of foreign policy for themselves. Whereas before, interest group activity was largely confined to bargaining over the domestic political agenda, since the Vietnam war foreign policy has also become a major arena of interest group competition. Furthermore, the strength of some of these private groups is such that sometimes it appears that they, and not the United States government, run foreign policy.

This interest group competition has sometimes become so intense and the positions taken so strongly felt that a coherent, rational foreign policy has often been difficult to carry out. We have become so pluralist a nation that we may have lost our attachment to any agreed-upon core of central foreign policy values. And with the democratization of foreign policy that the rise of these multitudes of vociferous and powerful private interest groups implies, the United States government runs the risk of losing control of its own foreign policy. More discussion of these controversial themes follows in the chapter.

FOUR QUESTIONS ABOUT INTEREST GROUPS AND FOREIGN POLICY

Unquestionably the United States is in a new era in terms of our system of interest groups, a system that goes considerably beyond the Madisonian conceptions of democracy and pluralism. While most Americans strongly support traditional notions of democracy and pluralism, the proliferation and strength of today's interest groups sometimes raise very serious questions about our capacity to conduct a serious, sensible, and coherent foreign policy. The strength, capacity, and legitimacy of the United States government seems gradually to be declining, while the power of private interest and societal groups is ascending.[1] In social science terms, *society* (the nation's multitudinous associations and interest groups) is becoming more influential than, or in some areas taking over, the state, with potentially disastrous consequences for American foreign policy.

Four key questions need to be raised at the beginning to guide the discussion in this chapter and to help us understand more broadly the workings, or the lack thereof, of American foreign policy.

1. Have some powerful interest groups taken over whole areas of foreign policy for themselves? Specifically, have big business, big agriculture, and big labor "hived off" and privatized certain areas of foreign policy having to do with international commerce, trade, and labor relations that previously were thought to be the proper responsibility of the United States government? And if these policy areas have been literally taken over by private interest groups, what are their relations with the United States government? Is there any accountability to the public on the part of these private groups? And what are the implications for democracy of our foreign policy becoming privatized in this way?[2]

2. Ungovernability? The second question is whether the sheer number of private interest groups "out there" is eroding the strength of American political institutions and making the country all but ungovernable.[3] In the last two decades, we have seen a tremendous proliferation in the number of interest groups, some of them with more clout in certain areas than the United States government itself. Does this sheer number of interests threaten to convert our valued pluralism into a chaotic free-for-all—anarchic, fragmented, and with little or no attachment to a nucleus of agreed-upon values or unity? Without any attachment to a central core, all these centrifugal interest groups are on the verge of spinning out of control. The system is becoming so divided and so

fragmented that there may no longer be enough unity left in the system to make foreign policy manageable, let alone effective.

3. Biases in the system? The third question involves biases in our interest group structure. There are far more activist interest groups on the left, on the liberal side, than there are on the right—some estimates put the proportions at about 80% liberal and 20% conservative. We will leave others to speculate on the reasons for this, but the fact is that far more lobbying groups exist on the left than on the right. In reaction to this imbalance, conservative interest groups have recently begun to mobilize and organize. But it still remains the case that liberal groups are far more organized than conservative groups by a ratio of about four to one—a pattern that does not reflect the division of the electorate and, therefore, is worrisome for democracy.

4. Tunnel vision? Finally, we need to be concerned with the multitude of new special interest groups that have grown up in the last decades, and that have a particularly narrow or tunnel vision of foreign policy. Here we have in mind the various religious groups, actors' associations, special interest lobbies, physicians' associations, committees in solidarity with the people of one country or another, ethnic lobbies, and so on—all of which have very strong ideological views on foreign policy issues that are sometimes beyond their fields of competence, but which are nevertheless able to influence and sometimes even hamstring and paralyze foreign policy. The proliferation of these groups has added greatly to our pluralism—and to the chaotic, sometimes unmanageable character of our foreign policy. At the same time, the fact that these views are very strongly held and put forward by such groups, usually without due regard for other foreign policy considerations, means that the big picture and the overall interests/good of the United States run the risk of being sacrificed. For example, many of these groups are very strongly committed to a foreign policy based on human rights. Now most of us are also committed to a strong human rights program, but if that focus is followed to the complete exclusion of other legitimate American interests—political, economic, diplomatic, strategic—it will be disastrous for United States foreign policy. That is what is meant by the dangers of tunnel vision or a one-dimensional foreign policy.

We shall have more to say on all these controversial themes in the discussion that follows.

BIG BUSINESS AND UNITED STATES
FOREIGN POLICY

Symbiosis is a term used mainly in biology to describe a situation in which two organisms live in intimate association, often feeding off each other and mutually serving each other's functions. That is precisely the relationship of big business, big agriculture, and big labor to American foreign policy. These big groups and the government live in intimate association, they feed off each other, and they mutually serve each other's interests.

Such a relationship goes considerably beyond what most of us think of as the normal role of interest groups—that is, lobbying for and influencing policy. By now, however, we are not talking about mere influence, although that is important too, but about the actual *incorporation* of interest groups into the decision-making apparatus of the state, the virtual *turning over* to these private interests of some areas of our foreign policy, and thus the *hiving off* of public policy functions and the sometimes near-monopolization of these functions by private groups. In the related political science field of comparative politics, the incorporation of private groups into public decision making and the granting of monopolistic control to these private interests over certain areas of public policy are called corporatism.[4] The question is, what happens to public accountability and democratic oversight when a large share of our foreign policy is dominated by private interests rather than the public agencies that by law and Constitution are supposed to be responsible?

Big business is probably a larger actor in American foreign policy than most of us suspect. Its influence extends far beyond what most of us think of as legitimate lobbying activities. At the same time, the role of big business in foreign policy does not really conform to simplistic Marxian categories either. Big business is not really an agency of "imperialism," nor is the United States government a tool of the large corporations, doing their bidding abroad or dictating that American foreign policy serve the interests of the multinational firms.

Although it still happens from time to time, the days when a large corporation like the United Fruit Company can seat and unseat governments in the Third World are pretty much over. Because of the debt crisis and the inefficiency and corruption of many Third World regimes, the major corporations are getting out of most Third World countries and putting their investments, naturally enough, where there is less grief and greater profits: that is, in Western Europe, Canada, the booming Pacific rim countries, and the United States itself. Nor is it the case that United States embassies and ambassadors serving abroad, or the State Department in Washington, very often feel the heat of pressure from big business or a giant multinational to take a decision or follow a policy to which the United

States government, an embassy, or the Department of State is opposed. The memoirs of numerous United States ambassadors all attest to this fact that rarely if ever do they get pressured by American companies to take an action to which the United States government is opposed. Things really do not work that way anymore—or at least not very often.

There are, of course, various nefarious acts in which some big companies still get involved abroad. These acts are headline-grabbers but they are not very representative. These may include the bribing of officials of another government to gain certain favors, the paying of "protection" money to local military officials, discouraging union activities in their plants, greasing the palms of bureaucrats to speed up the processing of needed papers and permits, and exercising influence—sometimes untoward—over the politics of the host country. However, because the stake of their investments is high and they can easily be nationalized or kicked out, most American companies try to be good neighbors in the countries in which they invest. Offsetting the sometimes wayward activities listed above are also the *facts* that American firms operating abroad tend to pay higher salaries than any others, help stimulate economic development, provide greater benefits in the way of housing and health care, and bring sorely needed capital, jobs, and investment that all Third World countries *must* have if they are ever to develop.

How then *do* the big companies go about exercising influence? The process is both more pervasive and more subtle than the heavy-handed tactics described in much of the literature. Here is where the symbiosis image with which we began becomes useful. For in fact what has happened is that big business has often insinuated itself directly into the official, United States government decision-making process itself. Big business does not need to influence the government, although it sometimes does that too; it *is* the government. Business has been incorporated into the decision-making apparatus of the modern state. Whole programs on which business has more talent and expertise than the United States government have been, in part, turned over to business. Certain agencies of the government have de facto become conduits to encourage and bolster American private business abroad. They, in effect, are public lobbying agencies for big business.

The range of activities of these government agencies on behalf of big business is broad. Let us provide a brief flavor of them. For example, the international division of the Department of Commerce is strongly oriented toward serving the interests of American businesses that already have or wish to invest abroad. The international division of the Treasury Department performs similar services as well as helping private commercial banks in the United States to weather the international debt crisis. The Office of the United State Trade Representative, which enjoys cabinet status, promotes further American trade, lobbies against protectionist legislation that will diminish trade, and helps American business overcome trade barriers thrown up by other countries. In addition, virtually all United States embassies abroad have commercial sections (along with the usual political, military, and cultural sections) that carry out studies of local economic conditions and assist American businesses in investing there.

Frequently the persons who staff these posts and agencies are recruited out of the business world and therefore tend to be very sympathetic to the needs of big business. Or else a person who serves in one of these government capacities may subsequently be hired by a big firm that will put his inside information on how the government works to good use. Later on, that same person may return to government at a higher level, say, at the assistant secretary or even secretary level, where he can continue to serve both the needs of the business sector and what he considers the public interest, which are often viewed as identical. After another stint in government, the person may again return to the private sector in what resembles a revolving-door system.

This process and system should not be viewed as either nefarious or even sneaky. It is not as though big business and big government are involved in some gigantic, secretive, complex conspiracy to subvert American values. Rather this is the logical outcome of the kind of nation we are. Compared with other nations, our government is very limited in terms of its size and resources. Furthermore, we are a nation that truly believes that most activities should be left to the private sector. In this case that means private business. At the same time we are a nation in which most jobs and the strength of the American economy depend on the health and prosperity of private business, not the government. Private business really believes—and public opinion backs it up—that it is the role of business to bring jobs and prosperity to other countries as well as to the United States through investment there. Meanwhile, the United States government, recognizing that *it* cannot provide jobs and prosperity abroad, facilitates the private sector in doing so. This is not conspiracy, but a mutuality of interests. Both business and government accept—even applaud—the role that private firms play in other countries, both in stimulating prosperity for them and in maintaining and increasing it for Americans at home.

The system may thus be looked at not just in terms of government agencies and personnel but also in terms of programs. For example, when it became necessary for President John F. Kennedy to build a private investment program and a program to train managers into his Alliance for Progress for Latin America, where else could he turn for assistance and people to run the program than to the private business sector? When Ronald Reagan created the Caribbean Basin Initiative to provide capital and assist the development of the poor and unstable nations of the Caribbean, he quite naturally turned to David Rockefeller of the Chase Manhattan Bank who set up a committee and rounded up his colleagues and fellow businessmen to get investment flowing again into that region. It is to be emphasized that, given limited government resources, none of these and many other programs would be successful without a major private business input.

It used to be that the National Association of Manufacturers and the Chamber of Commerce were the main interest groups one focused on when studying business interest groups. These are still important, but they have now been supplemented by hundreds of trade associations, one for virtually every industry in the country (pharmaceutical manufacturers, shoe manufacturers, and so on). In addition, the larger individual American firms now all have full-time Washington offices so that they can track the political currents, keep tabs on pending legislation, attend think tank receptions to learn of new research affecting their area, meet with government officials and the like. Many of these companies not only have their own legal staffs to protect their interests but also hire large and well-connected Washington law firms to help them wield influence. These lobbying agencies and their law firms are clustered in and around K Street in Washington and are known irreverently as the "K Street Bandits." They are not literally thieves, but they certainly know how to manipulate and take advantage of the system.

Why is the input of these business groups so important? Part of the reason has already been given. They alone have the knowledge, the experience, the skills, and the capital to make a successful investment or private sector program work. In addition, in an era of budget deficits and, hence, of declining United States public assistance, otherwise known as foreign aid, the United States government has turned to the private sector to provide the capital that the public sector no longer provides.

Finally, we need to look at the foreign policy logic of all this. We believe that economic growth in the Third World is absolutely necessary for stability, for democracy, and to keep out nefarious foreign influences. Without economic growth and possibilities, popular discontent is liable to grow, stability is likely to be undermined, democracy will flounder, and communism may triumph. Hence the absolute need for a continuous flow of capital and investment. There will *never* be enough public foreign assistance to fill the need; such capital can only come from the private sector. That is not only why the United States government relies heavily on the private sector for advice, capital, and personnel, but why the public and the private sectors work so closely together. Both are absolutely necessary for each other for the success of each other's basic agenda. That is also why we described their relationship as symbiotic, because both the public and private sectors in this sense feed off each other, depend on each other, and are so closely intertwined as to be inseparable.

Let us look a bit more closely at the means, both traditional and newer, by which the influence of big business in government is exercised.

1. Lobbying. Business both supplies information to and receives information from the government. Its lobbyists and lawyers ply the halls of Congress on an everyday basis. They meet with congressmen and especially their staffs. Particularly in the subcommittees of the Congress, where much of the legislation is actually hammered out, the lobbyists are omnipresent. They often know more about particular provisions than do the congressmen. Knowledge is power, and business provides a good share of the specialized knowledge to the Congress. Bills and hearings may run to thousands of pages, but the lobbyists go over every word. They try to get language incorporated that helps their particular industry, and sometimes even language that particularly benefits themselves. But in the overwhelming majority of instances, the relationship is symbiotic: the lobbyists need the congressmen and their staffs and they, in turn, need the expertise and insight that only the lobbyists and the firms or industries they represent can provide.

2. Campaign finance. We all know that political campaigns are expensive: a campaign for the House of Representatives can now easily cost $500,000 and one for the Senate in a hotly contested race can run to $10 million. Money is the lifeblood of a successful campaign, and 90 percent of the money comes from business firms and business associations. Much of this money is diverted to individuals and to political action committees (PACs) because of legal limits placed on corporate contributions. But of course we all understand that if 90 percent of the money comes from business corporations, the congressmen receiving such funds are beholden to big business—not usually in a direct way (money traded for votes) but to guarantee special access to business for the airing of its point of view and to make sure nothing really bad happens to a particular kind of business. Contrary to what some of us may have been taught when young, money *does* talk and carry influence. And increasingly, in this age of multinational companies and increased economic interdependence, more and more of the PACs and influence peddling are being devoted to international issues.

3. Interchange of personnel. Approximately two thousand former military officers are presently on the payrolls of the one hundred largest American corporations. At the same time, many of the top-ranking civilian employees in the Pentagon come from big business. This revolving door—and the contracts and insider knowledge that go with it—is what is often referred to as the military-industrial complex. Such back-and-forth movement between the private and public sectors is also prevalent in the civilian agencies—the Departments of Commerce and the Treasury, and the Office of the Trade Representative.

4. Private business running government agencies. We have already seen how whole areas of foreign economic assistance, such as the Caribbean Basin Initiative, are sometimes turned over to the private sector for management. In this way American business or its representatives run a great many ostensibly public activities abroad. It should also be noted that in the area of foreign aid, American firms, not necessarily the recipient countries, are often the chief beneficiaries: the companies provide the products that are sold abroad and frequently the personnel to administer these programs. Furthermore, the aid provided creates new markets for other American products because, by law, the countries to which we give our aid must usually use the money to purchase American products.

5. Advising. Many business advisory councils maintain very close relations with government agencies. The relationship is not only symbiotic, it is almost incestuous. For example, the National Petroleum Institute, a private lobbying group, serves as a key "adviser" to both the Interior and the Energy departments, providing them with data, political intelligence about the Middle East and other oil-producing areas, economic trend reports, and key personnel to staff these agencies. In the process, the distinction that we once used to make between the public and the private domains has been crisscrossed, fudged, and blurred—"hopelessly lost," in the words of political scientist Grant McConnell.[5]

6. Personal contacts. Many of the chief executive officers (CEOs) of large American corporations, as well as their board members, vice-presidents, and division or office heads, are on a first-name basis with their counterparts in the United States government: cabinet members, assistant secretaries, and so on. They go to parties and receptions together (no wine and cheese, please; only shrimp, oysters, ham, and roast beef); they know each other's past professional histories; and they share an interest in political stability, moderation, and economic growth. They are able to joke together, share stories together, and exchange "inside-the-beltway" (Washington, D.C.) gossip. At certain levels, therefore, lobbying and PACs are unnecessary; rather, this web of personal contacts and ability to simply pick up the telephone and call the appropriate government official (who, chances are, is also a friend or acquaintance from this same Washington social *cum* political circuit) will do just as well.

7. Power abroad. The influence of these large companies, especially when operating abroad in a small country, is enormous. General Motors, for example, has more sales than the budgets of all but 18 of the 160-odd countries in the world. The bigger companies have immense resources at their disposal; they can mobilize more lawyers, more CPAs, more public relations experts, and more diplomatic connections than can an entire small nation. Actually, even small countries are not without their own resources that they can mobilize against a big company, and many have done so very successfully. The relationships between small, dependent countries and big United States-based multinationals are not nearly as one way as some of the literature portrays. Nevertheless, it is still an asymmetrical relationship in which the big companies are able to wield considerable influence.

Big business, more than any other large interest group, is thus woven into the fabric of the American government, including those parts of it responsible for foreign policy. In this symbiotic relationship between private and public power, sometimes the private sector is dominant and sometimes the public; but whatever the case, there is no doubt that private big business is enormously influential. In many cases, big business can do the job better than can the federal government—another reason for its power. In other cases, if business senses a weak team at the State or Treasury departments or at the National Security Council, it will move in and almost (but not quite) literally take over some of these supposedly public sector activities itself. In these senses, business is almost always *in* power; even when it is not directly in charge it is so close to the surface of power as to be all but inseparable from it. Herbert Hoover once said that "the business of America is business," and a former secretary of defense, who had earlier been president of General Motors, once stated that "what's good for General Motors is good for the USA." There is hyperbole and exaggeration in these comments of course, but they are not as far off the mark as they once seemed.

Fully 40 percent of the profits of the nation's three hundred largest corporations are now earned abroad. Hence as the world continues to shrink under the impact of modern communications and transportation, as international trade increases globally and what has been called the internationalization of capital goes forward, and as more firms become *multinational* rather than located in one country, we can only expect that this percentage will go up. And so, too, will the influence of these gigantic companies on United States foreign policy increase.

BIG AGRICULTURE AND UNITED STATES FOREIGN POLICY

The United States is no longer a rural and agricultural country. Farmers currently number only about 3 percent of the total population and therefore lack political clout. Nevertheless, albeit on a smaller scale, the same trends and characteristics that we saw with regard to business also apply to agriculture—trends toward greater concentration, toward a more "corporatized" society and polity, and toward the privatization of certain areas of ostensibly public responsibility.

Although farmers constitute a small minority of the total population, agricultural products accounted for about 12.2 percent of United States exports in fiscal year 1987 and earned about $27.9 billion.[6] International agriculture is *big* business. The United States is the world's largest exporter of coarse grains and soybeans, and one of the largest suppliers of wheat, cotton, meat, and horticultural products. Nevertheless, the share of American agricultural exports relative to other nations' has been gradually decreasing in recent years because of competition from the European Economic Community and such Third World exporters as Brazil and Argentina. Even with this relative decline, however, agriculture is one of the few economic sectors in which the United States consistently registers a trade surplus.

American agricultural exports make an important contribution to our foreign policy objectives. The United States has been working to achieve a more open and equitable trading environment that would result in improved export opportunities for American agricultural products. Another priority is greater cooperation in food aid, food security, and agricultural economic development in developing countries—for the same political and strategic reasons (stability and growth) that we support private business investment there. But it should also be remembered that the United States is an important market for agricultural products from around the world, the total value of which rose from $17 billion in 1981 to $21 billion in 1987. Coffee is the single largest agricultural import.

Agriculture policy has become something of a political football in recent years. In 1980, President Jimmy Carter cut off grain sales to the Soviet Union in retaliation for the Soviet invasion of Afghanistan; but that market was quickly filled by Argentina, with the result that not only did we not hurt the Soviet Union but the USSR now bought its grain from Argentina and became Argentina's largest trading partner, to the detriment of the United States. In addition, American farmers suffered from the loss of the Soviet market. Food aid has also become controversial: we sent massive famine relief to Ethiopia only to find that its Marxist-Leninist government was withholding the aid from its own population for political reasons, or was channeling it to certain favored groups at the expense of others, or was turning it over to bureaucrats and military officers who were selling it for private profit.

The Targeted Export Assistance (TEA) program of the Department of Agriculture is illustrative of many of the problems discussed here. TEA was set up to help further American agricultural exports, but it is staffed heavily by persons either recruited from big agriculture or beholden to it. It has become a program mainly to subsidize, using taxpayers' money, luxury agricultural items—not wheat and corn but products like almonds and mink. It mainly helps large agribusinesses, not individual farmers. There is practically no accountability as to where its subsidies go. The major industry groups, such as the citrus growers, monopolized the funding available through TEA and then used the funds to promote the brand names of certain products—for example, Sunkist—instead of generic market development abroad, which was the intention of the program. One growers' group was reimbursed millions of dollars for expenses it had never incurred. A General Accounting Office investigative report (which in itself was quite unusual because most of these programs are never investigated) concluded that the program was beset by shoddy administration, had inadequate guidelines and safeguards, exercised favoritism, and was subject to abuse by private firms that had all but literally taken over the agency.[7]

The volume of world trade in agriculture actually declined during the 1980s. Improved agricultural technology and slower growth in demand were the primary factors, which in turn stimulated government policies and support programs aimed at cushioning farmers from the slower market. But that led to massive increases in farm subsidies, from $4 billion in 1981 to $26 billion in 1986 and $22.4 billion in 1987. At present the prices of most major crops—both those produced by the United States and those produced by other countries—are depressed by oversupply and the growing use of export subsidies.

The overall result of these and other changes has closely paralleled the transformations we saw with regard to big business. First, there has been a tremendous concentration of resources as more and more small family farms are swallowed up by large agribusinesses producing for a world market. Second, the Department of Agriculture, which oversees these policies, has become an increasingly important *political* actor in the foreign policy area. Third, a symbiotic and almost incestuous relationship has grown up between the Department of Agriculture and the large agribusinesses, in which the department in effect operates as a lobbying agency for large farmers within the United States government. The Department of Agriculture has become to farmers what the Department of Commerce is to big business: a spokesman in the United States government for private interests. And fourth, this means that big agriculture has literally captured and hived off for itself an entire department of the United States government, implying both the privatization and the corporatization of the system. Where the public foreign policy interest of the United States gets served in all of this is sometimes very hard to find.

BIG LABOR AND UNITED STATES FOREIGN POLICY

We are not used to thinking of big labor (the AFL-CIO) as having a major foreign policy role. But in fact big labor's role is often as important as a foreign policy instrument as is that of big business. Their roles are both complementary and mutually supportive—two sides of the same coin.

Both big business and big labor are no longer just private interest groups; rather they have become quasi-officially a part of the governmental system itself. Representatives from both sectors are almost always consulted on impending policy and regularly sit on the numerous boards, task forces, and commissions set up by the White House. Both have been given, or have hived off for themselves, whole areas of foreign policy, but without assuming much accountability or responsibility for their activities. The incorporation of both business and labor into semiofficial roles, supported and often financed by the government, is part of the "corporatization" (bigness, bureaucracy, inseparability of public and private functions) of American life. In addition we must ask: how well are these groups doing their job?

Big labor is still a powerful force in Washington, D.C., despite declining membership nationally. No politician, whether in the Congress or the White House, would dare to challenge, let alone cross, big labor. That costs votes, and no congressman wishes to lose votes. In addition, organized labor still exercises veto power over many appointments and programs. Hence big labor is always treated with kid gloves. That is why there is practically no oversight of its activities, including in the foreign policy area.

Industrial and labor relations are one of the main anvils on which the structure of the modern state, society, and economy is hammered out. Labor relations are hence every bit as important as diplomatic, political, and security relations. That is why the United States seeks to monitor closely and influence or even control if possible the labor relations systems of other nations. The chief purpose of course is to prevent Communist unions from gaining the upper hand and using their positions of strength within the labor movement to launch a Marxist-Leninist revolution or seize control of the organs of the state, which would be detrimental to American foreign policy interests. The task of preventing such Communist takeovers of union movements abroad has been in large part entrusted to the American labor movement.

The program got started right after World War II, at the beginning of the cold war.[8] Europe had been devastated by the war, both physically and emotionally; Stalin's armies were completing their takeovers of Eastern Europe; and in several Western nations in the immediate aftermath of the war the Communist parties and trade unions were stronger and better organized than their democratic counterparts. The fear was that, unless the United States helped out, Communist-led revolutions and takeovers might also occur in France and Italy, both of which had strong Communist labor movements and parties. Hence the American labor movement, using CIA money and sometimes CIA personnel, was enlisted to bolster and provide financial support to non-Communist trade unions.

The program was largely successful in the European context. American assistance helped build up the Christian-Democratic trade unions in Italy and the Socialist (but non-Communist) union movement in France to the point where their strength was equal to or exceeded Communist union strength. Along with the Marshall Plan, the program helped build up the economies of Western Europe, bolstered the working class, restored prosperity, and enabled Europe to get back on its feet. The non-Communist unions, supported by the American labor movement and the United States government, were able to serve as a check on the Communist unions and to prevent the possibility of Marxist-Leninist revolution in Western Europe. American foreign policy goals were thus served.

The success of the European efforts emboldened America's labor movement and the CIA to do the same thing in the Third World. The program got started in the late 1950s, corresponding to the sudden emergence of a variety of new nations in Africa and Asia and, in Latin America, to the triumph of the Cuban revolution and the emergence of the first Marxist-Leninist, pro-Soviet nation in the Western Hemisphere. The fear was that unless the United States helped fund and create non-Communist trade unions in the Third World, more and more of these countries would have Castro-like Communist revolutions. A new training program, the American Institute for Free Labor Development (AIFLD), was therefore established to carry out the program. The funding and often the personnel—the labor attaches sent to the American embassies abroad to work on creating anti-Communist labor movements—were still CIA.

Conditions in the Third World were quite different from those in Western Europe, however. The CIA and AFL-CIO had little experience in or understanding of the Third World, and seldom acquired the necessary level of expertise. In addition, the model of collective bargaining that was used, which was based on the generally nonpolitical, collective bargaining system of the United States, had little relevance in the Third World. The exceedingly conservative ideology of the AFL-CIO representatives who carried out the program was often unacceptable and inappropriate in the Third World. And CIA funding was counterproductive because when the funding source was eventually revealed, the labor group that received it was discredited and often destroyed as a result.

The AFL-CIO was in fact successful in many of its training programs for young Third World labor leaders. And the money it poured in was un-doubtedly useful to the recipient countries. To its credit, the AFL-CIO was energetic in many countries in criticizing governments that abused union rights. In some countries, it succeeded in bolstering democratic unions and keeping Communist or Fascist ones from coming to power.

But the balance sheet also contains many negatives. In quite a number of countries, AFL-CIO activities split and divided the labor movement, rendering it weaker. In some cases, AIFLD helped mobilize reactionary forces to overthrow left-leaning and prolabor governments. The AFL-CIO's imposition of an American model of labor relations failed to take account of local practices and conditions and was therefore unacceptable to the leaders of Third World nations.

In several spectacular instances, the AFL-CIO all but ruined the local labor movements, thereby stimulating more pro-Communist and anti-American sentiment, which was what the program was designed to prevent in the first place. The labor attaches brought in by the AFL-CIO and the CIA were often at odds over policy with other members of the U.S. embassy team, thus adding to our policy incoherence and disarray abroad. Frequently these labor attaches reported to Washington directly without going through the United States ambassador, and they carried out policy in the labor arena that was uncoordinated with and sometimes directly opposed to overall embassy policy. In addition, the later revelations that it was the CIA that was providing the funding was often the kiss of death to the local labor movement that accepted AIFLD assistance.

In the face of these numerous gaffes, mistakes, and sheer disasters, were there any serious investigations by the Congress, the White House, or the General Accounting Officer, which oversees foreign as well as domestic programs? Was there any attempt to cut off funds from the program or to take a hard look at its basic assumptions? The answer is, practically none. And the reasons, of course, are political. Given big labor's political, electoral, and financial clout, no politician wants to delve too deeply into these affairs. Those who do will be punished politically or electorally. That is not what politicians, who love being in Washington and at all costs want to avoid the voters sending them back to Hicksville Junction, want.

Hence in the case of our labor diplomacy, not only has there been no accountability for the AIFLD activities abroad (most Americans are not even aware that the AFL-CIO has its own foreign policy) and no responsibility to the public, but in many respects AIFLD has done a bad job besides.

We are told that the program is better now. CIA funding has been terminated; the AFL-CIO now gets its money directly from a congressional appropriation to the National Endowment for Democracy, a semiprivate agency established to help encourage democracy abroad. We are also told that the AIFLD is currently more sensitive to indigenous practices and no longer seeks to impose an American-style model of trade unionism on countries where it does not fit. In addition, the intense ideologues who guided the program in its early years have now died or largely faded from the scene.

Problems still remain, however. These include the takeover of another area of foreign policy by a private agency, the lack of public accountability and responsibility, and the fact that the particular private interest group involved does not appear to be doing the kind of job that is required. It is certainly valid to say that labor relations are a key arena of foreign policy and that the United States thus needs to be involved; but so far the results have been very mixed and the problems unearthed have added considerably to our foreign policy dilemmas and disarray.

THE PROLIFERATION OF NEW INTEREST GROUPS

Big business, big agriculture, and big labor are the major groups that we think of when we consider the influence of interest groups on policy. But by this time a host of new interest groups (religious bodies, human rights lobbies, ethnic groups, ideological interests, single-cause lobbies) have emerged, making our foreign policy much more complex and difficult than before. Foreign policy is far more participatory and democratic than before. Whether an effective foreign policy can function in this context, however, is still open to question.

Since Vietnam (again that watershed), American foreign policy has become far more intense and ideological. Whereas earlier most Americans were content to allow the government to carry out foreign policy without such intense citizen input, now the situation has been altered dramatically. There are literally thousands of new foreign policy interest groups operating in the political arena. It now seems that everyone wants to get into the act. Far more people than before have strong views about foreign policy issues. On virtually every controversial issue, conglomerates of interest groups line up on both sides.

Among the new religious lobbies involved in these and other conflicts are the U.S. Catholic Conference, the National Council of Churches, the United Methodist Board of Church and Society, the Lutheran Council, the historic "peace churches" (Quakers, Unitarian Universalist), and a variety of smaller denominations. The National Council of Churches, which is part of the World Council of Churches, has provided guidance and an umbrella organization for several mainline Protestant churches (Presbyterian, United Church of Christ-Congregationalist) to lobby over South Africa, Ethiopia, Central America, and other issues that loom hot from one moment to the next.

The main human rights lobbies, which often overlap with the religious bodies, include the Washington Office on Latin America (WOLA), Amnesty International, America's Watch, and the Council on Hemispheric Affairs (COHA). WOLA, for example, is closely associated with the Methodist Church, although its staff includes persons from several religious groups.

Then we have Physicians Concerned, which is preoccupied with nuclear disarmament, a radical activist organization of lawyers, a left-wing actors' association headed by Ed Asner (of *Mary Tyler Moore* and *Lou Grant* fame), various groups of faculty who have taken stands on major issues, and a large number of other activist organizations.

Almost all of these groups are on the left. They stem either from the old, hard-core American left which now has little electoral support but is very vocal and particularly strong among writers, artists, and intellectuals. Or they emerged during Vietnam, either as New Left organizations or as the old left rebaptized with new and more appealing names ("Human Rights," "Peace," "Solidarity"). A number of these groups still seem to be fighting the ideological wars of the 1930s or reliving the protests of the 1960s, which they seem loathe to give up. They appear to be wedded to ideological conflict whether or not it has much to do with the issues of the present day. Protests are heady stuff, it is fun to be in "the movement," and one wouldn't want to miss out on the latest action, particularly if one came late to the Vietnam demonstrations and didn't want to be left behind by the more recent causes.[9]

The influence, attention to, and success of the left obliged the right, often belatedly and weakly, to organize. A right-wing actors' association headed by Charlton Heston now functions alongside the left-wing one. The conservative and Evangelical churches and their interdenominational lobbies, such as the Assemblies of God, Moral Majority, and the Christian Voice, have similarly during the 1980s become active politically. Built upon the frustration, increasing alienation, and concern of millions of Fundamentalists and Evangelicals, the goal of these groups is to restore "God fearingness" to American politics. The conservative religious lobbies' foreign policy agenda is heavily concentrated on the Soviet Union, communism, and Communist incursions into Central America; on the home front they are mainly concerned with abortion, drugs, the absence of school prayer, and American moral decay.

Conservative political groups in Washington include the Conservative Caucus of Howard Phillips, the Committee for the Survival of a Free Congress of Paul Weyrich, the National Conservative Political Action Committee of Terry Dolan, and the direct mail fund-raising activities of Richard Viguerie. Most of these groups, as well as many of the left-wing ones, are very "thin," often consisting of one man, some fancy letterhead with an impressive listing of its "board of directors" (usually friends and cronies of the director), a mailing address in Washington, D.C., and several student interns. Hence when some of these persons appear on the evening news with the name of their organization underneath, we are often impressed because it sounds important and we think it must have a large popular following. But it turns out the "organization" consists of the person on the TV screen and that is about all. During the early months of Reagan's presidency, the administration was frequently hamstrung in carrying out its policies because it feared the reaction of the Republican right wing. Only slowly did it figure out that the Republican right wing consisted of only three or four individuals who were very clever at getting publicity for themselves and whose clout came only from the mistaken fear of people who thought that they represented powerful grass roots support. In Washington, D.C., there is often less there than meets the eye.

Most of us are taught as young people that hypocrisy is bad and that we should avoid it, but in Washington, D.C., hypocrisy is what makes the world go round. The suspicion is growing that some of the so-called human rights groups, for example (Amnesty International is a possible exception), are not so much interested in human rights as in a left-wing political agenda. They want to condemn right-wing regimes and conservative administrations; human rights is merely the vehicle—and a very effective one—for doing so. If these groups were really interested in human rights, then they must of necessity condemn abuses of human rights in left-wing regimes as well as right-wing ones; if they do not, then one can only conclude that their agenda is a political one, not human rights per se.[10]

The church lobbies have been particularly effective (often in alliance with the human rights groups); after all, what congressmen can resist seeing a nun, priest, pastor, or rabbi, particularly if he or she shows up in religious garb. The religious garb also lends a measure of sanctity and righteousness to the person wearing it and the obligation, presumably, to be taken seriously. Actually most religious political activists these days would not be caught dead on the streets in their religious garb, but when visiting congressmen it comes in very handy.

These comments are not meant of course to demean human rights as a policy area with which we should be concerned or to denigrate clergymen. But it is to suggest that in these as in other areas the real agendas are not always the stated ones; people are not always what they seem; and hypocrisy—as well as good intentions—often abounds. Nevertheless, as President Reagan's Assistant Secretary for Inter-American Affairs Langhorne A. Motley once stated, "Taking on the churches is really tough. We don't normally think of them as political opponents, so we don't know how to handle them. It has to be a kid-glove kind of thing. They are really formidable."

The role, structure, and influence of these groups deserve far more study than is possible here. Several further comments are required. First, it seems clear that these new groups have latched onto or rose in conjunction with the "new issues" in foreign policy: democracy, human rights, basic human needs, disarmament. New issues call for new interest groups, and a whole cottage industry of them has grown up.

Second, even though some of these groups are quite well organized at the top levels, and although a lot of "networking" interconnections exist among the leadership, the degree to which the leadership actually represents the rank and file is very much open to question. For example, although WOLA, a Methodist-sponsored group, has been strongly critical of United States policy and sympathetic toward the Sandinistas, approximately 80 percent of the membership of the Methodist churches voted for Ronald Reagan in 1984. It is clear from this and other data that the politics of these groups' leadership is not at all in accord with the politics of the parent religious body's membership. In fact, we know that the foreign policy positions of these religious lobbies is determined, not by their church membership, but frequently by a small cadre of leaders working in the central offices of these churches, who no longer worry about men's and women's souls but stand for a secular political agenda and political activism, and who often have a positive disdain for their churches' memberships. Once again, a word of caution is necessary, therefore, that the testimonies and pastorals that come from the churches are often not at all in keeping with what their membership believes. By 1989 the reaction in many of these churches to what their central offices were doing politically had become so intense that a major restructuring of national church activities was under way.

A third issue has to do with how often well-meaning people who inhabit the church organizations are used and manipulated by more experienced political operators.[11] We are all in favor of democracy and human rights as well as peace and nuclear disarmament. The questions is, what is the best means to achieve these desired goals. Is it by a careful, gradual process of negotiation, which achieves a relaxation of cold war tensions from a position of strong economic and strategic security; or by a precipitous and unilateral disarmament that ultimately leaves the United States weakened, emboldens and plays into the hands of the Soviet Union, and may in fact *increase the possibilities* of nuclear war? The first position is more attractive to most Americans, but it takes immense time and capital, including large defense budgets, so that we conduct negotiations from a position of strength, not weakness. The very difficulty and slowness of the process, however, often leads to impatience and an opting for the second or unilateral solution, as in the nuclear freeze movement. But that leaves the United States debilitated and potentially vulnerable, a condition that obviously works to the Soviets' advantage. Hence, while many of the so-called peace lobbies that have sprung up in recent years are undoubtedly sincere, they also have the potential to be (and sometimes are) manipulated by the Soviet Union or its various front organizations, not to achieve peace, but to undermine a careful and prudent American foreign policy and thus to serve the foreign policy goals of the Soviet Union.

Finally, we come to the new ethnic lobbies. Greek-Americans, for example, are more numerous and better organized than are Turkish-Americans, with the result that in the numerous issues of conflict between Greece and Turkey in the Mediterranean, the Greek position has been more effectively presented and Greek interests more strongly supported than Turkish ones. Among Irish-Americans, support for Irish unity is often strong, sometimes to the extent of going beyond the cause of protecting Catholic civil rights in Northern Ireland to supporting assistance to terrorist organizations in that blood-soaked territory.

Through such lobbies as Trans Africa or the Washington Office on Africa, American blacks and others have taken up the cause of the liberation of blacks in South Africa; the Congressional Black Caucus has also become interested in the fate and future of a number of predominantly black nations in the Caribbean as well as in Africa. The Cuban exile community, largely centered in South Florida, is very active politically, generally on the conservative side, and enjoys virtual veto power over United States policy toward Cuba. The rising Hispanic population in the United States, which in the 1990s will become our largest minority, is increasingly important politically as well, particularly in the American Southwest. But other than an abiding interest in their nations of origins, which many Americans have, no one is certain at this stage what the political and foreign policy impact of this rising Hispanic presence will be.

The relations of the American Jewish community to Israel is both an extension of this previous discussion of the impact of ethnic and religious groups on foreign policy and a special case in itself. In the first place, the American Jewish community is far larger numerically and more powerful politically than is the American Arab community—although the influence and political capacities of the latter have begun to rise. In the second place, many non-Jewish Americans have a lot of sympathy for the Jewish tragedy of the Holocaust and for the plucky state of Israel, which is surrounded and hated by far more numerous Arab states. Third, Israel has been a faithful ally of the United States and is the only state in the Middle East that has been consistently democratic and whose culture, politics, and human rights positions are in the Western tradition. We must also remember that while most American Jews generally support Israel, the Jewish community does not speak with one voice and is often sharply in disagreement over certain Israeli policies.

There are often problems in the U.S.-Israel relationship as well as, generally, good relations. First, Israel receives more United States foreign aid than any other country, even though it is by no means a poor country, and a strong case could be made for a more equitable sharing of the aid with other needy countries. Second, American secretaries of state have sometimes noted that Israel takes up an inordinate amount of their time, up to 50 percent, probably more than the size or strategic importance of the country would seem to indicate as appropriate. Third, there are worries that Israel's treatment of its Arab minorities is not consistently in accord with human rights standards that ought to be observed. This statement needs to be balanced of course by a consideration of the truly dismal human rights standards of some Arab states and of Arab terrorism practiced against Israel.

A fourth question is whether the United States is too closely allied with Israel at the expense of its relations with the far more populous Arab states. Should we be more evenhanded in our relations with Israel and the Arab states? Are our national interests best served by present policy? As a European diplomat once quipped, "How did you Americans get yourself into a position where you are allied with the only state in the Middle East that has no oil?" Finally, there are questions about the influence on United States foreign policy of the so-called Israeli lobby, which includes the American Jewish Committee, the American Jewish Congress, the Anti-Defamation League, B'nai B'rith, the Synagogue Council of America, the Union of American Hebrew Congregations and, most important, the America-Israel Public Affairs Committee. Is this lobby *inordinately* large and influential? Does it close off the possibilities for discussion of more evenhanded policies in the Middle East? Does the specter of a charge of "anti-Semitism" scare politicians into silence and, therefore, skew in one-sided ways the American policy debate? And is it really true that Israel's interests and those of the United States are the same, or can always be made compatible? Might there not be situations in which these interests are not compatible, situations in which hard choices will have to be made, and—as in the case of the American Jonathan Pollard, who was caught spying in the United States for Israel—some terribly wrenching decisions and conflicts of loyalty will have to be resolved?

These are difficult questions that involve hard choices. They also illustrate the terrible difficulties of our foreign policy process and the sometimes agonizing decisions that have to be faced. They further show the complexities of a foreign policy process in which ethnic and religious groups have come to play a major role. The question of divided loyalties has been most acutely raised with regard to the American Jewish community and Israel; but as other ethnic, religious and nationality groups became better organized and more powerful, it will be raised with regard to them as well. The role of these new ethnic minorities and their increasing assertiveness in politics are undoubtedly reflective of our increasingly democratic and pluralistic political system; but they also add still more sources of division and fragmentation to a political process that is already exceedingly fractious.

CONCLUSION

In conclusion, let us return to the four questions asked at the beginning of this chapter.

First, it *is* the case that some major interest groups have partially taken over, hived off, and privatized certain areas of foreign policy for themselves. Big business, big agriculture, and big labor have been incorporated into the structure of our national government; like other modern, industrial democracies, the United States has become "corporatized." But this is not all the result of power grabs by these private interests; in many cases these policy areas have been turned over to them because the United States government either needs these groups or lacks the expertise that these groups have. Some degree of privatization of foreign policy is probably inevitable in such a pluralist democracy as ours; however, the problem remains of the accountability of these groups, their responsibility to the public, and the sheer incompetence of some of their activities which, because of political fears, are not adequately overseen by Congress.

Second is the question of ungovernability. We have seen in the last two decades a tremendous proliferation in the number of interest groups concerned with foreign policy. This is in marked contrast to the pre-Vietnam period when consensus on foreign policy was more or less the rule and foreign relations were left largely to the experts. Now, however, the number of actors has so multiplied that it is exceedingly difficult to carry out a coherent, rational foreign policy. Whether the issue is Central America, southern Africa, the Middle East, or Soviet relations, the number of actors who get into the act is phenomenal. Often clever at getting their point of view across in the media or to Congress, these groups have for a time all but paralyzed American foreign policy on some issues. Undoubtedly we have become democratized in the process, but it remains a question as to whether we can carry out an effective foreign policy under these conditions.

The third question has to do with bias. Is the foreign policy debate distorted because some ideological or ethnic sectors of the political public are better organized and more effective than others? The answers are sometimes troubling. Greeks are better organized than Turks, and therefore their viewpoint often prevails. The American Jewish community is better organized and more powerful than the Arab community, and the political power of the Cubans is greater than those who would seek to normalize relations with Cuba. On Northern Ireland, Catholic voices in the United States are stronger than Protestant ones. On southern Africa, American blacks have made racial discrimination more the issue than American security considerations.

Politically and ideologically, the system has been heavily skewed to the left. The human rights groups, the religious lobbies, the disarmament groups all seem to be on the left. Writers groups, actors groups, publishing, the movies, and some university faculty also seem to be heavily concentrated on the left. The fact that, until recently, approximately four-fifths of the organized groups were on the left and only one-fifth on the right represents an imbalance in the political system. Ultimately, for pluralism to function effectively, the interest group balance must more or less reflect the balance of the electorate; but that has not been the case. President Reagan received record-high political mandates, around 60 percent in both 1980 and 1984; and yet if one read subsequently the position papers of the active lobbying groups, almost all of them were lined up against his policies. The conservative elements have now begun to organize for political action but they remain far behind the left. In the meantime, we have an interest group system that seems to be out of balance, skewed to the left, and not on many issues reflective of the American people.

Finally, there is the problem of tunnel vision. Almost all the groups surveyed here have one issue for which they stand and one issue only: Greece, or Israel, or human rights. They tend not to see or present both sides of the story, and they are often so preoccupied with their own single issue that they refuse to see other, often equally compelling interests or the large picture. Only by such balance can we have an effective and agreed-upon foreign policy. But in our present condition of more ideological, fragmented, divided, and tunnel-vision politics, our foreign policy, as a reflection of these conditions, has too often been incoherent, immobilized, and ineffective.

Notes

1. An earlier anaylsis of some of these themes can be found in James A. Nathan and James K. Oliver, *Foreign Policy and the American Political System* (Boston: Little, Brown, 1987).
2. Grant McConnell, *Private Power and American Democracy* (New York: Vintage, 1966).
3. Samuel P. Huntington, "The Governability of Democracies: USA," in *The Governability of Democracies*, edited by Michael Crozier, Samuel P. Huntington, and Joji Watanuki. (New York: Trilateral Commission, 1975).
4. On corporatism, see Reginald H. Harrison, *Pluralism and Corporatism: The Political Evolution of Modern Democracies* (London: Allen & Unwin, 1980); and Howard J. Wiarda, "The Latin Americanization of the United States," *The New Scholar* 7(1979):51–85.
5. McConnell, *Private Power and American Democracy.*
6. Department of State, Bureau of Public Affairs, *Agriculture in U.S. Foreign Economic Policy* (Washington, D.C.: GPO, 1988).
7. *Washington Post*, 24 May 1988, sec. A21.
8. For the history and background, see George Morris, *The CIA and American Labor* (New York: International Publishers, 1967).
9. Richard Cohen, "Getting Religion." *National Journal* 14 Sept. 1985, 1080–84.
10. Joshua Muravchik, *The Uncertain Crusade: Jimmy Carter and the Dilemmas of Human Rights Policy* (Washington, D.C.: Hamilton Press, 1986).
11. The best study is Guenter Lewy, *Peace and Revolution: The Moral Crisis of American Pacifism* (Grand Rapids, Mich.: William B. Erdmans, 1988); also Adam Garfinkle, *The Politics of the Nuclear Freeze* (Philadelphia: Foreign Policy Research Institute, 1984).

Suggested Readings

Bauer, Raymond A, Ithiel de Sola Poole, and Louis Anthony Dexter. *American Business and Public Policy.* Chicago: Aldine-Atherton, 1972.

Bergsten, C. Fred, Thomas Horst, and Theodore Moran. *American Multinationals and American Interests.* Washington, D.C.: Brookings Institution, 1978.

Cohen, Benjamin J. *In Whose Interest? International Banking and American Foreign Policy.* New Haven: Yale University Press, 1986.

Cohen, Richard. "Getting Religion," *National Journal.* (September 14, 1985): 2080–84.

Edel, Wilbur. *Defenders of the Faith: Religion and Politics from the Pilgrim Founders to Ronald Reagan.* New York: Praeger, 1987.

Holloway, H. "Interest Groups in the Postpartisan Era: The Political Machine of the AFL-CIO." *Political Science Quarterly* 94 (Spring 1979): 117–33.

Huntington, Samuel P. "The Governability of Democracy: USA," in Michael Crozier; Samuel P. Huntington; and Joji Watanuki, *The Governability of Democracies.* New York: Trilateral Commission, 1975.

Lewy, Gunter. *Peace and Revolution: The Moral Crisis of American Pacifism.* Grand Rapids, MI: Eerdmans, 1988.

Mathias, Charles M., Jr. "Ethnic Groups and Foreign Policy." *Foreign Affairs*, 59 (Summer 1981): 975–99.

Milbraith, Lester W. "Interest Groups and Foreign Policy." In *Domestic Sources of Foreign Policy,* edited by James N. Rosenau, 231–52. New York: Free Press, 1967.

Morris, George. *The CIA and American Labor.* New York: International Publishers, 1967.

Nathan, James A., and James K. Oliver. *Foreign Policy-Making and the American Political System.* Boston: Little Brown, 1987.

Ornstein, Norman J., and Shirley Elder. *Interest Groups, Lobbying and Policymaking.* Washington, D.C.: Congressional Quarterly Press, 1978.

Russett, Bruce M., and Elizabeth C. Hanson. *Interest and Ideology: The Foreign Policy Beliefs of American Businessmen.* San Francisco: Freeman, 1975.

Said, Abdul Aziz, ed. *Ethnicity and U.S. Foreign Policy.* New York: Praeger, 1978.

Truman, David B. *The Governmental Process: Political Interests and Public Opinion.* New York: Knopf, 1951.

CHAPTER SEVEN

Political Parties and Foreign Policy

✪
✪

Political parties in the United States have not historically been thought of as major actors in foreign policy matters. In part, this is due to the strong sense of isolationism and exceptionalism that has long been prominent in American political culture, and to the absence of serious attention to foreign affairs in the United States, which the parties both reflected and reinforced. This relative unimportance of the parties in foreign policy matters also stems in part from the fact that parties do one major thing in America: they put up candidates for elections. Since most American elections are decided on either local issues such as zoning, schools, property assessments, and municipal services, or national bread-and-butter issues such as jobs, inflation, taxes, interest rates, and the overall performance of the economy, foreign affairs have usually been considered of secondary importance. The wisdom of the professional politicians is that a candidate can *lose* an election on the basis of an inadequate knowledge of foreign policy (for example, in 1988 as Michael Dukakis was widely criticized by the Bush campaign as being inexperienced in foreign policy), but that a candidate cannot *win* an election just on the basis of his experience or views on foreign policy. He must have other things—that is, a prosperous domestic economy—going for him. Foreign affairs alone will not do it.

Now these truths are beginning to change. For one thing, our political parties and our domestic political debates are becoming more ideological than they once were. Clearly, as the controversies over Central America, southern Africa, and relations with the Soviet Union have shown, America's foreign policy toward these issues and regions has become part of this more impassioned debate. A second reason why foreign policy issues are becoming more important is that in the last two decades (since the first OPEC-induced oil price explosion of 1973) we have begun to realize just how economically interdependent we now are with the rest of the world: on OPEC for oil, on Japan for high technology and automobiles, on Latin America for raw materials and, now, manufactured goods, and on many other countries as well. At this stage, the United States could not retreat into

December 7, 1941   December 7, 1989

© Mike Luckovich. Reprinted by permission of Tribune Media Services.

isolationism even if it wanted to. A third factor is our realization of how dangerous the world is out there. In recent years, Americans have frequently been the targets of terrorist attacks, shootings, and kidnappings. In this new and more dangerous world, we have come to demand foreign affairs experience in our national leaders, especially our presidents.

These factors have made foreign affairs an increasingly important concern in our national consciousness and, therefore, in how we vote. Because foreign policy issues have become more important to voters, they have also become more important to our political parties, whose main purpose, after all, is to win elections. Thus while our two main political parties have not often paid serious attention to foreign affairs in the past, the signs abound that this is beginning to change. The changes are slow, but of the increased salience of foreign affairs issues to more and more voters there can be little doubt.

THE NATURE OF AMERICAN POLITICAL PARTIES

American political parties are very different from European political parties. European political parties tend to be national and centralized, ideologic, and programmatic, with broad functions, clear programs, and strong interests in foreign affairs. They also have the institutional structures—permanent foreign policy branches, for example—to play a significant foreign policy role. By contrast, American political parties tend to be locally and regionally organized, conglomerates of several interests rather than representing a single class or point of view, nonideologic, nonprogrammatic, very fluid, with limited functions, and with little traditional interest in foreign policy. While these conditions are now changing, as we see in more detail later in the chapter, these historic—and continuing—characteristics of American political parties serve to keep the parties from playing a strong and consistent foreign policy role.

First, American parties tend to be locally, state, or regionally oriented. The national organizations of our two major parties, headquartered in Washington, D.C., are the weakest links in the chain. The national parties all but go out of existence in the intervals between elections, greatly reducing their staffs and usually moving to smaller offices. This means that the parties lack not only a strong national central administration and staff but also a strong national program. The parties stand for different political principles in the North (more liberal) than in the South (more conservative); they focus on different problems in the East (urban issues) than in the West (farm and conservation issues). This regional basis to the parties helps explain why our politicians must talk out of one side of their mouths when in one part of the country and out of the other side when in another. The weak national organization and the corresponding focus at the local, state, or regional level also help explain why the parties are not very oriented toward foreign affairs. Foreign policy requires a single, clear statement that represents the position of the country as a whole—not something our decentralized American parties are very often prepared to offer.

Second, the two main American parties are conglomerates of various interests. Unlike many of the European parties, American parties do not represent the views of a single group or class. American parties are pluralistic and multiclass, cutting across class cleavages. Many scholars believe that the pluralistic and multiclass nature of the American parties—their seeking to be all things to all people—is a good and healthy ingredient of American democracy. But, again, because they are so pluralistic, it is hard for the parties to speak with a single voice on foreign affairs. That also explains why party platforms are typically vague on many foreign policy issues: the parties do not want to lose the support of any one of their constituent groups by staking out too strong a position that one or another of these groups might find objectionable. The parties try to settle for a moderate position that sounds good, with uplifting rhetoric, but actually represents the lowest common denominator.

Third, American parties have historically been nonideological. Again, the contrast with Western Europe is pronounced. The United States does not have a strong Communist party, a strong Socialist party, a strong Social Democratic party, a strong Catholic or Protestant party, a strong Conservative party, or a strong Monarchist party. In fact, in their quest to occupy the broad center of the American political spectrum, and hence to capture more votes, our parties have steadfastly avoided adherence to or close identification with any one single ideology or body of beliefs. Nor, until recently, have the American parties, because of their ideological diversity, had close ties with many like-minded parties abroad—there are no parties abroad really like the American parties. Because they are so diverse ideologically as well as in other ways, the American parties do not have a clear-cut position on foreign affairs either with which they are identified. Once more, the picture is one of diversity and cross-cutting loyalties rather than of any one single position.

Fourth, American political parties are fluid. Their programs and positions frequently change. They may stand for one thing one day and another the next. This feature, too, is related to the parties' preeminent purpose, which is to win elections. Therefore, the parties like to keep their positions ambiguous, to hold their cards close to their chests. That way, depending on which way the electoral winds are blowing, the parties can change their position quickly to garner the most votes. The parties therefore have few fixed foreign policy positions: rather, they prefer to stand for vague generalities whose meaning can be altered to suit the electoral circumstances. It is winning elections that the American parties are oriented toward, not remaining firmly attached to any one set of foreign policy positions.

Fifth, American parties have few important functions. The general, theoretical literature on political parties suggests that their role is to serve as "interest articulators" and "aggregators." That is, the party role is to articulate and present clear platforms, recruit candidates to run on those platforms, and bring together (the "aggregation" function) diverse interests and factions within the party. But we have already seen that the parties prefer to set forth vague platforms rather than clear ones. We know that candidates are selected by a variety of means, including self-selection, rather than through some recruitment process carried out supposedly by the parties. Finally, with interest groups often interjecting themselves directly into the political process rather than through the parties, it is doubtful that American parties actually perform the interest aggregation function either. That leaves winning elections as virtually the sole function that the parties perform. And in that overriding goal, the articulation of clear, precise, well-thought-out foreign policy positions rarely occurs.

The bald fact is that American voters—and, therefore, the parties—are often not very interested in foreign affairs. We have made these points previously, but they are worth repeating here. Isolationist sentiment is still strong in the United States, most Americans do not pay close and sustained attention to foreign affairs, and our elections are mainly decided on such bread-and-butter issues as the domestic economy and jobs. Since the voters are not preoccupied with foreign policy issues, neither are the parties. That explains why the American parties have weak international ties and why they have never developed—as their Western European counterparts have—regular branches of the parties specializing in foreign affairs.

These *historic* characteristics of American parties are all now changing. And the changes do not necessarily mean an improved foreign policy. As noted above, American parties are tremendously flexible. They can change quickly, bend with the wind, and adopt new positions quickly. So can the candidates which the parties put up for public office. All these features have been generally good for the pragmatic practice of American democracy.

Now, however, this flexibility seems to be giving way. The parties are becoming genuinely *national* parties, as regional differences in the United States are increasingly erased. Television and extensive news coverage make it harder for a candidate to say one thing in one part of the country and something quite different in another. The right wing of the Republican party and the left wing of the Democratic party keep pushing the parties in more ideological directions, wanting them to stake out clear positions and make their ideological differences permanent and manifest. They also want the parties to identify more closely with like-minded parties abroad, to assist like-minded parties in other countries, even to form two new *internationales* (like the Communist or Socialist internationales) of parties that share their philosophies.

All of these changes will certainly make our parties easier to identify ideologically. And it seems like a nice, neat, coherent, and rational scheme on paper, which is what often makes it attractive to party intellectuals. But lost in this process would be the flexibility, pragmatism, and capacity to change quickly what has been part of the genius of the American parties and of American democracy. A more ideological stance by the parties would lead to a greater hardening of political positions, more divisiveness, and less flexibility. While more clearly defined political parties may sound great, such a condition would have severely damaging implications as well. In fact, the calls for more clearly defined and ideologically consistent political parties are related to the general hardening, more polarized positions, and overall divisiveness of American politics in recent years, since Vietnam and Watergate. We may well move toward a more ideologically based political party system, but that is a very slippery slope, with strong negative consequences as well as positive ones.

POLITICAL PARTIES: ABOUT FACE

It used to be said that the Republican party was the party of isolationism and that the Democratic party was the party of internationalism. But now the two parties appear to have done an about-face and may have reversed their historic positions. Is that accurate? Is it only half true? If so, what is the other half?

Prior to World War II, the Republican party *was* strongly isolationist. It believed in a strong America, even a fortress America, but it did not want to get involved in the tangled and often murky everyday affairs of other nations. It stood for a strong economy and a strong defense. Moreover, even though isolationism has been strongly criticized in recent decades,

the early Republican isolationists had some solid and quite rational arguments on their side. They took pride in the fact that the United States was
a special nation with a unique moral role—a position that has come back
into favor with America's renewed policies in favor of democracy and
human rights. They wanted to avoid the entangling international politics of
Europe and its amoral *realpolitik;* they felt the United States should never
get itself involved militarily in a ground war in Asia (as, for example, in
Vietnam); and they did not think that the United States sufficiently understood the societies, cultures, and politics of the Third World to get involved
there. These are at least arguable, and not silly, premises. And it was, after
all, a series of Republican administrations in the 1920s that pulled the
United States military occupation forces out of a half dozen countries in
Central America and the Caribbean.[1]

The Democratic party, in contrast, has long prided itself on its internationalism. It points to President Woodrow Wilson and his idealistic internationalism; to President Franklin Roosevelt and his Good Neighbor Policy as
well as his successful management of American policy during World War II;
to the Marshall Plan and the North Atlantic Treaty Organization (NATO) of
President Harry Truman; and to the enlightened internationalism of John F.
Kennedy. But the picture is certainly more mixed than that—as the Republicans gleefully like to emphasize. After all, Presidents Wilson, Roosevelt,
and Truman also led the United States into major wars; Wilson sent
American troops into the Caribbean in the first place; the Kennedy-Johnson
assumptions about foreign policy led to United States involvement in
Vietnam; and America's extensive and ongoing relationships with the
NATO countries of Western Europe, with Asia, and with Latin America may
well have overextended our power and brought us not always the goodwill
of these peoples but sometimes their animosity.

During and immediately following World War II, the Republican party
began to switch positions, from isolationism to internationalism. It backed
President Roosevelt during World War II and laid the basis for a bipartisan
foreign policy, particularly in the context of war and national crisis.
President Truman's involvement in Greece and Turkey right after the war,
his inability to reach a postwar accommodation with the Soviet Union,
NATO, the Marshall Plan, and United States involvement in the Korean
war—all were causes for misgivings, dissent, and controversy within the
Republican party. But many Republicans, in the changed circumstances of
the cold war and the challenge of the Soviet Union, saw the need for the
United States to get more strongly involved internationally and to maintain
our readiness. This conflict was fought out most particularly in the 1952
Republican party convention when General Dwight Eisenhower, who
represented the party's internationalist wing, got the nomination over
Senator Robert Taft, who represented the isolationist wing. Thereafter,
regardless of whether they represented the conservative or liberal wing of

the party, the Republican presidential candidates—Richard Nixon, Barry Goldwater, Jerry Ford, Ronald Reagan, George Bush—*all* came from the internationalist side. With the recognition of the need for a strong defense, a strong economy, and a strong involvement in the world to protect America's interests, isolationism was dead within the Republican party.

Meanwhile, the Democratic party appeared to many observers to be going through just the opposite trajectory. The Democratic party had long been internationalist. Its leaders had been witness to the 1930s, when America's lack of involvement in Europe and the appeasement of Hitler fueled German ambitions and led to World War II. In the post–World War II period, it was the Democrats who first recognized the imperative of containing the Soviet Union, building NATO, and fashioning the Marshall Plan as further deterrents to Soviet expansionism. The Democratic party had also authored the Point Four technical assistance program, and saw the need, in order to fend off Marxist-Leninist challenges, for the United States to get involved in the developing nations. John F. Kennedy's Alliance for Progress, after all, was aimed fundamentally at preventing further (besides Cuba) Soviet advances in Latin America. It sought to accomplish this goal not by aiding dictators as in the past, but by assisting social and economic changes, as well as democratization, and by helping alleviate the causes of communism instead of simply responding after the fact to its effects—that is, the establishment of a full-fledged Communist regime. This was a sensible, prudent, enlightened policy—even though the implementation of the alliance left a great deal to be desired.

Then came Vietnam. The United States' protracted, frustrating involvement in that bloody war not only undermined the American consensus on foreign policy (Chapter 4), but it also destroyed quite a number of internationalist assumptions of the Democratic party. First, running on an antiwar platform, Senator Eugene McCarthy and then Robert F. Kennedy (before he was assassinated) challenged—an unheard of affront—a sitting president, Johnson, for the Democratic nomination in 1968. Next, the basic assumptions of American liberal internationalism came under strong attack. Did we have a right to be involved in Vietnam at all? Were we violating international law? Was Vietnam really a case of Soviet-supported Communist expansionism or simply a civil war to which we should not be a party? Did we really understand the culture of a Third World and non-Western society like Vietnam? In the process of trying to save that country, were we really destroying it with our saturation bombing? With the use of chemical agents, wasn't the United States becoming a war criminal, even a monster? These and other questions shook the United States—and the Democratic party, in power until 1968—to its foundations.

The results were some fundamental changes in the Democratic party. In 1972, Senator George McGovern won the Democratic presidential nomination on a highly moralistic "peace" platform. He was roundly defeated in the general election, but a new orientation within the Democratic party was now set. Meanwhile, many left activists and intellectuals within the party began to settle on a new agenda: curb the CIA because it engages in "immoral" activities; curb the power of the military because it represents a "war machine"; cut the defense budget and use the money for social programs. In addition, many of the party's leaders came to oppose United States involvement in Third World areas of conflict because it might lead to "another Vietnam"; some believed that the United States was an "evil" country that no longer had anything to teach the rest of the world; and quite a number accepted the intellectual approach called "dependency theory" which, in its more extreme manifestations, taught that most of the poverty and problems of the Third World were the United States' fault.

To many, it appeared that the 1960s "counterculture" seemed to have triumphed within the Democratic party, or at least among some of its most activist elements. They supported détente with the Soviet Union, believed that the cold war was over (despite Soviet gains in Afghanistan, Ethiopia, southern Africa, Southeast Asia, the Middle East, and Central America), stood for "peace" (often involving unilateral United States disarmament, with no parallel reduction required of the Soviet Union), and therefore allowed the United States' defense posture to deteriorate. This was essentially a formula for American withdrawal from the continuing exercise of strong leadership in the world. It represented a repudiation of basic United States strategic doctrine on which bipartisan consensus had existed since World War II, and meant that the United States largely stood idly by while the Soviets vastly increased their military capability during the decade of the 1970s.

These currents crested during the presidency of Jimmy Carter. President Carter was well-meaning but totally inexperienced in foreign affairs. He appointed a number of "romantics" to the United Nations who accepted the blame for the Third World's ills and went so far as to apologize for past United States actions. He gave the wily Soviet leader Leonid Brezhnev an affectionate, well-publicized kiss on the cheek while the Soviets were amassing a vast military arsenal and acquiring countries left and right. His wife ("Who elected her?" skeptics asked) prepared to lead an official delegation to Latin America by reading the Bible in Spanish. President Carter's human rights campaign was a noble one, but many critics said it came at the expense of other vital United States interests. In Nicaragua, the administration could not decide whether to support or oppose the Sandinista revolution; its disastrous temporizing in the name of promoting "ideological pluralism" eventually allowed a full-fledged Marxist-Leninist regime inimical to United States interests to consolidate its power. Meanwhile, Mr. Carter clothed himself in piety, talked of national "malaise" but did nothing about it, wrung his hands, and saw his presidency flounder on the shoals of Iran's seizure of the American hostages in 1979.

In fairness to President Carter, it should be said that he largely inherited the détente policy from the preceding Republican administrations of Presidents Nixon and Ford, and Secretary of State Kissinger. It should also be said that Carter in his last two years in office followed a more hardheaded and realistic foreign policy approach than he had in his first two years. Nevertheless, President Carter was widely seen as naive and inexperienced in foreign policy, well-meaning but ineffective, and leading from weakness (or at least the perception thereof) in dealing with the Soviets rather than from strength.

More moderate Democrats, those who were liberal on domestic social issues but also believed more strongly than the President in deterrence and a strong defense, became alarmed at the direction their party was taking. Such figures as Senator Henry (Scoop) Jackson, Senator Patrick Moynahan, Congressman Jim Wright, Professor Jeane Kirkpatrick, and several hundred others—all loyal Democrats—came together to form the Coalition for a Democratic Majority (CDM). The CDM contained some of the most sensible and respected people in Washington. They did not want to abandon the Democratic party but, because of its recent stances, they felt the party was abandoning them. They wanted to maintain a strong strategic posture and were especially concerned by the immense Soviet military buildup. Yet they were cut out of all the important foreign policy positions in the Carter administration and, when they met with President Carter, were lectured on the need to support his policies. Many in the CDM were so disillusioned by what they perceived as a leftward and neo-isolationist drift in the Democratic party that they, reluctantly, abandoned its ranks. In 1980 they either refused to support the party's candidate (Carter) or they joined the ranks of the neoconservatives and voted for Ronald Reagan. Not only these leaders but millions of ordinary voters joined what came to be called the Reagan Democrats.

It would not be accurate to label these recent, leftward tendencies in the Democratic party "traditional isolationist." No desire exists to return to the isolationism and "fortress America" mentality of the 1930s. Rather, this left wing of the Democratic party is becoming more like the British Labor Party: it believes in socialism or social democracy, it is closely tied to the peace movements, it sometimes seems to think the Soviet Union is full of people who are "just like us," some of its spokespersons believe the United States should exercise leadership and disarm first as a gesture of goodwill and moral right—even if the Soviet Union fails to follow suit, and it often suggests that most of the problems in the Third World are due to past "sins" of the United States. In a devastating speech at the 1984 Republican National Convention, Ambassador Jeane Kirkpatrick, herself a former Democrat, called this the "blame-America-first lobby."

It should be said that this leftward trend within the Democratic party does not represent majority sentiment within the party. Rather, it represents a minority, but a very vocal, activist, and intellectual minority. It therefore has influence beyond its actual numbers. Within the party also may still be found many conservative and traditional Democrats (Senators Sam Nunn of Georgia and Charles Robb of Virginia), many Democrats who are party supporters on domestic issues but are not very interested in foreign affairs, and a large number of persons who would like to bridge the gap between the party's left and right wings. However, the Democratic party may have reached a point now where its left or "progressive" wing not only holds veto power over the party's platform and program but is in a sufficiently strong position that a Democratic presidential candidate cannot win the nomination without the left's support. In long-range terms, that may be a dangerous position—electorally—for the party.

THE IDEOLOGY OF THE PARTIES

It has been part of the ongoing genius of American politics that our political parties were not very ideological. Rather, the American parties were catchall parties, political homes to diverse groups, regional interests, pluralisms of persons and their varied ideas. Now that is beginning to change as the parties, or at least some elites within the parties, become more ideological. The growing ideological differences between the parties have been a further factor in undermining the bipartisan consensus that used to exist on many foreign policy issues. It has also added to our divisiveness and fragmentation as a nation.

The year 1968 was the last time the United States had a presidential election *not* dominated by sharp ideological difference over foreign policy between the two major parties and their candidates. That year, Hubert Humphrey, who was liberal on domestic issues but strong on defense matters, was the candidate of the Democratic party against Republican Richard Nixon, who similarly stood for a strong defense. Both parties (the Democrats especially) were divided *internally* on defense and foreign policy matters, but the two presidential candidates both campaigned on a platform of continuing America's leading global role while also promising to end the war in Vietnam.

But in every election since 1968, the parties and their candidates have divided sharply over foreign policy issues and on a strongly ideological basis. In 1972 it was the incumbent Nixon against the Democratic challenger George McGovern; in 1976 it was Democrat Jimmy Carter against Republican Gerald Ford; in 1980 it was Carter versus Republican Ronald Reagan; in 1984 it was Reagan against Democrat Walter Mondale; and in 1988 the contest was between Republican George Bush and Democrat Michael Dukakis. Every one of these last five elections has been sharply contested ideologically, so we need to know what these ideological differences are.

In general, it may be said that the Democratic party has come to be seen by a large portion of the electorate as weak on defense while the Republicans are viewed as strong on defense. Democratic candidates are often preferred on domestic social issues, but in those elections in which foreign policy is an issue—that is, the election for the presidency—voters have recently tended to prefer the Republican position.

Let us provide some illustrations of these ideological differences over foreign policy. In 1972, Democratic candidate George McGovern campaigned on a platform of ending the war in Vietnam and of withdrawing United States forces; he seemed also to hold the United States (not the Communists in North Vietnam) as responsible for the continuation of the war, as well as for other ills in the Third World; and he favored reducing the defense budget and reallocating the money to domestic social programs. President Nixon, his opponent, also wanted to end the Vietnam war but in ways that left South Vietnam able, hopefully, to withstand Communist pressures, and that did not reflect disgrace on the United States or its military institution. He favored continuation of a vigorous, global American foreign policy and a strong defense capability. Nixon was overwhelmingly elected while McGovern carried only what came thereafter to be called irreverently "The People's Republic of Massachusetts."

The 1976 presidential campaign, pitting Republican Gerald Ford against Democrat Jimmy Carter, revolved mainly around domestic political issues (trust, honesty, morality) and not foreign policy ones, and therefore is not a matter for our detailed attention here. It should be said, however, that had incumbent President Ford emphasized in the campaign how dangerous the world had become and the need for a president experienced in the ways of Washington and of the world as compared with "a naive peanut farmer" (as he was sometimes called) from Georgia, he would have won. But he did not heed the advice that some of his advisers were giving him and so he lost. Ford's gaffe in suggesting that Poland was somehow not subordinate to Soviet military power—at that time, contrary to all the known facts—also made Ford look incompetent on foreign policy matters.

In 1980 candidate Reagan attacked President Carter as being naive, romantic, and wishy-washy on foreign policy. Carter and many of his advisers had shared the post–Vietnam fear of employing American military force, seemed often to believe the New Left's view that the United States was responsible for Third World poverty, were reluctant to use the CIA because it was thought to be "immoral," and believed that the United States did not need to have such a strong military defense. The Carter team placed its emphasis on human rights, but it also believed in nonintervention in the internal affairs of other nations; and it often could not decide between the two horns of this dilemma and thus appeared incompetent and indecisive on many foreign policy issues. Meanwhile, the Soviet Union during the 1970s was engaging in an immense military buildup, was acquiring new "satellites" (Vietnam, Ethiopia, Angola, Afghanistan, Mozambique, South

Yemen, Grenada, Nicaragua) in far-flung areas of the Third World, and seemed about to surpass the United States in world power and influence. Candidate Reagan strongly attacked what he called a policy of weakness in the Democratic administration. In 1980 and then again in 1984, Reagan, who favored a strong defense and was suspicious of Soviet intentions, won overwhelming (approximately 60 percent) electoral victories. Victories of that magnitude are usually referred to as "landslides."

In 1988 Bush and Dukakis faced off. Reflecting the by-then dominant tendencies in some important sectors of the Democratic party, candidate Dukakis called the Strategic Defense Initiative (SDI) a "fantasy," but eventually indicated he would continue limited research on the program; Bush promised both to research and deploy a missile defense system as soon as possible. Dukakis, who argued that the United States could no longer afford a $300 billion defense budget, opposed plans to increase American naval forces by two aircraft carrier groups. He also opposed the small Midgetman intercontinental ballistic missile and the deployment of the multi-warhead MX missile. After expressing reservations earlier, Dukakis later came out in support of the B-1 and Stealth bombers. By contrast, Bush supported all these new weapons and weapons systems.

Dukakis favored the immediate signing of a nuclear test ban treaty with the Soviet Union. But Bush argued that the Soviets' willingness to sign and abide by such a treaty grew out of American strength and the *buildup* of our own military forces, and not from weakness. Dukakis echoed Bush in saying that he did not "trust" the Soviet Union but he seemed more willing than Bush to give the Soviets the benefit of the doubt and to begin a process of United States disarmament without mutual and reciprocal steps by the Soviets. Dukakis favored bans on nuclear weapons testing and on in-flight testing of missiles; Bush said both kinds of testing were needed to keep American nuclear arsenals updated.

Dukakis opposed aid to the anti-Communist Resistance in Nicaragua and denounced the Reagan administration's Central America policy as a "fiasco." Instead, he favored working through the Organization of American States, an almost moribund agency that had not dealt seriously with a major issue in twenty years. Similarly he expressed strong support for the Arias Peace Plan (named after the Costa Rican president who formulated it), which called for an end to all foreign military assistance in the area but that was criticized by the Reagan administration as providing insufficient guarantees that the democratization of Marxist Nicaragua would proceed apace. Bush, in contrast, supported a multifaceted approach to Central America that derived from the 1983–84 Kissinger Commission: economic assistance as well as limited military aid, support for democracy and human rights as well as a program in defense of United States strategic interests, and public as well as private assistance. He favored the Arias Peace Plan so long as it was amended to take into account legitimate United States security concerns in Central America. Similarly, and consistent with his position on other issues, Dukakis favored a "multilateral approach" to solving the Latin American debt problem and believed that some proportion of the debts should be written off and forgiven, whereas Bush stood for a more cautious approach and was opposed to any plan that would pass the costs of Third World debt onto the American taxpayer. That, at least, is how Dukakis appeared to many voters.

Dukakis believed, as had President Carter, that American actions in the Third World often violated international law. Bush, in contrast, took a stronger position in defense of American national interests. Dukakis wanted the United States to impose further sanctions on the apartheid regime in South Africa, whereas Bush did not favor additional sanctions at this time and sought to balance his moral outrage at South Africa's racial policies with a concern of how vital American strategic interests in South Africa would be affected if the white government in South Africa were toppled and the Marxist-Leninist African National Congress (ANC) took over.

Meanwhile, in his home state of Massachusetts, the Republicans took pleasure in pointing out, Dukakis had declined during his ten years as governor all invitations to visit the major Air Force base there, had associated his name with various unilateral nuclear freeze efforts, and had opposed the Ground Wave Emergency Network (GWEN), an underground communications system designed to transmit warnings or presidential orders in case of a nuclear attack. In the case of GWEN, his critics were quick to argue, Dukakis apparently rejected the logic that what deters war is the strength and integrity of the United States military deterrent that includes an effective and fail-safe communications system, and instead seemed to accept the logic that the way to deter war is to be totally unprepared for it. These criticisms, of course, were not all or necessarily accurate renditions of Dukakis' actual positions, but they were effectively used by the Republicans during the campaign.

Dukakis did in fact have some simplistic views of the Third World which apparently were strongly shaped by his experience as a young university student in Latin America in 1954. That was the year the CIA financed and aided an exile opposition group that invaded and toppled the Marxist government (which included Communists in the cabinet and other key positions) of Guatemala. The United Fruit Company, a large United States banana-exporting concern, was also fearful of its landholdings being nationalized by that government and had lobbied strongly against it. Ever since this episode, literally thousands of undergraduate term papers have been written about it. Dukakis' foreign policy beliefs were so strongly influenced by these events (he was actually in Peru at the time, where the reaction against the United States action was particularly strong) that even thirty-five years later that remained his vision of Latin America and the United States role there. He continued to believe that it was the CIA and the United Fruit Company that really ran Latin America. That is patently absurd: United Fruit (as well as most other United States corporations) has gotten completely out of Latin America, while CIA operations (almost always carried out under orders from higher authorities—most often the president himself, although an effort is made to disguise that fact as we shall see in Chapter 11) in Latin America have been greatly reduced in recent years.

In short, Dukakis came to be widely seen by the electorate as having a naive, ill-informed, and often romantic view of United States foreign policy. In this he was similar to earlier candidates McGovern and Carter. He seemed also to share many of the counterculture's views, which hurt him politically: that the CIA, the Defense Department, maybe the United States itself was a "morally evil" force that needed to be reined in. All this was in contrast to Bush, whose basic policy of peace through strength was widely viewed as more realistic. Because of his stands on these various defense and foreign policy matters, Dukakis was sent during the campaign a highly critical "open letter," published in *Time* magazine, by James Schlesinger, a major intellectual figure who had served in the cabinets of both Democratic and Republican administrations and who had dealt with national security issues for every president since Eisenhower. Schlesinger told Dukakis that, on foreign affairs, "your record is not reassuring," a devastating critique that had a large effect on the campaign and was apparently the prevailing view of the electorate as well.[2]

These romantic and visionary views are not of course shared universally within the Democratic party. Moreover, it must be remembered that all during the 1988 campaign, Dukakis was haunted by the continued presence of the Rev. Jesse Jackson, who continued to pull Dukakis to the left even though the Democratic party candidate knew full well that he had to move toward the center if he wanted to win the election.

Periodically, usually in the lull and boredom between election campaigns, the Democrats get together to try to achieve more responsible foreign policy positions, ones that the electorate will support. They recognize the party is viewed by the public as antidefense and "soft" on communism, and they have tried to change those perceptions. At one of these Democratic party policy meetings, Senator Joseph Biden, himself a former presidential candidate, said that the United States has several "arrows" in its quiver—diplomacy, military force, and economic power—and that we [Democrats] should not be seen as afraid to use any one of them. Similarly, Virginia Senator Charles Robb has warned his fellow Democrats that "we need a foreign policy which neither renounces nor relies exclusively on the use of force, a policy tempered but not paralyzed by the lessons of Vietnam."[3] These are eminently reasonable statements that point the Democrats in the direction they need to go if they hope to win future presidential elections. But in recent elections, the Democratic candidates have seldom been willing or able to move in these directions—for reasons we discuss in the next section.

CAMPAIGNS AND PRIMARIES: THE VETO POWER OF THE RADICALS

Both the Republican and the Democratic parties have their radical factions. These radical factions are extremely important during the election campaigns and especially in the primaries. They are active and highly vocal. Often they can secure their respective party's nomination for one of their own—or, failing that, they can exercise veto power over other, more moderate candidates.

The Republicans have what is called the "Goldwater wing" of their party —so named after its 1964 standard-bearer, Barry Goldwater. This wing is often considered to be ultraconservative, even reactionary. It stands in contrast to the more moderate and centrist wing of the party as exemplified by Dwight Eisenhower, Richard Nixon, Gerald Ford, and George Bush. For a long time the accepted wisdom among political analysts was that when this faction is allowed to define the platform or choose the candidates, the party loses disastrously—as did Mr. Goldwater. Nevertheless, a moderate Republican candidate (Nixon or Ford) could not win the party's nomination unless he was acceptable to the party's right wing.

Then along came Ronald Reagan and all these givens changed. Reagan came out of the Goldwater wing of the party. It was said that he was the most conservative candidate the Republicans had had since Calvin Coolidge. Not only did Reagan, with the conservatives' support, win the nomination in 1980 but then he also, contrary to the earlier wisdom, went on to win the general election in 1980 and 1984 with landslide margins. With Reagan into office went a whole cadre of conservative activists known as "the movement." The tables within the Republican party had thus been reversed. Now it was the conservatives who had captured the party machinery and emerged as dominant within the party, while the moderates were on the outs. Moreover, on this basis the Republicans had won two straight presidential elections. The party seemed to be becoming more ideological and more extreme.

Under George Bush, however, another reversal occurred. Bush is a moderate and mainstream Republican. Winning the party's nomination and then the presidency in 1988, Bush moved to put his own supporters in charge of the party machinery. Although a moderate, he won the nomination because as vice-president he was the heir apparent to Reagan and seemed to offer continuity with the Reagan administration. Interestingly, the candidate of the conservatives, Congressman Jack Kemp, did not do well in the primaries in which the conservatives have always run strong. And when Senator Robert Dole tried to pick up the conservatives' mantle, he did not do well against Bush in the primaries either. Hence there seems to have been again a reversal: the moderates are now in charge and the conservatives have been brushed aside. They remain a major force within the Republican party but are no longer overwhelmingly dominant as they were under Reagan.

Bush, in addition, ran a smart campaign and did what a moderate Republican has to do to win *both* the nomination and the election. That is, he ran as a loyal Reaganite and a true conservative during the primaries. He did that so as not to antagonize the party's right wing. He thus retained the support of most of the Reagan conservatives. Once Bush had the Republican nomination sewn up, he then skillfully shifted course to appeal to the country's broad center and to moderate independent voters. But he did so without antagonizing the right. Through this delicate juggling act Bush kept the loyalty of the conservatives while also capturing the broad center of the political spectrum.

The Democrats have a parallel problem, except that their chief problem is on the left and not the right. Today, a Democrat seems unable to be nominated unless he is acceptable to the party's left or "progressive" wing. For the past sixteen years it has not been possible for the party's conservative or moderate wing, earlier represented by Hubert Humphrey and Senator Scoop Jackson and currently by Senators Albert Gore, Sam Nunn, and Charles Robb, to receive the nomination. That is because the progressives are the most vocal, most active, and most involved in the early primaries. Hence when the Democratic candidates early in a campaign go off into the snows of New Hampshire or Iowa, which are the groups that they must first please? The answer is: the party's left wing, the human rights groups, the liberal yuppies, the peace advocates, the university professors, and the progressive activists.These are the people who attend the caucuses and whom a would-be Democratic nominee must first win over.

There is nothing wrong with these groups or this activity, of course, except that it skews the selection process. The groups mentioned are not representative of the nation as a whole, yet their support is absolutely essential if a Democratic candidate is to garner early primary victories. Moreover, since Iowa and New Hampshire represent the first caucuses and primaries, a candidate must win there and establish momentum if he hopes to win the nomination. So a Democratic candidate can become a serious contender and maybe even his party's nominee just by appealing to its progressive wing—as McGovern did. Certainly he cannot be the nominee without that support. At the same time, the positions a candidate takes to gain the support of the progressives in these early primaries are not at all the positions he needs to take to win the general election. In fact, these positions are downright damaging to his presidential nomination and may well cost him the election.

In 1988 that is precisely what happened. The early leaders in the primaries—Senator Paul Simon of Illinois, Senator Gary Hart of Colorado, the Rev. Jesse Jackson, and Governor Dukakis—all came out of the Democratic party's progressive wing. They all took positions on foreign policy issues to satisfy and win the votes of the progressives that were often viewed as considerably to the left. These were positions on Central America, South Africa, and the Soviet Union that the general electorate could not support. Yet the Democratic candidates *had* to take these positions if they hoped to win these early contests and thus establish that all-important "Big Mo"—momentum. Meanwhile such moderate candidates as Albert Gore, who alone among the Democrats might have won in the general election against Bush, had no chance at all in the early primaries and was viewed as unacceptable by the party's left wing.

Especially at its activist core, the Democratic party is thus far more liberal than the rest of the voters. The activists want to end the cold war, get the United States' "boot" off the neck of the Third World, and get on with their (usually) prosperous, upper-middle-class lives and careers. If good schools, national health insurance, and a clean environment mean raising the tax rates to levels of European social democracy, so be it—even if the rest of the population cannot afford such high tax rates. If their priorities mean chopping the defense budget, that is good too—regardless of longer-term United States security considerations. Since populist and progressive groups are strong in the early primary states like New Hampshire and Iowa, an aspirant to the Democratic nomination must stake out a strong progressive position. But most Democrats in the South, as well as a majority of the electorate, consider these positions alien, extremist, and dangerous. To be quite frank about it, these voters prefer more missiles over homeless shelters, Baptist preachers and a scene of Mary and the baby Jesus at Christmastime in the town square over the American Civil Liberties Union, and tough talk to the Russians instead of kisses on the cheek. As the Democratic candidates are obliged to take progressive stands in the early primaries, however, they drive centrist and independent voters, where majority sentiment lies, into the hands of the Republicans.[4]

We are now in a position to see clearly what the Democrats' electoral dilemma is. The dilemma is that those positions and those candidates who can win the party's nomination have a very difficult time in achieving victory in the presidential sweepstakes. At the same time those candidates who could win a presidential election have very little chance in the primaries, since the more ideological activists are often in a position to determine the nomination. The Democrats have not yet figured out a way to resolve this dilemma. Until they do, it seems unlikely that they will be able to capture the grand prize, which is the White House. Moreover, with the Rev. Jackson as the early frontrunner among the post-1988 candidates, the party may well be destined to repeat again in 1992 the mistakes it has all too often made in previous presidential elections.

THE PARTIES AND INTERNATIONAL AFFAIRS: INSTITUTIONALIZING THEIR ROLE?

We suggested at the beginning of this chapter that out there in the hinterlands, among the general American public, and in many academic analyses as well, political parties are not accorded great importance. The United States is not like Italy, for example, where the two main political parties are almost part of the culture and where political party identification and presence are ubiquitous: Christian-Democratic and Communist barber shops, grocery stores, social clubs, taverns, even funeral parlors. Political party identification there implies a whole way of life, cradle to grave.

In the United States, we do not have such close contact with our parties: they run candidates every two or four years but other than that we do not see very much of them. At the local level, elections for mayors and town council members are often nonpartisan; partisanship is not a way of life for most Americans, and most communities do not have open and functioning party offices except during the few weeks before a national election. Academic analyses reinforce this overall view of American political parties as generally weak, emphasizing their fluidity, absence of clear ideological positions, low party identification on the part of voters, who are fickle and shift party allegiances, and the presence of large numbers of independent voters and even larger numbers who fail or refuse to vote at all.

If political parties have been weak on the domestic scene, they have been all but invisible in the international arena. The parties may adopt a foreign policy statement as part of their platform at their quadrennial conventions, and obviously the presidential candidates must take stands on foreign policy issues. But in between elections the parties, as parties, pay little attention to foreign policy matters, nor are they equipped institutionally with regular, functioning foreign affairs offices. Since American elections have usually been decided on domestic economic issues and only rarely on foreign policy ones, the parties have historically paid little attention to the latter. Individual candidates or members of Congress may and do take stands on foreign policy issues, but the parties rarely do except in the vaguest of terms.

Unlike their European counterparts, furthermore, the American parties are not members of some larger *internationale* (Communist, Socialist, or Christian-Democratic); nor do they have the range of youth groups, foundations, trade union affiliates, research centers, and so forth associated with them that European parties do and that enable them to play a much greater international role than ours do. By tradition, history, organization, and functions, American political parties are simply not equipped, set up, or oriented toward playing a serious, sustained foreign policy role.

Only recently have the two American parties begun to take on a larger and more institutionalized international role, and they are so new at it that it is hard at this stage to evaluate the new activities properly. As part of the legislation authorizing the organization of the National Endowment for Democracy (NED), a congressionally funded but semiprivate agency established to assist in the creation and nurturing of democracy abroad, the two main political parties have created two new international affairs institutes. These are the National Democratic International Affairs Institute and the National Republican International Affairs Institute. Both institutes operate on modest $2- to $3-million budgets that they receive from Congress through the NED.

Neither institute has precisely spelled out its range of functions yet, nor are the roles of these institutes entirely clear. The National Democratic International Affairs Institute has been chiefly running conferences on democracy for academics and government officials, but it is only beginning to get into the much harder business of actually helping institutionally to build and consolidate democracy. Often divided by conflicts over ethnocentrism and cultural relativism, and still paralyzed by the trauma of Vietnam, the Democratic International Affairs Institute has been reluctant to involve itself in the internal affairs of other nations. It is the same dilemma that often plagued President Carter's foreign policy. However, in Chile the Democratic Institute ran a major voter registration drive and helped the opposition to rally the No vote in the 1988 plebiscite held on his rule by the dictator Augusto Pinochet.

The Republican International Affairs Institute has been more aggressive than the Democrats in establishing ties with like-minded political parties abroad and—just the opposite of the Democrats—was for a time mainly concerned with advancing the Reagan Doctrine (involving assistance to resistance forces fighting against Marxist-Leninist regimes) by aiding opposition forces in Nicaragua. Recently, it too has aided voter registration drives and articulated a broader prodemocracy agenda.

But in the case of both party institutes, the activities and impact so far have been quite modest. Neither institute has the funds or the personnel to engage in vigorous or widespread international activities. The institutes represent a beginning foray by America's two parties into the international arena but, at this stage, with very limited results. The two parties' foreign affairs branches represent a new phenomenon well worth watching in the future, but for now they remain all but invisible internationally. It is not just that American parties are limited in their domestic impact and importance, therefore, but that their international roles are even more circumscribed.

ADVISING THE CANDIDATES—AND, WITH LUCK, A FUTURE PRESIDENT

It is the height of ambition for many academics, particularly if their field is foreign policy, to serve as an adviser to a presidential candidate. Academics do not themselves always make good political candidates—

among other things, they often see too many sides to an issue and are therefore indecisive—but they do often serve as advisers. And, who knows, if their candidate wins, they may also go along to the White House as a top-level policymaker.

Where do these advisers come from? How are they chosen? How do they attach themselves to a candidate?

There is no single answer to these questions, no one route to future presidential influence. If a candidate is from the House of Representatives or the Senate, he or she will already have congressional and committee staffs from which some aides and operatives will be recruited to also work on the campaign. If a candidate is a governor, he or she will similarly have a team of advisers already in place recruited from the state house. Typically these include political cronies, some law school and/or college buddies, members of the governor's or congressman's private or political staff, and often some academics from the local or state universities or who have gotten to know the candidate over the years. (Dukakis may have made a mistake in 1988 by recruiting his advisers almost exclusively from Harvard, which thereby antagonized academics from other Massachusetts institutions.)

Often such politically inclined academics will have made a practice over the years of sending their writings to budding politicians, hoping that if and when that politician becomes a candidate, he or she will remember the person who earlier had sent all those learned articles. Other advisers may be recruited from among business colleagues and acquaintances or from hometown officials or among family members.

The situation in the Ivy League universities is a special, but perhaps illustrative, case because (1) the Ivy League thinks of itself and is often considered *the* premier group of universities in the country; and (2) the Ivy League believes that if its personnel are not now, for some reason, ruling the world, or at least the country, then they surely should be. At the same time, all the candidates like to have Ivy League names attached to their roster of foreign policy advisers simply because that adds luster to their campaigns. It is not always that the candidate really wants to have that Ivy League person give him advice (presidential candidate usually presume to know the answers already); rather, he often just wants to put that Ivy League name on his foreign policy advisory list because it makes him look good by association.

All the candidates pass through the Ivy League campuses on their way to New Hampshire or the other early primaries. The system works like this: an Ivy League scholar will be sitting in his office when he gets a phone call from one of his colleagues. "Oh," the caller will say, "Paul Simon is coming through town next week and is looking for foreign policy advisers; wouldn't you like to go have lunch with him?" So off go ten or fifteen persons to have lunch at the faculty club with Simon, to press their ideas on him and, at the same time, to impress him, hoping to enhance their prospects of serving as one of his advisers. Then Simon goes off to a primary somewhere only to be rebuffed by the voters. There go the chances of these academics to someday serve as Paul Simon's future National Security Adviser.

But lo, the next week a call will come from the same or another faculty colleague who says, "Bob Dole is coming through town next week and is looking for foreign policy advisers; wouldn't you like to have lunch with him?" So off the faculty goes for lunch with Bob Dole, hoping for inclusion on his team. But then Dole goes up to New Hampshire and gets shot down in that state's primary by George Bush. So ends the Dole candidacy—and, along with it, the prospects for an important foreign policy position for those academics who had attached themselves to his campaign.

The next week it is Al Haig's turn to come to lunch, then Al Gore's, or Pete DuPont's, or Dick Gephardt's. All make their pilgrimages to the Ivy League schools. And the foreign policy faculty at these schools, in turn, try to latch onto the successive candidates, hoping to make it into the inner ranks of their advisers, and from there to Washington, D.C. On the campuses of the Ivy League institutions, "Potomac fever" (the desire to go to Washington) is both widespread and highly contagious. It is quite a little dance that goes on between candidates and would-be foreign policy advisers. The fact that Ivy League faculty members are often well-known academics, very bright, and first-rate scholars—and that the stakes are so high (being able to influence United States foreign policy)—gives this "dance" a very serious aspect as well as its lighter side.

Out of this experience, repeated now in several recent election campaigns, come several conclusions:

1. The faculty at a number of our most prestigious universities really believes that it should run American foreign policy, at the National Security Council and elsewhere.
2. Up until Reagan, all the recent National Security Advisers— McGeorge Bundy, W.W. Rostow, Henry Kissinger, Zbigniew Brzezinski—came from the Ivy League schools; the present senior faculty at these schools, naturally enough, believes this trend should be continued—even if they are now facing competition from academics from other, often state, universities.
3. There is considerable rivalry among the senior faculty on these campuses to be the National Security Adviser in the next administration.
4. The junior faculty are also involved in this game, attaching themselves to some among the senior faculty in the hope that if one of the stars is chosen for the National Security Council, the junior faculty member (a starlet?) will be able to go along as one of his assistants, perhaps responsible for Africa or the Middle East. Among

the junior faculty at some Ivy League universities the sense is widespread that if you haven't made it to the NSC by the age of twenty-six (or thereabouts), life might as well be over for you.

5. In these campaigns to become presidential foreign policy advisers, political loyalties are fickle and fleeting. The faculty NSC wanna-bes go from one candidate to the next on an almost weekly basis. They also often go from party to party, depending on who might be willing to employ their services. The conclusion one reaches is that it is not necessarily loyalty to principle or ideology that is at work here but often mainly loyalty to self and to private ambition.

6. The candidates similarly demonstrate narrowness of thinking. They do not often want fresh ideas, only confirmation of the conclusions they have already reached and an attractive Ivy League name to give intellectual gloss and a certain academic veneer to their campaigns.

7. The entire process—of academics mailing out their curriculum vitaes and latest papers to the candidates, of campaigning (almost as hard as the candidates themselves) for advisory and NSC positions, of cultivating the candidates, of changing one's political or ideological position quickly, depending on which candidate is coming through town—is more than a little demeaning. At the same time, it *is* how the system works. It will not seem an attractive route for some academics who value their truthfulness, are committed to their ideas, and worry about their integrity. On the other hand, the rewards in terms of power and influence of pursuing this path are great. For, after all, these are the people who, if chosen, will provide foreign policy advice to *the president.* Future candidates and NSC advisers will have to weigh these crosscutting pressures for themselves.

DIVIDED GOVERNMENT: A PERMANENT FEATURE?

Divided government refers to a situation in which the Congress (or at least one branch of it) is in the hands of one of our major parties, and the White House is in the hands of the other. Divided government often adds a further ingredient to our paralysis on foreign policy and other issues, and has been frequently lamented by academic analysts who see advantages in a concerted and coordinated decision-making apparatus (such as exists in a parliamentary system, in which the parliament and the prime minister must necessarily be of the same party).

But in the United States, we seem to be in an almost permanent condition of divided government. With the single exception of the one-term Carter administration, every government since 1968 has been a divided government. We have had divided government now continuously since 1980. Moreover, and astonishingly to many analysts, the American voters seem to prefer it that way. Voting returns are starting to show a conscious and actual preference for divided government. Voters seem to prefer a Republican in the White House and Democrats in control of the Congress as well as most state governorships and legislatures. They want a Republican president to run foreign policy and a Democratic Congress to run domestic social policy. Republicans win the White House on the basis of a platform of peace through strength, while Democrats have majorities in the Congress on the basis of "caring" and "fairness" issues.

Such a *conscious* preference and voting pattern for divided government is astounding if we value an efficient and coordinated foreign policy-making process. It seems to indicate a preference for checks and balances over consistency, coherence, and a "rational" foreign policy. At this stage, the pattern has been present only in most recent elections and only among some voters. So we do not know as yet whether this is a permanent feature or only a temporary one. But if it proves permanent, we will have to change a lot of the ways that we think about American politics.

Notes

1. Robert A. Taft, *A Foreign Policy for Americans* (New York: Doubleday, 1951).
2. The Schlesinger letter was published in *Time* 1 Aug. 1988, 22.
3. Quoted in *New York Times* 2 Nov. 1988, A21.
4. Paraphrased from Eric Alterman, "Democrats: Split the Party? There's No Way to Reconcile the Flag-Wavers and Quiche Eaters," *Washington Post* 27 Nov. 1988, D5.

Suggested Readings

Clausen, Aage. *How Congressmen Decide: A Policy Focus.* New York: St. Martin's, 1973.
Dahl, Robert. *Congress and Foreign Policy.* New York: Harcourt Brace, 1950.
Herrnson, Paul S. *Party Campaigning in the 1980s.* Cambridge, Mass.: Harvard University Press, 1987.
Hinckley, Barbara. *Stability and Change in Congress.* 3rd ed. New York: Harper and Row, 1983.
Hughes, Barry. *The Domestic Context of American Foreign Policy.* San Francisco: Freeman, 1978.
Mayhew, David. *Congress: The Electoral Connection.* New Haven, Conn.: Yale University Press, 1974.
McCormick, James M. *American Foreign Policy and American Values.* Itasca, Ill.: Peacock, 1985.
Pomper, Gerald M., with Susan S. Lederman. *Elections in America: Control and Influence in Democratic Politics,* 2nd ed. New York: Longman, 1980.
Sorauf, Frank J. *Party Politics in America.* Boston: Little, Brown, 1984.

CHAPTER EIGHT

The New Powerhouses:
Think Tanks and Foreign Policy

❂
❂

Think tanks are major new actors on the foreign policy scene, and they have become increasingly influential. The phenomenon of the think tank is a new one (the last thirty years) and therefore has not so far been adequately treated in the literature on American politics and foreign policy. Yet it can be argued that the major United States think tanks are every bit as influential in shaping American foreign policy as the political parties, interest groups, and other agencies surveyed in this book. The think tanks have taken their place among the most important foreign policy actors in Washington, D.C.

WHAT ARE THINK TANKS?

Think tanks are unlike other institutions with which we are more familiar. Think tanks are centers of research and learning but, unlike colleges or universities, they have no students (but do have student research interns), do not offer courses (but do hold lots of seminars and forums), and do not try to offer a smattering of expertise on all subjects but rather concentrate preeminently on key public policy issues. Nor are think tanks like foundations because they do not give money away; instead they try to raise money for their studies from the foundations and other sources. They are not corporations because, while they have a product (research), think tanks are not profit-making organizations. And they are not like interest groups because their primary purpose is research, not lobbying— although some think tanks do that as well.

Think tanks are research organizations that have as their primary purpose *public policy research,* and which are located in or have close connections with (at least the more important ones do) Washington, D.C., where they can more effectively influence the public policy debate. Think tanks contain no departments of English, art, or chemistry—although one of the more prominent "tanks" has a division of Religion, Philosophy, and Public Policy. Rather, think tanks focus chiefly on economic, social, and political policy issues and recently have concentrated on defense, security, and foreign policy issues as well. They seek not just to do research and write about these issues, however, but to influence the policy debate toward their point of view and to put forth their solutions to public policy problems.

What members of think tanks do is to *think* (and write, and publish, and also disseminate their products) about public policy issues; they also serve as *advocates* for their public policy positions. It is the think tanks— not so much the parties, the interest groups, the Congress, the White House, or even the media—that have come increasingly to set the public policy agenda and define the issues. It may sound ludicrous upon first hearing, but the fact is that these days neither congressmen nor presidents, nor their secretaries of state, have the time or the specialized knowledge necessary to think about, to do the research, and to fashion the recommendations on major public policy issues. So the think tanks often do it for them. It is the think tanks who have the ideas and expertise, can do the necessary background work and research, and are able to put their ideas into attractive form that is translatable into public policy proposals.

Think tanks have come essentially to do the government's thinking for it. The persons who work at the think tanks are experts in various areas of public policy analysis: housing, health care, education, the economy, or foreign policy. Their scholars either come up with the new ideas themselves, based on their own research, or they rationalize and put into articulate, public policy form the ideas and conclusions that other academics, politicians, and government officials had already arrived at but were unable for various reasons to put in a framework that policymakers can use. The think tanks tend also to perform an integrating role when the national bureaucracy is divided or when too many parts of it are involved in a policy issue and no coherence among them is possible. Then the think tanks may step forward and provide the integrating perspective that is necessary.

The think tanks provide an essential service. In an era when many books, statements, and speeches are ghostwritten by persons other than their purported authors; when the budgets of various government agencies are prepared not by the agencies themselves but by private contractors; and when even the testimonies of cabinet secretaries are often written not by the secretaries or their staff but by outside consultants, we should not be surprised to find the think tanks performing public policy work and not necessarily the government agency we would assume to be responsible for such work. The activities performed by the think tanks are part of what we will call the privatization of the American public policy process. Such privatization is widespread in the government and is a result in part of the bigness, inefficiency, and sheer lack of time to do long-range planning in the public bureaucracies. The work the think tanks do is essential; and if the government cannot or will not do it, then these private agencies will have to fill the void.

Implied in the above is the suggestion that there are risks and dangers involved in such privatization, as well as advantages. There is almost no public accountability or oversight of the think tanks' activities, a particularly risky situation when the think tanks start to perform quasi-public policy roles. Moreover, the proliferation of think tanks in recent years (there are now six or seven big ones but literally hundreds of more specialized ones) has meant that each think tank wants its point of view to be the dominant one. The proliferation of think tanks and their strong political positions all along the political spectrum from extreme left to extreme right means that the world of the think tanks is often as partisan, as ideological, and as divisive as is the nation as a whole. It is one of the main theses of this chapter that the think tanks both reflect and add to the politicization, fragmentation, and creeping paralysis that we have repeatedly seen as among the main—and dangerous—characteristics of contemporary American foreign policy.

WHY THINK TANKS HAVE SO MUCH INFLUENCE (in Contrast to Most Academic Scholars)

Many of us who teach foreign policy courses are frustrated policymakers. Here we are, knowing quite a bit about foreign policy issues and having written extensively about our areas of expertise, and no one calls on us for our advice! Many foreign policy instructors believe that, if only given a chance, they could do infinitely better at foreign policy than the present administration—whatever the administration. Many would much rather be making American foreign policy than teaching it, but no one has ever tapped them for a position. Hence many teachers are often caustic, and sometimes bitter, in their criticism of American foreign policy—especially knowing that they are better informed than the United States government officials responsible and that their knowledge should be put to use.

These paragraphs are not meant to be hard on our teachers in foreign policy courses. The fact is, there are often good reasons why scholars and intellectuals from our colleges and universities, and their expertise on foreign policy issues, are not often tapped by policymakers. These reasons have to do mainly with the contrast between how foreign policy issues are discussed on campus and how they are dealt with in Washington, D.C. A person who wishes to plug into this debate, or become a policymaker, should understand and come to grips with these differences:

1. The writings of academics tend to be too abstract and theoretical for most policymakers to deal with. For policymakers, academic writing is usually too far from political realities to be of much use to them. Hence they don't pay much attention to academic foreign policy writings.

2. Academics tend to be concerned with developing models and discovering general laws of behavior; policymakers tend to emphasize the concrete and the particular, and to be suspicious of "grand theories." Policymakers don't have the time, nor the inclination, to wrestle with grand theories like "dependency analysis" or "state-society relations"; they need to know how to vote or decide *today* on military aid to Pakistan.

3. Academic writing nowadays is often too far on the left for policymakers to feel comfortable with. Policy-making and policymakers, almost of necessity in a democracy, must stick close to the center of the political spectrum, to the mainstream. Otherwise they will lose public support and votes, and their policies will fail. By contrast, academics who do not have to face the task of explaining and gaining support for their recommendations among a skeptical public or of having to face the voters every two years, tend to write in an ideological vein that is not supported by domestic public opinion.

4. Academics are not usually aware of the bureaucratic limits that face the policymaker. The policymaker's range of choices is usually quite constrained and he must operate within a bureaucratic matrix of diverse interests and responsibilities. His options and freedom to chart new paths are very limited. Hence the advice the policymaker receives from the academic, who is not ordinarily aware of these bureaucratic pressures and constraints, is not often very useful to him.

5. Nor is the academic analyst always aware of the everyday political crosscurrents in Washington: who's up and who's down, who has whose ear and when, what the different factions in the administration are and their current jockeying for power, and the rivalries between the different foreign affairs bureaucracies. Without such knowledge (recall the discussion in Chapter 2 of the bureaucratic, organizational, and political models of policy-making), the academic's "rational actor" advice is likely to be of only limited utility.

It is precisely these flaws that the Washington-based think tanks, and the academics who serve on their staffs, can avoid. That is also why the think tanks have such influence and most college- and university-based academics do not. The think tank scholars tend to produce concrete

analyses and recommendations, not abstract ones; they are seldom preoccupied with general models; they do know the bureaucratic ins and outs;
and they keep current on the everyday political and bureaucratic changes
that their academic counterparts outside of Washington cannot possibly do.
Hence the think tanks know how to plug into the system in ways that
academic scholars generally do not.

Let us provide three brief illustrations of these points to make them
more concrete:

1. At a recent conference on defense strategy that brought together
academics, military officials, and foreign policy planners, a naval admiral
was saying what academics have long known but are often reluctant to
admit. "You academics should have no illusions that you have any influence on policy," he said. "The Navy *knows* what it wants; the policy papers
you prepare have not one iota of influence on policy." He continued: "If we
can use your papers in our fights with the Army or the Defense Secretary
or with the Congress over the appropriation for the Defense Department,
then we will use your arguments. But don't think you have any influence on
real policy because we have already decided which way we want to go."

The moral of this story is that academic writings may be used as
rationalizations for decisions already arrived at, or in internal bureaucratic
battles, but seldom to present a series of options to policymakers. Knowing
that will shape the kind of policy papers that academics, as in this case
denizens of the think tanks, will send to policymakers.

2. During the revolution in Portugal in 1974, the United States Ambassador to Portugal and the United States Secretary of State were in strong
disagreement about the nature of the revolution and what should be done
about it. The Secretary of State was convinced Portugal was lost to communism and that the American response should be to mobilize the CIA or
send in NATO forces. The Ambassador, in contrast, did not believe the
revolution was hopelessly lost to the Communists and wanted to give the
Portuguese a chance to work out a democratic solution to their own
problems. An academic who knew Portugal, and who was also acquainted
with this bureaucratic struggle between the Ambassador and the Secretary
of State, helped influence the outcome by feeding information about
Portugal and its institutions to the Ambassador, enabling him more
strongly to argue his case. The Ambassador won the argument—unusual
because an ambassador does not usually take on his boss, the secretary, in
this way. And the outcome was also favorable: Portugal is today a flourish-
ing democracy and faces little if any Communist threat.

The moral of this story, again, is that academics can influence policy,
but only if they know the bureaucratic struggle going on within the foreign
policy-making system and know how and in what format to channel
information into the system.

3. Two academic colleagues, friends as well as specialists on southern Africa, sought to influence the policy debate on that troubled region. The one stayed on campus, gave flaming speeches, issued ideological diatribes, and fulminated against the Reagan administration. He gained some student following, but his shrillness and ideological attacks had no influence on policy whatsoever. The other scholar also favored a more enlightened approach toward southern Africa. He went to Washington, joined a leading think tank, studied the statements of the administration to understand its concerns, wrote reasoned and sensible articles about the region, and eventually was recruited as a consultant into the State Department where he helped negotiate a settlement of the southern Africa dispute.

Here the moral is obvious: shrill criticism does not work (except maybe on campus), and may produce among the general population the opposite effects of those intended; but a person who takes the time to learn the system and to understand what motivates policymakers can be quite effective.

This discussion of how scholars can and do influence policy is also relevant to our discussion of think tanks and what they do. The think tanks are largely staffed by scholars who are public policy oriented, are often Washington insiders, and know how to influence the debate. In contrast to their academic colleagues in the universities, they know where the pressure points are, who's in and who's out, when the appropriate moment is to get their viewpoint aired, and how to go about doing so.

The think tanks play an especially important role in linking research to policy. In addition to their own independent research, the think tanks serve as a transmission belt, a broker, a link between academic work and policy-making. The think tanks thus perform liaison functions. They sift and filter the academic research for ideas that are useful and will "fly" in a policy sense. At the numerous conferences they put on, the think tanks often invite the best academic minds on the subject to Washington. Then it is the job of the think tank scholars to translate the generally abstract prose in which academics write into terms that a policymaker can deal with. They must cut out the theory, the "conceptual framework," and the models, and put the knowledge and information contained in the scholarly papers into concrete, practical language and recommendations. Rather than providing the abstract "position paper" with its required five options, think tank scholars make the academic research realistic and down to earth. They know the bureaucratic infighting, the political constraints, which ideas have a chance and which do not, and how, where, and when to feed these ideas in. In this way the think tanks can help make academic research look useful, reasonable, and workable to the policymakers. They define the options, give the arguments for them depth and sophistication, provide rationales for policy or help steer it in new directions. The think tanks can thus define the parameters of the debate, educate the public and the Congress, show what will work and what will not, and demonstrate how to get from here to there. Such work may not always be in accord with the "purity" of academic research, but it is infinitely more practical and certainly has a far stronger effect on policy.

In the analysis so far, we have drawn the lines rather sharply between campus-based academic research and the public policy research and dissemination done by the think tanks. While the general points made still hold, the argument needs to be qualified in certain ways. First, some academic scholars—primarily at the Ivy League universities but often those with specialized knowledge at other universities as well—*do* have an influence on policy-making. Second, at some institutions (Harvard's Center for International Affairs is the best example), specialized foreign policy research centers exist that represent hybrids between the university world of pure research and the think tank world of policy-oriented research—and which not only serve to bridge the gap between these two but are also influential policy centers in their own right. Third, the case can be made that while university-based academics usually have little influence on everyday policy, through their students as well as their writings they may have influence in longer range terms. Finally, many of the new recruits to top-level posts in the Defense or State departments and the CIA are former academics, often frustrated ones who want to *make* policy rather than just write or lecture about it. That is another way in which the line between academic work and actual policy-making is being increasingly blurred.

THE COUNCIL ON FOREIGN RELATIONS AND THE THINK TANKS: FROM AN OLD ELITE TO A NEW ELITE IN FOREIGN POLICY

For a long time in the post–World War II period, the Council on Foreign Relations was the dominant private organization in the foreign policy field. The council had actually been formed earlier, right after World War I, to help generate public support for the Fourteen Points of Woodrow Wilson's Versailles peace treaty. Centered in New York, the council attracted elite, establishment figures. It was not so much a think tank (although the council now does have its own research staff) as a gathering place for wealthy, well-placed New Yorkers who had an interest in foreign policy. During the period before and right after World War II, when the United States still had strong isolationist tendencies, the council was a center of internationalist sentiment. It put on programs, listened to speakers talk about various parts of the world, and published what was then the leading journal in the field, *Foreign Affairs*.

The membership of the council was by election only. Membership was thus kept select and limited. It consisted mainly of prominent Wall Street bankers and lawyers as well as diplomats. During the 1940s and 1950s, a large portion of the foreign policy leadership was recruited out of the council: Dean Acheson and John Foster Dulles, David Rockefeller and Douglas Dillon, Averill Harriman and John McCloy, and a large number of ambassadors and assistant secretaries. Although there were partisan differences, most council members thought of themselves as moderates and centrists. They were the backbone of the consensual, bipartisan foreign policy that prevailed up to the Vietnam war.

By the 1960s, criticism of the council began to be widespread. The economist John Kenneth Galbraith denounced it as "irrelevant" and resigned. It was said to be too WASPish, too old-fashioned, and with too few women, minority, and younger members. As a New York-centered organization, it was denounced by conservatives as a part of the "Eastern liberal establishment." And as a bulwark of post–World War II foreign policy, it was held responsible by leftist critics for the assumptions that led to American intervention in Vietnam.

In the 1970s and 1980s, the council vigorously moved to refurbish its image and its position. It recruited new members among women, minorities, and younger persons. It opened a branch in Washington and sought to recruit members from other parts of the country besides the East Coast. It has a more vigorous research program and its activities have expanded.

In the meantime, however, a fundamental transformation in foreign policy-making influence has been taking place. The center of foreign policy influence has shifted from the Council on Foreign Relations to the Washington-based think tanks. The council has lost its place as the dominant, or virtually only, private influence on foreign policy. That role has now been filled by the think tanks, with major impact on United States foreign policy.

Let us sum up the changes that this shift from the council to the think tanks implies:

1. Power in foreign policy has definitively shifted from New York, which once was dominant not only in banking but also in foreign affairs, to Washington.
2. It has shifted from Wall Street bankers and lawyers to the scholars and public policy specialists who inhabit the think tanks.
3. It has shifted from an older generation whose assumptions were based on the experiences of the 1930s, World War II, and the emerging cold war to a new generation shaped by the 1960s and Vietnam.
4. It has shifted from the middle-of-the-road and bipartisan elements who were predominant in the council to the much more partisan, ideological, and political elements who are in the think tanks.

It is this last change that is particularly worrisome from the point of view of the main theme of this book. For if American foreign policy appears already to be divided, fragmented, and often in disarray, then the think tanks, with the divisions between them and their more partisan and ideological approach, may well be further instruments of this divisiveness. That at least is the hypothesis with which we begin.

THE WORLD OF THE THINK TANKS

The world of the think tanks is fascinating and ever changing. Think tanks come in a variety of forms and locations. Some are located on or near university campuses, others are independent. Some serve basically as research centers for the United States government; others do not accept government contracts at all. Some are large and some are small. Some have a single focus or issue for which they are known, others work on a variety of subjects. Here we will be concerned chiefly with the large and influential Washington-based think tanks, since that is where considerable power lies.

First, let us look at what may be termed the "minor leagues" of think tanks, or what is sometimes referred to as the "feeder system"—so called because they often feed ideas and budding personnel into the larger think tanks. This league includes the Mershon Center at The Ohio State University, the Foreign Policy Research Institute in Philadelphia, and the Institute for Foreign Policy Analysis in Cambridge, Massachusetts. These are all small "tanks" with staffs of maybe ten to twenty people and budgets in the neighborhood of $1 to $2 million. They specialize in foreign policy and national security issues. However, because they are outside of Washington and therefore can neither know about nor directly influence the everyday insides of policy-making in the nation's capital, these think tanks tend to concentrate their efforts on publishing scholarly books and articles—on longer range policy analysis, in order to influence the scholars, editorialists, and others who *do* have a direct influence on policy.

A second category is the think tank that does most of its work for the government. Examples include the RAND Corporation, which used to be an Air Force think tank and now is more independent; CNA (Center for Naval Analysis), which does research for the Navy; or the BDM Corporation, a multimillion dollar private firm whose business is chiefly (90–95 percent) with the Defense Department and has recently been bought out by the even larger Ford Aerospace Corporation. But because these think tanks do chiefly contract research for the government and are not independent, general foreign policy think tanks, they are not our chief focus here.

A third category is major think tanks that have influence but are nonetheless (and almost a contradiction in terms) outside of Washington, D.C. The Hudson Institute was located in New York and headed by Herman

Kahn, a visionary thinker who specialized in futuristic studies. Kahn became famous for "thinking about the unthinkable"—that is, a rational, calculating approach to nuclear war strategy rather than a purely emotional one. He was practically a one-man think tank, although he did vastly increase the staff and the budget of Hudson. But Kahn has since died and the Institute has moved to Indianapolis; it keeps up its influence through a branch office in Washington, D.C.

Another one of the "biggies" outside of Washington is the Hoover Institution on War, Revolution, and Peace. Centered in three beautiful buildings on the lush Stanford University campus in Palo Alto, California, Hoover is one of the most influential and well-funded of the think tanks. It has a marvelous library (begun by President Herbert Hoover), wonderful facilities, a first-rate research staff, and aggressive, top-flight leadership. Although Hoover is known as a conservative think tank, its scholars are about equally divided between Republicans and Democrats and include many centrists, which means that its relations with the more liberal and often left-leaning Stanford faculty are often tense. Hoover sent some thirty of its personnel into the Reagan administration and is most famous for its research on economic and social policy as well as foreign affairs. Like the Hudson Institute, it has a Washington office; its California staff keeps in touch by often twice-monthly long plane rides between the West Coast and the East.

Our main concern here, however, is with the major, independent, Washington-based think tanks, of which there are five. These are, going from left to right on the political spectrum, the Institute for Policy Studies (IPS), the Brookings Institution, the Center for Strategic and International Studies (CSIS), the American Enterprise Institute for Public Policy Research (AEI), and the Heritage Foundation. There are numerous other smaller, usually more specialized think tanks in Washington but these are the bigger and more influential ones.

INSTITUTE FOR POLICY STUDIES

The Institute for Policy Studies (IPS) is the most left wing of the major think tanks. It was founded in the early 1960s by dissident government employees Marcus Raskin and Richard Barnett, who advocated a "radical critique" of American foreign policy and a dismantling of the capitalist system. It has three office buildings in Washington, D.C., numerous affiliates abroad, and a staff of about fifty. IPS was funded chiefly by the Samuel Rubin Foundation, Mr. Rubin being a founder of the Faberge cosmetics firm and a registered member of the American Communist Party. The Rubin family keeps a strong hand in IPS through daughter Cora Rubin Weiss and son-in-law Peter Weiss, chairman of the board of trustees. The institute says its budget is $1.7 million, but the suspicion is strong among Washington observers that some of its budget may be secret and come from the outside. It seems doubtful the IPS can have the staff, buildings, and activities it has on such a small budget.

IPS represents the "hard left" in American politics. It is not just liberal but often Marxist, with some of its associates veering off to full-fledged Marxism-Leninism. IPS pictures the United States as "the most evil society in history" and blames the United States and "capitalism" for virtually all of the world's ills. It sees its mission as liberating people from their "colonial" status and reconstructing society along socialist lines. It is against all defense measures and has consistently sided with countries hostile to the United States. It may not be a full Communist-front organization, but it has been characterized as "communoid"—awfully close to it. Because of its activities and the lingering suspicion that it is supported by the Soviet Union, IPS has been the object of repeated FBI and Internal Revenue Service probes. In turn, IPS is suspicious of and hostile toward outsiders who make inquiries about its funding and internal affairs.

IPS reached the height of its influence during the Vietnam war protest years; some of its stalwarts even found their way into the Carter administration. But during the eight years of President Reagan and the more conservative turn of the country, IPS became the think tank that time forgot—at least in Washington, although not on some college campuses. It was viewed in Washington as "flaky" and far too radical. But its fortunes rose somewhat in 1988 when its director, Robert Borosage, became Jesse Jackson's chief foreign policy advisor, when former Democratic presidential candidate George McGovern signed on as a fellow (as a way of luring social-democratic support for the institute as well as the hard left), and when a number of Jackson's other foreign policy advisors gained positions of influence within the Democratic party. IPS was especially effective in getting its personnel invited to speak at many American colleges and universities; and while its influence on Washington policy-making is small, it does have some support among radical students and faculty.

BROOKINGS INSTITUTION

On the moderate and eminently respectable left is the Brookings Institution. Brookings was founded in 1927 by a St. Louis businessman, Robert Brookings, although its roots may be traced back as early as 1916. Brookings occupies a splendid building on Massachusetts Avenue in the heart of Washington, D.C.; its budget in 1987 was $15 million (nine times larger than IPS's budget), which placed it right up there with the Hoover Institution and ahead of any of the other Washington think tanks.

Brookings became famous largely on the strength of its economics "faculty" who were champions of Keynesian economics as early as the 1950s and whose viewpoints triumphed during the Kennedy administration. Only later did Brookings begin to expand its foreign policy activities, focusing on nuclear strategy, the Middle East, and general foreign policy issues.

Over the years Brookings has moved steadily toward the center. That is where the money to support its research is and that is where the bulk of public opinion lies. Brookings now has a Republican president and a Republican vice-president, is recruiting more centrist scholars, and raises the bulk of its money from the same corporate sources as do the more conservative think tanks. Brookings has moved away from a strong ideological posture, and its foreign policy activities and publications are also serious, scholarly, and middle of the road. Most observers, in fact, have not seen very many ideological differences in recent years between Brookings' foreign policy positions and those of the Center for International Studies (CSIS) or the American Enterprise Institute (AEI). But as Brookings' moved to the center, that left a hole on the liberal left that no major think tank at present occupies.

CENTER FOR STRATEGIC AND INTERNATIONAL STUDIES

The Center for Strategic and International Studies was founded in the early 1960s as a foreign policy offshoot of and by two former associates of the American Enterprise Institute—Richard Allen, who was President Reagan's first National Security Advisor, and David Abshire, who later became an ambassador and presidential troubleshooter. CSIS was different from the other Washington think tanks (and more like the Mershon Center or Hoover Institution) in that from the beginning it was associated with one of Washington's leading universities, Georgetown. But the relations between Georgetown and CSIS steadily worsened (the Georgetown faculty was more liberal and faculty members were seldom brought in on the more lucrative research opportunities available at CSIS) until in 1987 they formally separated, a divorce that will probably be detrimental to both institutions.

For a long time CSIS had only a limited staff and resources, but in the late 1970s and 1980s it steadily grew until its budget reached $9 to $10 million. The affiliated staff includes a number of highly visible foreign policy specialists of cabinet-level rank: Henry Kissinger, Harold Brown, James Schlesinger, and Zbigniew Brzezinski. CSIS, unlike Brookings, has only a limited endowment, must raise virtually all of its operating funds every year, and therefore the staff often spends upwards of 70 to 80 percent of its time raising money for its various projects. Despite this time spent in money-raising, the CSIS staff still manages to produce an impressive amount of research and publications.

CSIS has been aggressively courting larger donors and expanding its seminar, publication, and outreach activities. It stands for a "realist" position in foreign policy, which probably defines it as centrist and somewhat conservative. Its foreign policy positions are not all that much different, therefore, from the American Enterprise Institutes—at least until recently.

THE AMERICAN ENTERPRISE INSTITUTE

The American Enterprise Institute for Public Policy Research was founded in 1943 as an advocacy agency for free enterprise; it later emerged as a full-fledged but still conservative think tank. During the 1950s, when Brookings took up the Keynesian cudgels, AEI remained committed to a free market approach. It is largely because of their orientation toward the role of government in the economy (broad for Brookings, limited for AEI) that Brookings was baptized the "liberal" think tank and AEI the "conservative" one. For a long time, in fact, AEI and Brookings were the two major (and virtually only) think tanks in Washington; both of them had large budgets approaching $15 million by the mid-1980s.

In the 1970s and 1980s, AEI began to build up its foreign policy staff to match its already stellar economics staff. It concentrated on defense policy, NATO, general foreign policy, Latin America, and the Middle East. The foreign policy staff was made up largely of centrists, liberal Republicans, moderates, and serious scholars. Although there continued to be differences between AEI and Brookings in their economic policy recommendations, in the foreign policy field AEI's research products were hardly distinguishable from those of Brookings and CSIS.

But that is what turned out to be precisely the problem for AEI. By the mid-1980s, AEI was in serious financial trouble. It was deeply in debt and plagued by major management problems. Some donors complained that with its increasingly centrist and pluralist foreign policy orientation AEI had lost its mission and sense of purpose. In addition, AEI was outflanked on the right by the aggressive Heritage Foundation, which began to draw the conservative money that used to go to AEI. Its budget shrank from $14 million to $8 million, and its president was fired.

In a series of purges that ran from 1985–1987, AEI let go or pensioned off almost its entire foreign policy staff. In their place it hired a number of persons referred to as "neoconservatives." Some analysts feel that AEI's foreign policy team is presently even more conservative than that of the Heritage Foundation, which has long been thought of as the major think tank on the political right. Meanwhile, AEI's research productivity and publications, and its reputation as a major center for foreign policy research and influence, plummeted as well.

Under new leadership, AEI had begun to recover by the late-1980s, was put on a sounder financial footing, and was managed on a leaner basis. But its research productivity was still much smaller than it had been in the earlier glory years and, on the outside, objective observers wondered if the institute's neoconservative position had a bright future either in Washington or, politically, in the nation as a whole.

HERITAGE FOUNDATION

The Heritage Foundation is a newcomer among the leading Washington think tanks. It is also the most conservative.

Founded in 1973 by two former congressional aides, Edward Feulner and Paul Weyrich, Heritage represented the far right or most conservative wing of the Republican party. A number of its early leaders and associates had been a part of Barry Goldwater's losing presidential campaign in 1964, and they sought to keep the conservative flame alive. By the mid-1970s, they had become followers of Ronald Reagan.

Heritage's initial funding came from wealthy sponsors like Joseph Coors, the beer manufacturer. It also tapped into "the movement," the large number of ideologically committed conservatives in the United States. Alone among the think tanks it used direct mailings to raise funds among small donors—130,000 persons who give perhaps $10 or $25 per year.

Heritage grew slowly in the 1970s but expanded meteorically in the 1980s when its man, Reagan, was elected president. It vastly expanded its staff to about 120, bought its own building on Capitol Hill, and began a vigorous program of seminars and publications. Its *Mandate for Leadership* volume provided a blueprint of policy proposals for the Reagan administration and, like the Hoover Institution and AEI, twenty to thirty of its personnel went into the administration. As a kind of clearinghouse for young committed conservatives of "the movement," Heritage found jobs for many others hot off the college campuses and eager to serve.

Heritage also benefitted from the decline of AEI during this period. The foundation had staked out a frankly conservative position to the right of AEI and began to attract more and more of the conservative financial support that had previously gone to AEI. Moreover, it was noticeable that after the mid-1980s, when foreign ministers, heads of state, and other visiting dignitaries came to town, they often went to Heritage to visit or hold a seminar. That was a measure of the fact that their embassies in Washington had adjudged Heritage to be a rising and influential power in the Reagan administration.

Heritage is still viewed by the other think tanks as a Johnny-come-lately, however. It is seen as more a lobbying organization committed to advancing its own policy agenda than a serious research institution. Unlike the other think tanks, Heritage has hired few academic stars, but lots of ambitious young people whose scholarly credentials are not yet established and whom it therefore does not have to pay very much. They are worked very hard producing what the other think tanks refer to derisively as "instant analyses"—hastily prepared reports culled from newspaper files that Heritage can place on the desks of congressmen within twenty-four hours. Many of these reports are heavily loaded ideologically and politically. For that reason, Heritage's research products in the past have had a dubious reputation among scholars. But it should be recalled that Heritage's main purpose has not been to produce original research; rather it wants to shape and influence the policy debate, and by that measure it has been phenomenally successful.

In many ways sad to say, and although scholars have not yet faced up to this reality, the fact is that most congressmen and their aides, as well as journalists, White House officials, and policymakers in the executive agencies, do not have the time to read the weighty, scholarly tomes that independent researchers or Brookings or AEI prepare. What Heritage does successfully is to produce short, pithy papers on very short notice that tell too-busy congressmen and their aides how they should vote. Congressmen and other policymakers cannot be expected to be informed on all the complex details of all the issues that come their way, so the brief, direct, and straightforward Heritage papers and recommendations are often a godsend to them.

With Reagan in the presidency, Heritage's influence expanded enormously. It shot past AEI as the largest conservative think tank and its budget reached the levels of the real biggies, Brookings and Hoover. Gradually over the years its research products have also improved to the point where scholars must now pay them serious attention rather than dismissing them as in the past.

As Heritage came closer and closer to being an Establishment think tank, its ideological fervor began to wane somewhat. In the foreign policy field, it may well be that AEI, after its neoconservative changeover, is now the more conservative (or Heritage the more liberal) of the two. Another question is what will happen to Heritage now that Reagan has left the presidency, and its once enormous access to policy-making has ended. It will almost certainly continue to do well, since its sponsors tend to feel more threatened by Democratic administrations, or even moderately conservative ones like Bush's and hence will continue to give more money. Under Republican or Democratic administrations, the Heritage Foundation will thus continue as a force to reckon with.

HOW THINK TANKS EXERCISE INFLUENCE

How do think tanks go about exercising their influence? Why do their books and studies have an influence on policy while so many of the studies produced by academic scholars do not?

Let us take the second question first. The fact is that so many books and studies are being produced on so many foreign policy subjects these days that even scholars cannot keep up with the writings on their country, area, or issue of expertise. Government officials, who are very busy and do not usually have the academic background in a field that scholars have, are far less able to keep up. So they pick and choose very carefully what they read.

Also there is a pecking order, a set of presumptions about who or what is worth reading. Whether it is a mistaken presumption or not, the fact is that the scholars who inhabit the Washington think tanks—especially Brookings and AEI—are presumed to be at the top of their fields, higher even than the Ivy League institutions. Parenthetically, we should say that in actuality such a rank order is probably exaggerated, that a good university department is probably as strong in terms of its research as the contingent of scholars at any of the leading Washington think tanks. But in Washington and in the country at large, it is often thought that the think tanks represent the top rung. And, of course, in this area as in so many others, what people think is often as important as what really is. So if you're a too-busy government official with only limited time to read, where do you turn first? The answer is, to the think tanks, because that's where it's believed the real expertise lies.

Now, how do the think tanks actually go about influencing policy? There are several methods, and the think tanks have become very adept and clever at getting their research products and message out there.

1. Lunches, seminars, dinners. Virtually every day the think tanks have programs on one subject or another. To these meetings are invited congressmen and their aides, White House and State Department officials, journalists, and other opinion-leaders. Not only are the food and drinks free, but if you are a policymaker and don't attend, you might miss something and then someone else will be one-up on you. Usually these forums offer an opportunity for scholars from the think tanks to showcase their ideas or a new study that they have just produced. For example at AEI, Judith Kipper's lunches and seminars on the Middle East were *de rigueur* for persons wanting to have a say or influence policy on that area.

2. Television and media. Think tank scholars regularly appear on such programs as *Nightline, MacNeil/Lehrer,* or the evening news. They are not necessarily better informed than scholars in Berkeley or Ann Arbor, but they are known to the media programmers, their offices in Washington are practically next to the television studios, and it does not cost the networks anything to bring them in compared with flying their own crews out to some college campus. For many of those same reasons think tank scholars are often quoted in the press.

3. Public appearances. Think tank scholars have virtually daily opportunities (if they wish) to speak before college and university audiences, seminars and forums, professional associations, State Department or other training programs, foreign exchange groups, or the audiences of fellow think tanks. This exposure makes them well known nationally and even internationally; hence at some future time when a policymaker is looking for someone to give advice, he will most likely call on the speaker he heard at one of these forums.

4. Access to policymakers. Think tank scholars have direct access to policymakers. They are in the White House, the State or Defense departments, and other government agencies for meetings on, again, a virtually everyday basis. Because of the presumption noted earlier that they represent the top ranks of scholars, think tank personnel are able to get through doors and see people that others are not able to do.

5. Congressional testimony. Think tank scholars often know personally the congressional staffers who schedule hearings, or are known to those staffers. Hence, when a committee or subcommittee is looking for testimony on a particular subject, it will usually call on persons from the think tanks. Also, since the Congress is itself a very partisan institution, its members know that by calling on representatives of the several think tanks they can get testimony that supports the conclusions they have already reached, which is always comforting to congressmen.

6. Advisory panels. Think tanks have high-level advisory panels for virtually all their programs. These consist of outside persons, usually prominent in the worlds of business, banking, and industry. In this way the think tanks can list many more important persons of wealth and influence on their letterheads and in their annual reports. These same persons help them raise funds and get their studies into the right hands.

7. Personal contacts. Think tank scholars, because of their presence in Washington, ordinarily have a vast range of personal contacts. These include not only fellow scholars from other think tanks and the universities, but also journalists, government officials, business executives (who often sit on the boards of directors of the think tanks), labor officials, foundation heads, representatives of foreign governments, and so forth. The range of people with whom think tank scholars come in personal contact is far broader and at a much higher level than is true of most university-based academics. Think tank scholars are able to take advantage of these contacts to get their message across.

8. Government experience. The think tanks are prime recruiting grounds for new government talent. Many longtime think tankers have gone in and out of government service several times. They go in when their preferred party comes to power and back to the think tanks when the other party is in power. There are few things more heady for think tank scholars than a chance in government to put the ideas they have been writing about and nurturing for so long into actual practice. And, of course, because they are already in Washington, are well connected, and have probably signed up to be on one or another of a presidential candidate's advisory teams far in advance, their chances of getting an interesting position at State, the National Security Council, or another agency are far greater than those of a university scholar who may be just as knowledgeable.

9. Studies and publications. The think tanks are very good at getting their products out to where they are read and paid serious attention. They maintain vast and highly specialized mailing lists that are constantly updated and that enable them to reach quickly virtually every well-known person in the country on any particular issue. They have publications and public relations offices that prepare press releases about the study, organize press conferences for a new book, do summaries that then appear on the op-ed pages in leading newspapers, get their authors on the talk shows, and send out endless free copies. After all, no study will have influence unless important people read it. The think tanks have facilities for bringing their scholars' work to the attention of opinion-leaders and decision makers. On Central America policy, for instance, the writings of CSIS and AEI scholars were important in returning the Reagan administration to a more moderate and centrist position. Quite a number of these scholars even have their own syndicated newspaper columns.

An informal but useful way to measure the influence of the think tanks (or of other scholarship) is the following. Government runs, in part, on the basis of memos. If a State Department or Defense Department official, or an analyst at the CIA or the National Security Council has your study in front of him and open at the time he is writing his own memo to the secretary or the director or perhaps the president himself—if, in short, he is using your ideas and analysis at the time he writes his own memo—then you have influence. If your study is not open in front of him or, worse, you do not even know who the responsible official is, you do not have influence. It is as simple as that.

THINK TANK DYNAMICS

If you are a scholar, think tanks are very nice places to work. They are like universities in their dynamism and intellectual excitement, but they have no students and hence no teaching obligations, very few of those endless committee meetings that plague university faculties, and no heavy layers of bureaucracy. Despite the fact, as we know, that most professors love their students, with no teaching, no committees, and no bureaucracies—what, the scholars of the think tanks often ask, could be better than that?

The staff salaries at the think tanks also tend to be far higher than in colleges or universities. There is an almost unlimited photocopy, postage, and long-distance telephone budget. Think tank scholars have research assistants (often several of them) and usually a private secretary. The larger think tanks have their own dining facilities, kitchen staff, editorial and publications staff, conference and travel staff, administrative staff, and fund-raising offices. It is far easier to be a productive scholar when all these facilities are at your disposal and when a friendly editor is right down the hall. Think tanks are nice places for student interns too.

But there are some drawbacks as well—although on balance the benefits seem to greatly outnumber the disadvantages. Foreign policy issues in Washington (South Africa, the Middle East, Central America) are very fickle, they often rise and fall with the headlines, and there is no permanent tenure at the think tanks. For example, one of the think tank presidents justified the expansion of Latin America programs at his institute by referring to Central America as a "growth industry." Crudities aside, this means it was great for the scholars in that program as long as Central America was seen as a critical policy arena; but once the attention had passed on to other issues—Eastern Europe, the Pacific Basin, Soviet relations—the program and the scholars associated with it could expect to be cancelled.

Some scholars will also feel uncomfortable doing public policy research (as distinct from value-free research), since public policy research is almost inevitably partisan, political, and somewhat one-sided. In addition, there is a growing tendency within the think tanks for management, not the individual scholars, to decide what topics are to be researched. The scholars may also be required to do fund-raising, an activity with which some of them may feel uncomfortable; and the management system in most think tanks tends to be top-down rather than grass roots and participatory as in most universities. And, as in most Washington agencies, the public relations officials tend to have more say than their talents or abilities would seem to indicate—sometimes more power in their think tanks than do the scholars.

Now let us turn to the issue of think tank influence in different administrations. If we position the think tanks on a political spectrum, the picture will look something like this:

Far Left		Center		Far Right
IPS	Brookings	CSIS	AEI	Heritage

If we next consider which of the think tanks have influence (measured in terms of receptivity to their ideas or the number of scholars who enter government) in a liberal-Democratic (Carter), administration, the loop would look something like this:

| IPS | Brookings | CSIS | AEI | Heritage |

That means that within a liberal-Democratic administration, Brookings will occupy the center, CSIS the right, and IPS will be given a few positions on the far left. AEI and Heritage will be excluded; however, AEI will be thought of as the "responsible opposition" and Heritage as "far out"—too far to have any influence at all.

In a conservative-Republican administration (Reagan) the loop of influence will look as follows:

| IPS | Brookings | CSIS | AEI | Heritage |

Note that here AEI is the center, CSIS the left, and Heritage the right. Brookings is now thought of as the "responsible opposition" and IPS thought of as the "nuts," the "bomb throwers," or worse.

In a centrist administration (Ford, Bush, Johnson) the loop would look like this:

| IPS | Brookings | CSIS | AEI | Heritage |

Thus CSIS becomes the center, AEI the right, and Brookings the left. IPS and Heritage are both excluded from influence in such a centrist administration.

Now, finally, if we superimpose these three loops, we also see some interesting things:

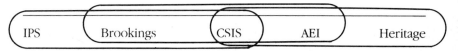

| IPS | Brookings | CSIS | AEI | Heritage |

Note that, as in a multiparty political system, the "party" of the center, CSIS, has influences in all administrations—just because it is in the center. AEI and Brookings have power in two-thirds of the cases and are thought as being influential even when their favorites are out of power. On opposite sides of the political spectrum, the situations of IPS and Heritage are also analogous: two-thirds of the time they are out of the loop and not taken very seriously. It takes special circumstances for either of these two more radical think tanks to exercise power: a sharp swing to the left of the Democratic party to bring IPS into influence, and a sharp swing to the right of the Republican party to bring Heritage to power. There is a political science maxim in all of this and that is that the center groups have power all of the time (usually out of proportion to their actual vote or strength), the moderately partisan or ideological groups have influence most of the time, and the radical elements are chiefly left out in the cold. Democratic politics and pluralism of necessity mean centrist politics.

This configuration and these loops of influence should not be thought of as immutable, however. The power and influence of these think tanks rise and fall. For a long time Brookings and AEI, the two great liberal and conservative antagonists (the "thinking man's think tanks," as they were sometimes called), had the field pretty much to themselves. Then along came IPS and CSIS in the 1960s and Heritage in the 1970s. All of the "big five" seemed for a time to be booming ahead in terms of larger staffs, more activities, and ever larger budgets. But IPS seemed to suffer a precipitous decline in the 1980s, AEI went into a downward slide from which it has since recovered (but at a considerably lower level of activities), and CSIS has also had budget difficulties.

In the meantime, a variety of new think tanks stand ready in the wings, hoping for a growth spurt in funding or a new idea that will propel them to prominence. These include the CATO Institute, which represents a libertarian position; the International Institute for Strategic Studies, which takes a moderate position; and the Carnegie Endowment, which is older but still small and aspires to fill the liberal-left position left open by Brookings' gravitation toward the center.

THINK TANK FUNDING

The question we raise in this section is the degree to which the sources of think tank funding bias the research work and product that come out.

Few of the think tanks raise much money "democratically"—that is, from the general public. Among the big think tanks, only Heritage has been able to develop and use effectively the device of direct mail solicitations. But of course Heritage appeals to a special ideological clientele, persons who have strong conservative views and support the foundation with small donations.

"Contract research" is another touchy matter. Brookings and CSIS accept a limited amount (about 15 percent of their budgets) of contract work from the government. But AEI has consistently turned down all contract work because it wants to maintain complete independence in deciding what topics to research and because it fears its research will be tainted if it agrees to accept government money.

Among the think tanks, only Brookings has a large endowment—that is, money donated to the institution with the understanding that it will be invested and only the earned interest will be used to fund current projects. Its large endowment makes Brookings virtually immune to ups and downs in other forms of giving. All of the other think tanks are trying similarly to build up a sizable endowment, but this requires time and the careful cultivation of large donors.

Support from the major foundations is also important for the think tanks, accounting for about 20 percent of their budgets. The think tanks tend to draw support from like-minded foundations according to ideological criteria: the more liberal Ford, Rockefeller, Mellon, and MacArthur foundations give mostly to Brookings and sometimes to IPS and CSIS, while the more conservative Scaife, Pew, Olin, Bradley, and Smith Richardson foundations give chiefly to AEI and Heritage. This pattern of ideologically based giving is clear, even though by their charters—to say nothing of the tax laws—the foundations are supposed to be "nonpolitical."

The biggest source of support for the think tanks is private business and business foundations. Such gifts are of course tax exempt. Upwards of 60 to 70 percent of the several think tanks' support comes from business. CSIS, AEI, and Heritage have traditionally received most of business' largesse because those are the think tanks most in accord with business' point of view. But now even the liberal Brookings is raising more and more of its money from the business sector, which is also having the effect of drawing its ideology more toward the center. IPS is antibusiness and anticapitalism, so it does not attract much support from big business, but it does get funds from some of the sons, daughters, and grandchildren of the earlier scions of industry who, although very rich, are often committed to capitalism's overthrow.

The relationship between the think tanks and big business is changing, however. First, there is an increasing tendency for business firms and foundations to designate their gifts for specific research projects rather than for general budgetary support as they had done in the past, thus muddying the distinction between contract and noncontract research. Second, the tax laws have changed, making it less attractive for companies to give money to the think tanks. And third, there is a tendency among business firms to give more money to local charities (the opera, the orchestra, parks, playgrounds, educational opportunities) and thus get back immediate credit for their generosity in their own "neighborhoods" rather than to give it to the think tanks where the returns are not so immediate or so obvious.

Above and beyond these issues is the question of bias. If so many of the think tanks are so heavily dependent on big business for such a large share of their support, doesn't that necessarily bias their research products? Money does talk, after all. And so the answer is yes, but not in blatant and obvious ways. That is, none of the larger think tanks are really lobbyists for big business, nor can business really "buy" a research result that it desires. But at the same time all the major think tanks (IPS is the exception, and it has little influence) tend to champion open, market, capitalist economies and to be suspicious of, if not in some cases hostile to, statism and central planning—all of which serves the interests of big business. While they do not lobby for specific business interests, the think tanks do refrain from criticizing big business and do provide an overall intellectual climate in which business can flourish. Indeed, one can explain the Brookings Institution's move toward the ideological center as a reflection of its efforts to attract business financial support. One could even suggest that the current absence of a major think tank on the liberal left is a reflection of the fact that such a think tank would not be able to obtain the business support necessary for its survival. That is another bias within the think tank system.

CONCLUSIONS

The analysis presented in this chapter tends to confirm the hypotheses with which we began:

1. Power in foreign policy has shifted from New York to Washington.
2. It has shifted from the Wall Street bankers and lawyers who were in the Council on Foreign Relations to the scholars and academic professionals who inhabit the think tanks.
3. It has shifted from an older to a newer generation.
4. It has shifted from middle-of-the-roaders to much more ideological and politicized analysts in the think tanks.

This last point especially deserves elaboration because it relates to a more general point raised in this book. The Council on Foreign Relations was an agency of bipartisan consensus in an earlier time, but the think tanks tend to be partisan and fragmented. They range up and down the political spectrum, from extreme left to extreme right. Hence the think tanks have become still one more set of agencies contributing to our foreign policy fragmentation and divisiveness. The point should not be exaggerated, since the several major think tanks often work together on various projects, their scholars tend to be personal as well as professional friends who attend each other's conferences, and at least among AEI, Brookings, and CSIS—the more centrist tanks—there has long been a considerable degree of consensus, especially in the foreign policy area. But at present even this may be changing. Hence we are left with a situation in which, instead of the single, bipartisan, consensual voice on foreign policy that we once had, now five major think tanks and hundreds of minor ones are competing for attention and trying to get their viewpoints across. This has led often to a more contentious, more partisan and ideological, and more fragmented and polarized foreign policy debate. The older unity has broken down and in its place has come a myriad of rival, often squabbling, voices. The think tanks have been both a reflection and a further agency of this greater divisiveness and disarray. This divisiveness will undoubtedly continue, even though under President Bush, an effort was made to recruit centrist foreign policy advisers and the influence of the Council on Foreign Relations seems once more to be on the rise.

The think tanks represent a whole new range of voices on foreign policy; in recent years they have also become very influential, providing ideas and publications as well as feeding their people directly into important government positions. At the same time their influence, while considerable, should not be exaggerated. The think tanks are only one of a great variety of sources (interest groups, political parties, and many others) that feed options, information, policy positions, and people into the United States government. Nevertheless, the think tanks have the power in some cases to alter perspectives, affect policy decisions, and exercise direct influence. They help define the boundaries of public policy debate, they offer agendas and options, they confirm changes already afoot in some areas and lead them in others, they catalyze and popularize new ideas, they help bridge the policy gaps between the executive and legislative branches and among a variety of agencies, they also bridge the gap between academic and Washington research, they are effective in formulating the position papers between administrations, and they serve to educate the media, congressional staffers, policymakers, and the general public. These are all important functions, and hence in the shifting kaleidoscope of influences that is our foreign policy, the think tanks have assumed a major role.

Suggested Readings

Destler, I.M., Leslie H. Gelb, and Anthony Lake. *Our Own Worst Enemy.* New York: Simon & Schuster, 1984.

Dickson, Paul. *Think Tanks.* New York: Athanaeum, 1971.

Easterbrook, Gregg. "Ideas Move Nations." *The Atlantic Monthly,* Jan. 1986, 66–80.

Feulner, Edwin J. *Ideas, Think Tanks and Governments.* Washington, D.C.: Heritage Foundation, 1985.

Hicks, Sallie M., et al. "Influencing the Prince: A Role for Academicians?" *Polity* 15 (Summer 1982):279–93.

Linden, Patricia. "Powerhouses of Policy," *Town and Country,* 99 Jan. 1987.

Powell, S. Steven. *Covert Cadre: Inside the Institute for Policy Studies.* Ottawa, Ill.: Green Hill, 1988.

Smith, James A. "Private Players in the Game of Nations." *The Washington Quarterly* 2 (Summer 1988):17–25.

Sundquist, James L. "Research Brokerage: The Weak Link." *Knowledge and Policy: The Uncertain Connection,* edited by Laurence E. Lynn, Jr. 126–44. Washington, D.C.: The National Academy of Science, 1978.

CHAPTER NINE

The Washington Social Circuit

✪
✪

Not all of Washington policy-making takes place within or through formal political institutions, of course. We know from our elementary reading that such institutions as political parties, interest groups, the Congress, and the presidency all have an important influence on policy, including foreign policy. These are the institutions that our laws and Constitution, as well as the introductory textbooks that we read, designate or point to as key actors in the policy-making process.

But all of us know, deep down, that the process also works through other, less formal means. The formal institutions are important, to be sure, but they are not the only way that foreign policy influence is exercised. Also important are the informal contacts, the lunch and dinner get-togethers, the social networks, the interpersonal relations, the clans, cliques, and friendships that Washingtonians maintain. Some would maintain that these informal gatherings are as important as—or even more important than—the formal institutions. We cannot here resolve that issue once and for all, but we can say that most Washington insiders tend to believe that *both* the formal institutions and the informal contacts are useful and, therefore, they take considerable pains to cultivate both.

The present chapter serves as a beginning guide to some aspects of the social scene in Washington, D.C. It contains some gossip, some travel information, and some tips about Washington social life. Some readers may feel that the treatment of these informal aspects is too breezy, reads too much like a travelogue, or treats serious subjects (foreign policy) at the level of party gossip. But in fact: (1) A great deal of *serious* foreign policy discussion *does* take place at this informal level; and (2) a great deal of Washington political life, including foreign policy, *does* revolve around gossip, interpersonal relations, as well as parties and informal get-togethers. This is not a chapter on foreign policy as it might be taught by Sally Quinn (a Washington novelist, woman-about-town, and editor of the *Washington Post*'s Style Section), but it does suggest that the Washington social circuit is far more important as a *serious* subject for discussion of how the foreign policy process works than any other text has been willing to acknowledge.

WASHINGTON, D.C., AS A CITY

For a long time, until the 1960s, Washington was considered a bit of a provincial southern capital. The real centers of power and influence in the United States were New York, Boston, Philadelphia, Chicago and, eventually, Detroit and Los Angeles; but not Washington, D.C. Washington was a small town by comparison with these others, with little to recommend it: little industry, little commerce, little banking, no stock market, limited power. In addition, the climate is terrible (steamy, muggy) in the summer; before the widespread use of air-conditioning, Washington and its institutions (Congress, the Supreme Court, the presidency) used to close down in June, flee to cooler climes, and resume again in the fall.

While Washington was a southern city, it was also a city of enormous contradictions. Washington had a large middle class, consisting chiefly of persons employed by the government or by government-related private organizations, but it also was a city of enormous poverty, with a large underclass. Some of its blacks were well off and highly educated, but Washington also had large ghettos within sight of the Capitol where homes often lacked indoor plumbing. Washington, the capital of the greatest and freest nation on earth, was also a center of grinding poverty in which over half the population was still subject to racial discrimination.

Nor did Washington have much in the way of a cultural life—no opera, one theater (the National), and a poor orchestra. However, it did have excellent chamber music and, since the 1920s, the truly great museums built along the Mall. The restaurants were not very distinguished nor was there much in the way of international cuisine. Educational excellence was also concentrated in the prestige universities of Philadelphia, New Jersey, New York, and Cambridge, not in Washington. Real money and social status were similarly concentrated in these other centers—Boston's Beacon Hill, New York's Park Avenue, Philadelphia's Main Line, Grosse Pointe outside Detroit, and Lake Forest outside Chicago. Washington was not a center of wealth or a very impressive social life. Elite social life was active but dominated by old families and less easily penetrated by newcomers and outsiders than today. And by international standards, Washington as a capital could hardly compare with London or Paris.

Even politicians did not stay in Washington any longer than they had to. They looked on Washington as a temporary assignment, not a place to live. Often they stayed in downtown hotels like the Willard or the Mayflower, and left their families in their real homes in their districts. They got out of Washington as soon and as often as possible; few thought of settling permanently in the city once their period in office was over.

But now all this has changed, making Washington one of the most attractive places to live in the entire country—if not *the* most attractive. Washington has even better museums than before and, by now, a rich cultural life. Its theater and music are outstanding. Air-conditioning has made it livable all year round. Many areas of the city feature beautiful parks and stunning architecture. Washington now has many fine restaurants; the underground Metro system is superb; and condos and apartments abound, although housing is very expensive.

There is now real wealth in Washington to rival and surpass that of other cities. The government, the think tanks, as well as the Washington universities have made it one of the nation's main centers of intellectual life—maybe the main center. Because its economy is diversified and intimately tied to government, which continued to grow even with an antigovernment conservative (Reagan) in the presidency, Washington—unlike Detroit, or Houston, for example—is virtually recession-proof. Despite these positive changes, however, Washington remains a city where there is widespread poverty, oftentimes tense race relations, a high crime rate, and social conditions that are sometimes akin to those in less-developed nations.

There is an aura of power about Washington that is especially attractive to persons interested in public policy. Washington is, after all, where government authority and decision making in the United States are concentrated. It is, in many ways, a wonderful place to live: vibrant, alive, exciting, stimulating. Every summer thousands of our best young and bright college and university graduates flock to Washington, looking for both personal advancement and an opportunity to serve. The social, intellectual and, of course, political life is virtually nonstop. The opportunities, the capacity to exercise influence, the chance to meet new friends and interact at the highest levels are enormously attractive.

Living and working in Washington give one a sense of importance and power. The White House and Capitol Hill act like magnets to the bright and the ambitious. It is a booming, vibrant, and dynamic city. It is fun to walk down the sidewalk and cross paths with persons that before one saw only on television: former Secretary of Defense Robert McNamara hurrying to work down Connecticut Avenue, ABC newsman Sam Donaldson berating his camera crew right there on the street, or a famous congressman who by chance shares an elevator ride with you.

Washington not only attracts thousands of young people every year, but more senior people have come to love the city and seldom go back to their old home districts once their appointments or terms in office are up. They find jobs as lobbyists or consultants and thus remain influential. They also serve as teachers of the young people coming in, showing them the ropes of how Washington works. Plus, with its abundant cultural life, its never-ending social life, and the rich network of opportunities for retired or out-of-office politicians and officials. Washington is a wonderful city in which to retire.

All these changes have made Washington a very attractive and seductive city that would not have been the case thirty or forty years ago. In addition, although now far more pluralistic than before, it remains a *Southern* city with the elaborate social graces, the importance of family connections, the clique and clan rivalries, and the informal ways of operating that are the focus of this chapter. The *Washington Post* understands the importance of all these social activities—it is often said that the real news in Washington is reported in the Style (or society) Section, not on the front pages; but our other great national newspaper, the *New York Times,* as well as most persons who live outside Washington, do not. The *Times* takes Washington politics deadly seriously at the policy level and in terms of the formal institutions of government, which is also where many of our early civics courses and government textbooks concentrate, but it does not cover well and often fails to understand the strenuous social life of the capital which many are convinced is just as important as the formal institutions.

INSIDE AND OUTSIDE THE BELTWAY

The Washington Beltway is a sixty-three mile, circular stretch of the interstate highway system that wraps completely around the District of Columbia. Inside the Beltway are located the White House, the Congress, the Pentagon, the State Department, virtually all other federal government agencies, as well as the headquarters of the political parties and almost all important interest groups. This is where the seat of government power in the United States is located.

But "inside the Beltway" is more than a geographic location; it is also a metaphor, a symbol, for a whole way of thinking. Washington, D.C., although now a diverse city, is the nation's political capital. Politics remains its main "industry" (that is chiefly why people go to Washington); politics is the chief subject of conversation in Washington; and for many Washingtonians, politics is an all-important and even consuming preoccupation. It is not so much literature or art or even the Redskins football team (Washington is without a major league baseball team) that people talk about in Washington but politics, politics, politics. Day or night, at work or at home, socializing or just riding to work, politics is the passion and the consuming interest.

There are endless stories, rumors, and gossip to pass around and discuss. Such political talk goes on virtually nonstop. All this constant political talk is not the main preoccupation in most of the country, where jobs, schools, family, and the local community are the main topics of conversation. But in Washington, politics is the main and almost only subject of conversation. That is, after all, what Washington people mainly do not only in their jobs but also in their lives.

People who work inside the Beltway thus have a set of understandings, jokes, stories, even a language—almost all of it focussed on politics—that is all their own. That is what being "inside the Beltway" means: being "in" on all this political gossip and information, loving it, and participating in it. People who live in other parts of the country seldom are aware of all these insider jokes and stories, nor do they care all that much. Outsiders tend to believe that things in Washington do, or ought to, work the way their textbooks, their civics classes, or the Constitution says. But persons who work inside the Beltway know better, know that it is informal or personal connections that count as much as the formal institutions. Further, they are not always willing to share this insider information with those who live outside the Beltway. The insiders prefer to maintain their own monopoly of information and thus to keep the rest of the country, so much as that is possible in our open, democratic society, somewhat in the dark. Such secrecy, they argue, helps maintain the mythology and legitimacy of the overall system. But it also helps keep outsiders out; it enhances the power of those who *do* know how the system really works, who do know all its skeletons and secret closets; and somewhat cynically we can say that it also enhances the insiders' speaker fees.

This insiders-versus-outsiders mentality breeds certain resentments. Outsiders frequently resent it when insiders keep them in the dark and refuse to give them full information. Insiders can be rude, patronizing, and condescending to outsiders. Because of these resentments, some politicians (Jimmy Carter, Ronald Reagan) choose to run *against* Washington, D.C., against the bigness, bureaucracy, and arrogance of Washington, knowing they could gain votes by this strategy. Jimmy Carter, however, maintained his hostility to Washington insiders even after his inauguration and refused to learn the ropes of how to get along in the city; it is no accident that his is usually considered a failed presidency. Reagan also ran against Washington; but once there he made his accommodation with the Washington establishment, worked and consulted with it, fit right in, and himself became a consummate Washington insider. The moral is: as a politician it is OK to run against Washington, but once you're in Washington you had better make your accommodation with its power centers and ways of doing things or yours will not be a successful administration.

Why are these considerations so important? First, Washington does not always operate strictly by law and Constitution; informal channels are also important; and to tap these channels a new president or administration must rely on Washington insiders who do know how things work. Second, to get your agenda passed, you've got to do more than just deliver formal messages to the Congress; you must socialize with them, share a bourbon at the end of the day, take time to listen to their stories, learn their personal problems and the pressures upon them. Third, a similar approach is required with the bureaucracy: you have to work with it to be successful in implementing your program, sympathize with its problems rather than just criticizing its inefficiencies, attend its functions, join the social swirl. Fourth, a successful administration also needs to cultivate the press, to be well liked, to project a favorable image—and once again socializing and becoming a Washington insider is enormously important for the success of your program. It is not by merit alone but also by the ability to get along and go along that administrations succeed or fail.

A fifth and very important reason for becoming a Washington insider and participating vigorously in the Washington social circuit is to learn new information. All those Washington parties that go on night after night (and by now, lunch after lunch and even breakfast after breakfast) are not just for the fun of it. Rather, that is where you pick up information, learn who is rising or falling in the power hierarchy, find out what kinds of pressures operate on whom, and catch up on the insider news that does not get in the papers or on the evening television broadcasts. It makes a difference to know who is falling out with whom, who is having a fight with whom and whether it's irreconcilable, who has begun a love affair with whom, who's changing to what job, who's coming to Washington and who's leaving, and what that all means. For example, if you know that a certain NBC reporter has begun an affair with a high-ranking member of the White House National Security Council staff, not only do you expect that this will probably bias her reporting but you also begin to watch her broadcasts for insider information about the White House that only her NSC friend could have provided. All this becomes grist for the Washington gossip and informal news network, providing tidbits of information that you store in the back of your head for use at some future time.

Perhaps the differences between a Washington insider and a Washington outsider can best be illustrated as follows. Outside Washington, people tend to say that the Carter administration did this or the Reagan administration did that—as if there were a monolithic, unified, single-minded administration in office. When Washington insiders hear such blanket statements, however, their eyes tend to glaze over. They want to know if it is the White House or the State Department that is the doer, if it is James Baker or Richard Cheney, which *faction* in the administration, and whether that is a sign that that faction is rising or falling in power or favor. Only a Washington insider knows all these factions, who's in them, what they stand for, and where the pressure points are. And only by being *in* Washington, on the social circuit, can one have the knowledge to know all these pressure points and, more than that, what they mean and how policy operates within and through them.

It may take a year or more (depending on the level) for a newcomer to become acclimated to this Washington social circuit, to get on the mailing and invitation lists, to learn how the system operates and who's in it, and to begin to operate effectively within it oneself. It takes time to learn the ropes, to build up one's file of phone numbers and addresses, and to acquire the expertise and knowledge that make people in Washington want to invite you to their functions.

The reverse process is much quicker, however. That is, once one leaves Washington, one loses touch with "the system" very quickly. Not only does the phone ring less and the invitations come more infrequently, but one's "inside" knowledge and understanding of how things work fades rapidly as well. Even for people with long Washington experience who do understand the system in general terms, it takes only about a month away from Washington for their understanding and analyses to begin to suffer. Once they're out of the Washington circuit, they very quickly lose touch with all the details of who's rising and who's falling. Once they leave Washington, they're cut off from the Washington information network, and their analyses and judgments reflect that cutoff. One almost *has* to attend those constant receptions and dinners to stay well informed and to remain current with what is really going on in Washington beneath the surface.

That has important implications as well for scholarship and for our understanding of how American foreign policy-making works. Many books are written on foreign policy-making by persons who have not spent adequate time in Washington. These books may cover some aspects of the process well, but they often leave one dissatisfied. They frequently lack the nuance and the understanding of the details and the informal processes that are also very important in policy-making. A more complete analysis can only come from trying to blend an understanding of the more formal aspects with more informal processes. That is our intention here.

LEVELS OF SOCIAL LIFE

Washington social life—and the political news and gossip that go with it—operates at many different levels. At the highest level are the White House state dinners, often for a visiting head of state—formal, quite stiff, often glitzy affairs. These are, of course, by invitation only, usually for sixty to one hundred persons, mainly persons of wealth and/or prominence, high government officials, and a handful of experts in the visitor's country. Such dinners may be fun once or twice because it is, after all, the White House and there is a lot of pomp and circumstance involved, and important because they may add to your knowledge about a visiting president or his country; but guarded as well and not the kind of gathering where a lot of informal conversation can go on. These are quite stylized affairs with severe limits on what one can say or do—although sometimes some of the guests may slip away for a private conversation of substance.

At the lower levels are the wine and cheese parties that college-age interns may attend. Most of these take place in private houses and apartments; but if you are a smart and ambitious intern and you work on Capitol Hill, you learn after a while which interest groups throw the best receptions and where you can get practically a full meal before you go home at night. Some interns and low-level employees on the Hill have a whole network of friends and contacts who report to each other during the day where the best receptions are going to be that evening. Sometimes congressmen as well as the lobbyists who host them also attend these events. But congressmen are persons of importance and they, of course, expect more than wine and cheese: they expect ham, roast beef, lobster, shrimp, and other niceties. Congressmen also learn which interest groups or which political action committees (PACs) put on the best spreads; the interest groups in turn learn that if they want to attract congressmen and important members of the administration to their parties, they had better make quality food and drink—and lots of it—available. Important persons are often invited to several dinners and receptions every day; hence they can afford to choose carefully among the invitations, or try to put in a brief, "political" (handshaking) appearance at several functions.

The Washington social circuit is important not only for its good food and drink (the "lubricators") but also for the rich information and gossip that are exchanged there. It is on the social circuit that you catch up with the news of the day, find out who's doing in whom, exchange ideas and impressions, establish new interpersonal relationships as well as cementing old ones, talk about programs as well as personalities, discuss how programs are faring in the Congress, hear about the latest administration moves or appointments. This is also where new books are discussed, ideas evaluated, and personalities dissected. All this is essential information that every Washington mover and shaker must have. Hence everyone who is anyone or wants to become someone *must* attend—whether such a vigorous social life is your cup of tea or not—because that is where the action is and because you know that if you're not there, your rivals and competitors will be. And as a result, they will be better informed than you.

Most of Washington social life thus takes place somewhere between the high-level glitter of the White House and the down-'n'-out reception with wine and cheese. It is important to remember that the kind of hosts is also changing, which similarly tells us something about Washington and the organization of power there. The analysis that follows is thus not meant simply as a set of social tips but, more importantly, as an analysis of the levels of social life, what goes on there, and how these relate to the informal channels of foreign policy.

First, let us focus on the institutions that are becoming *less* important. These are often the kinds of gatherings portrayed in movies made by producers who don't know or understand Washington. For example, embassy cocktail parties are on the way down. The embassies often have lavish food and parties (especially the Middle Eastern and some Latin American countries); but they are seen as stiff and formal and, except for a few embassies (British, French) and a few occasions, they are not viewed as places of lively conversations. These are often large and sometimes noisy affairs; but some news may be exchanged in a brief encounter, and the important guests may at times slip away to a private room for further conversation.

Washington's famed hostesses have also largely faded away. These were usually wealthy women (the stereotype is Perle Mesta), often widows of important persons, who had the money, the servants, and the large houses that enabled them to throw elaborate dinner parties for several score of persons. Such hostesses thrived in an earlier era (the 1950s) when Washington was still a small town and all of its important people could be fitted into one party. But the big-time hostesses have died or "retired," the town has changed (no longer can all its movers and shakers fit into one room), few persons have servants or mansions anymore, and no longer do such gatherings attract many of the city's real powerhouses.

The famed Georgetown dinner party is also in decline. It has not disappeared and never will, but there are far fewer than there used to be. Many Washington people still entertain at intimate dinner parties (no longer necessarily in Georgetown; wealth has spread to the suburbs), but seldom at the pace of once a week or once a month as in earlier times. The size is now eight or ten people (what most dining rooms will hold) rather than twenty or more as in the past; it costs a great deal to have even that many people over on a frequent basis; spouses are unwilling or unable to spend two days cooking and cleaning in preparation; maids and cooks are in very short supply; caterers are very expensive; and most persons are too busy to do this more than a few times a year. It should be said that at very wealthy and high-prestige levels (the cabinet or agency heads), such small and intimate dinner parties are more frequent since these people have both money and "help"; but among the majority of upper-middle-class persons who have important positions in Washington, the "Georgetown" dinner party is no longer an everyday or every week event.

Another reason for the decline in importance of the private George-town dinner party is that the ten or so most important foreign policy "wise men" who could be expected to gather at one of these dinners are no longer around. Up through the 1950s American foreign policy was dominated by a handful of experienced persons with vast backgrounds abroad and who knew each other well: Dean Acheson, George Kennan, Robert Lovett, Charles "Chip" Bohlen, John J. McCloy, Llewellen Thompson, Averill Harriman, and a few others. The nation's foreign policy expertise could not only all be gathered in one room but literally at one dinner table.

But now this has changed as well. Along with the Washington hostesses, this older generation of foreign policy generalists has passed from the scene. Foreign policy knowledge has become so detailed and specialized that it is impossible now for a half-dozen men to hold it all in their grasp. Specialized knowledge as well as the elaboration of a broad framework of foreign policy has passed to the think tanks and the executive agencies. And all these persons cannot be included in a single Georgetown dinner party as was the case with the smaller corps of generalists in the old days.

Nor have government agencies picked up the slack. In the age of Gramm-Rudman budget restraints, the agencies do not have a lot of surplus funds, and among the first items to be cut are their entertainment budgets. The State Department is especially known for its cheapness. At the conferences it hosts, guests must go out and buy their own coffee and doughnuts as well as their own lunches. When the State Department hosts a reception, someone else—usually a private interest organization—must usually pay for it. Nor do the CIA and Defense Department entertain lavishly, although they do at least provide coffee and doughnuts to their conference participants—and sometimes even lunch.

As individual entertaining has declined, institutional entertaining has increased. That is in fact where most of Washington's social life now takes place. It is no longer in the homes of the few or the wealthy but in and among some of the new Washington institutions. Here we have in mind Washington-based interest groups who, to get their message across effectively, do a lot of entertaining; the think tanks, who also have a message to deliver; the PACs; and such research cum action agencies as the Carnegie Endowment for International Peace and the Council on Foreign Relations.

One or another of these agencies holds a reception, a dinner, a sit-down lunch, or a breakfast virtually every day. They bring together persons from the think tanks, from the administration, congressmen and their legislative assistants, lobbyists, media people. What attracts these people is not just good food and drink but usually a presentation by a high-level policymaker, the launching of a new book or research project, a seminar or conference, or the visit of a foreign dignitary. In other words, Washington social life is intimately tied to political and policy discussions. That is what makes Washington go around: good entertainment *and* policy discussions and ideas. Just as these agencies (think tanks, PACs, research organizations, lobbying agencies) have become among the major new actors in the city's political life, they have also become the primary centers of social life. Moreover, with the cost of food and drink to entertain lavishly so high, only institutions (no longer individuals) can afford to put on these sorts of meetings. The power structure in Washington has changed since the 1960s, and so has its entertainment.

What happens at these events? First, there is usually a social hour or half hour. That is where you greet your friends, have a drink, and start to catch up on the news. Then usually there is a speaker, or a panel of persons dealing with a certain subject—for example, NATO or United States policy in the Middle East. That is often followed by dinner and more chance to converse informally. Then comes a period of questions and discussion. If it is a dinner meeting, it will usually begin at six o'clock and be over by nine o'clock. And remember, this goes on virtually every single night.

Who comes to these meetings? They are almost always by invitation only. But new members are also welcome and brought in if they are occupying positions of influence in Washington. Power, position, and influence are what count, not family background or social position. The guest lists usually include persons from the government, congressmen, ambassadors and State Department officials, former presidential candidates (George McGovern, John Anderson, and Walter Mondale are regulars on the circuit), scholars and think tank personnel, lobbyists of various kinds, and journalists. It is a diverse group but often very high level, made up of highly intelligent and experienced persons, whose discussion tends to be factual and noninflammatory rather than intensely ideological. Washington insiders quickly learn, despite their political or ideological disagreements, to get along with persons of all points of view and not to insult them, because the person you insult one day may be the same person you need a favor from, or will have to work with, the next. In Figure 9.1 we have included a list of persons attending one of these gatherings to illustrate the program and the affiliations of the participants.

Figure 9.1
An Example of Institutional Entertaining

Carnegie Endowment for International Peace
FACE-TO-FACE DINNER DISCUSSION
DECEMBER 8, 1988

SUBJECT: Prospects for Pluralistic Democracy in Mexico

SPEAKER: Mr. Cuauhtémoc Cárdenas
                       Party of the Democratic Revolution

GUESTS: Mr. Frederico Heroles
                       National University of Mexico

                       Mr. Sture Graffman Huburech
                       Advisor to Mr. Cárdenas

PARTICIPANTS:

Nancy Agris   John Allen
House Subcommittee on Western   Central Intelligence Agency
Hemisphere Affairs
                                     Bernard Aronson
Adolfo Aguilar   The Policy Project
Carnegie Endowment

Peter Askin
Agency for International Development

W. Tapley Bennett
Ambassador

Lawrence Berlin
University of Pennsylvania

Larry Birns
Council on Hemispheric Affairs

Pat Breslin
Inter-American Foundation

Morris Busby
Department of State (S/SE)

Samuel Campos
Campolo News Service

Cynthia Carlisle
Overseas Development Council

Michael Casella
U.S. Department of Commerce

Sara Castro-Klaren
Johns Hopkins University

Christina Cerna
Inter-American Committee on
Human Rights/OAS

Foster Collins
Yale University

Stephen Cooney
National Association of Manufacturers

Michael Czinkota
U.S. Department of Commerce

Judith Davison
Joint Economic Committee

Richard Deutsch
Voice of America

Dorothy Dillon
Consultant

Betty Dukert
Meet the Press

Raymond Duncan
State University of New York

Arthur Endres, Jr.
House Judiciary Committee

Patricia Weiss Fagen
UN High Commissioner for Refugees

Ava Feiner
Consultant

Robert Fisk
Attorney

Kenneth Flamm
Brookings Institution

Jonathan Fredman
Attorney

Alfred Friendly
World Bank

Anne Greene

Margaret Daly Hayes
Inter-American Development Bank

Roger Hickey
Economic Policy Institute

Anne Howard
Anne L. Howard & Associates

Benjamin Huberman
Consultants International Group

Thomas Hughes
President, Carnegie Endowment

Lars Hydle
Open Forum

Frederick Jasperson
World Bank

Victor Johnson
House Subcommittee on Western
Hemisphere Affairs

Michael Johnson
Office of the House Minority Leader

William Knepper
Council of the Americas

Jennifer LeBrecque
Face-to-Face

Brian Latell
National Intelligence Council

Robert Leiken
Harvard University

Jerome Levinson
Inter-American Development Bank

Louise Leif
U.S. News & World Report

George Lister
Department of State (HA)

Jane Lowenthal
Carnegie Endowment

Milton Lower
Economic Policy Institute

Kate Lusheck
Face-to-Face

Alan Madian
Erb & Madian

Edward Marasciulo
Pan-American Development
Foundation

Richard Marshall
U.S. Information Agency

James Matlack
American Friends Service Committee

Gary Matthews
Kiplinger Washington Editors

Doris Meissner
Carnegie Endowment

Joanna Mendelson
The American University

Carl Migdail
Free-Lance Writer

Irving Mintzer
World Resources Institute

Edward P. Morgan
In the Public Interest

Wilson Morris
Office of the Speaker

Geoffrey Pyatt
Inter-American Dialogue

Stephen Quick
Joint Economic Committee

Thomas Quigley
U.S. Catholic Conference

Patricia Ravalgi
Council on Foreign Relations

Adelina Reyes-Gavilan
National Endowment for Democracy

Charles Robb
Hunton & Williams

Martin Roeber
Central Intelligence Agency

William Rogers
Arnold & Porter

Richard Solomon
Department of State (S/P)

Daniel Stein
Federation for American
Immigration Reform

K. Larry Storrs
Congressional Research Service

Peter Swiers
Director, Face-to-Face

Deborah Szekely
Inter-American Foundation

Frank Tapporo
Office of the Secretary of Defense

Margaret Thompson
National Republican Institute
for International Affairs

Irene Tinker
The American University

Terence Todman
Department of State (EUR/NE)

Irving Tragen
Organization of American States

Melville Ulmer
University of Maryland

Viron Vaky
Carnegie Endowment

Robert Vickers
Central Intelligence Agency

Elizabeth Weiner
Business Week

Allen Weinstein
Center for Democracy

Patricia Weir
House Subcommittee on Western
Hemisphere Affairs

Howard Wiarda
American Enterprise Institute

David Williams
Council on Hemispheric Affairs

James Wilson

Maurice Wolf
Wolf, Arnold & Cardoso, P.C.

Clay Woods
U.S. Department of Commerce

Robert Zimmerman
Consultant

Even though the United States is a large country and Washington a big city, the actual number of movers and shakers in various policy fields is quite small. Everyone who counts almost literally knows everyone else who counts. For example, in the areas of Middle Eastern or Latin American affairs, it is probably the case that the number of key policy influentials in each area is no more than sixty or seventy persons. These lists of area specialists often overlap the ranks of overall foreign policy generalists in Washington who have influence, whose number is probably not more than five hundred. That is a very small number. It means also that through these frequent social gatherings the members of the foreign policy community in Washington get to know each other very well. It is also from these ranks that the foreign policy personnel of the next administration—whatever the party—are likely to come.

These considerations return us to the broad purposes of all this social life. It is not just food, drink, gossip, and the exchange of ideas. Other important purposes are also served. For example, in these frequent informal gatherings bad ideas are often winnowed out from good ones, and solid and sensible personnel from the opposite kind. A political process is at work here by which the Washington foreign policy community sorts out people as well as programs. Persons who regularly attend these get-togethers know who would be a good person in what key government positions and who not, what ideas will work and what not. That is why when a new administration (Carter or Reagan) comes to power after having run against Washington, and brings with it foreign policy advisers whom the Washington community does not know, Washington starts to shudder. Neither these people nor their policies have gone through the Washington winnowing process. Thus, we are likely to get all manner of inexperienced people with some "nutty" ideas—and we usually do, to the detriment of our foreign policy.

The Washington foreign policy community can be seen as an "establishment." It is centered in the think tanks, the interest groups, the journalistic community, the research agencies, and the Council on Foreign Relations as well as in the government itself. Since it is an establishment, that breeds resentment on the part of those who are not members of it. On the other hand, it is not a closed establishment and is always open to new members and new ideas. But in the winnowing process we have described, this establishment does tend to force policy back toward the middle of the road. Individuals with highly partisan or ideological points of view tend to have to compromise with those whose assumptions are different, and the result is a tendency toward centrism in foreign policy. It is no accident that both Carter and Reagan started off with very ideological administrations (one on the left, the other on the right) but eventually—as this foreign policy establishment reasserted itself—gravitated toward the center. Democratic politics, we have seen, is almost by definition centrist politics. By pushing foreign policy back toward the middle while also being open to new ideas, this foreign policy establishment and its web of informal interconnections perform a useful service.

WASHINGTON "FRIENDSHIPS"

If you want a friend in Washington, you should buy a dog, or so says an old adage.

Washington is a city of fickle tastes, of fleeting friendships, and of passing policy preoccupations. South Africa is "it" one day, Central America the next, the Middle East the third, then Japan, NATO, China, or the Soviet Union. In addition, Washington is a city of recent arrivals: few people have deep roots there or strong family ties. Most people are newcomers to Washington who migrated to the city because a job, a cause, or a political campaign brought them there. Washington is not usually where you grew up, where your strongest friendships are, where your family is, or where people accept you (warts and all) just because you are you.

Washington is a friendly city, a Southern city, a city of often gracious hospitality; but friendships there tend to be based more on your political position than on anything else. You are important for the power and position that you hold, not necessarily for your intrinsic worth as an individual. That means that friendships tend to be temporary, politically connected, and usually short-lived.

This is disconcerting to many Washington newcomers who are used to the warmth, serenity, and permanence of *real* friendships. Such newcomers, if they are elected or appointed to important positions, are often lionized at first, leading them to believe that they have many "good" friends. They are flattered, invited out to dinner often, cultivated by the press, and played up to by other persons. What such newcomers forget is that in Washington such expressions of friendship are more political than personal. People make friends with you because of the important position that you hold or the influence you are thought to wield, and not always because people genuinely like you. They like you because you are important and they need or want to get something from you—or simply to get along with you out of necessity. Genuine friendship, however, is very rare.

The acid test of real friendship in Washington comes when you fall from or lose power. *Then,* count the number of friends you have, the calls you receive, the number of persons who flatter you, the amount of attention you are paid. The answer is: almost none. Because as soon as you leave, another person will fill your position and that person will begin receiving all the attention. Once again it is the position that is all-important, not so much the person occupying it. True friends are those who still call after you've fallen or are on the outs; but in Washington, D.C., with its emphasis on position more than person, such friendships are rare indeed.

Now this is not an altogether bad system—as long as one knows ahead of time what the givens are. But many Washington newcomers mistake the flattery that comes with their new position for genuine friendship, and they often turn bitter toward former colleagues who do not call them any more once they no longer occupy their old posts. If one understands the givens ahead of time, however, one can avoid the bitterness that ensues after a political friendship has gone by the boards. One simply comes to accept the fact that some friendships are real, some are political, and the two types should not be confused.

OTHER CHANNELS

In addition to the parties, social circuits, and informal channels already mentioned, several other channels of influence need to be noted here. Few of these have received the scholarly attention that they deserve, but their importance makes it necessary for us to discuss them briefly even in the absence of detailed information.

One of the most important of these new influences is the large Washington law firm. Many of these firms now are home to several *hundred* lawyers (the three- or four-person partnership has largely gone by the boards) and have branches in several American cities and abroad. The fees for these Washington firms are very high, and the firm's business may exceed $100 million yearly. These are big outfits with major influence, doing important work. As the United States in recent decades has become a more legalistic and litigious nation, and as our legislation and regulations have become more complex, the role of these large firms has grown enormously. Many have clients (including governments) abroad, which means they tend to become lobbyists as well as counselors. In fact, that is one of the new features of Washington that is worth further study: the merger of lobbying and legal activities within the same gigantic firm. In one recent notorious case, for example, the law firm of Arnold and Porter took the lead in trying to arrange the overthrow of General Manuel Noriega in Panama; sometimes the firm worked with the United States government, but at other times it went ahead on its own. Most large Washington law firms, however, try to wield their considerable influence quietly and behind the scenes rather than so up front.

American (and sometimes foreign-based) interest groups are a second major informal influence. As we saw in Chapter 6, virtually every American interest group worth its salt now has a Washington office. In addition, most foreign governments have both law firms and public relations agencies to represent them. Some of these are large organizations employing scores of persons and, as indicated, often overlapping in many complex ways with the large Washington law firms. The fact that these interest groups now concentrate far more strongly than before on foreign policy issues reflects the growing interdependence of the United States with other nations. Representatives of these interest groups prowl the corridors of Congress and the executive agencies, keeping track of legislation as well as new regulatory rules and interpretations that affect their or their clients' interests. Oftentimes these interest groups are better informed than the congressmen or executive agency personnel who are supposed to keep tabs on them, and between them and their regulators a complex, symbiotic relationship has grown up. An "iron triangle" connects the interest groups, executive agencies, and congressional subcommittees. The interest groups want and require government help, while the government could not well function without these groups' expertise. Many areas of public life have thus been "privatized," while numerous private activities are carried out in conjunction with public agencies. In these ways the public and the private domains have often merged. The results of this "corporatization" of the American polity are not yet certain, but of the increasingly important role of these interest groups there should be no doubt.[1]

A third category of informal power wielders is individual operators who know Washington intimately and have a knack for getting things done, for making the wheels turn. Examples include Clark Clifford, the debonair lawyer who has served virtually every president since Truman; Robert Strauss, a Texas entrepreneur, lawyer, and consummate wheeler-dealer; and Joseph Califano, a former cabinet member under Lyndon Johnson. These men are power brokers: when their (usually high-priced) clients have a problem, they know whom to call, what buttons to press, how to get the bureaucracy to move and take action. Usually these individual power brokers are lawyers, lobbyists, ex-campaign chairs, and former high-ranking government officials—or all of these at once. They know how to "fix" things; they maintain good connections in the press and in government; and they have friends in all the important agencies whom they can turn to for assistance.

The fourth category of informal influences to be mentioned here is a catchall category. It includes patronage networks, usually government officials who brought their own former students or underlings into government with them and who maintain contact with them in the form of a system of ongoing interpersonal relationships even after they leave office.

It includes alumni associations, such as the University of Michigan Alumni Association, which was particularly strong and active when one of its own, Gerald Ford, was president. And it includes other networks: women's networks, old school ties, political networks, religious connections, ethnic linkages, and the vast web of associations that is so much at the heart of American pluralist democracy.

IN FRONT OF AND BEHIND THE CURTAIN

Most Americans understand the role of the formal institutions in American politics, what the Constitution says, and the role of the president, Congress, and the political parties. Often more vaguely, they also understand that there are interest groups "out there" that similarly play a role. What is often completely unknown to outsiders, however, is the role of informal, interpersonal connections and of the Washington social circuit. These influences are not often reported on, they are the hardest to learn about, and many Americans are unaware of their vast importance. For, as emphasized here, all these social gatherings are not just fun and games; they are intimately a part of the broader political process. As Max Friedersdorf, a former legislative assistant in the Reagan administration, once put it, "You have to go to parties to stay informed."

The image that should be used to try to understand Washington policy-making is that of a stage in a theater production. In front of the curtain is what we all see: the actors (president, Congress, parties, and so forth) carrying out their roles, publicly, visibly, according to the script (the Constitution). But behind the curtain, backstage, all kinds of other things are also going on: stage hands and production managers running around, improvisation as some of the actors forget or botch their lines, informal meetings by some of the actors who are temporarily offstage, advance meetings with or phone conversations to reviewers and critics. What goes on behind the curtain is often not at all the same as what the public sees in front of it.

So with Washington policy-making. What goes on in front of the curtain is visible, public, plain for all to see. But behind the curtain may lie an even vaster range of activities: plots and counterplots, endless telephone calls, private meetings upon private meeting, snippets of usually incomplete information filtering in, and all kinds of personal and political considerations and networks coming into play. In all this, the Washington social circuit plays a major role, for it allows policymakers to unwind at the end of the day, catch up on the latest news, exchange stories and gossip, hear some new ideas, size up people and policies, forge new coalitions or cement old ones. The president's life is too public for him to engage in all these activities, but his aides certainly do—and virtually every day. In this way the Washington social circuit, which remains almost completely un- studied in the political science and foreign policy literature, begins to acquire an importance that rivals—and maybe even surpasses—that of the formal institutions with which we are far more familiar.

Notes

1. "Corporatization" here means the incorporation of the private interest groups into the public or governmental structures, by formal or informal means, so that the private and the public domains become virtually inseparable. For more on this subject, see Gerhard Lehmbruch and Philippe C. Schmitter, eds., *Patterns of Corporalist Policy-Making* (Beverly Hills, Calif.: Sage Publications, 1982).

Suggested Readings

Alsop, Stewart. *The Center.* New York: Harper & Row, 1968.

Berne, Eric. *Games People Play.* New York: Ballantine, 1964.

Broder, David. *Behind the Front Page.* New York: Simon & Schuster, 1987.

Brzezinski, Zbigniew. *Power and Principle.* New York: Farrar, Straus, & Giroux, 1983.

Cannon, Lou. *Reagan.* New York: Putnam, 1982.

Cater, Douglass. *Power in Washington.* New York: Random House, 1964.

Fiorina, Morris P. *The Keystone of the Washington Establishment.* New Haven, Conn.: Yale University Press, 1977.

Gotlieb, Sondra. *Wife of. . . .* Washington, D.C.: Acropolis Books, 1985.

Haig, Alexander M., Jr., *Caveat.* New York: Macmillan, 1984.

Hess, Stephen. *The Ultimate Insiders.* Washington, D.C.: Brookings Institution, 1986.

Macpherson, Myra. *The Power Lovers.* New York: Ballantine Books, 1975.

Peters, Charles. *How Washington Really Works.* Reading, Mass.: Addison-Wesley, 1981.

Quinn, Sally. *Regrets Only.* New York: Ballantine Books, 1987.

Reed, Julia. "The New American Establishment." *U.S. News and World Report* 8 Feb. 1988.

Sabato, Larry. *The Rise of Political Consultants.* New York: Basic Books, 1981.

————. *PAC Power.* New York: Norton, 1984.

Smith, Hedrick. *The Power Game.* New York: Random House, 1988.

Stockman, David. *The Triumph of Politics.* New York: Harper & Row, 1986.

Weatherford, J. McIver. *The Tribes on the Hill.* New York: Rawson Wade, 1981.

Witcover, Jules, and Jack Germond. *Blue Smoke and Mirrors.* New York: Viking, 1981.

Young, James Sterling. *The Washington Community.* New York: Columbia University Press, 1968.

CHAPTER TEN

Congress and Foreign Policy

❂
❂

With this chapter we begin to look at the actual institutions (Congress; the president and the National Security Council; the executive departments of State, Defense, and Treasury; the CIA and others) of the United States government that are responsible for foreign policy. Moreover, in this chapter we move from those groups and interests that *influence* policy to those institutions that actually make policy. Having previously examined the background, context, and sociopolitical influences over policy, we now move to an analysis of the actual decision-making process itself. We are thus moving to the heart of the foreign policy-making system.

In terms of the two metaphors, the funnel and the concentric circles, with which we began this book and that we have used for organizational purposes, we are also moving along. At this point, our funnel of foreign policy-making influences narrows considerably; in terms of the series of concentric circles, it is also clear that we are now getting very close to the center. For in treating the Congress, we are dealing with only 535 persons (435 in the House of Representatives, 100 in the Senate). That number is considerably augmented if we also include the mushrooming congressional staffs, now totaling about 15,000 persons, some of whom are more influential even than the congressmen for whom they ostensibly work. The tremendous growth of congressional staff—and its important implications—is a theme to which we return later in the chapter. Nevertheless, it is still the case that we are now dealing with a smaller number of persons of influence, and that Congress is one of the places in the United States system in which foreign policy decisions are actually hammered out and made.

WHO'S IN CHARGE OF FOREIGN POLICY?

In the last twenty years, Congress has moved aggressively to play a larger role in foreign policy. The causes of this new congressional aggressiveness are complex (and explored in detail below), but of the fact that Congress is playing a greater role there can be no doubt. First, during the

1970s Congress moved on a variety of fronts to check and curb presidential authority and independence in foreign policy; then in the 1980s Congress began to move to a position of virtually coequal status with the president on foreign policy; and finally, in the case of United States policy toward Nicaragua, the Congress staged what could almost be called a takeover of a part of the running of American foreign policy for itself. Because Congress likes to play such a larger foreign policy role, and because its position as a major foreign policy actor has now been institutionalized in law and practice, it seems unlikely that we will soon go back to the older system of congressional quiescence in foreign policy.

While Congress has undoubtedly helped to democratize our foreign policy in various ways, serious questions remain as to whether we can have an effective foreign policy run on that basis and whether it is appropriate for Congress to play such a strong foreign policy role, to the extent of trying literally to micromanage virtually every aspect of policy. Here are some of the key questions that arise out of the new assertiveness of Congress in foreign policy and that run through the discussion in this chapter:

1. Can we really have a foreign policy run by a "committee" of 535 persons, without the central direction and coherence that only the executive branch can provide?
2. Will not a foreign policy run by Congress lead to a situation in which we have almost literally 535 secretaries of state, with all the fragmentation and incoherence that provides?
3. Congress is a highly partisan body, even the embodiment of partisanship in the American system; won't such a body inevitably politicize our foreign policy in inappropriate ways?
4. Congress is fickle in its attention spans, it follows the headlines in its concern with foreign policy issues, and its membership turns over every two years; how can we have any constancy and continuity in our foreign policy if Congress continues to play such a large role?
5. Is Congress institutionally equipped to run our foreign policy and what will be the consequences of a too-strong congressional role?
6. What then should be the proper role of Congress in our foreign policy-making?

These are the troubling questions with which we begin and that run through our discussion of Congress and foreign policy.

CONGRESS AND PRESIDENT: AN INVITATION TO STRUGGLE

In actuality, the situation that prevailed immediately after World War II, in which the president took the definitive lead in foreign policy and the Congress generally ratified his decisions, is unusual in American history.

The postwar executive dominance in foreign policy grew out of the cold war with the Soviet Union; out of the emergency situations in Greece, Berlin, Iran, China, and Eastern Europe right after the war; and out of the sense, which Congress shared, that in this era of instant communications as well as the potential for instant missiles and instant nuclear war, only the president had sufficient information and authority to make the quick decisions that foreign policy now called for. But it should be remembered that this era of executive dominance in foreign policy—except, of course, in wartime, when the president always was expected to take charge—was the exception rather than the rule in our history.

The Congress has long played an important role in American foreign policy. The debates in Congress over foreign policy have been spirited and rambunctious because these issues do after all affect the fate and future of the nation. Throughout our history, Congress has often questioned the president, thrown roadblocks in his way, and frustrated his designs. In the past, such congressional involvement in foreign policy matters could be tolerated because the stakes were low and American security was shielded from the major conflicts by thousands of miles of protective oceans. When war broke out, of course, Congress tended to close ranks and rally around the president, looking to him to provide leadership, and generally curtailing its criticism.

That is what made the cold war era so different, for the cold war was a condition of almost permanent conflict and crisis that seemed to demand permanent presidential leadership. Congress chafed sometimes, but it did not really challenge the president—until recently. These new challenges arose both out of a distrust of presidential leadership since Vietnam and, more recently, out of the sense that the cold war was virtually over and, therefore, there was no longer such a strong need for the Congress to defer to presidential authority. So now we are back to the position in which we have often been in American history, a position of conflict between the Congress and the White House over foreign policy, but in an era of continuing foreign policy crises it is still not clear if we can afford all the wasted time, conflict, and partisan bickering and posturing to which this rivalry gives rise. Our celebrated checks and balances seem to be producing deadlock, not effective government.

The roots of this conflict between congressional and executive leadership in foreign policy of course go back to the Constitution. The president is the commander in chief, but only the Congress has the power to declare war. Are the sending of troops to Lebanon, the fleet to the Persian Gulf, or military trainers to El Salvador therefore acts of war that require congressional approval? Or do they lie within the realm of presidential discretion? Therein lie some of the great controversies of our day. Similarly, the president may negotiate treaties but, by the Constitution, the Senate must approve them. What, therefore, of "executive agreements" that take the form of treaties—must they also have Senate approval? Again, the president

"Unfortunately, our hands are tied. Congress won't let us take part in any covert operations that will risk global annihilation."

appoints top-ranking foreign policy personnel, including ambassadors, but the Senate must approve those. What if the Senate, or an individual senator, holds them up for a while—or even permanently? The president is charged by the Constitution with being responsible for foreign policy, but of course Congress has power over the purse and is in charge of appropriations; and the simple fact is that without money for foreign aid, an adequate State Department budget, or sufficient funds for the Defense Department or the CIA, we cannot have much in the way of a foreign policy.

The United States Constitution contains such a complex system of checks and balances, and many of its articles are sufficiently vague, that it is impossible to say definitively who is in charge of foreign policy. Plus, the relations between Congress and the presidency may vary over time, depending on a president's mandate and popularity, the national mood, the reputation of Congress, the individuals involved, as well as foreign circumstances. What we can say about the Constitution, therefore, is that it provides an "invitation to struggle" to both the legislative and executive branches, without itself resolving the issues or stating definitively where final power in foreign policy-making lies. There has been, is, and always will be tension between the Congress and the president over foreign policy. Such tension and conflict should be looked on as the norm and not the exception.

So we will just have to live with the fact that United States foreign policy will always be less coherent, less unified, less consistent, more conflict prone than the foreign policies of most of our allies who have different kinds of political systems. The uneasy relationship, even rivalry, between the Congress and the White House will go on, since it is built into our system of government, our checks and balances. There will always be competition and conflict between the two because the Founding Fathers wanted it that way. Hence the disputes that arise between them can only be resolved in the political process through elections and interest group struggles and changes in national political sentiment. Such imprecision and vagueness may leave some of us uncomfortable, but that is the nature of the American system and it is precisely what the designers of the Constitution had in mind. Since we cannot do much to change these things, we will just have to cope with and work through the system we have, however inefficient and sloppy that system sometimes is.

CONGRESS: POLITICS, AND PARTISANSHIP

In Chapter 7 we saw that political parties in the United States have not played the same important role that parties play in Western Europe, and that their functions—other than the electoral one—are quite limited. The fact that American political party organizations are weak, ephemeral, and fluid, have not sunk their roots or functions deep into the American psyche or consciousness, perform few activities (most of which we could just as soon do without), and have played only a very limited international role—all this leaves us unprepared for the importance of political parties and partisanship in Washington, D.C. In the nation's capital, political parties and partisanship are a big thing—in ways that they are not in the rest of the country. Here parties matter. Votes are often decided along strictly partisan lines; appointments to key positions are determined on the basis of party affiliations and loyalty; friendships and allegiances are often made along party lines; witnesses at congressional hearings are chosen on the basis of the party "lines" they will present—and all this partisanship frequently at the expense of merit considerations or achieving a truly sensible, reasonable, and bipartisan foreign policy position. The rest of the country may think that parties are in decline and have limited functions, and that excessive partisanship is strange and not a little bit silly; but in Washington, party affiliation and a strong commitment to partisan positions are what get you ahead in politics. Congress is the embodiment of this partisan spirit.

Academic experts and others who are called to testify before Congress and who spend a lot of time preparing a balanced statement, for example, soon discover that the congressmen are not always interested in a balanced statement. They want a partisan statement, a club that they can use to beat over the head members of the other party. Congressmen are like the admiral quoted in Chapter 8: they already know the answers, know what they want. They want arguments that reinforce their own point of view, rationalizations for a decision already made that they can use to justify their own positions or to attack those of their opponents. Except in rare situations, a careful, balanced, nonpartisan position paper will leave them cold, quizzical, and inclined to let the paper sink into oblivion—grist for the term papers of the student interns who inhabit these hearing rooms, but with little real effect on policy.

Readers are asked to recall the discussion at the beginning of the book regarding "rational actor" and "political" models of decision making. Probably most of us are willing to acknowledge that politics plays a part in foreign policy decisions. But we would still much prefer the process implied in the rational actor model, and we still do not like to admit that politics—not rational calculation, merit, or the best and most compelling arguments—is often the determining factor, having far greater importance than we are prepared to acknowledge. That is in fact one of the main themes of this chapter: how politics has come to overwhelm sensible and rational calculations of the national interest—to the detriment of our foreign policy. Politics is not just a factor; in some cases, it is *everything*.

Let us demonstrate this axiom by focusing on the general question of why congressmen vote the way they do. The answer may be surprising to some readers, an answer that is well documented in the political science literature. As a political scientist, this author is not sure how much "scientific" certainty political science has contributed to the world; but on this issue, the evidence is overwhelming. That is, when you hold all other factors that might be thought of as explaining congressional voting constant—the party of the congressmen, their religion, whether their districts are rural or urban, their gender, and so forth—there is one factor that explains voting behavior better than any other, and that factor is the desire to be reelected. In other words, among all the factors that help explain why congressmen vote the way they do, voting to ensure their own reelection is a more powerful explanatory factor than any other. If we keep this fact firmly in mind, it goes a long way toward explaining the troubles of American foreign policy.

A few examples of how this works will be instructive. When Jimmy Carter was trying to get the Panama Canal Treaty, which turned over control of the canal to Panama in the year 1999, through the Congress—usually cited as the major foreign policy accomplishment of Carter's presidency—the administration discovered that it was only a handful of votes short. Usually only the Senate must ratify treaties (by a two-thirds vote); but in this case, because United States territory (the Canal Zone) and other issues were involved, the House of Representatives determined that its approval was also necessary. It was not logical, rational argument regarding the merits of the treaty that won over the few additional congressmen. Rather it was a presidential promise of vast federal spending in their states and districts that secured their votes, plus the promise that these congressmen would vote for President Carter's bill if he would support their pet projects later on—projects that had nothing whatsoever to do with Panama. In short, a deal was struck: the congressmen supported the President on Panama even though they knew little and cared even less about the Canal treaties, and he in turn supported them on something else. Votes were simply bought and sold (not literally for money, of course) on a strictly "you scratch my back and I'll scratch yours" basis. Merit and rational argument had virtually nothing to do with explaining how the Panama Canal treaty was ratified by the Congress.

Let us take another example. In 1982–83 the debate over United States policy in El Salvador was waxing hot and heavy. The Reagan administration was arguing in favor of both economic and military aid to the country as a way of preventing a Communist takeover, while the Democratic opposition, under pressure from religious and human rights groups (see Chapter 6), wished to restrict aid until El Salvador improved its human rights situation. President Reagan then went on national television to bring his case to the American public, but the real message—directed at Congress—was contained in the speech's last two paragraphs. We in the White House have a long memory, he said, and we keep track of every congressman's vote. If you in the Congress vote against my aid package and El Salvador falls to the guerrillas, we will not hesitate to use that against you in your next election campaign. We will brand you as "the congressman who lost El Salvador." For congressmen who want above all else to be reelected, that was a very serious threat indeed. Many congressmen switched quickly and President Reagan's bill passed easily—again on a basis that had little to do with the country under question but everything to do with reelection considerations.

But then the Congress and House Speaker Thomas P. ("Tip") O'Neill turned the tables on the president. It voted just enough aid to comply with the request for assistance to El Salvador, but not enough to win the war. In effect the Congress said to the president, "OK, Mr. President, we've voted for your aid, so you can no longer blame us politically for 'losing' El

Salvador. But since we voted for your aid, now it's your war to win or lose, Mr. President. And if you lose it, then we won't hesitate to use that fact against you when *you* run for reelection." In short, the Congress now put the president up to his neck in the political quagmire that is El Salvador and told him to either swim or sink. Where El Salvador or the reality of the conditions prevailing there ever fit into this dispute was not entirely clear. What occurred was hardball politics between a Republican president and a Democratically controlled House of Representatives, but how this debate and deal served the national foreign policy interests of the United States remained something of a mystery.

Nicaragua provides another recent case. The debate over United States policy toward Nicaragua has now dragged on for over ten years. Candidate Reagan and his advisers in 1979–80 blamed the Carter administration for "losing" Nicaragua—to say nothing of Afghanistan, Ethiopia, Iran, and Grenada. In turn, all during the 1980s, the Democrats in the Congress used Nicaragua as a stick to beat the Republican administration over the head. The polls have shown that most Americans do not favor United States military aid to the armed Nicaraguan resistance (popularly known as the Contras), do not favor CIA intervention in that country, and above all do not favor the sending of American troops to Central America. The Democrats have paid scant attention to the genuine security problem that the United States has in Central America because they wish to use the issue to embarrass the president on these other grounds. By focusing on the human rights violations committed by the Contras, the principle of nonintervention, and the Arías Peace Plan (who could be against "peace," especially when it has the additional blessing of the Nobel Prize Committee?), the Democrats tried to seize the moral high ground while leaving Reagan to wrestle with the messy dilemma of what to do about Nicaragua. It is a close debate, with the votes about evenly divided on the issue that has come up repeatedly over the last several years of aid to the Contras; and of course when the votes are close and a lot is at stake, that gives individual congressmen even greater bargaining power to squeeze favors first out of the Democratic leadership (in the form of reelection campaign funds and other favors) and then out of the White House by offering to vote in favor of the president's program in return for benefits to the congressman and his district.

Actually, a lot more consensus exists in Congress on what the United States should do in Central America than the spirited debate and divisions we have had over the years would indicate. Just about everyone recognizes that we need some economic aid, some social programs, some military assistance, some aid to struggling democracies, and a decent human rights policy. While almost everyone acknowledges this (although still disagreeing about the relative balance between those different components of policy), the leadership of both major parties think that they can embarrass the other over Central America and use it as election campaign fodder. The Republicans think they can use Central America to portray the Democrats as "soft" on Communism especially in "our" hemisphere, while the Democrats think they can portray the Republicans as uncaring, weak on human rights, and running the risk of getting "our boys" involved militarily in Central America.

The leadership of both parties, however, has concluded that it can get political, ideological, and reelection mileage out of Central America, and therefore the debate and the conflict goes on. It goes on also because both parties have concluded that there are no costs—electorally—to them in Central America. That is, unlike Greeks, Jews, or Irishmen, few El Salvadorans or Nicaraguans vote in this country. So the electoral cost to a congressman of saying or doing something stupid on Central America— unlike the Middle East, for example—are minimal. That is why Central America is such an attractive issue to congressmen: they can get political and reelection mileage out of it at no or very little costs. Meanwhile the wars and conflicts in Central America go on. It is United States *politics* that is the issue, not Central America per se. Indeed the interests of Central America are seldom taken into account because the "higher order" political interests of the two parties is to use the issue for partisan purposes and to gain political advantage, not to help the long-suffering countries of Central America. Indeed Central America is often sacrificed on the altar of the American political process and the effort by politicians on all sides not to solve the problem but to prolong it for partisan purposes.

We suggested above that partisanship may prevail in some areas and on some issues more than others. It is generally on issues concerning Latin America and Africa (how many Zambians, Angolans, Mozambicans, or Ugandans vote in this country?) that congressmen have the least to fear electorally and therefore can say and do things for partisan advantage that they cannot do in other areas. South Africa is another matter, however, because of its apartheid system; that issue *does* have resonance among American voters. The Middle East is dangerous not only of itself but also politically (the Israeli lobby), so politicians are very careful what they say and do about that area. And the Soviet Union, alone among the nations in the world, has the capacity to destroy us, so politicians are usually cautious there as well. But even on Soviet affairs, as witness the debate over the interpretation, ratification, and future steps in disarmament negotiations (nuclear as well as conventional), Congress plays politics with the issues. It is at one and the same time disgraceful, downright dangerous, and as American as apple pie. But the politics and partisanship about foreign policy issues will not go away soon or ever; in fact, it is precisely our point that such partisan posturing and electioneering over foreign policy issues has been increasing in recent years.

How we carry out an effective and sensible foreign policy from time to time in this preeminently political context is often not a little short of miraculous, and of course is sometimes not achieved at all. And that is precisely our dilemma.

THE NEW CONGRESSIONAL ASSERTIVENESS—CAUSES

Congress has certainly become more active and assertive in foreign policy matters in recent years—of that there can be no doubt. The more interesting questions are why and how. Here we look at the causes of the new congressional assertiveness; in the next section we analyze how and in what foreign policy areas—human rights, oversight of intelligence activities, etc.—the Congress has come to play a larger role.

The reasons behind Congress having a bigger part in foreign policy are complex. They involve not just congressional power grabs but institutional changes within the Congress itself as well as broader scale changes in American culture, society, and politics. Let us enumerate the changes.

Decline of the Seniority System

It used to be that under the seniority system in Congress, congressmen or senators who had served the longest—usually Southerners from safe, one-party states—held the most important positions and wielded the most power as committee chairmen: of Foreign Affairs, Defense, Ways and Means. But in the mid-1970s, under the pressures of a new generation of young congressmen eager to rise to the top and impatient with the old leadership, Congress' internal ways were changed to allow younger members to go up the escalator of power more quickly. By coincidence, a number of the elderly chairmen died about the same time, or retired, or were replaced.

At this stage, while the seniority system is still in effect, it has been greatly weakened. The result is that new and younger persons can rise to the pinnacles of power in the Congress more quickly. These younger persons tend to be more partisan and ideological, eager to make their mark, and less willing than the old leaders to defer to presidential authority on foreign policy or other matters.

Proliferation of Specialized Subcommittees

Along with the decline of the seniority system and of the power of the old committee chairmen has come the tremendous growth in the number of subcommittees. Most of the work and hearings that were formerly done in the full foreign relations committees (Foreign Relations in the Senate, Foreign Affairs in the House) are now done in the more specialized subcommittees: on Latin America, Africa, refugees, and so forth. The mushrooming of subcommittees means Congress can get into more things than it used to (including into trouble and into areas where it probably does not belong). It also means that virtually every congressman now has a subcommittee of which he serves as chair. There is a story of one congressman who, when asked how he remembered the names of all of his 434 colleagues, replied: "I don't. I just address them as Mr. Chairman, knowing that in 95 percent of the cases, that greeting will be the correct one."

Larger, More Politicized Staffs

In the last fifteen years, the size of congressional staffs has increased enormously. Table 10.1 illustrates the changes.

Table 10.1   Growth of Congressional Payroll

	House		Senate	
	Committee	*Personal*	*Committee*	*Personal*
Year	*Staffs*	*Staffs*	*Staffs*	*Staffs*
1947	167	1,440	232	590
1976	1,680	6,939	1,201	3,251
1986	1,954	7,920	1,075	3,774

Source: Norman Ornstein et al., *Vital Statistics of Congress,* 1987—88.

During the last several decades, while the size of the House and Senate has remained the same, the size of the staff has increased anywhere from *five to ten times.*

In their personal offices, the size of the individual congressman's personal staff has grown from about ten or eleven in the old days to about twenty-five today. The size of personal congressional staffs is still regulated by law, but Congress has gotten around this through the enormous growth of committee staffs. So, in addition to their personal staffs, congressmen may have many other staff persons who work for them on the committees or subcommittees on which they serve. This means that an important senator like Ted Kennedy may have several specialists on Latin America or Africa working for him whose expertise rivals and at times may exceed that of the State Department. This enables the senator to challenge the secretary of state on virtually all areas of foreign policy and with a level of knowledge garnered from his staff that competes with that of the executive branch.

Not only have the staffs multiplied in size, but the staff members tend to be *very* hardworking and to be younger and often more ideological than the congressmen whom they ostensibly serve. The staff may thus push a congressman farther in some direction than he wants to go or to issue statements on his behalf that are heavily loaded. Or the staff may in effect carry out his own policy preferences, in the congressman's name but with only minimum oversight from him. The staff may be more zealous in promoting the person they work for (that is the name of the game for staff, after all) than he himself may wish. These activities and the sheer growth of the congressional staff have often polarized the differences between the Congress and the executive more than is healthy for the republic, have added to the fragmentation and disarray of our foreign policy-making, and have gotten the Congress into the micromanagement of foreign policy that ought really to be left to the president.

Declining Party Discipline

It used to be that the leaders of the two parties in the Congress (speaker, president protem, majority and minority leaders, whips) could enforce discipline on their members and tell them how to vote. No more. Congress is not quite a free-for-all but it comes close. The party leaders can no longer control their own members. Congressmen tend to vote more as individuals or as blocs (Black Caucus, Reform Caucus, Boll Weevils, etc.) than according to the dictates of party leaders. Not only can't the president keep the "troops" of his own party in line, but the opposition is fragmented as well. Deals can still be cut, favors traded, and the threat of cutting off funds for future campaigns used to get the congressman to vote the way the leadership wants. But it is far harder now, and the result is that congressmen are "all over the lot" on some votes, harder to count on to line up behind the leadership, and far more likely to vote their individual or bloc interests than their party lines.

Technical Expertise

In addition to their larger staffs, congressmen now have available to them a range of specialized agencies and expertise on whom they can rely for advice, wise counsel, and even policy position papers. Those agencies include the General Accounting Office (GAO), the Congressional Budget Office (CBO), and the Congressional Reference Service (CRS). These agencies help give the Congress a level of expertise and oversight abilities that rivals that of the executive branch.

On virtually any issue—including foreign policy—the Congress can now challenge the executive on an almost equal footing. It can mobilize almost as much knowledge and expertise as the State or Defense departments, the CIA, or the National Security Council. Because in today's modern, complex world knowledge is power, this gives the Congress advantages it did not have before.

The GAO now issues its reports of occasional corruption, inefficiencies, and misdeeds in the conduct of United States policy directly to Congress as well as to the executive, thus giving Congress an added weapon to wield over the executive. Moreover, the GAO has recently gotten into the area of making foreign policy recommendations, not just overseeing the process. The CBO gives Congress its own budget arm, independent of the White House's Office of Management and Budget, by which Congress can check into an administration's spending, set forth its own projections about the future performance of the economy, and supervise closely the immense and often stupefying budgets of the Department of Defense. The CRS, a division of the Library of Congress, provides the Congress with its own research branch and enables any congressman to call up from the CRS's pool of researchers an informed, twenty-page position paper on any subject within twenty-four to forty-eight hours. The CRS enables even uninformed congressmen to sound like they know what they're talking about on almost any foreign policy issue.

These agencies have given the Congress a level of technical expertise—and hence of power—that it never had before.

Youth and Ambition

The 1970s and 1980s have brought to the fore a whole new generation of congressmen. These are congressmen who do not have to fight the seniority system to gain influence, who are often contemptuous of the old party leadership and wish to go their own way, who tend to avoid strict party labels and emphasize their own independence and individuality. Quite a number of the new congressmen are products of the Berkeley and Vietnam-era generations who question and distrust authority, are suspicious of United States foreign policy objectives, and do not always accept the foreign policy assumptions that guided an earlier generation of policymakers. Their reactions on foreign policy issues are sometimes emotional and knee-jerk; at the same time that they want to grab more power, however, they are often less responsible about exercising it. Some congressmen—a handful—have even allied themselves with our enemies and want the United States to lose and be humiliated at every opportunity.

The new congressmen are often themselves products of the "me generation." They are looking out for number one—themselves. They are ambitious and want power, and are impatient to wait the many years it often takes for a freshman congressman to rise to the top. For the sake of serving their ambitions, they are often willing to ride roughshod over party and congressional rules, over the executive branch, and sometimes even over the best interests of the United States. This enables them to leapfrog over the usual congressional procedures and decorum and vault themselves into the limelight—often before they are ready or fully informed on the issues. Such ambition and power seeking on a grand scale have often been destructive not only of party loyalty and congressional understandings but also of American foreign policy interests. The best interests of the United States have too often been sacrificed to the self-seeking motives of these younger congressmen.

Television

The agency that enables these young congressmen to leap to the forefront is, of course, television. As seen in an earlier chapter, television provides instant stardom. It enables an otherwise obscure congressman to go on national television and share equal time with a secretary of state or even the president. Appearing on television is the fastest way to achieve national recognition and stature. For the ambitious and power-hungry young congressmen, television is the name of the game.

Not all Americans know that Congress now has the benefits of its own television studios, right on Capitol Hill. A congressman no longer has to go down to the main network studios in the center of Washington; instead, the filming and taping can be done without the congressman ever leaving his office complex. This is tremendously advantageous to the congressman not only in terms of time but also in terms of positive image: because studio employees are hired by Congress itself, no congressman will ever have to face an unfamiliar setting or be made to look bad on the "tube." The congressman can do short takes here for the national news, or he can do longer filming for his home district television stations, which frequently present these segments unedited as if they were presenting real news. The whole operation is wonderfully advantageous for congressmen; it also enhances their reelection possibilities.

But the preoccupation with television appearances also has its downside. It often lowers the level of the debate to that of the thirty-second "sound bite"—a glib phrase or sentence that sometimes passes for more serious discussion. It gives rise to instant analyses—because television needs a comment *that* night—rather than more measured and careful discussion. It has been destructive of party unity, seniority, and congressional integrity, enabling a low-level congressman to say whatever he wants regardless of the party leadership. And it has brought to the fore a new kind of congressman—glib, superficial, good "face men" (rather like the TV anchors themselves), tanned and well coiffed, cool but shallow and, once one gets beyond the sound bites, not very well informed. These are the new congressmen—assertive, ambitious, and too often the masters of public relations rather than of substance.

Air Travel

Another cause of greater congressional involvement in foreign policy-making, one which we seldom think of, is the revolution in communications and air travel in the last thirty years. Congressmen now routinely fly off on investigative trips for the weekend to Central America, which from Washington, D.C., is only four hours away. Leaving Friday evening, they can be in four or five capitals by the time they fly back on Sunday afternoon. When he was seeking to arrange the departure of strongman Ferdinand Marcos from the Philippines, Congressman Stephen Solarz seemed almost to be commuting to Manila on a weekly basis. Europe is similarly within reach for a weekend jaunt; and when Congress is not in session, congressmen and their wives, friends, and staff regularly take longer junkets to more distant countries. Communications satellites enable these roving congressmen to appear in their favorite television spots even when they are thousands of miles away. In fact, their presence in a foreign country is what helps get them on TV.

All this traveling, together with the personal contacts they may have developed in the place of destination, plus the staff aides with expertise of their own who travel with them, enable congressmen to develop the information sources and the firsthand knowledge that at some levels match those of the State Department. The congressmen's experience abroad and hands-on expertise are very likely to be greater than that of the president himself or his advisers. Modern jet travel, as well as instant communication via satellite and other means, have enabled congressmen to thrust themselves to the forefront of the foreign policy debate and to put forth alternatives that are based on a level of expertise and firsthand knowledge that rivals the executive branch.

Distrust of the President

Because of Vietnam and Watergate, when the president not only mishandled the crises but also lied about them, the Congress has come to mistrust the president. Vietnam especially in the foreign policy area led Congress to think the executive branch could not be trusted to carry out a sensible American foreign policy, one that defended our interests while also remaining true to American ideals. And, let us face it, the presidents we have had since then—Gerald Ford, Jimmy Carter, Ronald Reagan—have not always given the Congress abundant reason to be confident of prudent, informed, humane, and practical foreign policies emanating from the Oval Office.

The result is a profound distrust of the president—of a series of presidents—on the part of the Congress. Distrust—it is as simple as that.

The fact is, the Congress simply doesn't trust the American president to carry out foreign policy. This factor, perhaps above all others, explains the congressional resurgence in foreign policy in the last two decades. For if the president cannot be trusted to carry out foreign policy, then Congress must do so.

THE NEW CONGRESSIONAL ASSERTIVENESS—EFFECTS

It is one thing to talk about, as above, the broad causes leading to a new congressional assertiveness in foreign policy. But now we need to turn to what the Congress has actually done to express that assertiveness. In fact, there has been in the last fifteen years a rash of legislation coupled with new practices by which Congress has given itself a greater foreign policy role. But this has not led necessarily to any greater efficiency or good sense in our foreign policy, only to a mishmash of conflicting jurisdictions, constant battles between Congress and the White House, a foreign policy that is contradictory and inconsistent, and a further element of paralysis added to our already conflict-prone foreign policy.

The War Powers Act

Many of the legislative acts of the last two decades that served to limit the president's role in the foreign policy area and to enhance that of Congress grew directly out of the Vietnam experience. Foremost among these is the War Powers Act of 1973. It will be recalled that the Vietnam war was an undeclared war, that then President Lyndon B. Johnson had interpreted the Gulf of Tonkin Resolution of 1966 as providing congressional approval to his war efforts in Vietnam, but that Congress had never actually declared war. The War Powers Act sought to remedy that gap in our policy-making process.

The War Powers Act, which was passed by both houses of Congress over President Nixon's veto, provides that any commitments of United States military forces to any global hot spot for longer than sixty days must receive the approval of Congress. The legislation thus permitted a president, as commander in chief, to respond to genuine emergency situations by the rapid dispatch of American forces for a short time; but any commitment longer than sixty days had to be subjected to congressional scrutiny—presumably the power to disapprove and call the troops home as well as to approve.

The problems with the War Powers Act are many, which is why its actual implementation has been an almost complete failure. First, it may well be unconstitutional, representing an unwarranted congressional interference in the president's constitutionally mandated foreign affairs responsibilities. But so far the issue has not been brought to the Supreme Court because (1) the Congress, fearing it will lose, wants to maintain even the limited influence (really, only bargaining power with the executive) over presidential discretion in the sending of troops that the act gives it; and (2) the White House, needing congressional votes on budget and other issues, has not wanted to force the issue. But someday soon, someone, somewhere will challenge the War Powers Act in the courts and then we will have to wait and see how the Supreme Court decides.

Second, the War Powers Act is ambiguous. In addition to the sixty-day limitation, the president is supposed to "consult" with the Congress before sending troops; but what precisely does that mean? Does "consultation" mean informing a handful of sympathetic congressmen as President Reagan did before sending United States forces into Grenada; does it mean consulting Congress after or before the sending of troops; does it mean providing limited or complete information—what? No one knows. Now, suppose the president sends the navy (not United States ground forces) to patrol for longer than sixty days the dangerous waters of the Persian Gulf, but still within international waters, for the purpose of enforcing commonly understood rights of international passage—is that a violation of the War Powers Act? Again, no one knows. The act is full of ambiguities such as these.

Third, the War Powers Act is politically difficult for Congress to carry out. Suppose the president sends American troops to war-torn Lebanon and then asserts that they must stay beyond the sixty-day limit because the lives of American hostages there will be in even greater danger if they are pulled out. Who in the United States Congress in those circumstances is going to invoke the War Powers Act and thus run the risk of the American hostages being killed, the responsibility for which will rest upon the heads of the congressmen who voted such invocation? Or, if the president asserts powerfully that United States interests or the lives of "our boys" are at stake in some troubled area, who in the Congress can afford to publicly say otherwise? The answer is, no one.

Because of the ambiguities and political difficulties in the War Powers Act, the Congress attempted to correct it through a series of amendments proposed by Democratic Congressman Edward P. Boland of Massachusetts. The problem is that there are at least five different Boland amendments, with considerable confusion and further ambiguity between them. Yet these are the provisions under which Col. Oliver North was tried in the Iran-Contra affair. North was accused, among other things, of violating the Boland Amendment, but it was never clear which variation of Boland he had violated; he was also accused of violating the War Powers Act, which is itself ambiguous and may well be unconstitutional. It is therefore not surprising that the North trial generated a great deal of political and constitutional controversy; and that when the jury reached a verdict, it convicted North on some lesser charges but not on the charges of violating the War Powers Act or the Boland Amendments.

The questions about and the ineffectiveness of the War Powers Act have led to considerable rethinking. Congress is studying the act and will be proposing new amendments. The White House, meanwhile, operates almost as though the act does not exist, knowing it can get around it either by legal or political means. At the same time, the threat of Supreme Court action hangs overhead. So War Powers remains in limbo for now, neither an effective piece of legislation nor one that can immediately be gotten rid of. No one is satisfied with the act that we do have; yet Congress cannot simply reverse itself by repealing it, and every president since Nixon has been opposed to it and generally operated as if it didn't exist. The result is confusion, uncertainty, and another contentious issue hanging between Congress and the White House.

The Legislative Veto

Another area in which the Congress has sought to expand its authority is in the use of the legislative veto. As its name implies, the legislative veto was an attempt by Congress (actually, only a limited number of congressmen) to check presidential foreign policy prerogatives by voting against *particular* aspects of the executive's policies. By a simple vote of Congress, presidential initiatives could thus be disapproved and, hence, "vetoed."

But, as every freshman knows, the United States Constitution gives the president the power to veto acts of Congress; nowhere does it give the Congress express powers to veto acts of the executive. Hence, despite the efforts of some congressmen and a number of constitutional lawyers to rationalize and justify the congressional veto, it did not come as a great surprise to very many people when the Supreme Court struck down this effort by Congress to exercise greater power as unconstitutional.

Intelligence Oversight   Another legacy of Vietnam, of CIA attempts in Chile to destabilize the Socialist/Communist regime of Salvador Allende, and of the general congressional feeling that the CIA was an "invisible" and an "uncontrolled" agency out there wreaking havoc on unsuspecting governments and heads of state, was the attempt by the Congress to exercise greater oversight over United States intelligence activities, especially over covert (secret) actions. The legislation grew out of the hearing and investigations of Senator Frank Church in the mid-1970s of alleged CIA involvements in the assassination of such notorious dictators as Trujillo in the Dominican Republic and Diem in Vietnam, attempts to put poison in the beard of Fidel Castro, and other secretive and allegedly nefarious activities.

Actually, as we shall see in more detail in the next chapter, most scholars of foreign policy do not believe the "invisible government" thesis.[1] That thesis suggests that the Central Intelligence Agency is some rogue agency, out of control, that goes around *on its own* conducting dirty tricks and worse, without the approval of elected representatives. Although the CIA does occasionally carry out some covert operation without express presidential approval, that is not the situation in the vast majority of cases. In almost all cases, the president or his representatives approve CIA operations beforehand, although of course these are not broadcast publicly, and elaborate steps are sometimes taken to protect the president from having to admit that he approved an activity that somehow went haywire. The CIA does not ordinarily act on its own; in virtually every case it receives prior presidential approval for its activities—although under the doctrine of "plausible deniability" it has to be possible for a president to deny that he approved it.

The new legislation led to the creation of House and Senate intelligence committees designed specifically to oversee the CIA. Under the old system, which was probably too lax, CIA reporting to Congress was usually left to a handful of trusted senators and representatives in the armed services committees who were known to be sympathetic to the CIA and who could be counted on to be discrete and always to vote approval of the CIA's budget. Now, there are separate oversight committees to which the CIA must report, some of whose members and staffs are frankly hostile to CIA activities.

The result is a continuing controversy not unlike that which surrounds the War Powers Act. Information that the CIA director or his lieutenants give in closed or secret sessions to the congressional oversight committees can usually be counted on to be leaked and on the front pages of every newspaper in the country by the next day. It is usually leaked by hostile congressmen or their aides for the purpose of discrediting the CIA or of scuttling a particular CIA operation of which the congressman may disapprove. Because of the leaks, CIA directors have become wary of sharing very much information with the Congress and often supply incomplete or even misleading information. That of course makes the Congress even unhappier, and it next accuses the CIA of "hiding" information. Meanwhile, foreign governments and informants also stop supplying information to the CIA because they know that what they tell the agency on the basis of confidentiality will likely appear tomorrow in the *Washington Post* or *New York Times*. It is a royal mess, which leaves all parties dissatisfied, and adds one more element to our foreign policy conflict and paralysis.

Human Rights Certification   Jimmy Carter touched a chord in his foreign policy by emphasizing human rights; congressmen also like human rights not only because they believe in the policy but also because it enables them to wax indignant about torturers, dictators, and murder-ers—at no cost to them and obviously to some political advantage because who, after all, can be against human rights. The Congress therefore enacted legislation that requires the Department of State to certify every six months that country X is making "progress" on human rights or else American aid to the country will be cut off. Human rights progress must even be demonstrated in countries that are in the midst of civil wars or where revolutionary guerrillas are seeking to destroy the nation's economic infrastructure—such as in El Salvador. Only the governments of such countries are obliged to demonstrate human rights progress; there is no check on the guerrillas who are also out there murdering innocent civilians—often more so than the government forces.

The result is often a complete charade. Every six months representa-tives of the State Department must go before the Congress and, with elaborate documentation that takes immense amounts of staff time to compile, try to demonstrate that there is human rights progress in country X—when everyone knows there may have been no or little progress. Moreover, the purpose of the congressional hearing is not usually to get an honest evaluation of the human rights situation in country X but only to use the opportunity to lambast the administration which is in the hands of the other political party. The hearings are partisan rather than objective, and everyone knows that both the administration defending American aid to country X and its congressional foes are dissembling. Hypocrisy abounds—but of course in Washington, D.C., that is what makes the world go round.

The goal is certainly a noble one: we all want the human rights situation in country X to get better. But the questions are: Can you fight a guerrilla civil war and improve your human rights situation at the same time? How can the government forces be expected to clean up their human rights act if the guerrillas continue to murder and maim? And, is it possible for human rights to be improved anywhere if the debate between Congress and the White House is so partisan, so rancorous, and so hypocritical? These issues have not by any means been fully resolved but it is the case—surprise, surprise—that in part as a result of these hearings both the war against the guerrillas and the human rights situation in El Salvador and other countries began to improve.

Controlling the Purse Strings   One of the hallowed rights of Congress is to initiate all money bills and to control appropriations. The president may initiate measures all he wants but unless Congress votes the funds, the president's agenda will not get anywhere. In the past this power of Congress was exercised with restraint and prudence, allowing the president to lead, especially in foreign policy, and with the Congress, usually with modest grumbling or amendments, voting the funds necessary for his program.

But now, the power of the purse is exercised much more tightly and in far greater detail. Congress has even begun to use its power over appropriation not just to modify presidential initiatives but to change them around or even to reverse them. Thus, while Congress cannot itself constitutionally take the lead in foreign policy-making, it can do so de facto through its domination of the appropriations process. For example, Congress has cut off United States assistance funds to regimes of which it disapproves, thus provoking a shift in United States policy toward such regimes; it has forbidden arms exports to certain offending countries; it has tacked amendments requiring certain human rights reforms on a bill dealing with trade with the Soviet Union; it gives "most favored nation" blessings (and thus access to American markets) to countries which it favors and withholds them from others; and it appends various trade and aid requirements to legislation that may or may not have anything to do with foreign affairs.

Congress has always had power over the purse, but now that power has been vastly expanded and reinterpreted to give Congress ultimate and de facto control over vast areas of foreign policy. Moreover, these appropriations matters are often handled haphazardly when it comes to foreign affairs and by committees and subcommittees that may be responding to domestic constituent concerns and not seeing the broader foreign policy implications of their acts. Protecting domestic sugar beet growers may be a laudable political goal, for example, but it may also have the effect of ruining a whole group of economies in the Caribbean and the Pacific, and thus prove disastrous for United States foreign policy. Many foreign policy analysts are troubled by Congress' considerable expansion of its power over appropriations as it affects foreign affairs, particularly the haphazard exercise of that power; but it is likely that Congress will continue to use and expand its control over the purse strings to check further the executive and to enhance its own authority.

Treaties and Executive Agreements   The United States is a party to some 966 treaties (as of 1983), but it has signed roughly *seven* times that number of executive agreements with various countries. Treaties of course require Senate approval, but executive agreements do not. The original intention of executive agreements was to serve as supplements to larger treaties or to deal with small issues that need not be covered by full-scale treaties. However, the sheer number and details of many recent executive agreements have led Congress to conclude that they were really treaties but were called "executive agreements" simply to avoid the requirement of congressional advice and consent—or dissent.

The result has been congressional pressure on the executive to con-

sider executive agreements as treaties that, by Constitution, require senatorial approval. The White House has resisted this because it likes the
flexibility that executive agreements provide and, frankly, because it would
prefer not to have to go through the trouble of securing congressional
approval. This issue will continue to be a matter of contention between the
two branches although, as with the requirement of human rights certification, there has been some progress toward resolution. The president will
remain free to sign binding executive agreements with other countries
because successful foreign policy-making requires the flexibility and capacity to respond quickly that such agreements provide. On the other
hand, there is considerable consensus in Washington that there are far too
many executive agreements, that some of them have been used as a device
to avoid congressional review, and that at least the more important executive agreements ought to be considered as if they were treaties—i.e.,
requiring senatorial approval. While this movement toward accommodation and compromise between Congress and the president is to be applauded, it still leaves room for a lot of fuzzy areas of potential conflict—
such as which executive agreements will in fact be treated as treaties and
who will decide which ones are to be so considered.

Military and Police Assistance   The United States has long provided military and police assistance to various countries to help them in
maintaining public order and in resisting armed guerrilla movements. But
in the 1970s, sentiment began to grow that the military and police forces
whom we assisted were gross violators of human rights and that the
equipment we provided sometimes enabled military movements to overthrow elected civilian government and to repress their own peoples.
Hence sentiment in Congress, on this issue as on so many others influenced by the Vietnam experience, began to shift toward opposition to
military and police assistance. Specifically, the Congress enacted legislation that prohibited military and police assistance to regimes such a
Guatemala's, which used its armed forces to quash not only Communist
and leftist groups but also, sometimes, human rights.

The dilemma was this: while everyone knew the Guatemalan regime
sometimes violated the human rights of its citizens, that regime was also
locked in a battle with Marxist-Leninist guerrillas whose human rights
record was not exactly unblemished either. By cutting off military aid the
United States not only ran the risk that the guerrillas might win, but it also
lost whatever chance it had to influence the Guatemalan regime for the
better. Military aid at least gave us a lever to try to reform the Guatemalan
military; by cutting off such aid, our own hands would be clean but that
would not lead to any improvement in the human rights situation in
Guatemala. In fact, without our aid and hence our influence, the human
rights situation there and in other countries where we cut off assistance
soon became worse.

The issue once again proved acrimonious and divisive, with the administration arguing that by cutting off aid we were losing influence abroad and running the risk of still more countries falling to communism, and the opposition arguing that we were aiding human rights violators and thus adding to the condition under which radical, Marxist-Leninist appeals would grow. It was a partisan standoff that eventually evolved into a number of compromises: military aid would be continued but on the condition that the human rights situation in country Y be improved. And, lo and behold, that is what happened: not only did the human rights situation improve because of United States pressure, but with an improved human rights situation the war against the guerrillas went better as well.

Nominations   The appointment of American ambassadors and diplomatic officials is still another area in which Congress has flexed its muscles. By Constitution, the Senate must approve the appointment of United States ambassadors who are about to be posted abroad, and also must ratify the appointments of other high administration officials (secretaries, undersecretaries, and assistant secretaries). Such Senate confirmations used to be more or less routine (assuming the appointee was not obviously a crook), but that is no longer so.

Now such ambassadorial and administrative appointments are closely scrutinized in the Congress—not so much on the basis of merit or competence but on political and ideological grounds. On the right, Senator Jesse Helms frequently holds up ambassadorial and other appointments on the grounds that they are not sufficiently conservative or as a way of prying some concession for him or his state out of the administration. On the left, senators refuse to ratify administration appointments in part because they find them ideologically unacceptable but mainly to embarrass the administration and to get some partisan advantage out of the hearings.

It is sad to see American foreign policy so intensely politicized in this way because the ultimate result will be (and already is) even less competence in our foreign policy-making machinery than exists at present. At the same time, such a highly partisan and politicized foreign policy process is now a given, the context in which we now operate, so that we had better be prepared to deal with these new realities.

Micromanagement of Foreign Policy   Foreign policy has traditionally been thought of as mainly the prerogative of the executive. Congress also has its power in the foreign affairs area, as we have seen, but that has usually been limited to oversight and review functions. No longer.

The trend in recent years has been for Congress to try to micromanage our foreign policy. That is, instead of Congress exercising the broad oversight that it exercised in the past and leaving the details of policy up to the executive and the State Department, now Congress often seeks to get involved in every detail of policy and even to manage it on an everyday basis. It is of course impossible for a body of 535 persons in the Congress, a body that is so highly partisan and political—perhaps more so than any other institution in the country—to micromanage foreign policy in this way; but that is the reality in which we now find ourselves. Congress now sticks its nose into, and of course seeks to use for partisan advantage, nearly every detail of foreign policy.

For example, the usual ratio of economic and military assistance in our foreign aid programs is two to one. That is, for every two dollars in economic assistance that we provide, we give one dollar in military assistance. Having established this general guideline, Congress then usually left it up to the executive (the State Department and the Agency for International Development) to decide on which specific programs the money would be spent. After all, it is the State Department and AID (not the Congress) that have long backgrounds in these areas, that have people in the field in the recipient countries on a long-term basis, and that know how to carry out policy in a complex foreign environment. Now the Congress and its numerous subcommittees, rather than exercise only oversight functions, are inclined to look into every detail of these complex programs and to presume to offer instructions to AID and State Department officials on how to carry them out. Moreover, Congress now desires to receive reports on how these programs are proceeding on an almost daily basis, to fine-tune their details in the same way that the Federal Reserve Board might try to fine-tune the money supply, and furthermore to have members and staff fly off to the country in question on a weekend junket to get firsthand experiences for even more intimate fine-tuning.

Such micromanagement by the Congress of our foreign policy is of course related to the changing trends discussed in the earlier part of this chapter: modern jet travel, greatly expanded staff, a more assertive and independent Congress, distrust of the president, and so forth. But it is doubtful whether a successful foreign policy can be managed by a legislative body in this way. On one side, Congress lacks the detailed expertise, the in-depth knowledge, the continuity, or the background in foreign affairs that is so essential in today's complex and interdependent world; on the other, Congress is too partisan, too political, too polarized, and just too diverse and large to carry out effective foreign policy. Congressmen like to play this foreign policy role since it gets them headlines and television spots, and therefore it seems unlikely that micromanagement of foreign policy by the Congress will end anytime soon. At the same time, we should recognize the dangers involved and how damaging to our foreign policy such deep involvement by the Congress is.

Biased Hearings   When Congress holds hearings on a major foreign policy issue—the Middle East, Soviet relations, Central America—we as citizens expect those hearings to be balanced and all points of view to be heard. Out of such careful and balanced considerations, we expect the congressmen to make up their minds. This is, again, the rational actor model of foreign policy-making.

But that is no longer the way it works. In this more politicized era, even hearings are preeminently political events. They are designed to support the views of the dominant party and to embarrass the opposition. The staff and the congressmen often purposely choose the witnesses for those purposes. True, the minority party usually is allowed one witness, but the weight is wholly on the other side. Since the congressmen already have their party positions firmly fixed, they look for witnesses who support their conclusions, not unbiased and balanced assessments. The hearings are not intended as a careful and judicious presentation of alternatives but as a "show" designed to make the committee or subcommittee chairman and his party look good. When the hearings are covered by television, these characteristics of the hearings and their fundamentally partisan nature are even further emphasized.

The result once again is a charade. Hearings are not designed to elicit balanced views but to reinforce highly partisan positions. The system of hearings has been so politicized that it sometimes resembles a circus rather than a serious effort to arrive at sensible policy. The situation in some committees and subcommittees has gotten so bad that many of our leading scholars refuse to participate. If their views are not taken seriously or are used solely for partisan purposes, then what is the point of lending one's name and reputation to this "show"? Scholars do not get paid for those congressional appearances, and it takes a lot of time for a serious scholar to prepare in-depth testimony. But if no one is listening or if the Congress wishes to use the testimony only for partisan purposes, then there is not much point in going to all this trouble. With more and more leading scholars refusing to lend their names and give their time to such charades, the result is that lesser scholars or partisan hacks are brought in as witnesses. And that, of course, lowers the level of the debate still farther. It is not a happy situation; with their highly partisan purposes, congressional hearings are no longer the effort to get at the facts and arrive at serious policy conclusions that they once were.

A Congressional Takeover of Foreign Policy   For a long time Congress has been nibbling at the edges of executive predominance in foreign policy, asserting its own prerogatives, and trying—as we have seen—to tip the balance in executive-legislative power back toward the legislative branch. In the process, Congress has over the last twenty years gradually been augmenting its authority in the foreign affairs area to the point where Congress must now be thought of in some areas as virtually coequal with the president in foreign policy matters. But in 1987 Congress took a step that went considerably beyond parity in foreign policy-making and staged what only could be considered as a takeover of United States Central America policy. In a move that carries grave consequences for the future of United States foreign policy, Congress all but swept the president and his secretary of state aside and began conducting foreign policy independently and on its own.

Some background is necessary. Quite a number of congressmen had long been dissatisfied with President Reagan's Central America policy. They wanted to move the policy along from one of conflict and confrontation with the Sandinista regime to one of negotiations. At the same time, House Speaker Jim Wright, having recently replaced Tip O'Neill, needed to shore up his position with House Democrats, especially its more liberal wing. In addition, Wright spoke some Spanish and felt that, as a Texan, he had some special understanding of Central America.

So, on his own, without consulting the president or the secretary of state, Wright launched his own foreign policy in Central America. As if he were head of state, Wright met with the presidents of Costa Rica and Nicaragua. He worked out a plan that he presumed would bring "peace" to Central America. Of course, like apple pie and motherhood, no one can be against "peace"; Wright also had the advantage of working with a recipient of the Nobel Peace Prize, the president of Costa Rica. He threw the prestige of the Speaker's office plus that of the United States Congress behind this particular plan; and campaigning on the "peace" issue, Wright was able to undercut the administration's own efforts in the region. In effect, Wright took the ball away—indeed stole the whole court—from the White House. He had staged a congressional power grab of United States Central America policy, leaving the president on the sidelines, fuming, and out of the play.

Now, it can be argued that something was needed to get the administration's Central American policy off the ground. But the last time any of us looked at the Constitution, it was not the Speaker of the House who was in charge of foreign policy. Wright not only took over a whole area of foreign policy for himself but he also pushed it in a particular direction that is not likely to be advantageous to American national interests. At the same time, his actions undermined secret negotiations that were then going on between the White House and the Central American countries. In long-range terms, such a power grab by the Speaker is bound to be disastrous for the future conduct of United States foreign policy. It is inconceivable (except that it happened) and unconscionable that a Speaker of the House should conduct his own foreign policy, independently of the president and secretary of state, and undermine other aspects of United States policy in the process. Such coups d'etat are assumed to happen in "banana republics," not in the United States of America—unless we too have become something of a banana republic.

CONCLUSION

Congress is often not looked on kindly by specialists in foreign policy analysis. Congress is thought of as usurping functions that properly belong to the executive, as dangerously pandering to the public by telling it only what it wants to hear, and by introducing divisive partisanship into foreign policy—the one arena in this complex, dangerous, and interdependent world where bipartisan policy is necessary. At the White House, the terms often used to describe Congress are even more derogatory: "clowns," "incompetents," "meddlers."

But we must remember that most congressmen are very shrewd persons politically. That is how they got to be congressmen in the first place. They keep their ear to the ground and they try to respond to the demands—now more vocal and intense than ever, in our more highly politicized political system—of their constituents and of pressure groups. Moreover, they generally take their roles as brokers between national policy-making and local politics seriously—that, after all, is what gets them reelected. They must try to interpret national policy to their constituents; at the same time, they must convey the public opinion of their constituents to national policymakers. Policy-making cannot plunge too far ahead of public opinion, nor can it lag too far behind, nor can it be too much at variance with sentiments at the grass roots level—and if it is or becomes so, that is when policy gets in trouble. The problem for congressmen, of course, is that they have no job security and are hence always running for reelection—and that also raises problems in terms of a coherent and consistent foreign policy.

But oftentimes—as on Central America—public opinion as well as White House policy are unclear or confused. The congressmen want to please their constituents and they do not like to cross the White House; but if their constituents are uncertain about what they want and the president's policies are not working, that also leaves the congressmen unclear and uncertain about which way to vote. Such lack of clarity or certainty on an issue also gives congressmen greater leeway in terms of their own actions. So it is not the case that congressmen are "clowns" (a few may be) but that they must respond to constituency pressures; the demands on them are intense, and in some circumstances both constituency pressures and White House policy are unclear, leading to uncertainty, indecision, flip-flops, and confusion.

Nevertheless, there has been a significant increase in congressional assertiveness and power in the foreign policy realm in recent years. While the new congressional assertiveness has produced decidedly mixed policy results, it is unlikely to be reduced soon. Congressmen enjoy playing this larger foreign policy role, it serves their ambitions to qualify for future even higher office, and they have larger staffs who also want to expand into greater foreign policy visibility. In addition, there are now structural and procedural arrangements in place (War Powers Act, human rights requirements of certification, others we have discussed) that oblige the Congress to continue playing this larger role. Furthermore, in its response to the human rights requirements, the limits on aid, and so forth, the executive branch—even though it may not like many of these new arrangements—has nonetheless adjusted to them. With the institutionalization of Congress' expanded role going forward, and with the president, however reluctantly at times, adjusting to these new procedures, it seems certain that in the future Congress will be more of a coequal partner in foreign policy-making than previously. We cannot and will not go back to the older tradition of overwhelming executive predominance. Whether these trends are a good thing for American foreign policy, however, remains very much in doubt.

Not only has Congress come to play a far larger role in foreign policy-making but that has meant also a far more partisan and politicized foreign policy. In considerable measure that is the result of having a situation of a divided government, where the White House is under the control of one party and the Congress of the other. But the bitterness and nastiness between the White House and the Congress are now so deep that the problem would not be fully overcome even if one party were in control of both branches. The sniping and rivalry would still continue. Hence there can be little hope in the foreseeable future for the restoration of those golden, halcyon (pre-1965) years of a truly unified and bipartisan foreign policy. That era, given our changed societal and political conditions in the 1970s and 1980s, is probably gone. It was an exceptional period in any case and may have been romanticized, for there were divisions then as well. Hence what we have to look forward to is a continuation of the partisan bickering, the conflict, and the backbiting that has characterized our foreign policy in recent years. At best what we can hope for is some greater capacity to manage and cope with these conflict-prone currents.

At the same time one can make a strong case that the new congressional assertiveness and role in foreign policy have in some ways been beneficial, that the system is working. After all, neither presidents Ford, Carter, nor Reagan were known for their foreign policy expertise or acumen. Hence when the White House went off in some mistaken or excessive directions, it was the Congress' right *and obligation* to step in and provide a corrective. It was not that Congress was always interested in power grabs (although that was sometimes true as well) but that the executive was pursuing wrongheaded objectives or taking the country in what the Congress—with its contacts with public opinion—believed to be wrong directions. Hence on Central America and other issues, many congressmen felt they *had* to step in to correct what they felt were mistakes by the administration. Congress can claim some credit—despite all the huffing and puffing—for forcing the administration back toward a more centrist foreign policy position, toward greater emphasis on human rights, and toward a better balance between socioeconomic aid and military assistance. In this sense one can say that the system worked—despite all the imperfections our chapter has pointed out.

Meanwhile, the "invitation to struggle" between the executive and legislative branches will go on. Congress is more powerful than before on foreign policy issues, but the actual impact of all this new legislation and new practices of the last fifteen years on actual foreign policy-making is probably less than all the attention it has received would lead us to think. The new legislation mandating a greater congressional role, such as in the War Powers Act, contains many ambiguities and escape clauses; and there have been very few instances in which the Congress has been able to completely frustrate, let alone reverse, a skilled White House determined to have its way. Power within Congress, in addition, is too fragmented and dispersed for that institution to be the dominant one in foreign policy, and the lack of interest by the American public in most foreign policy issues is a further discouragement to a larger role.

Thoughtful members of Congress themselves recognize that Congress cannot lead in foreign policy, that the institution is too cumbersome and inefficient, that there are limits on Congress' role in foreign policy, and that any renewed effort to develop a congressional veto over foreign policy would certainly be ruled unconstitutional. Hence the fears that some have expressed that we are fashioning an "imperial Congress," as contrasted with earlier writings on what was called an "imperial presidency,"[2] are not likely to be realized. With all the changes in recent years toward greater congressional involvement, it is still the president and the executive branch that remain the hub and vortex of our foreign policy-making system. The president must consult and share power with the Congress in as yet not fully defined ways, but ours is still a White House-centered system of foreign policy decision-making. Hence it is toward these inner circles in our design of concentric circles, toward the narrowest part of our funnel of causality, that the analysis next turns.

Notes

1. After the title of the book by David Wise and Thomas Ross, *Invisible Government* (New York: Random House, 1964).
2. Arthur Schlesinger, Jr., *The Imperial Presidency* (Boston: Houghton Mifflin, 1973).

Suggested Readings

Abshire, David, and Ralph D. Nurnberger, eds. *The Growing Power of Congress.* Beverly Hills, Calif.: Sage Publications, 1981.

Crabb, Cecil V., Jr., and Pat M. Holt. *Invitation to Struggle: Congress, the President and Foreign Policy.* Washington, D.C.: Congressional Quarterly Press, 1984.

Destler, I.M., and Eric R. Alterman. "Congress and Reagan's Foreign Power." *Washington Quarterly* 7(Winter 1984):91–101.

Dodd, Lawrence, and Bruce I. Oppenheim, eds. *Congress Reconsidered.* Washington, D.C.: Congressional Quarterly Press, 1985.

Fisher, Louis. *Constitutional Conflicts Between Congress and the President.* Princeton, N.J.: Princeton University Press, 1985.

Franck, Thomas M., and Edward Weisband. *Foreign Policy by Congress.* New York: Oxford University Press, 1979.

King, Anthony, ed. *Both Ends of the Avenue: The Presidency, the Executive Branch, and Congress in the 1980s.* Washington, D.C.: American Enterprise Institute for Public Policy Research, 1983.

Pastor, Robert A. *Congress and the Politics of U.S. Foreign Policy, 1929–1976.* Berkeley: University of California Press, 1980.

Spanier, John, and Joseph Nogee, eds. *Congress, the Presidency and American Foreign Policy.* New York: Pergamon, 1981.

Turner, Robert F. *The War Powers Resolution: Its Implementation in Theory and Practice.* Philadelphia: Foreign Policy Research Institute, 1983.

Whalen, Charles W., Jr. *The House and Foreign Policy: The Irony of Congressional Reform.* Chapel Hill: University of North Carolina Press, 1982.

CHAPTER ELEVEN

Bureaucratic Politics I:
State, Defense, CIA

❂
❂

Foreign policy, as we saw in Chapter 2, is not just a "rational" process in which options are set forth, the pros and cons of each option duly considered, and a presumably rational and coherent choice made by the president or his secretary of state. Rather, politics in its broadest dimensions—partisanship, logrolling, electoral posturing, the servicing of private political ambitions—is also involved. In the discussion of public opinion, the mass media, parties, interest groups, think tanks, to say nothing of the Congress, we saw how intensely politicized the entire foreign policy-making process has become.

But in addition to the political interests affected, we learned that bureaucratic interests are also involved. That is the focus of the present chapter and the following one, reflecting how important the subject of bureaucratic politics in foreign policy has become. Here we focus on the traditional foreign policy-making agencies: the Department of State, the Department of Defense, and the Central Intelligence Agency. In the next chapter, we will be dealing with the Department of Treasury, the Department of Commerce, the Department of Agriculture, and the Department of Justice—particularly the Drug Enforcement Agency and the Immigration and Naturalization Service.

Here are the issues and why they are important. On the one hand, such agencies as the State Department (diplomacy), Defense (military), and CIA (intelligence) are all supposed to perform separate but interrelated foreign policy functions, which are then supposed to be coordinated and harmonized by the president and the National Security Council. But in fact these separate agencies are not well coordinated, they have different subcultures that cannot be easily harmonized, they as often compete with one another as cooperate for the common purpose, and they often go in separate foreign policy directions or are at loggerheads with one another in ways that produce conflict and gridlock. Moreover (and also demanding our attention), the relative influence of these departments has changed over time, with very important implications for foreign policy. The general consensus among analysts is that since the 1950s the State Department has lost a lot of power relative to other Washington agencies, while the Defense Department and the CIA have gained.

Another important factor is that while State, Defense, and CIA have long been the main foreign policy-making departments of the United States government, in recent years a variety of other agencies have become increasingly important. The rise of these other agencies is related to the changing American position in the world and to the recent emergence of new, especially economic, issues. For example, the Treasury Department only began to be a major international actor about a decade ago as trade issues loomed larger, the issue of unpaid (and payable) Third World foreign debts became important, and as the United States economy became more interdependent with the rest of the world. The Justice Department became a major "player" in foreign policy as the drug and immigration issues loomed larger. And so with other agencies.

Part of the problem is that many of these departments newly involved in foreign policy issues lack experience in foreign policy, which leads to major gaffes. Another problem—the bureaucratic one—is that these agencies sometimes also compete with each other as well as with the more traditional wielders of power, such as State. These problems of coordination and conflict among the now many bureaucratic agencies involved in American foreign policy have become so important that they merit two chapters: this one, which concentrates on the traditional bureaucratic wielders of foreign policy influence, and the next one, which deals with the newcomers.

DEPARTMENT OF STATE

The State Department has many problems. In Washington, the question is often raised as to whether the department is totally hopeless or, with major reforms, is still salvageable. That rather overstates the case; however, the fact is, State has many severe critics, and few objective observers believe the department actually does a good job.

Nevertheless, it *is* the only Department of State we have and, hence, every incoming American president in recent times has felt compelled to make a speech early in his term indicating that the Department of State will be his main instrument of foreign policy. As predictable and recurrent as is this speech, however, is the fact that within one year of being in office the same president is certain to have despaired of and denounced the department and declared that he and his own staff, usually meaning the National Security Council, will henceforth run foreign policy from the White House.

The State Department then fades again into oblivion, to be used mainly as a messenger service and to handle routine issues, but not matters of important substance. Why is this so, and how did this sad state of affairs come to be?

History

The history of the State Department may be divided into three distinct periods: before 1940, from 1940 to 1960, and from 1960 to present.

Before 1940, the State Department was small, with few personnel and limited activities. The limited activities reflected the low level of United States participation in world affairs—except perhaps for Latin America, the Caribbean, and Western Europe—prior to World War II. There were sporadic and usually short-lived excursions into the global arena (such as during World War I), but the United States generally tried to stay out of entangling international obligations.

We were still an isolationist country at that time, and the limited activities at the State Department reflected that fact. State's responsibilities were confined to routine consular (visas, passports) and some diplomatic affairs, but the department was not often involved in the great issues of world affairs. Its small number of personnel tended to be generalists and troubleshooters, without great experience or expertise in any of the world's areas but with a smattering of knowledge about each. Department personnel were assigned to problems and areas as they arose, often on an ad hoc basis, and they were obliged to learn as they proceeded. While these people were often intelligent and skillful, they tended to conduct foreign affairs unsystematically, impressionistically, and by the proverbial "seat of the pants." Unfortunately for State, these traditions and practices are often still characteristic of the department today.

During and in the aftermath of World War II, State became a much more active player in United States foreign policy and on the world's stage. This is the second phase in State's development. The war pulled the United States into the world arena and made it a truly global power. Then, in the aftermath of World War II, the cold war began. The United States could not just disband its military forces after the war, abandon its global role, and revert to isolationism. The ongoing conflicts with the Soviet Union; Communist challenges in Eastern Europe, Greece, Italy, France, Iran, and elsewhere; NATO; the Marshall Plan; the Chinese Communist revolution; the reconstruction of Western Europe and Japan; the Korean war—all these events meant the continuation and expansion of vigorous diplomatic activity.

The State Department hence expanded from a few hundred professional foreign service officers (FSOs) to several thousand. At one fell swoop in the 1950s, large numbers of civil service personnel were assigned to the department and given status as foreign service officers, doubling the department's size. Reflecting its expanded responsibilities as a global superpower, the United States now had a far greater need than ever before in its history for a large, professional foreign service.

Not only did the size of the department vastly increase, but so did its functions. To an unprecedented degree, State began to get into cultural affairs, commercial relations, civil-military affairs, the activities of foreign labor movements, and a variety of other matters that went considerably beyond what we think of as normal diplomatic activities. Eventually State moved out of its cramped quarters next to the White House in the Old Executive Office Building (which for a long time also housed the Departments of the Army and the Navy under the same roof), consolidated its many activities, which by the 1950s were in buildings scattered all around Washington, and moved into its own new and immense office building three-quarters of a mile west of the White House in that Washington neighborhood known as Foggy Bottom (so named, not because of State's alleged fuzzy or foggy thinking, but because, before being drained, this area consisted of swampy bottom land near the Potomac River that was usually foggy). Today State itself is often referred to by that same shorthand term, "Foggy Bottom."

Even with State's rapid expansion in size and functions, its historic problems remained. Its career officers continued to "fly" and make decisions "by the seat of their pants" rather than systematically. State tends to see every issue or problem as distinct, discrete; it is not good at mapping general patterns, and it has long been opposed to systematic scholarly analysis that emphasizes the general and the comparative over the specific. State continued to prefer liberal arts generalists who could see the entire world in broad terms rather than the area and issue specialists who are now so required in today's more complex world.

The rapid expansion of the department and the difficult issues with which it had to grapple in the post–World War II period also led to tensions and problems. The State Department was not very accurate in predicting Soviet expansionism and behavior; only a handful of analysts predicted the outcome of the great Chinese revolution of the 1940s (and they were then villified and purged during the McCarthy era); its record during the Korean war of the early 1950s was not distinguished; and on other issues and countries its ability to predict and shape the results was seriously flawed. In 1953 Senator Joseph McCarthy of Wisconsin accused the State Department of having scores of Communists in its ranks—worse, of coddling them and then covering up these facts from the American public. McCarthy's charges, only part of which were true, and his tactics of smearing people with the "Red" or "Pinko" label because of their mere association with Communists helped undermine morale in the department and contributed to its discrediting in the eyes of the American people. State, which had long been mocked because of its fancy "cookie pushers" and "striped pants diplomats," was now thought of as "disloyal" besides.

The third era in States history, its decline, dates from the 1960s. There is no one single event that precipitated this decline, nor can we say that it began in any one year. Rather, the causes were long term and gradual. Three major factors may be identified. The first was State's own bad decisions and intrinsic problems—we discuss these in more detail below. The second was the rise of the Department of Defense and the Central Intelligence Agency, which began more and more to take over foreign affairs responsibilities, including in those areas—such as diplomacy and political relations—once reserved for State. The third was presidential distrust of the State Department that led to the vast expansion of the National Security Council (NSC), a "mini state department" located in the White House upon which presidents came to rely more and more for carrying out foreign policy. This process began in the early 1960s under Kennedy, and it reached its apogee in the late 1960s when the NSC under Henry Kissinger became preeminent, and State was almost completely eclipsed.

More recently, the State Department has attempted to make a comeback. Under secretaries Vance (Carter), Shultz (Reagan), and Baker (Bush), State played a more assertive role and began to recover some of its lost influence. But compared with the other main foreign policy agencies, State's power remains quite circumscribed.

Structure

The Department of State is organized in a typical bureaucratic pyramid (see Fig. 11.1). At the top is the secretary of state who sets the overall tone for the department and is, next to the president, the country's key decision maker in the foreign affairs area. The secretary is charged with the responsibility for the overall guidance, coordination, and supervision of foreign policy. His responsibilities include advising the president, testifying before Congress, serving as spokesman for American foreign policy, negotiating and implementing policy, as well as running the department. The secretary of state also has a deputy secretary, the second most impor tant person in the department, who is the secretary's alter ego and serves as his stand-in to run the department when the secretary is away.[1]

Below the secretary and the deputy secretary are four undersecretaries of state: an undersecretary for management who helps administer the department, an undersecretary for economic affairs, an undersecretary for political affairs, and an undersecretary for security assistance, science and

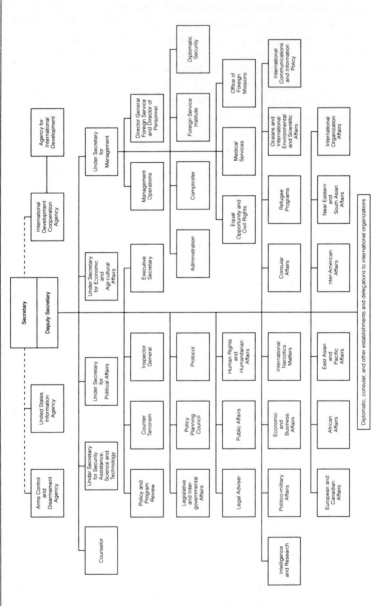

Figure 11.1
Department of State

technology. At this level, too, is the department's counselor who provides legal advice to the secretary. Other key officials at this level are the persons who manage the paper flow into the secretary's office and assign issues to the distinct bureaus. All these key offices are located on the seventh floor of the department where the most important decisions are made. The seventh floor has its own dining rooms, reception areas, as well as a nice view of the Potomac River.

The seventh floor also houses the department's Policy Planning Staff. This office sounds impressive, and is often the office to which academic foreign policy specialists are appointed. Policy Planning has gone through several incarnations and reincarnations in recent years, but it has seldom been an effective or influential agency. For one thing, the State Department subculture (more on this below) is often suspicious of and hostile toward long-range planning and the social science research that undergirds it; for another, foreign service officers are hostile to outsiders (academics and otherwise) who come into the department on a noncareer basis, and they have therefore devised ways of bypassing the Policy Planning Staff.

At the next level in the hierarchy are the assistant secretaries of state, of which there are fourteen. Five of these are in charge of regional bureaus (which are small bureaucracies in themselves); and nine are called functional bureaus. The five regional bureaus (for Europe, Africa, East Asia and Pacific, Latin America, and Near East and South Asia) are generally thought of as more important than the functional bureaus (Congressional Relations, Consular Affairs, Intelligence and Research, etc.). The assistant secretaries who head bureaus are key officials because they have a strong influence in the formulation of policy affecting their particular area, as well as in its implementation. We can usually tell what the foreign policy line of a particular administration will be, as well as its effectiveness, by studying closely the appointments at this level. For example, under President Carter, *all* the assistant secretaries came out of the left, McGovernite, or romantic wing of the Democratic party, and none out of the center or right wings of the party, a fact that quickly got Mr. Carter's foreign policy in trouble.

Each assistant secretary has several deputy assistant secretaries. Deputy assistant secretaries are often chosen both for their knowledge and for the specific political requirements they satisfy. For example, of the four deputy assistant secretaries in the Bureau of Inter-American (Latin America) Affairs, it is common practice for one to be a Hispanic, one a political appointee favored by the White House, one a specialist in economic affairs, and one a foreign service officer who actually knows something about Latin America.

All of the above positions (deputy assistant secretary and higher) are "political"—that is, they are subject to presidential appointment and removal. Below these levels (and often aspiring to these higher jobs) are the professional or career foreign service officers (FSOs) of which there are about eight thousand. FSOs serve in the various bureaus; they handle the flow of information coming in from the countries in a particular region (country desk officers); they work at bureaucratic jobs; or they may serve in the United States missions abroad. The life of a young FSO is often a frustrating one since the FSO often does menial bureaucratic tasks for many years before qualifying for a more important position; and then, just when he or she qualifies for a higher position, that job may be given to a political appointee.

In addition to these jobs at the State Department in Washington, the United States has representation at over one hundred thirty embassies and one hundred fifty other diplomatic posts (such as consular posts in major cities) throughout the world. The embassy is normally headed by an ambassador, with his deputy chief of mission (DCM), and contains several subdivisions responsible for economic affairs, political affairs, and often labor and military affairs. These overseas missions serve as the official links between the United States government and the foreign nations of the world. The job of the ambassador and the FSOs that are part of the mission is to represent the United States abroad, assess local conditions and report back to Washington, and implement policies decided by the president or the secretary of state.

The ambassador is, of course, the head of the United States mission; but in an era of instant satellite communications, shuttle diplomacy by the secretary of state, and vast amounts of information flowing in from the country via the press, interest groups, and roving Americans, the ambassador's role has become more circumscribed in recent decades. Another problem is policy coordination; while the ambassador is nominally in charge of the entire family of United States official relations in that country, in fact the military mission in the embassy may report directly to the Pentagon without fully informing the ambassador, or the CIA mission may report directly to CIA headquarters in Langley, Virginia, without giving the ambassador full information. In this way, the bureaucratic politics and rivalries between foreign policy agencies that go on in Washington, D.C., are repeated in the United States embassies abroad. The result is a further lack of coordination of American foreign policy.

Three other agencies deserve mention in this context, because they are linked to the State Department but are not entirely coordinated with it, which adds further to the bureaucratic confusion. The Arms Control and Disarmament Agency (ACDA) "reports" to the secretary of state and yet is a separate agency, with its own personnel system, its own responsibilities in the arms control area, and its own channel to report directly to the president rather than through the secretary of state. The United States Information Agency (USIA), which disseminates information about the United States abroad and also runs cultural and exchange programs, is similarly connected with State but at the same time independent from it. Its personnel are often looked down on by the State Department's FSOs. Similarly with the Agency for International Development (AID): it is physically located within the State Department but it is not always well coordinated with it and its employees are often treated as second-class citizens by the FSOs. Once again, the theme is fragmentation and lack of coordination of United States foreign policy.

Department Subculture

The State Department (as with other agencies) has its own subculture. Often referred to as the "fudge factory" and by other derogatory terms, State is viewed by many as a very funny place to work. It is widely thought of as aristocratic, snobbish, undemocratic, narrow, haughty, stuffy, phony, and effete. The department tends to be hostile to outsiders, inward looking and limited in its perspectives, often anti-academic and anti-intellectual, favoring generalists over specialists and intuition over scholarship. Its personnel are often accused of using the mask of a quiet, reserved demeanor and a reluctance to speak out forthrightly to hide their lack of knowledge about various subjects. These are the main stereotypes applied to State and, as with most stereotypes, there is some truth to them as well as some exaggeration.

For many decades, State Department personnel came overwhelmingly and disproportionately from the Ivy League campuses. This background gave credence to State's reputation as elite, snobbish, and effete. In the last two decades, however, State Department personnel have come increasingly from public universities, and the department has tried—albeit sometimes halfheartedly—to recruit women and minorities. But the old attitudes persist so that even among the public school graduates the department often inculcates a stiff, reserved, condescending air.

State Department personnel often share what may be called (with due respect to that great university) "the Princeton syndrome." That is, they often assume that all that is needed to be a successful FSO is natural intelligence and a B.A. degree (probably in history) from Princeton (or another Ivy League institution). That degree enables one to understand the broad outlines of Western civilization and history which, presumably, all other countries will and must follow if they are to be successful. This view is terribly ethnocentric and old-fashioned, but it is widespread within the State Department.[2] It helps explain why the department so little comprehends the Third World (which is often non-Western and will not, palely and retardedly, imitate the United States), why it does not value advanced or specialized training leading to the Ph.D. degree (although that is beginning to change), and why State Department reporting on foreign countries and foreign situations is often weaker and less sophisticated than that of other agencies. The State Department can't conceptualize, as Henry Kissinger used to complain; it seems incapable of going beyond individual cases to see general patterns; it prefers intuition over serious scholarly research; and it makes decisions impressionistically rather than by more rigorous, social-scientific means. These practices help explain why, in comparison with the CIA or the Department of Defense (which do, increasingly, hire Ph.D.'s), the State Department's reporting and assessment tend to be the weakest of the three. These weaknesses also help explain the working rule that many reporters and scholars follow when abroad: that if you want to know what's going on in a particular country, stay away from the State Department representatives.

More than other agencies, the State Department is particularly hostile to outsiders. Its own entrance requirements are very difficult and department personnel are therefore often antagonistic to those who bypass these processes; in addition, for the sake of the career opportunities of its own people, the department does not want outsiders taking the better jobs that would otherwise go to FSOs. The department hence reacts strongly when a president makes political appointments to ambassadorial posts; it also does not want academics and other outsiders appointed to positions within the bureaus or the Policy Planning Staff. Frequently, outstanding scholars and knowledgeable people have been vetoed for department appointments not on the basis of merit but simply because State does not want outsiders coming in. To a degree, of course, one can understand these resentments; but the overall result has been to isolate State from outside and beneficial influences, to keep out talent and ability, to reconfirm State in its own stuffy ways, and to harm the quality of American foreign policy-making.

As an elite corps, the State Department often presumes to know what's best for American foreign policy. It resents it when elected officials, including the president, try to tell it what to do. Sometimes it tries to change a president's policies, or to run rings around them, or to scuttle them entirely. As a result, no recent American president has fully trusted State. That helps explain the phenomenal growth of the National Security Council in recent years and the desire by a succession of presidents to locate foreign policy in the White House (the NSC) and take it out of the hands of the State Department.

State thinks of itself as *the* repository of foreign affairs knowledge and continuity, while elected officials insist that State ought also to follow the election returns. When a president gets 60 percent of the popular vote as his mandate, the State Department ought to acknowledge that fact as also providing, in a democracy, certain instructions about the preferences of Americans in the foreign policy area. But instead, State seeks to ignore the election returns and, often, to subvert a new president's policy. These practices have led to the charges that State is a disloyal agency and does not adequately carry out the president's foreign policy (both Mr. Carter and Mr.

Reagan had this problem with State, although from opposite sides of the political spectrum: Carter thought it was too conservative and Reagan, too liberal). Obviously we want continuity in foreign policy as reflected in the career foreign service, but we also require a foreign policy that reflects democratic preferences. In this country we have not yet achieved the appropriate balance between the professionalism and knowledge often-times found in the State Department *and* the desires of the country as expressed at election times.

Another problem at State is that it has not yet recognized and come to grips with the more democratic character of recent American foreign policy. As a somewhat elitist institution, State thinks that it can continue to make policy in a vacuum, as if the rest of the country didn't exist. But we have seen earlier that religious, human rights, ethnic, and other lobbies are increasingly out there "in the streets" working for their own visions of foreign policy. The State Department, however, refuses to go down to this street level, believing that, since it presumably knows best, it can continue to make policy regardless of what the public thinks or however interest groups lobby.

When the department did finally in the mid-1980s create a more elaborate Office of Public Diplomacy, oriented toward public relations and getting the department's message out, it did so reluctantly and over the nose-up objections of many FSOs. But the department needs to recognize that if it wishes to get its policy positions out there and to have its often reasoned views prevail, it needs to campaign and lobby for them. We are no longer in a situation domestically where the State Department's views will prevail just because State *says* they are superior. Rather, in this new, more democratic context, State must get out there in the universities, the churches, the town meetings and argue its case in public forums just like everyone else. Only by this route can the department's policy recommen-dations on Central America, Soviet relations, nuclear issues, and so forth gain the public support and legitimacy that are required. Such an exercise in public education and diplomacy would not only be good for the country but it would also be enormously healthy for that staid and elitist bureauc-racy that is the State Department.

The department's Foreign Service Institute (FSI)—State's teaching arm, designed to give language and area studies training to the FSOs—illustrates many of these problems. First, FSI is a low priority in State's pecking order, so that when the Department must absorb budget cuts, FSI is the first to feel the blow. Second, the leadership at FSI is weak, often consisting of about-to-be retired diplomats who are being put out to pasture. Third, the language training has long been weak, helping explain why so few FSOs in our embassies abroad can function effectively in the local language.

Weaker still, fourth, are the area studies programs designed to prepare a young officer for the culture, society, and politics of a new country. The courses are mediocre, poorly designed, and seldom taught by outstanding people. The courses consist of once-a-week lectures or seminars lasting for about two hours and running up to sixteen weeks. This is a woefully inadequate number of hours for a person to even begin to absorb the culture of a new country and how it works, let alone to understand how to function effectively overseas. There is little rigor in the classes, no required reading, and the instructors are not able to evaluate the FSOs either on their classroom performance or their suitability to serve the United States abroad. Frankly, some of these FSOs should never be permitted to represent the United States.

Attendance in these classes is not consistently required and many FSOs and ambassadors are able to bypass the course either completely or by taking a two-week "short course." This stands in marked contrast to the West German and other foreign services which spend two to three *years* training a person before sending him to a new posting. Having taught several courses at FSI, this writer can attest that it is a very frustrating teaching experience and does not at all prepare FSOs for the countries to which they will soon be sent. Doubtless this inadequate preparation also helps explain why State Department reporting about the countries is so superficial and so often marked by the absence of understanding, and why our foreign policy is so often inadequate.

A Department in Decline?

A career in the foreign service sounds exciting and romantic, but is it really? Far less so than used to be the case. For one thing, so much of the work is routine—standard operating procedures or SOPs. Young FSOs can expect to spend their early years licking stamps and fetching paper clips or serving in boring consular jobs. Even as they move up in the hierarchy, about 80 percent of the work is routine, while the remaining 20 percent may be creative and rewarding. But that is probably true for most jobs, and it may be that the 20 percent that is creative is well worth the struggle.

Second, State has a host of intrinsic problems as outlined here. The State Department has probably been the most studied and the most reorganized of all the Washington agencies. The problem is not the organization, however; instead it is the people and the particular subculture at State. The latter is so troublesome that many people, including most recent presidents, have all but given up hope of changing the place.

Third, State has lost power relative to other agencies. Its policy influence has been gravely weakened since the 1960s. Not only has it declined in influence relative to the Department of Defense and the CIA (both considered below), but currently it is also losing influence compared with the Department of Treasury, the Justice Department, and the Commerce Department (considered in Chapter 12). State has enjoyed a limited recovery in recent years, but it will not likely recoup the influence it had in the 1940–60 period.

Finally, it needs to be recognized that State has almost no domestic constituency. This is another factor in State's decline. The Agricultural Department has a symbiotic relationship with American farmers, the Commerce Department is closely intertwined with American business, the Labor Department has organized labor, and the Defense Department has the so-called military-industrial complex. But who speaks for, supports, defends, depends for contracts on, or has a symbiotic relationship with the State Department? The answer is, no one. That is disastrous for State—and for American foreign policy. For in this era of more "corporatized" politics, where government agencies and private interests are closely intertwined at all kinds of levels, the State Department has no interest groups with which it can interface, that support it, and that give it a constituency. Foreign affairs has no constituency and, therefore, neither political support nor political clout in the United States. But that is emphatically not the case with the department we consider next.

DEPARTMENT OF DEFENSE

The debate often waxes hot and heavy in the United States over which agency is more rigidly bureaucratized and less amenable to reform: the Department of State or the Department of Defense (DOD). With its $300 billion budget and over three million employees (two-thirds of whom are in uniform; the rest, one million, are civilians), the Defense Department may be the world's largest bureaucracy and one of its most cumbersome. Any agency that large is virtually impossible to administer, let alone to reform. Reformers have often despaired of getting the Defense Department to reform itself, to say nothing of the difficulties of changing it from the outside. Nevertheless, even a bureaucracy as huge and unwieldy as this one does change over time, adapt, and go through some major sea changes. DOD may not be as "hopeless" as the critics sometimes charge; it moves, as one senator put it, like a boulder—one inch at a time.

Nor should anyone doubt the utility of the nation's defense forces as an instrument of foreign policy. The United States military, at its most fundamental level, serves as a deterrent to outside and hostile aggression. This is its most basic role. It defends the country. It serves to protect America's friends and allies. It guards vital sea lanes, such as in the Persian Gulf, which if closed would choke the economies of Western Europe and Japan as well as the United States, cause massive unemployment, close down many social programs, and provoke enormous chaos throughout the world. The world's nations and our interdependent economies cannot permit this to happen. In addition, and at a very serious level, the United States defense forces serve as protectors of the American way of life, ward off the possibilities for Soviet or other enemy subversion and attack, and function as the ultimate guarantors of our freedoms and liberties.

The key principle of American deterrence strategy is that our military capabilities must be sufficiently strong that they need not be used. This proposition is difficult for many Americans to grasp since it is based on a seeming paradox: a strong defense is necessary to prevent our having to use it. Our military capability needs to be so strong that no enemy would dare to attack us.

The United States is not an aggressive or a territory-seeking nation; we try to protect our interests but we seek no global conquests. Rather, as an affluent and democratic nation, the United States much prefers to live in peace and harmony with the world, on the assumption that our own and other countries' economic, social, and political development are compatible and can go forward hand in hand.

Hence our military strategy is primarily defensive; even our offensive capabilities are designed to support the deterrence strategy of preventing others from attacking us rather than our aggressively attacking them first. Deterrence strategy has its problems, both logical and practical, and we can argue about whether an effective deterrence requires military superiority to all other nations or merely parity. But the overwhelming majority of Americans support the general principle of remaining strong militarily in order to prevent war and not wage it; and until something better is found, an enlightened deterrence strategy is likely to remain our basic and fundamental defense posture. The question for debate is not whether to have such a military deterrent (which virtually everyone accepts) but rather how much deterrence is enough.

There will be times when the United States will need to use force; but for the most part, the strategy is to use the *threat* of force rather than the real thing. However, when exercising even the threat to use force as a deterrent to actually having to use it, certain ground rules apply. First, we must recognize that the use of or threat to use force is not appropriate in all circumstances and that we must be very careful and discriminating when we decide to employ it. Second, civilian politicians must understand the military as well as the force threat and how to use them. Third, the armed forces must be involved along with the civilians in planning for a proposed maneuver right from the beginning. Fourth, the threat to use force must be credible or believable. Fifth, the display of strength must be overwhelming to be effective. And sixth, the purposes as well as limits to a display or limited use of force must be clear to all involved. That helps explain, incidentally, why it is the United States Navy that is involved in

approximately 80 percent of all such displays of force: navy :
visible, they can represent a potential threat to some host
while sailing in international waters (and thus avoiding
sovereignty), and they can be brought in and pulled out rather quickly and
easily (as compared with American ground forces, for example).

In this way, military pressure should be seen as only one of several
possible arms of United States policy—the others being summits, jawbon-
ing, diplomacy, political pressure, the mobilization of international opinion, covert operations, or economic pressures. Military pressure may have
to be resorted to when these other levers do not work or, sometimes, in
combination with them. The military is thus a foreign policy instrument;
however, it cannot be substituted for a sound political and diplomatic
strategy, and it must be used sparingly, reinforcing other actions, and only
when the chances of success are high. Military pressures, echoing the
conclusion of the foremost classical theorist of war, Carl von Clausewitz,
should thus be seen as politics and foreign policy carried out by other,
sometimes more violent, means.

Clausewitz goes on to argue that war is seldom an independent action
in itself but only an extension of politics or diplomacy. Nations do not
usually fight for the sake of fighting but for other causes that are generally
political in nature. As long as there is political conflict, there may also be
violent conflict, or war. However, to use the military does not need to mean
that violence will occur. Rather, it is the *threat* of violence—preparedness,
often just a demonstration of strength—that will be sufficient to accomplish
the objectives. It is for this reason, the logic of deterrence, that the United
States, in an essentially anarchic international environment devoid of very
much effective international law and with a (at least heretofore) hostile,
aggressive, and implacable foe in the form of the Soviet Union, must
continue to maintain a strong military force. We do not wish to attack
anyone; on the other hand, world conditions are not yet such that we can
unilaterally disarm and turn our "arms into plowshares" either. Until the
world changes or the human race's sometimes aggressive interests are
curbed, the United States must be prepared to defend itself, including with
military means. It is in this prudent and broad middle position, based
neither on aggression nor on one-way disarmament, that United States
deterrence strategy rests. True peace in a sometimes violent world comes
from American strength, not weakness.

History

The United States, like other nations before it and since, has learned
these principles of deterrence and the need for a strong military defense
from history and experience. At first the new nation that was the United
States in the eighteenth century had hoped that it would not need a

military; but troubles on the frontier, conflicts with such large European colonial powers as France and Spain, threats to American trade, and then the British invasion of the United States in 1812 and Britain's larger imperial designs dispelled this romantic idea. Nevertheless through the mid-nineteenth century the United States kept its military forces small, dispersed, and away from the seat of power in Washington, D.C. Only on one occasion (1860–64) prior to the twentieth century did the United States mobilize large military forces, and that was in a civil war, not an international conflict. Throughout the 1800s the United States remained a small, weak power, isolationist, exceptionalist, and preoccupied not with foreign affairs but with continental expansion.

As the United States became a major industrial power after the Civil War, it also acquired larger international ambitions and newfound military might. Admiral Alfred Thayer Mahan, the apostle of American sea power, laid the theoretical and strategic groundwork in the 1890s for the United States to emerge as a major global power. The United States built up its naval and military forces. By the 1890s, the United States was challenging the dominant British position in Central America, and in 1898 the United States defeated Spain and acquired her last remaining colonies in the Caribbean (Puerto Rico as well as a protectorate over Cuba) and the Pacific (the Philippines). The United States had emerged as a major world actor.

But even as a global power, the United States remained a reluctant warrior. Our policy was still generally isolationist and noninvolved. Unlike the other great powers, we did not maintain a large standing army. Rather, the American posture was to mobilize a large military force in times of genuine national crisis—and then demobilize once the crisis of the moment had passed. That is how we fought both World Wars I and II. We recruited a large army, fought for the defense of our principles and national interests, defeated our enemies, and then packed our bags and went home. We did not maintain large *standing* armies after the war ended. And after World War I, we refused to get involved in the League of Nations, the predecessor of the United Nations, because we did not wish to stay involved in foreign entanglements and wanted to distance ourselves from European conflicts. We fought heroically in both world wars, but we did not desire to maintain a large peacetime army or to serve as the police force of the world. After both of these wars, we demobilized and sent the troops home.

World War II was different, however, because the cold war with the Soviet Union began in its immediate aftermath. President Truman wished to keep a sizable contingent in uniform to serve as a check on Stalin's aggressive intentions, but in the immediate aftermath of the war he was unable to do so. The domestic pressures to "bring the boys home" and return to "normalcy" were just too great. So essentially what the United States did was to demobilize after World War II and then slowly mobilize again in the late 1940s as the cold war got under way in earnest.

The period of the late 1940s was a key turning point in United States military history. Not only did the cold war begin and the United States move, for the first time, toward the creation of a large, standing, peacetime army; but this was a period of reevaluating and reformulating United States strategic thinking to deal with the Soviet and Communist threat *and* of the most far-reaching restructuring of the United States military organization that we have ever experienced. For this was the time (1947) when we created the Department of Defense, the Joint Chiefs of Staff, and the office of the Secretary of Defense. Now the United States was truly a global superpower—not just on a temporary basis during wartime but on a permanent, standing basis.

Structure

Through World War II, the three main services (army, navy, and air force) continued as separate agencies. The war effort revealed the need for closer cooperation and coordination between them. Hence, in 1947 Congress passed the National Security Act.

The National Security Act was one of the most important and far-reaching pieces of legislation ever enacted. The act created both the CIA (discussed below) and the National Security Council or NSC (treated in Chapter 14). Although the act contained a number of compromises that had to be introduced for political reasons, and although it left a number of bureaucratic and interagency differences unresolved, it provided a basic framework for what was almost a revolution in the organization of the American national security system. The most controversial provisions of the act were those dealing with the military services.

The act created a National Military Establishment (changed in 1949 to the Department of Defense or DOD) that consisted of three executive-level service departments (army, navy, and air force), each headed by a civilian secretary. The three service departments were in turn subordinated to (and this was the real revolution) the new Office of the Secretary of Defense (OSD), headed by a civilian who would have cabinet rank. For the first time in United States history, the separate services were to be under a single administrative structure whose administrator (the secretary) must, by law, be a civilian. In addition, the act created the Joint Chiefs of Staff (Army Chief of Staff, Chief of Naval Operations, and Air Force Chief of Staff; 1952 legislation authorized the commandant of the Marine Corps to sit with the JCS as an equal when matters affecting the Marine Corps were to be discussed). Under the 1947 act, the Joint Chiefs were to serve as the primary advisers to the president, the NSC, and the secretary of defense on defense matters, and to function as intermediaries, brokers, and transmission belts between the armed services and the civilian defense secretary.

The Department of Defense has grown to be a very large and very powerful foreign policy influence (see Fig. 11.2). DOD is not just an implementer, in the military realm, of decisions made elsewhere (by the president, presumably, or the secretary of state) but is in fact itself a major actor in the *formulation* of foreign policy decisions. The precise influence of DOD is both controversial and variable over time: some analysts argue that it is just one influence among many in the making of American foreign policy, while others say it has surpassed the State Department and other agencies to become *the* dominant voice in foreign policy. However, no one doubts that the Defense Department (in contrast to State) has significantly increased its influence in the decades since 1947.

The secretary of defense has become increasingly important over the years. Amendments to the 1947 National Security Act in 1949, 1952, and 1958 added new under- and assistant secretaries to the secretary's office, enabling him to expand his staff and increase his power. The secretary was also given the power to transfer, consolidate, and even abolish functions among the military services. The early secretaries of defense in the 1940s and 1950s tended to be administrators of the huge Defense Department; but under Robert McNamara in the 1960s not only were power and decision making affecting the services consolidated more and more in the secretary's office but McNamara also emerged, in the context of the accelerating conflict in Southeast Asia, as a principal adviser on foreign policy, rivaling and often surpassing the secretary of state. From that time to this, the secretary of defense has generally been able to command as much or more influence over foreign policy as the State Department, and, with the exception (and even that may be controversial) of the Kissinger years, to have as much or more influence as the national security adviser.

If one focuses on the administrative *Office* of the Secretary of Defense and not just the secretary himself, the reasons for this rising influence will become clear. A glance back at Figure 11.2 may help to illustrate the point. Below the secretary of defense is a *vast* bureaucracy—considerably larger than that of the State Department and so vast that most of it is not even pictured in this diagram. Not only does the secretary of defense have an Executive Secretariat and an Armed Forces Policy Council, but he also has under his administrative authority *all* of the services, the office of the Joint Chiefs of Staff, all of the specified commands (Atlantic, Europe, etc.), and all of the myriad defense agencies (National Security Agency and the like).

If one then looks just below the boxes for the Secretary and Undersecretary of Defense in Figure 11.2, one finds a large box called Undersecretaries and Assistant Secretaries of Defense. This broad category obscures what is a vast panoply of bureaus that largely repeat, in the Defense Department context, the same regional and functional bureaus of the State Department. In other words, DOD administratively has everything State has—and then some! These bureaus, furthermore, are not just agencies to oversee military activities but also have important political, diplomatic, intelligence, and economic functions as well. Defense not only overlaps

Figure 11.2
Department of Defense Organization Chart

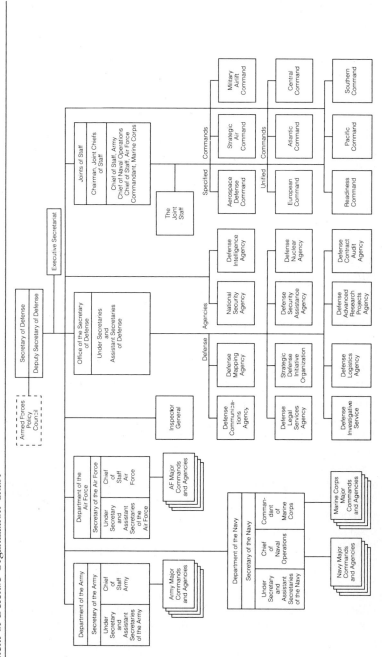

the political and diplomatic functions of State but, with its immense budget, can often outinfluence State as well.

Two of these agencies help illustrate the vast range of the OSD's influence and its incursions into civilian policy areas. The Office of International Security Policy (ISP) does planning (like State's Policy Planning Office) on strategic issues, recommends policy on arms control issues, and monitors political and economic as well as military trends having to do with NATO and East-West trends. Even more important than ISP is DOD's Office of International Security Affairs (ISA), which deals with security assistance, United States military missions abroad, international energy and economic issues, and the oversight of agreements with other nations. ISA's responsibilities are very far-ranging and, more than that, ISA provides a broad political component to the military assessments done by the Pentagon. For this reason, ISA is often referred to as the "little State Department," with functions and a budget that again may overshadow State's own. A further DOD incursion into the realm of political-diplomatic affairs came in 1977 with the creation of the position of Undersecretary of Defense for Policy, whose tasks are to integrate DOD policies with overall national security goals and to coordinate all DOD activities relating to political-military affairs.

The Joint Chiefs of Staff (JCS), which brings together the heads of the four services, plus a chairman, was created to provide a link between the professional military and the civilian DOD leadership. The chairman of the JCS is the president's top military adviser, while the JCS itself is supposed to provide strategic planning, a unified military voice, and coordination between the services. In practice, however, the JCS has been less influential in shaping policy than have the civilians in the Office of the Secretary of Defense. One reason for this is that the joint chiefs still represent their respective services and do not always present the coordinated view that is necessary. Another reason is that the presidents and secretaries of defense we have had have not always found the JCS's advice helpful and some have even tried to reduce the JCS's policy impact. Recent reorganizations have sought to overcome these obstacles and enhance the authority of the JCS.

Despite the ongoing problems of effectively utilizing the joint chiefs, there can be no doubt concerning the enormous accrual of Defense Department power in the foreign affairs area in the past four decades. Not only has DOD influence grown, but it has often come at the expense of other agencies, principally State. For along with the growth of DOD's military and strategic responsibilities has come the parallel enlargement of this department's political, economic, and diplomatic functions, which frequently encroach on State's territory. DOD can, in effect, duplicate everything State does—and, with its immense budget and bureaucratic infrastructure, can often do more or do so more effectively. It is small wonder that State has resented these incursions and sought to protect its turf. Perhaps it should not be surprising therefore to learn that some of the most protracted and complex fights in recent years have been not between the United States and its enemies but between our own departments of Defense and State.

The Defense Department Subculture

The military services, the Department of Defense, and the United States military academies and (postgraduate) defense colleges contain some of the nicest, smartest, most capable people to be found anywhere. The problem here is not the people, who are often very talented, but a system and a bureaucracy that are often frustrating, debilitating, and wasteful. Moreover, these inefficient features are often the standard operating procedures (SOPs) within DOD—so much so that very careful and articulate observers often despair of the system ever being repaired. This is not a criticism of the military or its personnel but of a *system* that has become unwieldy and, perhaps, unmanageable.

The first thing to say about the subculture of the military institution is that it is gung ho and has a great deal of *esprit*. Since the despiriting encounter in Vietnam, the military has come back. A generation has passed since that discouraging war, which played havoc on the military in the field as well as its reputation at home. The new enthusiasm within the military is reflected in the fact that the number of recruits is up, applications for the academies are way up, and Defense Department budgets have been up. Contrary to some notions that a few persons hold, the American military is not eager to get into a new war nor is it training the recruits to be "killers." Rather, this is a military that is highly professional and *prepared:* well-trained, well-equipped, and with a renewed enthusiasm for its role of providing for the common defense. It is doubtful if the spirit within the military has ever been as high as it has been recently, and certainly not in the last twenty years.

A second feature of the American military is that it is politically conservative, but not rabidly so. There are a few extreme right-wingers within the armed forces, but the dominant position is centrist or moderate Republican. These are prudent, practical persons, not ideologues. Since, as we saw in Chapter 7, the modern Republican party is widely perceived to be strong on defense issues and the Democratic party weak, it should not be surprising that military personnel should vote in overwhelming numbers—probably upwards of 95 percent in 1988—for the Republican presidential candidate. Although they strongly supported his defense buildup and the mood of renewed faith and optimism he brought to the country, many military men were nonetheless skeptical of some of Ronald Reagan's program and ideology. They want a practical and prudent leadership, not one that is heavily ideological. Moderately conservative they tend to be, but right-wing "nuts," no.

The military is conservative in another way: it wants to avoid "another Vietnam." Not only was Vietnam a terrible defeat, but it also reflected discredit on the military institution itself. Hence when the United States sent troops into Lebanon in the early 1980s, it was the State Department that pushed for this policy and not Defense. When United States naval forces were sent into the Persian Gulf, it was the Defense Department and Secretary Weinberger that put some limiting conditions on their use. And when the Reagan administration contemplated using United States ground forces in Central America, it was the military—to the administration's surprise, since it assumed that the strongest supporters for its policies would be found in the Pentagon—that strongly resisted. The modern American military wants no part of armed action unless (1) the objectives are clear; (2) the public is unified behind the policy; and (3) the objectives can be accomplished quickly, before American public opinion, which is notoriously impatient, tires of the conflict. These conditions were of course absent in Vietnam, and they were absent in the early Reagan administration policy toward Central America; the result was that DOD did not support the policy option of sending troops to the area.

A major problem in the military subculture remains the divisions between the services. Even after forty years under a single secretary of defense and with the creation of the integrating Joint Chiefs of Staff, this problem has still not been resolved. The problem is not just good-natured rivalries between the services and their respective academy football and other teams but goes deeper than that. It involves overlaps between the services, costly duplication, and enormous waste of money, men, and materials. For instance, each of the services now has its own special forces units, each has its own intelligence arms, its own airplanes, its own helicopters, and so forth. In every conflict—Vietnam, the Iranian rescue operation, Grenada—each service wants to get into the act to add glory, combat experience, and medals to its ranks—whether that service is needed or useful in that particular conflict or not. In both Iran and Grenada, the desire for all the services to be involved resulted in some *fatal* incompatibilities of machinery, methods, and technologies.

Moreover, each service has its own particular way and procedures for doing virtually everything—SOPs—which make it virtually impossible to streamline or coordinate them. Often such duplication is done consciously for the purpose of enhancing the overall Defense Department budget; the services never criticize each other and are in collusion to ensure that each gets what it wants. The system is so cumbersome, so deeply ingrained, that reformers have all but given up ever doing much about it—short of destroying the services themselves, that is. And that cannot be permitted, so the system persists and continues to limp along despite its many deficiencies.

Another problem (really a whole set of problems) concerns United States strategic thinking. Since the onset of the cold war, United States strategic thinking has always assumed that, if there is ever a conflict, it will be with the Soviet Union. This conflict will take the form either of a nuclear exchange or a more conventional war between the United States and its NATO allies *and* the Soviet Union and its Warsaw Pact allies, fought out on the plains of Central Europe. These are the kinds of wars we are, in a strategic sense, most prepared to fight. But our experience since World War II would seem to indicate that these are the *least likely* conflicts we will be called upon to engage in. Since 1945 *not a single* atomic weapon has ever been used in war, nor have there been any invasions across the plains of Europe. It is far more likely that the American military will be called upon to deal with messy, murky guerrilla wars in such peripheral areas as Southeast Asia, southern Africa, or Central America. Yet these are the kinds of wars, involving political, social, and psychological factors as well as military ones, with which we are least well equipped to deal. United States strategic thinking badly needs to be updated and modernized to deal with these kinds of conflicts as well as those of the other kind.

The bureaucratic inefficiency and ineptness of the Defense Department is also a problem. The system is slow, overloaded with paperwork, and numbing. It may take years for a paper to be shuffled or for a good idea to find its way through the bureaucratic labyrinth. The elaborate procedures and system that are DOD are terribly discouraging to bright, young, able military officials. Many have given up on it, preferring to play the game, collect their salaries, and qualify for a comfortable retirement rather than continuously butting their heads against stone walls. A number of able young academy graduates are opting out after their minimum five years of service—a terrible waste and loss to the country—rather than continuing to live with their frustrations. Many analysts blame this stifling bureaucratic system, within DOD as well as within and between the services, for a series of recent United States humiliations and disasters in Vietnam, Iran, Lebanon, and other places.

Still another problem is the symbiotic relationship of the Defense Department with defense contractors. This is the military-industrial complex about which President Eisenhower warned, a relationship between the Defense Department and its suppliers that is so cozy that it is impossible to separate DOD from the giant industrial base that supports it. The relationship often goes beyond symbiosis to encompass downright parasites as well. That is, it involves considerable graft, enormous inefficiencies, stupendous cost overruns on major weapons systems, cover-ups of shoddy materials and procedures, special favoritism to firms that do the contract work, and some whole companies that have only a single customer: the Defense Department. In any bureaucracy as large as DOD, many of these inefficiencies are all but inevitable; and with that immense $300 billion budget, some outright graft is likely too. But many analysts believe we could do far better in this area than we do and that we are not getting enough "bang for our bucks." The problem is compounded by the fact that congressmen want military bases in their districts because they bring money and jobs (every $1 billion in defense expenditures means forty thousand jobs), and these congressmen dominate the armed services and appropriations committees where decisions affecting the military are made. The Defense Department, the defense contractors, and "interested" congressmen constitute another "iron triangle" of influence in Washington that is extremely difficult to change.[3]

In other areas, however, there have been major improvements in the armed forces in recent years. Recruiting is way up ("It's a great place to start," as the commercials put it), and the quality of the recruits is also significantly improved. The United States military academies (West Point, the Naval Academy, and the Air Force Academy) have become first-rate academic institutions, attracting the cream of the crop of American young people and with entrance requirements that make them competitive with our most prestigious universities. Scores of at least 600s on both components of the Scholastic Aptitude Tests (SATs) are required or a person has almost no chance for admission. In addition, the morale of armed forces personnel is much higher than in past years and especially when compared with the Vietnam era. Finally, the immense defense buildup of the 1980s has given the United States a large and powerful military, better equipped and better prepared than at any time in our recent history.

Nevertheless, some key problems remain. First, while an overwhelming majority of Americans believe in the principle of peace through strength, we have also become weary of the cold war after forty years and tired of the large drain on our national budget that military expenditures represent. Some of this weariness is reflected in the rise of the peace movement in the 1980s, and also in the growing sentiment that we bring some of our defense forces back from Europe and Korea, or at least get our NATO allies and Japan to share more equitably in the defense burden. Given these pressures, it seems unlikely that we can sustain indefinitely the high level of defense expenditures that we currently have.

A second question involves the actual fighting capacity of our armed forces and whether they are being trained for the right kinds of wars. Many of the new recruits joined the armed forces because, for young persons just out of high school, it provides a job, education, and some hope for the future. Similarly with the officer corps: they enroll in the military academies in part, because these are prestigious academic institutions, their education is free, and they get first-rate professional training. But the idea that these young officers should in some future emergency have to occupy the oil fields of southern Mexico, go to fight in Central America or Korea, or have to stand up against a Soviet onslaught is the last thing that crosses their minds. Moreover, it is no longer Napoleonic tactics, military strategy, or how to fight a war that these young people are learning at our military academies but modern management, public administration, and international trade. These are all subjects that broaden the young officers' education and teach them about the modern world, but whether it also prepares them to fight and to defend the United States is another matter. Then, too, as already indicated, whether this training prepares them for the kind of political-psychological guerrilla conflicts with which we will most likely be involved in the future is similarly open to question.

A third issue has to do with the winding down of the cold war. If the Soviet Union is really in the process of reducing its commitments abroad, of terminating its expansionist tendencies, of turning inward and concentrating on its domestic problems, and of ending or at least reducing its cold war rivalry with the United States, this will have enormous implications for the United States military as well. If the Soviet Union is a diminished and now inward-looking superpower, it will be very hard for the United States to maintain its own readiness, the present military budget, and the size and equipment of our own armed forces. How the American military, indeed how the United States itself, reacts and responds to the immense changes presently going on in the Soviet Union and Eastern Europe will undoubtedly be one of the major questions of the years ahead.

A Department in Flux

The United States Department of Defense has been a rising force in American foreign policy since World War II. Its roles are not just the traditional military ones but have expanded into the areas of diplomacy, intelligence, international politics, and international economics—activities that in the past were carried out by other agencies. In the bureaucratic politics that is foreign policy decision making in Washington, D.C., the big loser in this process of expansion and aggrandizement of power within DOD has been the State Department.

The Defense Department is now a coequal participant with State in most foreign policy decisions, and in many areas DOD's voice is stronger than State's. The United States military hit a low point in the 1970s after the humiliation and discrediting brought on by Vietnam, but in the 1980s it strongly recovered in terms of morale, budgets, and readiness. Nevertheless, as a critical actor in the foreign policy arena, the Defense Department still faces major problems, both those intrinsic within the military institution and those that relate to its changing role and its need to adjust to modern-day trends. The young officers within DOD, however, are very impressive: highly educated, with advanced degrees, pragmatic, and often more open-minded than their counterparts at the State Department. Hence while it seems unlikely that State will anytime soon reform itself from within, in the Defense Department a major transformation in thinking and ideas is already well under way.

THE CENTRAL INTELLIGENCE AGENCY

The Central Intelligence Agency (CIA) is one of the most maligned and misunderstood agencies in the United States government. The image many Americans, to say nothing of most foreigners, have of the CIA is that it is a secretive spy organization whose operatives are like the title character in James Bond movies: dashing, ignoring or flouting the law, operating independently and without any control over their actions by higher political authorities. CIA agents are widely thought to roam the world, undermining unfriendly governments (especially leftist ones), assassinating people who get in their way, and riding roughshod over international law as well as the norms of acceptable moral behavior.

This image of the CIA has its roots in many of the early books about the agency and in a number of popular movies (*Three Days of the Condor*, *State of Siege*, *Missing,* etc.) purporting to offer "factual" dramatization of CIA activities. The images these books and films portrayed were those of an "invisible government,"[4] out of control, destabilizing or attempting to destabilize progressive regimes in Iran, Guatemala, Cuba, Nicaragua, and Chile. The CIA was pictured as acting autonomously, outside of the law, and without presidential approval or oversight.

The actual situation is, of course, far more complex than this. First, the CIA is a big, bureaucratic organization like the others considered here: most of its activities (maybe 80 percent), as in all bureaucracies, are normal, routine, and downright boring. They involve chiefly paper shuffling, not James Bond-like derring-do. Second, the main functions of the CIA have to do with the analysis of data, not covert operations. Most people who work as analysts for the CIA do research and write reports, not unlike their State Department colleagues; covert operations are actually quite a small part of the CIA's activities.

Third, the CIA rarely initiates a significant action without presidential approval. It is not an agency "run amok" or with "rogue" agents operating entirely on their own. Rather, CIA operations must generally be approved at the highest levels of the United States government—although elaborate pains are often taken to be able to disguise that fact. This is the doctrine of "plausible deniability," by which a president approves an action but for which a "cover" is provided so that the president can plausibly deny his involvement if the operation goes awry. After all, there is no reason why the president or the entire American government should be discredited because of the failure of some isolated covert operation. All of the most famous CIA operations—in Iran, Guatemala, Cuba, Vietnam, Chile, etc.— had this kind of presidential approval but with a smokescreen provided in case they failed. "Plausible deniability," however, is a quite different thing from saying that the CIA operates out of control and without the president's (or other high officials') approval.

The problem is that there are a lot of gray areas. While the president or the National Security Council generally approves major CIA initiatives, some of these are left up to the discretion of the CIA director. Or, while the NSC may authorize a covert operation, details and implementation are often left to lower level officials. In addition, some covert operations are buried deep within the CIA bureaucracy where there is little responsibility or accountability. And there is, on occasion, the problem of rogue operations—that is, CIA operatives acting on their own without approval from higher-ups.

Even though there will always be in a democracy tensions between the need for an open society and the need to conduct covert operations, few informed foreign policy practitioners would want to do away with covert operations altogether. Covert operations occupy that niche that lies between diplomacy and military force. It is one arrow among many in the American quiver of foreign policy activities. And there are numerous occasions when a good, CIA-run covert operation would be useful. For example, there came a time in the 1980s when the United States government decided that the dictator Augusto Pinochet of Chile was polarizing his country, providing an opportunity for the Communists and, therefore, ought to leave power. Normal diplomacy and pressure had failed to nudge the dictator out of power or toward democracy, and it was unthinkable that the United States would use military force against Chile. In those circumstances, a well-planned covert operation to force Pinochet out of office would look very attractive—and ironic, since the CIA is often blamed for bringing Pinochet to power in the first place. But because of the new restrictions on its activities enacted in the 1970s, the CIA was unable to play the role that might have been appropriate in this case.

Or, on the opposite side of the ideological spectrum, take the case of Marxist-Leninist Nicaragua. Diplomacy had not succeeded in nudging the Sandinista regime toward democracy, the use of military force was largely ruled out by American public opinion, and a third option, the funding of the *Contras*, had been terminated by the Congress. In that context, American policymakers would like to have the option of covert activities—except that these too had been largely ruled out by the Congress. That is among the major reasons United States policy in Central America was so frustrated and frustrating, because *none* of the arsenal of United States options was available, politically feasible, or workable: no diplomacy, no use of American military force, and no covert operations either.

Most analysts of foreign policy processes see the CIA as providing the United States with a third option. Where diplomacy doesn't work, and yet where a military action is also ruled out for various reasons, covert activity provides a middle way. "Middle" in the sense that it is stronger than diplomacy but more limited than a military operation. And, there are *numerous* instances in an uncertain and sometimes crazy world where policymakers would love to have this middle option available to them—against Quadaffi, for example, or the Iranian leadership, or other hateful characters and regimes. But, useful though they are, such covert operations cannot often be used because (1) the Congress has put severe restrictions on them; and (2) we lack the language and area specializations to carry very many of them out successfully; and (3) America is such an open and porous society that it is doubtful that we can run a covert (which means secret) operation even if we wished to. In the United States there are very few secrets anymore, or operations that can be kept secret for long, so that even our most successful covert activities very quickly end up as overt operations.

History

The United States does not have a long history or experience with secret, spy, and covert operations; and we are still not very good at it. Part of the problem lies in our Puritan heritage which insists our foreign policy be "moral"; but the fact is, intelligence operations cannot always be such. Part of the problem lies in the nature of democracy itself, which is based on open decisions and not on secret activities. In addition, part of the problem lies in our strong sense of guilt about international affairs, our desire to do good in the world, to avoid evil, and to atone for past "sins," all of which make it very difficult for the United States to engage in some questionable covert practices. And part of it lies also in that strong sense that "gentlemen do not read other people's mail," that covert activities are by definition sleazy and therefore to be avoided.

Before World War II, the United States had almost no spy activities or covert operations; and what it did have, it often felt uncomfortable about. But during the war, seeing the need to gather intelligence and run secret activities, especially after the attack on Pearl Harbor by Japan caught the United States by surprise, the Roosevelt administration created the Office of Strategic Services (OSS). The OSS was headed by a person whose reputation later grew to epochal proportions, William ("Wild Bill") Donovan. The OSS was small, creative, innovative and, during the war years, able to operate with considerable autonomy and derring-do. Its feats during the war later became the "stuff" of movies and legend. Many of the young operatives who would later serve as directors of the CIA—Allen Dulles, Richard Helms, William Colby, and William Casey—got their start with the OSS.

The Central Intelligence Agency was created by the same National Security Act of 1947 that created the National Security Council, the Department of Defense, and the Joint Chiefs of Staff. The CIA thus came into existence at the beginning of the cold war as the United States determined that it could not completely disband its wartime agencies and that the struggle with the Soviet Union would be an ongoing and protracted one. The CIA was created originally to operate under the NSC. It was not designed to replace the existing military intelligence agencies, the Treasury Department's secret service, or the FBI. Nor was the CIA supposed to set overall intelligence policy; that was reserved for the president and the NSC. Rather, the CIA was supposed to *advise* the NSC on intelligence matters, make recommendations to the NSC on the coordination of the several intelligence services, and itself coordinate and disseminate to appropriate government agencies intelligence information having to do with national security. Additionally, the CIA was to perform "other functions and duties" related to national security that the NSC might direct. It was on the basis of this vague phrase that the CIA got into the area of covert operations.

During the 1950s the CIA flourished. Ike liked and supported it. Its accomplishments were significant: curbing the rise of Communist trade unions and political parties in Western Europe, restoring the Shah to power in Iran, and ousting the leftist government in Guatemala. Under Allen Dulles, brother of Eisenhower's secretary of state, the size of the CIA bureaucracy grew rapidly. Ex-President Truman, however, became critical of the agency because of its size and its expansion into covert operations.

"The Company," as the agency was sometimes called, eventually moved into sparkling new headquarters in the Washington suburb of Langley, Virginia, directly under the route of commercial and private airplanes heading down the Potomac to land at National Airport. The leadership of the CIA, like that of the State Department at this time, tended to come from Ivy League and "Little Ivy" (Amherst, Williams, Wesleyan) colleges; but the rank and file of analysts and operatives was heavily weighted toward exiles from Eastern Europe. These persons had recently had their countries overrun by Stalin's armies so they were fervently anti-Communist; but their disproportionate representation within the agency led it to concentrate almost exclusively on European affairs and to ignore the potential trouble brewing in the Third World.

The 1960s was not a good decade for the agency—and then things went from bad to worse. The decade began with the CIA-sponsored invasion of Marxist-Leninist Cuba at the Bay of Pigs in 1961, an operation that ended in disaster and was called by one analyst a "perfect failure." Thereafter President Kennedy was hostile toward the CIA, believing that it had given him erroneous information about conditions in Cuba, and concentrated greater foreign policy in the White House while reducing his reliance on CIA intelligence. In the mid-1960s came the revelations that the CIA had been sponsoring, both domestically and abroad, numerous foundations, magazines, student and labor groups, publishing houses, cultural centers, academic institutions, and political training programs—revelations that reflected no glory on the CIA and discredited the organizations that had been the beneficiaries of CIA money. Finally, in the late-1960s the CIA was further discredited because of its early, mistaken assessments about the Dominican Republic (where the U.S. intervened in 1965) and Vietnam, and because many persons had come to believe that the CIA was operating out of control and becoming involved in immoral activities not only in Southeast Asia but elsewhere in the Third World. Or else, when the CIA did have later a correct and generally pessimistic assessment of American prospects in Vietnam, the political leadership (Lyndon Johnson) refused to listen and chose to ignore the agency.

If the 1960s were bad for the CIA, the 1970s were even worse. Vietnam remained a major albatross around the agency's neck. The efforts of the CIA to destabilize the leftist government of Salvador Allende in Chile attracted a great deal of adverse publicity. A series of books, by Wise and Ross, Agee, and Marchetti and Marks (see Suggested Readings), portrayed the CIA in the worst possible light. Then, in part because of these sensationalist books, came congressional hearings headed by Senator Frank Church (D-ID) that revealed CIA participation in the assassinations of several heads of state, as well as other CIA "dirty tricks." Hence the Congress moved to place restrictions on the CIA, to establish special intelligence committees to keep tabs on the agency, and to put in place an elaborate system by which the CIA was to report its covert activities to the Congress. These plans were sometimes leaked by the congressional committees, which of course ended their covert character and made for further bad relations between the CIA and the Congress.

Finally, the CIA suffered from undistinguished leadership during a part of the 1970s. William Colby was fired by President Ford as director because he had lost the support of the agency's own personnel and because morale was falling; Colby had not stood up strongly enough to the congressional probes and seemed himself at times to be a party to reducing the agency's activities and influence. Particularly under President Carter, the CIA's director, Stansfield Turner, pared down the size of the agency, let go a large number of its ablest operatives, and all but terminated covert operations. This was in keeping with Mr. Carter's and his advisers' moralistic view of foreign policy; but it all but destroyed the agency, lowered morale still farther, and left many agents confused and bitter.

Under Ronald Reagan and his CIA Director William Casey, the agency began to recover. Casey was a veteran of the OSS and had a flair for intelligence operations. He also had direct access to his good friend, the president. Morale increased again, recruiting went forward, and the CIA began to attract some of our best young persons. But Casey also recruited a number of ideologues into the agency whose hasty conclusions were not always supported by hard facts and, in involving the agency in Colonel Oliver North's "cowboy" arms-for-hostages operation ("Iran-Contra"), the CIA again suffered a setback. Casey's successor, former FBI Director William Webster, brought a needed period of calm and settling down to the agency—even though some of its personnel complained that Webster spent too much time on the tennis court and in pursuit of a good public relations image for himself, as distinct from devoting all his time and energy to the job. Under President Bush, however, Webster was asked to continue as director so that the calming process could continue.

Structure

Although the CIA is often assumed to be *the* intelligence-gathering arm of the United States government, in fact there is a whole *family* of intelligence agencies out there. Each of the armed services has its own intelligence unit, and the Department of Defense has the separate Defense Intelligence Agency located across the Anacostia River in Washington, at the Bolling Air Force Base and Naval Station. In addition, the departments of State, Energy, and Treasury each have separate intelligence services. The FBI concentrates on domestic crime but it sometimes overlaps into the international area as well. The highly secret National Security Agency, a branch of the Department of Defense (and not to be confused with the National Security Council, located in the White House), has responsibility for monitoring global communications through satellites and advanced listening and computer technology.

At the core of this diverse collection of intelligence agencies, each with its own separate but sometimes overlapping responsibilities, is the Director of Central Intelligence, or DCI. Under an executive order issued by President Reagan in 1981, the DCI was given considerably greater control over intelligence matters than was the case in the original National Security Act of 1947.

The exact size of the intelligence agencies and their budgets are closely guarded secrets. For example, the CIA budget is hidden inside the larger Defense Department budget so that precise figures are difficult to arrive at. In the early 1970s, it was estimated that the total number of employees of the several intelligence agencies was about 106,000, with a total yearly budget of about $6 billion. By the mid-1980s, the total number of employees had increased 25 percent to 130,000 and the total budget was about $12 billion.

The CIA itself has about 16,000 to 17,000 employees. These are divided into four directorates. Administration is the largest of the four, with about 6,000 employees; it is responsible for the everyday running of the agency. A second directorate is called Science and Technology; it has close to 2,000 employees. The Science and Technology directorate, like the NSA with which it sometimes overlaps, monitors foreign radio and television broadcasts and publishes the *Foreign Broadcast Information Services* (*FBIS*), a daily summary of broadcast news from around the world. This directorate also administers the U-2 and other spy planes and tries to keep the air force from encroaching on this turf.

The Intelligence directorate has around 4,000 to 5,000 employees. This is the principal work of the agency: contrary to popular conceptions, the CIA is not mainly a spy and covert operations agency (although it does those things too); rather, its main activities involve analysis. Persons who work in the Intelligence directorate read foreign newspapers, gather information from operatives in the field, and write papers analyzing trends and prospects—not unlike what scholars and their students do.

These are *overt* employees: that is, they can now say publicly whom they work for but cannot specify the exact subject of their work. For example, in the old days at professional meetings of foreign policy specialists one could always spot the CIA people because their name badges always said vaguely "U.S. Government," but now their name badges say simply and explicitly "Central Intelligence Agency." Many of these overt CIA analysts are now permitted to publish the results of their research in scholarly foreign affairs journals, although such work must be scrutinized by the agency beforehand to ensure that classified sources or intelligence information is not being compromised. The Intelligence directorate is divided into regional and functional offices that run parallel to those at State and Defense.

The CIA has recruited very able analysts and scholars for its Intelligence directorate in recent years, many of them at the Ph.D. level. These analysts are, for the most part, specialists in a region or functional subject area, in contrast to the generalists at State. They usually stay in place longer, concentrating on their particular areas, than their counterparts at State. Moreover, they can conceptualize—see things in a larger and broader pattern—again in contrast to State's often-lamented inability to do so. For these reasons, it is universally agreed in Washington among persons who have access to all three that the analytic reports that the CIA produces about foreign countries and its assessments of foreign trends and situations are generally superior to those of either State or Defense. State's analyses are often superficial, brief, without any conceptual understanding, and at the level of political journalism; while DOD's reports are always suspect because they are so strongly shaped by interservice rivalries. The CIA's, in contrast, tend to be much more analytical, balanced, comprehensive, and sophisticated—the best reports produced by any of the foreign policy-making bureaucracies.

The fourth directorate at CIA is Operations. It has about 4,000 to 5,000 persons working for it and is involved in clandestine activities. Even though this is only one part of the CIA's activities, covert activities are what we think of when we think of the CIA. These are the activities that have received all the publicity. Actually, the CIA engages in hundreds of generally small-scale covert activities every year—most of them useful and successful. But the agency cannot talk about its successes. It is only the handful of failures over the years that receive attention—in large part because only the failures become public knowledge. For the most part, the CIA has been inordinately successful over the agency's lifetime in its covert operations; but when there are failures, they tend to be spectacular.

The Operations Directorate at CIA is a gung ho bunch, somewhat like the special forces in the armed services. They pride themselves on their can-do spirit. They like to brag (chiefly to each other, of course) that they can go anywhere and do anything. There is a certain "Lone Ranger" attitude prevailing in Operations that is generally good, given the nature of this branch's activities, but that sometimes gets it in trouble. As in the Iran-Contra caper, some of the operatives are so gung ho for the cause they are pursuing that they sometimes go beyond the law and without presidential authorization. It may be that in some cases, for the good of the country, CIA Operations *do* have to go beyond the law; but that is also what may land them and the agency in deep trouble. However, as with CIA mistakes, these unauthorized cowboy exercises are the exception rather than the rule. Most CIA operations are authorized by the proper officials—the president, the NSC, or the director of Central Intelligence—although quite often the line between full authorization and CIA implementation gets rather fuzzy.

The Agency Subculture

The CIA is, after all, an intelligence organization. Many of its activities are secret—necessarily and properly so. As long as there are proper authorization, review, and oversight procedures by the appropriate officials (Congress and the executive branch), we as citizens probably do not need to know everything there is to know about the CIA. Not only would such openness rule out many CIA operations and be a threat to our national security, but most Americans would rather not know all the time what the CIA is doing—indeed we are probably happier and better off *not* knowing.

The secretive nature of the CIA, however, sometimes verges on paranoia. For example, the CIA headquarters in Langley for a long time permitted no pictures on the walls for fear that listening devices ("bugs") could be hidden in them. The buses that took employees and visitors to the agency did not stop at regular bus stops or indicate on their itineraries what was the final destination. Meetings with CIA officials were often conducted outside the agency, on street corners, with strangers wearing hats that covered their eyes and trench coats with the collars turned up—straight out of James Bond. Once inside the Langley headquarters (or in other office buildings around Washington that the expanding CIA now occupies), visitors must be escorted at all times and cannot be let out of sight for even a moment. Even going to the bathroom requires an escort! One of course understands the need for security at the CIA, but some of the rules and regulations are a bit much. Although the atmosphere is more relaxed now than it used to be, the agency is still quite paranoid about some things.

As noted earlier, Eastern Europeans were heavily overrepresented within the CIA in its early days. This lent an excessively conspiratorial air to the agency as the Eastern Europeans at times carried on their own historic feuds, rivalries, and conspiracies within the organization. Everything— even the most open and justifiable of operations—appeared furtive, secretive, back-alleyish. The full panoply of Eastern European languages and dialects were spoken within the agency. For good or ill, the agency's reputation in Washington and its relations with other agencies were strongly shaped by the early personnel makeup of the CIA.

But since then, the agency has become thoroughly "Americanized." In wanting to be acceptable in Washington and at interdepartmental gatherings, CIA personnel now look and act just like everybody else. In many respects in fact, especially given the large percentage of Ph.D.'s among its personnel, the CIA has come to look like a college campus. Its analysts are often tweedy, casual, and pipe smoking. Unlike in the old days, one can no longer spot the CIA people at a reception or academic gathering just by their appearance.

There remains, however, a considerable rivalry between the Intelligence and Operations branches within the CIA, and also between the civilians and the numerous military personnel that have recently come over to the agency. There are, in fact, two "cultures" (analytic and covert), two ways of thinking and behaving within the Company. The Intelligence people tend to be highly educated, tweedy, college types who take pride in their analytical skills and think that analysis ought to be the CIA's main focus. They tend to look down on the "cowboys" in the Operations division and are sometimes not a little bit ashamed to be in the same agency with them. Operations people, by contrast, sometimes think that they are the last line of defense keeping international communism from overrunning the bulwarks of democracy; and they tend to look down on the Intelligence directorate as effete, professorial types who fail to understand the world's harsher realities and even whose loyalty to the United States may sometimes be questionable. In addition, although there has long been a number of retired or serving (called "secounded") military personnel within the agency, their numbers seem to have increased in recent years, causing some resentment among civilian employees as well.

The CIA is in many ways a very interesting place to work because (1) its analysts have access to rich materials and fascinating data that persons outside the agency will never have a chance to see, and (2) the CIA has become one of the key players in the Washington foreign policy-making game and one of the few places where decisions and actions are actually taking place. The other agencies (State, Defense) have become so tired or so big or so bureaucratized that they are often very frustrating places in which to work. The CIA is also big and bureaucratic, but there are times—as in the early 1980s under William Casey and when Casey had direct and personal access to President Reagen—when a person working within the agency could actually have an important impact on policy. This is heady stuff and always attractive to would-be policymakers.

Yet there are costs as well as benefits to working for the CIA. In some quarters, just working for the agency brands one as a "spook" who is presumably involved in some evil and nefarious activity. For this reason, many CIA employees even on the overt side do not like to admit that they work for the agency and are afraid of "coming out." Moreover, the faculty academic climate on many American college campuses is such (antimilitary, anti-CIA) that once you do work for the CIA, even if only as an analyst, you can probably never go back to being a credible faculty member again. You cannot get an academic job, and many of your old academic colleagues will shun you. So even though there are marvelous research and analytic opportunities available in working for the CIA, many academic scholars shun the agency either on political grounds or because they know that, once tainted with a CIA association, they can't go back to a university position. This situation is in many ways unfortunate, preventing some of our best foreign policy analysts from working for the CIA, while also depriving our campuses of the insights that experience at the CIA provides.

A Summing Up

The CIA provides the United States both with essential intelligence and, through covert operations, with another set of instruments in our foreign policy arsenal. Covert operations provide something more than diplomacy but short of military intervention. They give the policymaker a set of tools that do not involve the controversial sending of American troops but that are often more effective than diplomatic discussions and negotiations. CIA-run covert operations are frequently faster and more effective than anything the State Department can do, while a DOD operation may be too big, too visible, and too expensive. Covert operations thus provide a middle position, a range of options between doing too little and doing too much. For example, if the United States could have mounted an effective covert operation, it would not have needed to give aid to the Contras—and thus we could have avoided all the nastiness and divisiveness that issue has provoked over the years. In addition, because covert operations are by definition secret, a president cannot be blamed if something goes wrong with one. That is why covert operations are so attractive to the White House or to a president: failures cannot be assigned but successes can usually be claimed. No politician can resist that logic.

But there are problems in this area too. Covert operations are sometimes so attractive to White House political operatives for the above reasons that a president may easily become overly reliant on them. Moreover, covert operations always carry the stigma of being run by the CIA, with the usually negative stereotypes that implies. In addition, the United States is such an open society and there are so many leaks that many serious analysts doubt whether we as a nation can carry out covert operations anymore. In the United States, many covert operations very quickly become overt operations. Finally, there are the difficult problems of overseeing CIA activities and of assigning responsibility so that we avoid inappropriate cowboy operations like Iran-Contra. All these comments are not meant to rule out covert operations, only to say that, like a military display of force, they should be used sparingly and with appropriate caution.

A FINAL CONCLUSION

Within the "family" of foreign policy agencies (State, Defense, CIA) considered in this chapter, it is plain that over the course of the last three decades State has been the big loser. In the bureaucratic rivalries or "bureaucratic politics" that constitute Washington, D.C., policy-making on foreign affairs, the Department of State's influence has been declining while that of *both* the Department of Defense *and* the CIA has been rising. In fact, CIA Director William Casey used to argue that by the 1980s the CIA had become the *only* effective foreign policy agency, that the others were, in his words, "too bottled up." There is truth as well as some exaggeration in Casey's statement. But no one doubts that in the bureaucratic turf battles of Washington and in the jockeying for influence, the relative power of these agencies has changed over time: State has declined while DOD's and CIA's influence has increased. These changes in the relative power of the main foreign policy bureaucracies carry enormous implications for the shape and conduct of American foreign policy.

State, Defense, and CIA have long been the main agencies involved in foreign policy. But now the bureaucratic politics and rivalries among these agencies have been made even more complicated by the rise of a variety of other agencies who have also jumped into the foreign policy arena. These include the Departments of Treasury, Justice, Labor, and Commerce, as well as the Environmental Protection Agency and others that have recently built up their international divisions. We turn our attention to them next in Chapter 12, "Bureaucratic Politics II."

Notes

1. The best analysis of how the Department of State works and what it does on a day-to-day basis is Anthony Lake, *Somoza Falling* (Boston: Houghton-Mifflin, 1989).
2. Howard J. Wiarda, *Ethnocentrism in Foreign Policy: Can We Understand the Third World?* (Washington, D.C.: American Enterprise Institute for Public Policy Research, 1985).
3. Hedrick Smith, *The Power Game: How Washington Works* (New York: Random House, 1988).
4. After the title of the book by David Wise and Thomas Ross, *The Invisible Government: The CIA and U.S. Intelligence* (New York: Random House, 1974).

Suggested Readings

Ackley, Charles W. *The Modern Military in American Society.* Philadelphia: Westminster Press, 1972.

Agee, Philip. *Inside the Company: CIA Diary.* New York: Bantam Books, 1984.

Ball, George. *Diplomacy for a Crowded World.* Boston: Little Brown, 1976.

Barrett, Archie D. *Reappraising Defense Organization.* Washington, D.C.: National Defense University, 1983.

Borklund, C.W. *The Department of Defense.* New York: Praeger, 1969.

Briggs, Ellis. *Farewell to Foggy Bottom.* New York: McKay, 1964.

Campbell, John. *The Foreign Affairs Fudge Factory.* New York: Basic Books, 1971.

Cline, Ray. *The CIA Under Reagan, Bush and Casey: The Evolution of the Agency from Roosevelt to Reagan.* Washington, D.C.: Acropolis, 1981.

Clotfelter, James. *The Military in American Politics.* New York: Harper & Row, 1973.

Colby, William. *Honorable Men: My Life in the CIA.* New York: Simon & Schuster, 1978.

Destler, I.M. *Presidents, Bureaucrats, and Foreign Policy.* Princeton, N.J.: Princeton University Press, 1974.

Hadley, Arthur T. *The Straw Giant: Triumph and Failure—America's Armed Forces.* New York: Random House, 1986.

Jordan, Amos A., and William J. Taylor, Jr. *American National Security.* Baltimore: Johns Hopkins University Press, 1981.

Kirkpatrick, Lyman. *The U.S. Intelligence Community.* New York: Hill & Wang, 1973.

Korb, Lawrence J. *The Fall and Rise of the Pentagon.* Westport, Conn.: Greenwood Press, 1979.

Lake, Anthony. *Somoza Falling.* Boston: Houghton-Mifflin, 1989.

Luttwak, Edward N. *The Pentagon and the Art of War.* New York: Simon & Schuster, 1985.

Marchetti, Victor, and John D. Marks. *The CIA and the Cult of Intelligence.* New York: Dell, 1974.

Pringle, Robert. "Creeping Irrelevance at Foggy Bottom." *Foreign Policy* 29(Winter 1977–78):128–39.

Ransom, Harry Howe. *The Intelligence Establishment.* Cambridge: Harvard University Press, 1970.

Rapoport, Anatol, ed. *Clausewitz on War.* New York: Penguin Books, 1968.

Rubin, Barry. *Secrets of State.* New York: Oxford University Press, 1985.

Tillema, Herbert. *Appeal to Force.* New York: Crowell, 1973.

Wise, David, and Thomas Ross. *The Invisible Government: The CIA and U.S. Intelligence.* New York: Random House, 1974.

Wriston, Henry. *Toward a Stronger Foreign Service.* Washington, D.C.: Government Printing Office, 1956.

Yarmolinsky, Adam. *The Military Establishment.* New York: Harper & Row, 1971.

CHAPTER TWELVE

Bureaucratic Politics II:
Treasury, Justice, Commerce, et al.

❂
❂

The previous chapter examined the role of the main foreign policy-making bureaucracies—State, Defense, CIA—in the formulation and implementation of American foreign policy. We saw that not only are these agencies critical in the making of foreign policy, but also that they frequently compete with each other, adding to the fragmentation and paralysis of policy-making and, further, that the relative balance of power among them has changed over time. This competition and jockeying for power among the leading foreign policy departments is called "bureaucratic politics."

In recent years, a large number of other bureaucracies in Washington have increasingly taken on a foreign policy role. These include the Treasury Department (on international debt and trade issues), the Justice Department (on drugs and immigration issues), the Labor Department (on international labor issues—treated in Chapter 7), the Commerce Department (on international business issues), the Environmental Protection Agency (on acid rain and other efforts to preserve and clean up the environment), and a *host* of other agencies—too many to deal with here in one chapter.

Two major global phenomena have caused the rise and insertion of these departments and agencies into the arenas of foreign policy, arenas that we usually think of as reserved for the State Department, the Defense Department, or perhaps the CIA. The first of these is the growing importance of international economic issues. Whether we are talking of Korean or Yugoslav cars, Japanese technology, Middle Eastern oil, Italian or Brazilian shoes, or Mexican vegetables—to name only a few—it is clear that the United States economy is no longer self-sufficient but is now far more interdependent with much of the rest of the world in all kinds of complex ways. We import food and raw materials as well as, now, manufactured goods from Latin America; we depend on Middle Eastern oil for our economic survival; we import high tech and a large variety of other products from Asia; we buy more and more of our shirts and pajamas from abroad; our banks and financial institutions are caught up in debt and international financial issues; and, of course, we ourselves must export agricultural products, raw materials, and industrial goods to pay for all these imports and to survive economically. Our increasing economic interdependence internationally was brought home to us, in spades, during the two great OPEC (Organization of Petroleum Exporting Countries)-imposed oil crises and price hikes of the 1970s; and, if anything, our economic interdependence has been increasing since that time. Such economic interdependence has brought to the forefront agencies (such as Treasury and Commerce) that never played much of an international role before but that now, by force of circumstances, must deal with international economic issues. To do so, they have been expanding and must continue to expand their international divisions.

The other global phenomenon is the emergence of new issues—pollution, drugs, international debt, immigration, to name just a few—onto the front burner of our foreign policy concerns. It is not that these new issues have pushed the more traditional ones—the cold war, the balance of power between nations—completely aside, but that the new issues have grown up and achieved importance alongside the older ones, and sometimes overlap them. These new issues, rather like the international economic ones, have elevated the agencies responsible for them (the Justice Department in the case of drug trafficking and immigration, the EPA in the case of pollution) into leading positions among the agencies responsible for foreign policy. In other words, a variety of cabinet-level departments as well as other agencies, whose responsibilities have in the past been chiefly confined to domestic matters, are now involved in foreign policy issues as never before.

This phenomenon of more and more agencies of the United States government having international responsibilities has added a variety of new dimensions and layers of complexity to our foreign policy that we have not experienced before. Two questions come immediately to mind. The first is, How well equipped in terms of personnel and programs are these traditionally domestic-focused agencies to deal with international issues? The second is, How has the rise of these new agencies and issues affected the traditional foreign policy agencies and the competition and bureaucratic politics between them? What we shall see is that the intrusion of all these other agencies into international affairs has made our foreign policy-making even more complicated and divisive than before.

It should be said also, in terms of the overall plan of the book, that as we consider these executive departments—State, Defense, and CIA in the last chapter; Treasury, Justice, Commerce, et al. here—we are getting very close to the center of our foreign policy-making system. Our concentric circles are becoming smaller; the funnel is growing narrower. After the consideration in this chapter, we have only the epicenter yet to consider:

the presidency (Chapter 13) and his own White House foreign policy staff, the National Security Council (Chapter 14).

THE TREASURY DEPARTMENT AND THE INTERNATIONAL DEBT ISSUE

The Treasury Department made its big splash onto the global scene during the 1970s. Richard Nixon's flamboyant Treasury secretary, John Connolly, who also had presidential ambitions, as well as Jimmy Carter's Treasury secretaries, Michael Blumenthal and William Miller, led the charge. The OPEC-imposed oil price jumps of 1973 and 1979 were the most dramatic events in stimulating these changes, but other gradual and long-term trends relating to the American economy were also under way. The United States had become increasingly dependent on a large number of nations for a large number of imported products; the rise of Japan, the European Economic Community, and a variety of other nations provided for stiff trading competition in the world; some of our own historic industries (such as steel) were becoming obsolete and noncompetitive; as a nation we were consuming more while saving and producing less; and overall the United States had begun to lose its place of overwhelming economic supremacy in the world. All these and other global forces began to thrust the United States Treasury Department into the forefront of our international relations. In the process, Treasury stepped on many toes (particularly those of the State Department, to say nothing of many of our friends and allies) and added several layers of new complexity and divisiveness to our foreign policy.

In this section we focus on the international debt issue to illustrate these Treasury-related foreign policy dilemmas, although some other issues in our trade and economic relations could be used to demonstrate the same points.

The international debt of Third World countries burst onto the world scene as a major international issue in the early 1980s. The biggest Third World debtors are located in Latin America (Brazil, Mexico, Argentina), but such countries as the Philippines, Nigeria, and many others are also deeply indebted to banks and international lending institutions in the United States, Western Europe, and Japan. The size of this unpaid debt is astounding: around $500 billion in Latin America alone—big enough to represent a serious threat to the private commercial banks and to the entire international financial system.

The causes of the international debt crisis are several, and responsibility rests among several parties. The big banks in the 1970s were flush with money, eager to lend, and not too particular about the creditworthiness of some of their customers. The Third World countries were eager to borrow, but they often used the money in wasteful ways. The United States government was then in the process of cutting back its foreign aid and saw these private bank loans to the Third World as a substitute for public assistance.

The interest rates on these loans in the late 1970s were very high (18 to 22 percent); but as long as the Third world economies were also booming, the debtor countries could repay them and there seemed little cause for worry. Besides, new loans could always be made available to cover the payments. Then came the global economic downturn of the early 1980s. Markets for the Third World's products dried up. The countries could not pay. In addition, new loans were no longer so readily available to help pay the old ones.

Today many Third World debtor nations cannot pay back the debts contracted earlier. The prognosis is, moreover, that they will *never* be able to pay them back. Certainly they will not be able to repay the principal— most Third World debtors cannot even keep current on the interest charges. The question is no longer when and how they will pay but how to deal with the fact that they cannot pay. Meanwhile, Third World debtor nations are struggling under the burden of intolerable interest payments and strict belt-tightening that hurts most the poorest people in these societies.

Because this is an international financial issue and because it affects most immediately American private commercial banks, the issue has been dealt with so far almost exclusively by the Treasury Department. But should it be? Is Treasury the appropriate place to deal with the issue?

The Treasury Department is staffed, naturally enough, almost exclusively with businessmen, economists, and specialists in finance. This is as true of its international division as it is of the department as a whole. And, superficially, having Treasury deal with this issue seems plausible. After all, debt does seem to be an economic issue that presumably should be dealt with by economists and financiers.

Treasury's response to the debt issue reflects that department's economic focus and orientation. Treasury says that the debt is a matter between the private banks and the countries affected and that it should be dealt with by them, without the United States government playing a significant role. Moreover, it argues that the problem of the international debt must be treated like any other debt: it represents a contractual obligation and it must be paid back. So the Treasury Department has, in general, stayed aloof from the crisis. When it has gotten involved, its primary obligation, as it sees it, is to help rescue American banks as well as the endangered international financial system, whose stability would be upset if a large-scale default should occur. Thus Treasury views the banks and the international financial system as its main clients, not the Third World countries who are obliged to pay their debts—or else!

The problem is that the international debt is no longer a purely economic or financial issue. Once the conclusion has been reached that the Third World countries cannot and will not pay, then it becomes primarily a political issue. The question now is not repayment—that is hopeless—but rather how we deal with and manage this huge, unpaid, and unpayable foreign debt. Those are questions that require political answers, no longer purely financial ones. Of course, we shall also have to continue to deal with the debt on an economic and financial level, but the biggest question—what to do about it—requires political answers.

The problem is that the Treasury Department is not equipped to deal with the debt or other international issues on a political level. There are few, if any, political scientists working for the Treasury Department and no foreign policy specialists. Treasury feels uncomfortable when those by definition more-imprecise political variables or factors are introduced into their equations. Moreover, Treasury resents it when other bureaucracies—in this case, the State Department—begin to intrude on its turf by suggesting that there are political and foreign policy interests at stake on the debt issue as well as economic ones.

What are these political interests? The Department of State has put these forward, in contrast to Treasury's overriding economic considerations. First, the United States has an interest in seeing that the nations of the Third World remain stable and viable and not go down the financial *or* political drain. Second, the United States has a stake in maintaining democratic government in many of these Third World debtor nations, and in seeing that these governments not give way to authoritarian or radical-populist regimes, which seems quite likely if the debt issue continues to fester. Third, the United States has an interest in the present moderate regimes in many of these countries, most of which have been quite pragmatic and friendly to the United States, and would not like to see them replaced by anti-American regimes. Fourth, public opinion in many of these countries is turning against the United States, blaming us for the hardships through which their peoples are going because of the debt burden—a trend that it is in our interest to reverse. Fifth, the Soviet Union is likely to score increased gains in the Third World by playing on the rising anti-Americanism unless the United States moves more quickly to ease the debt burden.

A close reading will reveal that these are all political and foreign policy reasons for being concerned with the debt issue. Indeed, a strong case could be made that the political and strategic considerations involved in the debt issue are even more important than the economic or financial ones.

So far, Treasury's attitude has been largely one of hands off. It insists that the debtors pay—unmindful of the fact that that will ruin the economies *and* governments of the Third World debtors. Only in emergency cases, such as next-door Mexico, has Treasury been willing to step in with major bailouts to help the faltering Mexican economy and its shaky political system. Treasury has sometimes been helpful in postponing the inevitable reckoning and in urging the banks to reduce fees, overlook late payments, and roll over the debt with new, so-called bridge loans. It has suggested a "menu" of options to nibble at the edges of the debt problem but not to reduce it overall. It has also suggested some level of "forgiveness" of the debt, but then left it up to the bankers and the debtor countries to negotiate the details. In this way, Treasury has involved itself in the debt crisis in limited ways, but it has not solved it. Of course, Treasury has also recognized that, if there is to be relief for the debtor countries, someone else will probably have to pay the bill. That somebody will undoubtedly, by direct or indirect methods, be the American taxpayer. And that is an outcome for which neither the Congress nor the executive branch has been willing so far to bite the bullet.

So how should we solve the debt issue? First, we must understand that the Third World debtors need themselves to *grow* out of their economic troubles—no amount of assistance or debt relief on our part can eliminate that fact. Second, we should, in general, continue to follow the careful, prudent steps initiated earlier by the Treasury Department. But third, we need to go beyond those useful but still modest steps. We need to recognize the preeminently political nature of the debt and to be prepared to deal with it in a political way. The reason for that is because our *own* national interests are affected by the onerous debt crisis, not just the banks or the Third World countries. So we will need to come forward with some kind of additional debt relief for the Third World, probably in the form of an international agency that absorbs and guarantees a large share of the debt, and that can be used to disguise from the American taxpayer that he or she is paying. That is not a very pleasant prospect, and it may be a hypocritical one; but there may be no other way to solve the problem. Note, however, that we will opt for such a solution because *our* interests are affected in Latin America and elsewhere in the Third World, although it will sometimes seem (and doubtless such arguments will be put forward by some politicians) that all we are doing is bailing out the banks and some corrupt, irresponsible governments.

The international debt issue is a very complicated one; we have only provided some of its broad contours here. Nevertheless, the issue illustrates a number of the main themes of this chapter. The first is that on this critical international issue the Treasury Department has emerged as a new actor and, so far, the most important one. But second, we have seen that, while Treasury has been quite clever in managing the economic facets of the issue, it has not yet faced up to its political facets—nor is it equipped to do so. Third, Treasury's stand on the debt issue—focusing on the purely financial aspects—has brought it in conflict with the State Department (hence, the bureaucratic rivalries and politics of this issue), which does see the debt in political terms as causing our relations with Latin America and the Third World to deteriorate badly and, therefore, as being harmful to our national interests. But so far, in terms of policy, it is Treasury's view that has prevailed and not State's—although the balance seems to be changing. And fourth, the issue has become enmeshed in our domestic politics, where the political pledge of "No new taxes" may ultimately prevent us from resolving the debt issue in ways that benefit both the United States and the Third World.

THE JUSTICE DEPARTMENT AND THE DRUG ISSUE

Drugs and drug trafficking have recently become a major issue in American politics. Some polls show drugs to be the number one issue among American voters.

Most of the drugs flowing into the United States come from abroad. They come from Europe, the Middle East, South and Southeast Asia, and—at this stage, the most important source—Latin America.

The agency that has the chief responsibility for dealing with the drug problem is the Drug Enforcement Agency (DEA). DEA is located bureaucratically in the Justice Department, which is headed by the attorney general, the nation's chief law-enforcement official. Herein lies the first set of problems in dealing with the drug issue:

1. The Justice Department is overwhelmingly a domestic affairs agency; like Treasury, it has a very short history of dealing with international issues and is woefully ill-equipped and ill-prepared, in terms of personnel and experience, to do so.
2. Ditto for DEA: it has always heretofore seen drugs as chiefly a domestic, or consumption, problem and lacks experience in the international realm.
3. Both the Justice Department and the DEA are essentially law-enforcement agencies. That is how they approach the drug problem. Hence if some foreign countries or their officials are breaking the law, then they should be punished and the weight of the judicial system thrown against them.
4. But, of course, as soon as one enters the international arena, things are never that simple. The drug traffickers may be breaking United States laws, but are they breaking the laws of the countries in which they reside? Is it appropriate for the United States judicial system and the weight of United States law to be extended to other, presumably sovereign, nations? And what if other American interests—economic, political, diplomatic, strategic—are in conflict with our interests on the drug issue? How will these conflicts be resolved, and by whom?

Let us examine the situation in Latin America, where most of the drugs now come from. As we do so, we will see why this issue has become so complicated and hard to deal with; why the policy that the DEA and Justice Department have followed so far has not been successful; and why, in fact, they may be the wrong agencies to deal with the problem—or at least the wrong agencies to deal with it by themselves.

First, drug production and use are part of the historic culture, especially among the indigenous populations, in many Latin American countries. Certain drugs are associated with religious beliefs and practices; drugs (such as the chewing of cocoa leaves) are also used by poor people in the region to numb the pain of hunger. Drugs are a common, normal, everyday part of life.

Second, because of the above, drugs in Latin America are not viewed as a law-enforcement problem, as they are in the United States. There are few prohibitions against their production or use. Nor is there a sense, as in the United States, that drugs are sinful. As a part of the culture and the religion, drugs are not seen as a matter calling for legal sanctions.

Third, and again following from the above, drugs are seen by Latin Americans as mainly an American problem, not a Latin American one. Most Latin American countries (Colombia is the major exception) do not have a "drug problem" as the United States does—that is, with violence and crime mushrooming as a result of drug use. Drugs are not ruining their youths or society as in the United States—although this too is now beginning to change. Hence, Latin Americans tend to view the drug problem as an American dilemma, a dilemma for the United States to solve in its own country, and not by forceful methods applied in Latin America, which has little or no problem.

Fourth, the production of drugs is quite rational—and downright profitable—from the point of view of the peasants and farmers producing them. Farmers may get anywhere from *fifteen to twenty times* as much money from growing the plants from which drugs are produced as from producing such traditional crops as coffee, bananas, potatoes, or beans. Hence, when DEA talks about solving the drug problem by finding alternative crops for Latin American farmers to produce, the agency runs up against the dilemma that none of these alternatives will produce anywhere near the profits that drugs will.

Fifth, and related, the national economies of these generally poor, Third World countries also benefit from drug production. Drugs help bring in sorely needed foreign exchange; they help raise the country's gross national product; and they thus benefit the country as well as bring in added revenues to the governments themselves. For example, drugs have now replaced coffee as the principal export crop of Colombia; and, if one knows something of Colombia's history and the importance of coffee to the country's economy, that is really a massive transformation. Hence, not only for individual farmers but also for whole countries and their governments, it is quite rational and beneficial to encourage drug production and to take advantage of the market that exists—regardless of its effects in the United States.

Sixth, it needs to be emphasized how widespread drug production is in Latin America and the physical impossibility of wiping it out on the production side. Like corn in Kansas or wheat in Nebraska, the slopes of the South American Andes, stretching across at least six countries, are one great shimmering field of drug plants. The territory under drug cultivation is so vast and the number of countries involved so large that no one could ever hope to wipe out the production physically. At the same time, the "factories" that actually produce the drugs are so small and technologically simple that they can be moved easily. The drug producers are gone by the time a military helicopter spots a plume of smoke in the jungle, finds a place to land in the thick forests, and the troops get to the scene. The producers avoid arrest by simply packing up their tubs and vats on mules and moving a mile away to a new spot. The production facilities are so simple (a fire and some large pots) that they can be moved quickly and easily, and the jungle is so impenetrable that the troops cannot find them even if they are only a scant hundred yards away.

Seventh, in many Latin American countries, government officials themselves are involved in the drug trade, or in the protection of those who are. They receive gratuities to supplement their often meager official salaries, a not uncommon practice in the region, in return for not scrutinizing drug activities too closely or even for helping in their export abroad. Such gratuities, moreover, are looked on as a form of patronage—a favor for a favor—not as graft or illegal bribery as they are viewed in the United States. Frequently, this kind of corruption reaches to the highest levels of the government, to the cabinet or to the president himself.

Eighth, not only are civilian officials implicated but so, frequently, are the armed forces. Local commanders may provide "protection" to the drug traffickers, look the other way as regards their activities, and in some cases even allow the use of military trucks, airstrips, and airplanes to help transport the drugs. Such profiteering, again used to supplement modest military salaries, may not be limited to local commanders but may reach to the highest levels of the armed forces.

Viewed in the Latin American, or producer, context, therefore, the drug problem is a much more complicated one than it appears from an American perspective.

The Justice Department and the DEA, however, have taken none of these complexities or their international ramifications into account. Their approach, naturally, given their focus and historic responsibilities, is to treat the drug problem purely from a law-enforcement point of view. Drugs are illegal (in the United States) and, therefore, must be stamped out. Drug trafficking is a crime, so therefore the drug lords as well as those who protect them must be thrown in jail.

Hence, DEA's approach to growing drugs abroad is to burn the crops—with no consideration for the economic consequences to the local economy. Or, DEA wants to spray the drug fields with Agent Orange, the chemical defoliant used in Vietnam and known to cause cancer—with no consideration for the peasant farmers of Latin America. DEA has assisted in kidnapping Latin American drug traffickers in their own countries and spiriting them to the United States to stand trial under United States laws—with no consideration for the sovereignty of the countries whose citizens have been kidnapped. And in the field in Latin America, DEA officials have frequently run roughshod over local law-enforcement personnel, shunting them aside, treating them with disdain, and acting as though they were guests and bystanders in their own nations instead of the other way around.

The greatest rub has come over DEA's desire to indict and arrest local officials who may or may not be involved with the drug trade. In keeping with their law-enforcement approach, the DEA officials now assigned to many United States embassies abroad want to put in jail anyone connected in any way with drugs—even if that means state governors in Mexico, cabinet officials elsewhere in Latin America, armed forces officers, or maybe even the president himself.

Here is where the bureaucratic politics of American foreign policy again enters in. The law-enforcement approach of Justice and DEA runs up against the more restrained and political approach of the State Department. State's job, after all, and that of our embassies abroad, is to get along well with different foreign governments and enhance our relations with Latin America. Good relations are not enhanced by putting the top leadership of these countries in jail, or even by threatening to do so. State's diplomatic responsibilities, therefore, are often directly contradictory to those of Justice and DEA, whose mission is equally valid. In Washington, D.C., therefore, there have been some hard bureaucratic conflicts between State and Justice over this issue, while in our embassies abroad the fights between State Department personnel and DEA officials have been intense. State Department FSOs barely conceal their disdain for the insensitive DEA officials whom they think of as ruining our relations with Latin America, a sentiment that is reciprocated by DEA officials who think the State Department is shielding criminal activities. The impasse is almost total.

It is not our intention here to provide an answer to the drug problem—that is for others to determine. But it is plain from the analysis presented that no solution will be successful that focuses on the production side alone. Drug production is too rational from the producing countries' point of view; it is too widespread; eradication is virtually impossible; and the protection system is both all-pervasive and reaches to the highest levels of the producing countries' governments. No, the solution has to come on the consumption side, in improved education in the United States about drugs and their debilitating effects, in the breakup and arrest of drug distribution gangs in the United States, and finally in changed consumer habits and mores in the United States itself. Or perhaps solutions can be found that emphasize both the consumption end *and* the production end, but that deal with the production side in more enlightened ways than we have seen from Justice and DEA so far.

The main points deriving from this discussion of the drug issue as regards foreign policy are:

1. The newness and inexperience of Justice and DEA in the foreign affairs area;
2. Because of this, as well as the law-enforcement subculture in these agencies, the inappropriateness of the solutions pursued so far and the damage they have done to our foreign relations;
3. The bureaucratic conflicts that have been provoked with the State Department;
4. The almost total lack of coordination between the main departments involved in this issue, each of which has legitimate interests and even the obligation to try to deal with it.

When so many competing bureaucracies are all trying to deal with the same issue but with almost no coordination between them, however, the result can only be damaging to United States foreign policy interests. In this sense, there are striking parallels between the debt issue, the drug issue, and others still to be analyzed. The creation of a "drug czar" may help solve these political and bureaucratic problems of coordination, but we will have to wait and see if the policy becomes more enlightened.

COMMERCE, TREASURY, AND THE UNITED STATES TRADE REPRESENTATIVE: THE CONFLICT OVER TRADE POLICY

Many scholars and practitioners of foreign policy are convinced that in the next decade, if not already, international economic issues will come to have more importance than international political or security issues. Two main trends are occurring: first, in this increasingly interdependent world, international trade and commercial and economic issues are achieving greater importance than ever before; and second, the cold war conflict with the Soviet Union is presently less intense and may be winding down, with the result that less attention and energy are likely to be devoted to military, political, or geostrategic issues and more to economic ones.

United States policy has historically been based on the principle of free trade—now amended to "free but fair" trade. By that amendment, the United States means that, while our markets will generally remain open and free of tariffs imposed on products from abroad, the markets of other countries must also remain open and free to our products. High tariff walls should not be constructed by other countries to protect local industries while keeping out American products; bureaucratic rules and regulations should not be designed by these countries to serve as a substitute for high tariffs and thereby keep out American products by other means; and in international competition, American companies should be allowed to compete freely without having to face companies from other countries that are strongly subsidized by their governments.

The United States supports free trade for the same reason it supports such principles as democracy and human rights: (1) because it is morally good to do so, and (2) because it is in our interests to do so. At the moral level, the United States stands for free and open trade as it stands for free and open governments, because that is the ethical and principled thing to do. We also believe that free trade helps benefit the countries and peoples of all nations and stimulates national development. At the national interest level, the United States favors free trade because our economy, industry, and efficiency have long been such that we would be in a position to benefit more from a free trade regime than almost anyone else. The ideological principle of free trade has sometimes served as a smoke screen to disguise these more self-interested motives, although there is no doubt that the principle of free trade is strongly ingrained in the American consciousness.

Most American trade abroad takes place at the private level, by *private* United States companies and multinationals (multinational corporations, or MNCs). Unlike many countries, the United States does not have very many large, state-owned enterprises or state-run corporations. The United States is really, in accord with its historic ideology, essentially a free market, laissez faire, free enterprise economy. It is private companies that are most important in our foreign trade, not the United States government.

The United States government does get into the act, however, chiefly as a facilitator and sometimes a regulator or policeman of trade. The United States government helps encourage private American companies to invest and trade abroad but the government—again unlike many other countries—is not normally a direct participant or partner in this trade.

The United States government supports private American companies in their commercial and trade activities abroad because that is in our interests. First, such activities strengthen our own domestic economy. There is a multiplier effect in international trade that is greater than that in domestic commerce: for every one dollar invested in trade, it results in a two-dollar increase in the gross national product, which translates into jobs and prosperity. Second, private investment and commercial activity abroad help bring economic growth and stability to many Third World countries that the United States would like to see remain stable and prosperous. Third, trade and private investment abroad give American foreign policy an added handle, another lever of influence, to go along with our political, diplomatic, and military levers.

At the same time, it should not be thought—contrary to some interpretations—that American foreign economic policy is a prisoner of private economic interests and operates only at their behest. The United States encourages investment abroad because that serves our economic as well as political purposes and because it gives American foreign policy added leverage, not because the United States government is somehow an agent of private "imperialistic" interests. American ambassadors and State Department officials, past and present, are unanimous in agreeing that American foreign policy and American private investment most often work harmoniously together abroad, but almost never are embassy personnel pressured by American companies to intervene on their behalf with the government officials of foreign countries—nor do our diplomats have any reason to think of themselves as the agents abroad of American private companies.

On the domestic side, three main agencies are involved in trade and foreign economic relations. These are the Treasury Department, and particularly Treasury's Undersecretary for International Economic Affairs; the International Trade Administration of the Department of Commerce; and the Office of the United States Trade Representative, a cabinet-level agency that lacks the status of a full department (and, therefore, seldom is as powerful as Treasury or Commerce) and has a small staff compared with the other two. The Department of State also has a Bureau of Economic and Business Affairs, but it lacks the clout of any of the previously listed three—again, causing problems of coordination and bureaucratic rivalries.

These agencies have to wrestle with a large number of issues, quite a few of which are incompatible. In addition, as with drugs and debt, many of these issues are political as well as economic. They should not be dealt with just by the main economic agencies (Treasury, Commerce, Trade Rep) but, in their political aspects, by the State Department and the National Security Council as well. In addition, Treasury, Commerce, and the Trade Rep's Office do not always grasp the full political and strategic consequences of the policy decisions that they may make on quite rational economic grounds.

Here are some of the difficult issues that we have to wrestle with in this area. The United States stands for free trade, but many Third World countries believe that they will only be swallowed up by the powerful and more efficient United States economy in any free trade arrangement; hence, they believe that they must build protectionist tariff walls to protect their fledgling industries and to ensure their national economic survival. The United States is also against subsidization of many industries by other governments, believing that subsidization puts American companies at a competitive disadvantage; but in much of the world, the line between private and public is far more blurred than in the United States. Subsidization is such a longtime and widespread practice in these countries that we will almost certainly not be able to change it and, furthermore, without such subsidies from the state, industry in many countries of the world cannot survive. These countries cannot sacrifice their national industries just because the United States accuses them of unfairness.

The United States opposes protectionism abroad while practicing it oftentimes at home; and the pressures in Congress stemming from constituents whose jobs are threatened by foreign competition to increase protectionism to keep out foreign products, even at the cost of harming our relations with these countries, is very powerful. A policy of free trade may well cost American jobs, which means that our foreign policy interests and our domestic requirements are often in direct contradiction. In addition, the United States at times pressures foreign countries to streamline and privatize their economies; but that means the likelihood of the privatized companies being swallowed up by richer American companies, which those countries do not want. It also means the sacrifice of a large number of patronage jobs by which these countries help keep unemployment down and by which they may also keep afloat politically. Thus it is clear that there are two, even many, sides to these issues, not just the one side we often hear about in the United States.

The United States favors the abolition of nontariff trade barriers in other countries; but from these countries' points of view, these barriers help keep their own industries—and maybe their political systems, too— alive, if not entirely well. The United States has an elaborate system for deciding when another country may be engaging in unfair and illegal trade practices and, hence, when the United States should retaliate or impose penalties. The process is enormously time consuming; definitions of "fairness" and "illegal" may be quite different from country to country; and the process seldom solves the problem but does produce more ill will between the countries. Meanwhile, the United States has itself been running very large budget deficits and has become the world's largest debtor nation. As we borrow to pay those debts, furthermore, we are sucking up the savings and investment capital of many other nations. They argue that it is time the United States got its own fiscal and economic house in order before it criticizes the policies of other nations.

These conflicts point up the problems in fashioning a coherent United States trade policy:

1. We have a private sector-dominated economy and not one in which the government has ever played a very great role.
2. As a nation, we have long prided ourselves on our self-sufficiency and are not yet used to all the compromises and accommodations necessary in an interdependent global economy.
3. The agencies primarily responsible for economic and trade policy (Treasury, Commerce, Office of the Trade Rep) have little understanding of the political sensitivities to which their strictly economic policies give rise, nor do they always understand well the domestic motivations and political requirements that oblige other countries to act as they do.
4. One of these agencies (the Trade Rep) is considerably less powerful than the full-scale departments, making it difficult to stand up to them in conflicts; and even Commerce's and Treasury's international bureaus and constituencies are weaker than their domestic divisions.
5. The State Department is quite weak in the area of international economic policy and is often unable to provide the political counterpoint to the strictly economic perspective provided by the other departments.

It should go without saying by this point that there is a lack of overall coordination between these several agencies and that frequently they are in conflict with each other.

THE JUSTICE DEPARTMENT AND THE IMMIGRATION ISSUE

The Immigration and Naturalization Service (INS) is located administratively in the Justice Department. The INS, like the Drug Enforcement Agency, was organized under the Justice Department back when things were easy, when all these issues were purely domestic issues and did not carry such strong international implications. Moreover, as with drugs, Justice's whole orientation toward immigration is to treat it as a law-enforcement issue (that is its mission and responsibility, after all) rather than as a complex sociological, political, economic, international, *and* law-enforcement issue all rolled into one. By concentrating on only one aspect of the issue, we largely miss the other important ramifications, which helps explain why policy often goes astray; yet our agencies (in this case, Justice), because of their compartmentalized specializations, often lack the expertise to see the issue in all its complex dimensions.

While the United States has been called a "nation of immigrants," historically most of these immigrants have come from Europe—or, in the case of black Americans, from Africa. But in recent years, more and more immigrants have been coming from the Middle East, South and Southeast Asia, East Asia, and Latin America. Latin America has become overwhelmingly the largest source of recent immigrants to the United States—so much so that in the decade of the 1990s, Hispanics will come to outnumber blacks as the largest minority in the country.

The "problem" of Latin American immigration into the United States is viewed differently in different parts of the country. New York City, always a mecca for recent immigrants, has become the second largest Puerto Rican, the second largest Dominican, the second largest Jamaican, et cetera, et cetera, city in the world. In south Florida, and especially Miami, the Cuban and other recent Latin American immigrants have turned that city into a predominantly Spanish-speaking city, raising complex questions about what should constitute our national language and culture. In the American Southwest, the problem is seen as floods of poor, illegal immigrants from Mexico and Central America who are overwhelming the local school systems and social services and causing the crime rate to soar. Meanwhile, in Washington, D.C., the problem of immigration is seen as a sign of the potential destabilization of Mexico and of other of our southern neighbors.

No one should doubt that as a nation we have a major problem on our hands in terms of immigration. On the one hand, we want to remain open to the poor and the oppressed of the world. That was in part the basis on which the United States was settled, and most Americans do not want to pull up the bridges and block our borders entirely to future immigration. On the other hand, the flow of immigrants into the United States has become such a mighty stream that we are unable to control it; our economy cannot provide jobs for them all; our schools and social services are overburdened in many parts of the country; and most of the recent immigrants come not by way of the doors of legal entry still remaining open to many, but illegally by swimming the Rio Grande, by sailing across the Florida Straits, or by walking across the desert into New Mexico, Arizona, or California. The problem is not immigration per se but the fact that it is out of control, chaotic, and often illegal.

Immigration is not just a foreign policy issue but a domestic one as well. At one level, it affects local communities—New York, south Florida, the Southwest—as we have already outlined. At another level, it affects our future and character as a nation in that the United States is fast becoming something of a Latin American nation, linguistically, ethnically, and in other ways. Third, it is changing our politics, as more and more Hispanics register to vote and put forth the issues that are important to them. And fourth, it affects our domestic interest-group struggles: organized labor wants strict enforcement of the immigration laws to protect the jobs of Americans against this low-paid, foreign competition, while agricultural growers want the Hispanics to come in because they provide a cheap, abundant labor supply.

The issue is even more complicated internationally. Should we let in El Salvadorans, many of whom are fleeing the terror of right-wing death squads, or Nicaraguans, who are fed up with the Marxist regime in their country? Each of these groups, of course, has its political champions in the United States who seek to use the fact of immigration to score points in the domestic debate over Central America. Another problem is Mexico, a large country on our southern flank that shares a 2,000-mile border with the United States and which is the last country in the world we would want to see destabilized. While immigration from Mexico causes certain domestic problems in the United States, it can also be seen as a safety valve for excess Mexican population (Mexico has one of the highest birth rates in the world), and for the excess populations of other Central American and Caribbean nations. Without such an open American safety valve for their excess population, a number of these countries could well explode in violent revolution, with dire consequences for American foreign policy.

The INS, like Treasury on the debt or the DEA on drugs, is just not equipped to deal with all the complexities of these problems. INS is basically a law-enforcement agency: its main goal is to carefully police the border, to enforce United States immigration laws, and to send the illegal immigrants back. But those measures only deal with part of the problem: they do not enable the United States to respond to the complexities of the issues and, in some respects (if they cause a social explosion in Mexico), may lead to an exacerbation of the problem.

In 1986 Congress passed and the president signed the Simpson-Mazzoli immigration bill. Not perfect by any means, and although many interest groups found, often for different reasons, provisions to which they objected, Simpson-Mazzoli provided a handle to begin to deal with this issue. Among other things, the bill made provision for many illegal immigrants already in this country to qualify for United States citizenship; it gave the INS stronger tools for patrolling the border and keeping out future illegal immigrants, while at the same time it allowed for the "safety valve" aspect of legal emigration from Mexico and Central America to continue. Simpson-Mazzoli has not solved the United States immigration problem, but it does provide some means for doing so; it represents a start in enabling the United States to regain control of its own borders, and it begins to recognize the complexities, both domestic and international, of the issue.

But many of the problems with which we have become familiar in this chapter remain. The agency responsible for dealing with immigration issues, the INS, is not well equipped to do so. It concentrates on one aspect of the issue—enforcement of United States immigration laws—but is not set up to deal with the issue's complex international dimensions. In addition, little policy coordination exists between the INS and other agencies—presumably the State Department—that can speak to the international issues. As a result, there is often more conflict among these competing bureaucracies than there is cooperation. Meanwhile, the problems continue to fester and grow worse.

We have focused in this chapter on some of the most important issues of policy fragmentation, lack of coordination, and often downright conflict among competing agencies: Treasury and the debt issue; Justice and the drug issue; Treasury, Commerce, and the Trade Rep on international trade issues; and Justice and INS on the immigration issue. These are some of the key problems, but there are many more. The Environmental Protection Agency (EPA) now also has an international arm that is trying to put filters and scrubbers on other countries' industrial smokestacks but without the language skills, the understanding of foreign countries, or the experience abroad to do this effectively and well. The Interior Department and other heretofore exclusively domestic agencies also now have international bureaus; by one count, no less than sixty-five agencies of the United States government presently have international divisions and responsibilities.

CONCLUSION: BUREAUCRATIC POLITICS AND THE NEED FOR POLICY COORDINATION

As the United States economy has become more interdependent with those of the rest of the world in recent decades, and as we have lost both our self-sufficiency and our position of absolute economic preeminence, economic issues—or, better, issues of political economy—have come more and more to the forefront of international controversy and discussion. At the same time, a host of new international issues—debt, drugs, trade, immigration, pollution, and others—have registered on our consciousness and acquired an importance that they had never had before. Both these trends—toward greater international economic interdependence and the rise of new issues—have thrust into the limelight agencies of the United States government that have never before played a significant international role and are often ill-equipped to do so.

In every one of the policy areas examined here, the main themes that came out were remarkably parallel. These were: (1) the inexperience and lack of history of all of these agencies in dealing with foreign affairs issues; (2) their lack of understanding of foreign areas, foreign countries, foreign languages, foreign ways of doing things; (3) the tunnel vision or unidimensional way of seeing things of all these agencies—Treasury's purely economic approach to the debt issue, Justice's strictly law-and-order approach to drug and immigration issues; (4) the lack of coordination between these agencies and others, such as the State Department, that, hopefully, *do* understand the larger political and international implications of these issues; (5) the many bureaucratic rivalries and turf battles between the different agencies of the United States government that exist on all these issues; (6) the confrontation, gridlock, and paralysis that exist; and finally (7) the lack of an effective, reasonable, *coordinated,* long-term policy for dealing with many of these issues.

The discussion needs to be broadened, however, to include the more traditional foreign policy bureaucracies discussed in the previous chapter: State, Defense, and CIA. There, too, the main themes were competition among the several bureaucracies, lack of coordination, intense rivalries, turf battles to control various domains of foreign policy, gridlock, paralysis and, ultimately, ineffective policy and a stymied foreign policy-making process. Experts in foreign policy, to say nothing of our allies, were appalled at the fragmentation of foreign policy-making that occurred under President Carter. The Reagan administration tried strenuously to overcome these faults, only to evolve toward a situation of fragmentation that was similar to Carter's. Can we ever again hope to have a clear, coherent, consistent, and at least more-or-less coordinated foreign policy system in this country?

Actually, there is in place an elaborate plan and system for coordination among all these foreign policy agencies. The questions are: Does it work? If not, can it be made to work?

Beginning in the mid-1960s, a number of mechanisms were established through the National Security Council for better interagency coordination on foreign policy. These included the Senior Interdepartmental Group (SIG), headed by the undersecretary of state and including undersecretaries from other departments; and the Interdepartmental Regional Groups (IRGs) at the assistant secretary level. The main aim of the SIG and IRGs was to gain input and advice from the several departments involved in a foreign policy decision and to coordinate policy between them better. A typical IRG, for example, might consist of an assistant secretary of State, of Defense, as well as representatives from the Joint Chiefs, the CIA, and the National Security Council. The higher level SIG had the added responsibilities of coordinating the several IRGs and reporting to the NSC or the appropriate secretary.

Over the years this structure of interagency coordinating groups has been changed several times. Later presidents changed the IRGs to interdepartmental or interagency groups (IGs). When he was national security adviser, Henry Kissinger reorganized and centralized the IGs to concentrate greater foreign policy control in his own hands. The Reagan administration reorganized the system again, creating three SIGs: one for foreign policy, one for defense policy, and one for intelligence activities. Each SIG, in turn, created its own series of lower level IGs, corresponding rather closely to the regional and functional bureaus of the State Department, Defense Department, or intelligence community, respectively. For example, the SIG for foreign policy, which is under the general direction of the secretary of state, would have an IG for Latin America, one for political-military affairs, and so on. Each IG included representatives from other agencies. Then, Bush revamped the system once again.

The *theory* of all these SIGs and IGs was that they would serve to better coordinate American foreign policy among the several bureaucratic fiefdoms. Their lines of responsibility run to the departmental secretaries and, ultimately, to the national security adviser and, hence, to the president. These interagency groups are not well known among the American public, even though they have the potential to be very important. If managed effectively, these interagency groups can serve as a means to coordinate policy and even manage conflict among the several, often contending, foreign policy agencies.

But theory is a long way from actual practice. In practice, many of these groups meet infrequently and some of them not at all. They lack decision-making authority, which is still lodged at higher levels with the secretaries of State or Defense. When they do meet, it is usually for the purpose of one agency (the chairing agency) sharing some limited information with the others, not for effective policy coordination. That is still done—when it is done at all—at higher levels, by the secretaries, the national security adviser, or the president. Moreover some agencies such as Treasury or Justice—precisely the ones that need to be represented on the new issues discussed here—are very seldom represented. So at best the SIGs and IGs remain information-sharing bodies, and even that function is carried out irregularly and often incompletely. Moreover, if one looks closely at the Reagan system, one sees that the three SIGs and their many IGs simply perpetuated the divisions that already existed between State, Defense, and CIA. An even higher interdepartmental committee would have to have been created to coordinate the three SIGs. Hence, while the idea of interagency cooperation and the better coordination of the many bureaucracies involved in foreign policy remains a noble one, its actual implementation remains a long way off.

At the highest levels of the decision-making pyramid, at the pinnacles of power, it is, of course, the president and his National Security Council that are ultimately responsible for policy coordination and implementation. That is where the buck finally stops in the American system. In the next two chapters, we deal with foreign policy decision making at this last and final level.

Suggested Readings

Aho, C. Michael, and Marc Levinson. *After Reagan: Confronting the Changed World Economy.* New York: Council on Foreign Relations, 1988.

Bagley, Bruce Michael. "The New Hundred Years War: U.S. Security and the War on Drugs in Latin America," *Journal of Inter-American Studies and World Affairs* 30(Spring 1988):161–82.

Bergsten, C. Fred. *Toward a New World Trade Policy.* Washington, D.C.: Brookings Institution, 1974.

Cohen, Stephen D. *The Making of United States Economic Policy.* New York: Praeger, 1988.

Craig, Roger. "Illicit Drug Traffic," *Journal of Inter-American Studies and World Affairs* 29(Summer 1987):1–34.

Destler, I. M. *Making Foreign Economic Policy.* Washington, D.C.: Brookings Institution, 1980.

_____. *Presidents, Bureaucrats, and Foreign Policy.* Princeton, N.J.: Princeton University Press, 1972.

Feinberg, Richard. *The Intemperate Zone: The Third World Challenge to U.S. Foreign Policy.* New York: Norton, 1983.

Goldwin, Robert A., ed. *Bureaucrats, Policy Analysts, Statesmen: Who Leads?* Washington, D.C.: American Enterprise Institute for Public Policy Research, 1980.

Hilsman, Roger. *The Politics of Policy-Making in Defense and Foreign Affairs: Conceptual Models and Bureaucratic Politics.* Englewood Cliffs, N.J.: Prentice-Hall, 1987.

Lee, Rensselar. "The Latin American Drug Connection." *Foreign Policy* (Winter 1985–86); 142–59.

Makin, John. *The Global Debt Crisis.* New York: Basic Books, 1984.

McCormick, James M. *American Foreign Policy and American Values.* Itasca, Ill.: Peacock, 1985.

Mills, James. *The Underground Empire.* New York: Doubleday, 1986.

Spero, Joan Edelman. *The Politics of International Economic Relations.* New York: St. Martin's Press, 1977.

Watkins, Alfred J. *Till Debt Do Us Part.* Washington, D.C.: Roosevelt Center for American Policy Studies, 1986.

Wiarda, Howard J. *Latin America at the Crossroads: Debt, Development, and the Future.* Boulder, Colo.: Westview Press, 1987.

CHAPTER THIRTEEN

The Presidency and Foreign Policy

○
○

The presidency is *the* focal point, the epicenter, the hub of the American system. Given our increased global commitments and responsibilities in recent decades, the presidency may be not only the most important job in the United States but also in the world. The presidency is at the narrowest point of our metaphorical funnel of foreign policy influences, at the center of our rings of concentric circles. Along with his foreign policy staff largely centered in the National Security Council (NSC, treated in the following chapter), the presidency is where the decision-making buck must stop.

There is an unmistakable aura that surrounds the presidency and the White House. Part of it lies in the pomp and symbolism of the presidency, which is not far removed from that of monarchy; part of it derives from the enormous power that is concentrated here, the power to make or break nations, the power to decide almost literally the demise or survival of humankind. One senses this aura in the faces of the thousands of tourists who come every day to tour the east wing of the White House, in the effort of every interest group and organization to find a location within blocks of the White House, and in the glow and murmur that fills a room whenever the president walks into it.

If one works in the White House, even in the Old Executive Office Building right next door or in the New Executive Office Building a half block away on 17th Street, where the offices of the NSC staff are concentrated, the same aura pervades. It is a feeling of immense power and responsibility. The first time one walks into the White House's West Wing (where the president's offices are), the first time one eats in the White House mess or visits the Situation Room in the basement, or the first (or second or third) time one walks into the Oval Office, one is liable to be mesmerized and tongue-tied by the experience. Even strong-willed and highly articulate persons are often so awed in the presidential presence that they fall silent or forget the lines they had carefully prepared to deliver.

There is a reasonable explanation for this. Because we are a democratic nation and a nation of immigrants, in contrast to other nations where the possibility of serving at the presidential or prime ministerial level is usually closed off to people without means or special family connections, when we finally make it to the White House by dint of hard work, merit, much studying, achievement, and not a little bit of luck, we cannot believe that we are there. Here we are, a little boy or girl from Grand Rapids, Paducah, or wherever, and we have made it to the very pinnacle of the American system. It is a very heady and awe-inspiring experience, and it usually takes a while to settle down and behave as one would in any other job. But, of course, by then one has gotten used to the perks—the parking spots, the access, the deference, the helicopters, the trips to Camp David, the sheer power and influence that go with a White House position. There is a magical aura that surrounds one's entry into the White House, but the letdown of leaving all that influence and importance behind is also great. Once you've worked for the president and served in the White House, no other job seems quite so important.

While the power and importance of the presidency are immense, there are also enormous limits on presidential authority. Ours is a system of checks and balances, and the president is frequently frustrated by his inability to get his agenda through the Congress. He is also frequently frustrated by his inability to get the bureaucracy to carry out his policies, to line up a coalition of interest groups to support his initiatives, or to shape public opinion in his favor. In addition, while most Americans revere the presidency, in a country of limited central state power such as ours, their lives, jobs, and families are seldom strongly affected by what goes on in the White House. From their point of view, it matters, in terms of pride, competence, and other imprecise measures, whether George Bush or Michael Dukakis occupies the White House—but not all that much. In addition, even with all his immense power, the American president cannot change other countries; cannot create institutions abroad where none exist; cannot change the political culture of divisive, bloody nations like Lebanon, Haiti, or El Salvador; and cannot manipulate the levers abroad as easily as it often appears from the banks of the Potomac.

HISTORY AND BACKGROUND

Although the Congress and the White House have long vied for dominance in foreign policy, it is usually and historically the president who has been supreme. Although, as we saw in Chapter 10, the United States Constitution offers an "invitation to struggle" to both the legislative and the executive branches, it is the president who has long been predominant in the foreign policy arena. Congress has become a resurgent power in foreign policy-making in the past two decades; but despite all the new congressional assertiveness, the presidency remains the main power in the American system.

Under the United States Constitution (Article II), the president is the chief executive. He is also commander-in-chief of the armed forces. He is further granted the power to be the chief negotiator and the chief diplomat, although his appointments and the treaties he may sign must receive the advice and consent of the Senate. With these three major powers—chief executive, commander-in-chief, and head diplomat—the president would appear to have sufficient constitutional power to prevail in foreign policy.

It was clearly the intention of the Founding Fathers to enhance the powers of the presidency, including in foreign policy. The Constitution of 1787 stood in marked contrast to the earlier Articles of Confederation under which Congress dominated foreign policy through a Committee on Foreign Affairs. But the system proved unworkable, as both the Congress and the writers of the Constitution realized, hence the vesting under the Constitution of broad powers in the executive branch. As Alexander Hamilton noted in *Federalist No. 70*, the presidency was made into a one-person office because in that way "decision, activity, secrecy, and dispatch" would all be enhanced. These were qualities that the founders associated with sound government and quick decisions, especially in the field of foreign affairs. The broad powers granted the president constitutionally as well as the supplemental writings of the founders make it clear that the executive was expected to dominate in foreign affairs. The Congress was supposed to check and oversee his authority, to share in some important powers, but not itself to take the lead.

In addition, over the intervening two centuries, the power of the president in foreign affairs has generally been enhanced rather than weakened.[1] At least five factors are involved: the setting of new precedents by the presidents, Supreme Court decisions, congressional delegation and deference, growth of the executive apparatus, and international and emergency factors such as war or threats of war.

With regard to precedents, George Washington made it clear that he would be the one to represent the United States abroad, to negotiate international agreements, to recognize other states, and to initiate the conduct of foreign policy. President Jefferson negotiated the Louisiana purchase, and President Polk was able to force the hand of the Congress in declaring war on Mexico. President Lincoln blockaded the port cities of the South during the Civil War; and Presidents McKinley, Roosevelt, Taft, and Wilson sent United States forces abroad without congressional authorization. The sending of United States military forces to Korea by President Truman was done without a congressional declaration of war (but not without controversy), and recent American presidents have sent United States forces abroad on numerous occasions to protect American citizens, restore order, or patrol international waterways—all without congressional authorization, although usually with some congressional grumbling. The large number of executive agreements, as distinct from treaties, that the United States has signed with other nations has also added to the list of precedents by which executive power in foreign policy has been enhanced.

A second factor in explaining the enlargement of presidential leadership in foreign policy is Supreme Court decisions. In *United States* v. *Curtiss-Wright Export Corporation et al.,* a 1934 case involving the sale of machine guns by a private company to Bolivia, the Court held that the Congress could delegate power to the executive, that the president was the representative of United States sovereignty in foreign affairs, and that the president's leadership prerogatives went beyond the actual constitutional listing of his powers. In *Missouri* v. *Holland* (1920), the Court upheld the supremacy of the president in making foreign policy over against the powers of the states. In *United States* v. *Belmont* (1937), the Court held that executive agreements were the law of the land, even if they had not received congressional approval. In these and other cases, historically, the Supreme Court generally has held in ways that strengthened the foreign policy-making capacities of the executive.

A third factor is congressional delegation and deference. In the Formosa Resolution of 1955, the Congress delegated to the president the power to use American armed forces to defend Formosa, as well as some smaller island near mainland (Communist) China, *as he saw fit.* The famous Gulf of Tonkin Resolution of 1964, which passed the House by a vote of 416 to 0 and the Senate, 89 to 2, authorized President Johnson to deploy United States military forces in Southeast Asia without a congressional declaration of war. In these ways Congress *delegated* its war-making power to the president. In many other instances, the Congress has simply deferred to presidential leadership. Whether talking about United States entry into the United Nations, the Marshall Plan, the formation of NATO, the test ban treaty, aid to such Communist countries as Poland and Yugoslavia, the sending of American forces to Lebanon or the United States fleet to the Persian Gulf, the Congress has (until recently) virtually always deferred to presidential leadership.[2] Such delegation and deference on the part of Congress have had the cumulative effect of adding still further to presidential leadership in foreign policy.

A fourth factor contributing to rising presidential influence in foreign policy is institutional growth within the executive branch. Parallel to the staff growth in the Congress—only more so—is the staff proliferation within the executive branch. All the main executive departments—State, Defense, Justice, Treasury—are far larger now than they were thirty years ago. This gives the president an enormous staff and expertise on which to rely. Then there is staff growth within the White House itself. The president's personal staff of advisers, assistants, and so forth is now similarly larger by far than previously, overflowing the White House, filling both the Old and the New Executive Office Buildings, and spilling over into the elegant townhouses around Lafayette Park across the street from the White House as well as into numerous other offices around Washington. Nor should we forget the creation of such specialized foreign policy agencies as the Central Intelligence Agency, the National Security Administration, and the National Security Council—all of which operate under executive authority and, therefore, tend to enhance the expertise, knowledge, and political and bureaucratic clout of the president. For the first time, in addition, the president has his own polling agency located in the White House as well as his own public relations office.

A fifth factor has to do with actual foreign affairs and their effects on the American presidency. To begin, every single war that the United States has fought over the past two hundred years has served, inexorably, to increase presidential power in foreign policy. Wars are emergency situations, and in emergencies we have simply felt it necessary to allow and trust broad presidential discretion. In addition, war necessitates flexibility and quick decisions; in such times, only the president is thought to have the capacity to run the country and conduct foreign affairs. The cold war with the Soviet Union, which is not like other wars with a definite beginning and a definite ending but has been waged virtually constantly since 1945, has resulted in an enormous increase in presidential foreign affairs authority. Since World War II, we have been on an almost perpetual war footing with the Soviet Union, although sometimes the conflict has ebbed while at other times it has been intense. But in this entire forty-five-year history, it is the president who has been the chief repository of increased foreign policy emphasis and to whom we look for leadership—so much so that we became used to taking presidential dominance in foreign policy for granted. Even the recent resurgence of the Congress to a position of greater influence in the foreign affairs field (which was largely the norm prior to World War II) has not yet resulted in a significant erosion of presidential authority, let alone a position of equality between the two branches—although the rising power of Congress *has* been sufficient to often frustrate a president and led to increasing paralysis in foreign policy-making.

TRAINING FOR THE PRESIDENCY

American presidents have been, for the most part, ill-equipped to handle the responsibilities of managing the foreign affairs of the most powerful and influential nation on earth. Unlike their European counterparts, for example, American presidents tend to come to office entirely inexperienced in foreign affairs. It is small wonder that our foreign policy produces so many gaffes and misdirections. The skills an individual acquires while being a politician and campaigning for the presidency are not at all the skills he will need to conduct a successful foreign policy. American presidents—with very few exceptions—have to learn about foreign policy while on the job. That strikes most foreign policy experts as both a very dangerous situation, in the sense that an inexperienced president may make a mistake that will lead to disaster, and a powerful explanation of why our foreign policy so often goes astray. The wisdom among the experts is that what has saved American foreign policy over the decades is that the Soviet Union has often been even more bumbling than we.

Part of the problem of presidential inadequacy and inexperience in foreign policy is that our presidents, naturally enough, tend to be reflections of the nation as a whole. That is, they have very little capacity in foreign languages, have seldom traveled abroad except on brief vacations, often share the condescension and patronizing attitudes toward other nations ("We are better than you"; "You should follow our example"; etc.) that are common in the nation at large, and have seldom developed the empathy necessary to understand other nations on their own terms. These attitudes, in turn, have grown out of the historic isolationism of the United States, the notion that we don't need other nations and can do just fine on our own, and out of the sense that the United States can simply proceed unilaterally with or without our allies. Unfortunately, our presidents have often shared the ethnocentric and isolationist sentiments that are pervasive in the American historical experience.

A second factor working against presidential knowledge and experience in foreign policy is the career patterns of politicians themselves. The career of most American politicians is, first, local or county office (councilman, selectman, commissioner, mayor); then state office (legislative, governor); next, federal office (House or Senate); finally the possibility of the presidency itself. Note that never and nowhere in this career ladder is foreign affairs experience or living abroad ever possible. In fact, interviews with congressmen about this problem reveal that politicians fear that their careers will be hurt or at least postponed if they live outside the country for a while. The result is that few congressmen do, in fact, ever spend time abroad, which helps explain why our presidents (as well as others constituting the pool of potential presidents) are so inadequately prepared for foreign policy issues once they reach the pinnacles of the American system. *Nothing* in their entire careers has ever prepared them for dealing with foreign affairs.

An opposite but still serious problem afflicts those congressmen, such as Senator Christopher Dodd and former Senator Paul Tsongas, who earlier served in the Peace Corps. They have foreign experience, language skills, and empathy; but their Peace Corps experience was almost entirely from the worm's-eye view, from the bottom up. They tend, therefore, to be almost automatically hostile to United States policy at the national or embassy level and to be forever suspicious of the elites of the capital city—including American diplomatic personnel—who seldom get out to the countryside and seldom realize that their policies have no effect whatsoever in the boondocks, where the Peace Corps young people are stationed. The Peace Corps experience provides a marvelous vantage point to see and learn other cultures, and that is to the good; but, of course, that is not the only vantage point and it leads frequently to hostility and suspicion toward United States policy exercised at other levels.

Let us run through the list of American presidents during and since World War II to illustrate their lack of prior foreign affairs experience. President Franklin Delano Roosevelt had once been secretary of the Navy but he nevertheless had limited foreign affairs experience before becoming president, had to learn on the job, and, while he is generally applauded for leading the nation through World War II, is widely thought to have come out on the losing end of the wartime negotiations with Stalin. President Truman had *no* foreign affairs experience and had previously been the owner of a small men's furnishings shop in Missouri; yet, he managed to pick good secretaries of state (George Marshall, Dean Acheson) and his accomplishments were many: the Marshall Plan, the Berlin airlift, NATO, Point Four, resistance to Communist aggression in Greece, Iran, Turkey, and Korea. Dwight Eisenhower, because of his experience as commanding general in World War II, had lived abroad and had more foreign affairs experience than any other recent American president. His administration is widely thought to have been the most successful in the foreign policy area during the post–World War II period.

With Presidents Kennedy and Johnson, we return to the tradition of presidents who had no previous foreign policy experience and, hence, who committed many goofs and outright disasters (the Bay of Pigs, the Vietnam war) in foreign affairs. President Nixon, along with his main foreign affairs adviser, Henry Kissinger, was a wily practitioner of *realpolitik,* who had learned from Eisenhower while serving as vice-president and who had also spent a large part of his years out of office between 1960 and 1968 traveling abroad and getting to know the world's leaders. Nixon's foreign affairs accomplishments were many (detente with the Soviet Union, the opening of China, an end to the Vietnam war), but he eventually had to resign because of the domestic scandal known as Watergate.

His successor, Gerald Ford, again had no experience in foreign affairs; Ford's brief administration was characterized by few accomplishments and few goofs either (the most notable of which was his saying emphatically during the nationally televised presidential debate with candidate Jimmy Carter that the Soviet Union had no troops and no control over its satellite, Poland). Carter himself likewise had almost no experience in foreign affairs but nevertheless had a moralistic and missionary attitude toward foreign issues and nations; his administration is widely thought to have foundered on the shoals of foreign policy disasters, principally the anti-American Islamic revolution in Iran and the seizure of the American embassy hostages there. Although on the opposite side of the political spectrum from Mr. Carter, President Reagan also had strongly felt beliefs about foreign policy but very little experience. Both these more ideological recent presidents went through a learning process that began to produce better policies about half way through their terms, but whether the nation could afford such on-the-job training remained very much an open and, to some, a scary question. With President Bush, who had been director of the CIA as well as ambassador to China, we return again to foreign policy experience in the executive branch.

This brief survey of our ten most recent presidents does not lead to very many encouraging conclusions. Of the ten, only three (Eisenhower, Nixon, and Bush) could be said to be prepared, in a foreign policy sense, for the job. The rest were inadequately prepared, often woefully so—although Truman was successful despite his inexperience, and perhaps Reagan will be so judged also.

Two corollaries follow from the preceding analysis. The first is that, while the presidency is the focal point of our system of government, that is often where the least expertise on foreign policy lies. The fact is, most foreign policy issues are handled more or less routinely, at lower levels, within the foreign affairs bureaucracies, where most of the real expertise is located. Only the biggest and most important issues get bumped up to the White House where the president must deal with them. But that is also the level where there is liable to be the least knowledge and understanding of the issues. That also explains why foreign policy at the White House level so often is misdirected or produces mistakes. It is sometimes a frightening paradox to realize that only the largest and most dangerous foreign policy issues find their way to the Oval Office, and yet that is where the least experience and background are often brought to bear on the issue.

The second corollary follows from the first. Because of presidential inexperience in foreign policy, we now increasingly pay attention not just to the rival candidates but to their whole teams. We want to know who advises the candidates on foreign policy and who will accompany them into office if elected. That is why, increasingly, presidential candidates have felt it necessary to form foreign policy advisory teams far in advance of the election, and to announce publicly who is on them. In this way, experienced observers can tell what to expect from a new administration even if the candidate is personally inexperienced. Washington insiders—those who follow these events closely—and increasingly the informed electorate now know months and even years in advance who will fill the main foreign affairs posts in the next administration. In this modern, complex era where so much is at stake, we need to examine and elect not just the candidate but the candidate's circle of advisers as well. More and more we are voting for a whole team of players, not just a single candidate.

THE POWERS OF THE PRESIDENCY

The president has broad formal power in the area of foreign policy-making. In addition, he has wide informal power that will vary over time, depending on the personality and political skills of the particular president. The president is similarly limited, both formally and informally.

First, the president is the commander-in-chief.[3] The Constitution states that the president is commander-in-chief of the United States Army and Navy and obviously, by implication, the more recently created Air Force and Marine Corps as well. Although there has long been disagreement as to what precisely the phrase "commander-in-chief" means, most presidents (as well as Congress and the public) have interpreted it widely, giving the president vast power over military and foreign policy.

The president is checked by the fact that the Congress must declare war; but, in fact, the United States has been involved in more than one hundred thirty hostilities in its history and in numerous other small episodes or near hostilities. Of these one hundred thirty and more, Congress has declared war in only five of them—the War of 1812, the Mexican War of 1846, the Spanish-American War of 1898, World War I, and World War II. All of the others—the vast majority—have been either undeclared wars (Korea, Vietnam) or police actions (sending United States forces to the Dominican Republic in 1965, to Lebanon in 1982, or to Grenada in 1983, and so on). The large number of actions in which Congress did not declare war and yet American forces were committed illustrates the vast powers of the president to act independently as the commander-in-chief.

In addition to the power to deploy American military forces, the position of commander-in-chief has been interpreted in ways that give the president even vaster power. First, it is the president, along with the Defense Department, who decides military strategy—Roosevelt in World War II, Truman in Korea, and Johnson in Vietnam. Second, the president may make decisions concerning the deployment and patrol functions of the military that may actually lead to greater hostilities—for example, Kennedy's naval blockade of Cuba in 1962 or Reagan's decision to escort tankers and other ships through the Persian Gulf in the face of Iranian opposition. Third, it has been the president's responsibility to decide when hostilities in any conflict situation should end and how and when negotiations for a settlement should begin.

In all of these areas, the president as commander-in-chief has vast power. Only during the Vietnam war, as well as more recently over Central America, did these presidential prerogatives and responsibilities come to be seriously questioned.

A second major power of the president is in treaty making. The president, by Constitution, has the power to make treaties "by and with the advice and consent of the Senate, provided two-thirds of the Senators present concur." It is not clear from this whether the president should seek the advice and consent of the Senate only *after* the treaty is negotiated and signed or during the process of discussion itself. Historically, the president has sought senatorial concurrence only after the treaty was signed, but in recent years, the requirements of politics and the need to assure confirmation have meant the involvement of the senators during the earlier process. Jimmy Carter "consulted" with over seventy senators in the process of negotiating the difficult and divisive Panama Canal treaties; and in the Strategic Arms Limitation Talks (SALT II), over twenty senators and forty-five House members sat in at various times during the negotiations in Geneva. Clearly, the treaty-making process has become more complicated and politicized, with the president having oftentimes to engage in simultaneous negotiations: one set of negotiations with the other party and another set with the Congress.

Treaty making is not cut and dried; there is an entire political process that is involved. First, the treaty is negotiated and signed by the representatives of the parties involved, a process that may be lengthy, may involve the media, may involve public opinion, and may be controversial. Once signed, the treaty is submitted to the Senate where it may be approved, rejected, amended, or approved but with reservations and further understandings. These changes may, of course, make it unacceptable to the other party or to the administration that negotiated it. The president also retains initiatives in this process: he may withdraw the treaty, may ask for further changes from the other party, or may refuse to sign it even after it receives Senate approval. While the political process thus described unfolds, the treaty may acquire a political life of its own so that even if a president still has reservations about a treaty, the power of public opinion (particularly if the treaty provides for nuclear disarmament, relaxes the tensions with the Soviet Union, or leads to some form of "peace" in southern Africa or Central America) may force him to sign it anyway.

A third major power of the president is his ability to sign executive agreements with other nations. Such agreements can be written or oral, public or secret. They are binding agreements between heads of state, but they do not require Senate approval. Some executive agreements are actually submitted to the Senate, but then only a majority vote is needed, not the two-thirds required by treaties. One can appreciate, after understanding the complexities of the treaty-making process, why presidents would *much* prefer to operate on the basis of executive agreements rather than going through the hassles of treaty ratification.

Most executive agreements are written, formal documents that resemble treaties; and as we saw in Chapter 10, the distinction between treaties and executive agreements is not crystal clear. We might assume intuitively that formal treaties are more important and more fundamental; but, in fact, executive agreements can also deal with fundamental war-and-peace issues. The Yalta and Potsdam agreements at the end of World War II, the Camp David Accords in which President Carter sought peace in the Middle East by bringing Menachim Begin of Israel and Anwar Sadat of Egypt together, and the SALT I Interim Agreement were all executive agreements involving momentous decisions.

The real difference between a treaty and an executive agreement is thus not so much in their relative importance as in the flexibility they provide a president. The president has a great deal more room to maneuver and to reach an understanding with a foreign power without everyone getting into the act—that is, without the entire, complex, divisive, and frustrating American political process entering in—through an executive agreement than through a treaty. But Congress believes the number of executive agreements reached without congressional consent has become excessive and, therefore, it has moved to have more executive agreements considered as treaties.

A fourth power of the president in foreign policy is the appointment of high foreign policy officials. These include the secretaries of state and defense, the undersecretaries and assistant secretaries, the director of the CIA, the director of the United States Information Agency (USIA), and all ambassadors. All these nominations must receive the approval of two-thirds of the Senate, but it is important to understand that many other presidential appointments do not require Senate approval. The list includes members of the president's personal White House staff, all members of the National Security Council, even the director of the NSC—who is a key foreign policy-making official and, in modern times, has become the president's chief foreign policy adviser.

In the past, Senate approval of high-level presidential appointments was more or less routine. The operating assumption was that a popularly elected president was entitled to assemble a team of his own choosing for foreign policy matters. Other than manifest and obvious incompetence and malfeasance, the Senate seldom put barriers in the way of persons the president wished to have. And even when there was opposition in the Senate, by forcing the issue a determined president could almost always have his way.

However, the system has become much more politicized in recent years. Appointments that used to be routinely approved are no longer so.

A president can still get most of his appointments through the Senate, but the barriers are now greater. Sometimes, as in the case of Carter's desire to appoint Kennedy speech writer Theodore Sorenson as director of the CIA, the president is told beforehand by the Congress not even to bother to submit the name. The opposition to Reagan's initial nomination to head the Office of Human Rights and Humanitarian Affairs in the Department of State was so strong that the candidate, Ernest LeFever, was forced to withdraw his name even before it came to a vote. The president's national security adviser must often submit to a grilling by the Senate, even though congressional confirmation is not legally required. Ambassadorial and other appointments are now routinely held up by the Senate, often for months or even years, on political or ideological grounds. During the last years of Reagan's presidency, a large number of his appointees was held up indefinitely and left hanging because Democrats in the Senate refused to schedule their confirmation hearings, hoping that a Democratic president would be elected in 1988 and that Democrats would thus be appointed to take over these unfilled positions. Meanwhile, while the Senate dilly dallied, key foreign policy positions remained unfilled. Partisanship seems to know no bounds in these matters, even if it comes at the expense of United States foreign policy.

Fifth, the president also has the authority to grant, withhold, or withdraw recognition to foreign states. The Constitution says that the president "shall receive ambassadors and other public Ministers," from which is derived the power of recognition. The president in the United States is the head of state, and by hallowed custom foreign diplomats are accredited to him personally. He has the power to receive them or not, to allow them into the country or to kick them out.

Recognition of other states has also taken on increasingly political overtones. Most other countries of the world grant diplomatic recognition to a government on the basis of whether it is in de facto control of its country, not on the basis of its political or moral purity or worth. For a long time the United States also followed the former practice. The question, hence, was not *how* a government came to power, whether it was by constitutional or extraconstitutional means (revolution or coup d'etat), but only whether it was in control of its own national territory.

More recently, however, political reasons have become increasingly important in the policy of granting or withholding recognition. For example, even though the Communists were in de facto control of mainland China by 1949, the United States did not recognize the People's Republic until 1979—thirty years later—because we disapproved of the Communist regime and wished to use nonrecognition to isolate and extract some leverage from the regime. The United States broke relations with Communist Cuba in 1960 similarly because we wished to isolate and stigmatize the regime of Fidel Castro. In several Latin American countries, the United

States tried to use nonrecognition (either the threat of or the reality) to head off coups d'etat or to preserve or reinstall democratic governments. The strategy did, in fact, have some deterrent effects, particularly when the threat of nonrecognition was accompanied by a cutoff of American aid; but the usual pattern was for a military government to claim that it was threatened by "communism" and the United States would then quickly restore both aid and recognition. Like sanctions, nonrecognition of existing governments has not been a very effective tool to secure our desired outcomes in other nations—although in some times and circumstances it has been moderately successful.

Sixth, the president may be said to have certain inherent powers. Since he is, by Constitution, the head of state, he is the individual with whom foreign governments have official contact. The president may be seen as the *only* official voice in the United States in foreign policy matters. In the major *United States* v. *Curtis-Wright* case cited earlier, the Supreme Court affirmed that the president "alone has the power to speak or listen as a representative of the nation." The Court made a sharp distinction between foreign (where the president is the chief authority) and domestic affairs (where other participants—Congress, the states, local governments—may also get involved). Said the Court, the president is the "sole organ of the federal government in the field of international relations."

As American foreign policy has become more and more politicized and "democratized" in recent years, these clear and sweeping statements by the Supreme Court have been increasingly undermined. They are undermined by House Speaker Jim Wright's seeking to undertake his own foreign policy in Central America, regardless of the elected president's policy and, in fact, contrary to it. They are undermined by State governors who, in addition to the quite legal trade and economic development missions that they send to various countries, sometimes conduct their own foreign policies abroad. And the Court's clear statement of presidential preeminence in foreign policy-making is also undermined by the efforts similarly of various towns and cities in the United States to conduct their own foreign policies: by the designation of their towns as "nuclear-free zones," by the establishment of "sister city" relationships in countries that are in conflict with American foreign policy goals, by their collective and usually highly partisan town-sanctioned resolutions on foreign policy issues, and by the designation of their communities as "sanctuaries" for refugees from countries in which they oppose United States policy actions. So far, the United States government has chosen largely to ignore these local initiatives, even though they sometimes conflict with the clear constitutional prerogatives of the executive branch in foreign affairs matters while they also add to the perception of confusion in American foreign policy.

The phenomena described above reflect the growth of what may be called local foreign policies (encompassing both local and state actions in these areas).[4] Clearly, such actions violate the Supreme Court's rulings on presidential predominance in *United States* v. *Curtis-Wright;* but, on the other hand, such local participation in foreign policy has been growing in the past decade and there are historic precedents for such grass-roots involvement. We await, therefore, a new Supreme Court ruling on such local involvements; in the meantime, with governors, mayors, town councils, to say nothing of the Speaker of the House, carrying out their own foreign policies, a further element of division, fragmentation, and paralysis has been added to our already deeply divided foreign policy-making process.

In thinking about the changes analyzed above with regard to presidential decision making on foreign policy, one factor stands out: how politicized the process has become. In every one of the six areas of presidential power that we have discussed, it is clear that politics infuses and is at the heart of all of them. Our discussion points to the conclusion that the president cannot just decide and decree foreign policy decisions anymore and expect the rest of the system and the country to fall into agreement. That was one of Jimmy Carter's gravest mistakes as president. As an engineer, technocrat, and "detail man," he expected that, once he and his advisers had pooled all their expertise and arrived at the "right" conclusion, everyone else would follow along. But because others saw the facts differently, operated from different assumptions, used alternative logics, or simply had different political interests, they did not always share Carter's conclusions. The president was often unable to recognize truths other than his own, and he was often unable to compromise his deeply felt beliefs. Hence, his foreign policies were seldom successful.

In the new, more politicized environment in which we find ourselves, hence, the president must also play the political game. He must not only present good and acceptable policies, but he must campaign politically for them. He must guide, instruct, cajole, persuade, and lobby. He must go on national television to present his case; meet with Congress to explain his policies; mobilize public opinion behind his programs or people; line up a supporting coalition of interest groups; get party support; enlist the aid of United States allies; be willing to compromise; send his spokesmen out into the universities, churches, and synagogues. The president cannot just issue orders and expect everyone to fall into line like in the army; instead, he must engage in political activities of the sort that in the past had largely been confined to domestic politics. For a president to be successful at foreign policy in the changed circumstances of the United States in the 1980s and 1990s, he must become actively engaged in the political process, just as his opposition is.

This is what political scientist Richard Neustadt meant in his celebrated pronouncement that the president was essentially a "clerk."[5] Given the aura that surrounds the presidency and its vast powers, Neustadt's notion that the president was not all powerful came as a shock to many of his readers. But, in fact, what Neustadt was suggesting was precisely what we have indicated here: that even the president must politically *bargain* his policies into existence and toward implementation and success, and not just issue them as a set of marching orders the way a general would. America, including the Congress, the bureaucracy, and other agencies, is too diverse, too pluralistic, and too independent for that to work. Neustadt's analysis was chiefly oriented toward the president's role in domestic policy-making, but now we know the same rules apply to foreign policy-making as well. As foreign policy has become increasingly politicized, the president also must "go into the political pits" to gain allies and support if he wishes his policies to succeed.

PRESIDENTIAL CHARACTER AND PERSONALITY

In recent years a new approach to studying the presidency—almost a cottage industry—has sprung up, which is frequently referred to as the study of presidential personality, or psychohistory. A spate of books has come out about each of our recent presidents, probing their early histories, their relations with their parents, early conflicts and political experiences, and so on.

The assumptions of this new approach are that every individual has strengths, weaknesses, a distinct personality derived from early experiences, and distinct traits; and that, in some ways, his performance in the executive office will be an extension of this early history and of the presidential personality. The argument is that the early experiences of a president will provide us with clues to the presidential character and, hence, to how he will behave in office. Hence, psychohistorians study early successes, behavior, style, and failures to try to predict how a person will act and respond in the presidency. Will he be an independent personality or will he rely heavily on advisers; how does he respond to challenges, to successes, to failures?

Now, few of us doubt that presidents (as well as the rest of us) are the products, in some ways, of earlier training, upbringing, race and class origins, education, parents, early formative experiences, and doubtless other factors. The trouble begins when presidential analysts try to draw a one-to-one relationship between a person's behavior early in life and his behavior as an adult, or when they draw neat correlations—usually without knowing, maybe fifty years later, all the facts and factors involved—between crises and responses during the president's youth and his responses to crises at the international level. No doubt such early influences are important, but psychohistory is also fraught with dangers and potential for gross misinterpretations (few psychohistorians, for example, are also trained psychologists or psychoanalysts) and, therefore, we need to be cautious in the use of such analyses.

One psychohistory approach, for example, has emphasized the distinction between crusaders (who are set in their ways, moralistic, with fixed and unyielding views) and pragmatists (who value alternatives and choices). Another approach has focused on authoritarian personalities versus democratic ones. Is the personality competitive or collegial? Is the person a rabble-rouser who likes to stir things up, or a creator and theorist who is often also a moralizer, or an administrator who lacks creativity and operates according to standard operating procedures? Did the person in early life exhibit hostile-aggressive behavior? Is there need for power? Or is there a desire for achievement and affection? Is the person a loner or a more social being, at home in the relaxed activity of everyday conversation among friends and colleagues? Does the person operate by consensus or insist on going his own way? These are only some of the issues and the categorizations set forth by different psychohistorians.

Perhaps the most interesting set of categories directly applicable to the presidency has been set forth by political scientist James David Barber.[6] Professor Barber distinguishes, first, between positive personalities and negative personalities. Positive personalities are those with optimistic, forceful, dynamic, enthusiastic outlooks on life, usually stemming from early successes with overcoming adversity. Negative personalities, in contrast, tend to be lonely, withdrawn, full of complexes, with chips on their shoulders. Professor Barber then adds another matrix: the president's attitudes toward public policy, which can be passive or active. Active public policy (foreign or domestic) is based on the rational setting of clear goals, the willingness to use the political clout of the White House to achieve them, and strong leadership on the part of the president. Passive public policy, in contrast, comes from a president who is not an initiator, who is somewhat withdrawn from the political conflict, who reacts to the ideas of others rather than initiating new programs himself.

Professor Barber then combines these two matrixes—one assessing personality and background, the other assessing attitudes toward public policy—into a table with four boxes, as in Figure 13.1.

Figure 13.1
Presidential Personality and Public Policy

| | | Personality Traits | |
		Positive	Negative
Public Policy	Active		
	Passive		

He then attempts to categorize our recent presidents in terms of where they fit into these several boxes.

Barber finds that President Truman had both a positive outlook on life and was a forceful, activist leader in public policy. This is clearly Professor Barber's favorite presidential type, although he recognizes that such a personality may be too hasty in trying to get results. A person with a negative personality but an active attitude toward public policy, in Barber's view, is the most dangerous type of presidential leader because he not only is full of complexes and carries a chip on his shoulder but also may act compulsively—as negative-active personality types, Barber has in mind a Lyndon Johnson (Vietnam) or Richard Nixon (Watergate). A positive-passive president (his example is Reagan) has a positive/optimistic attitude toward life but dislikes the discord and controversy of public policy; he also favors a laissez-faire attitude toward public policy and does not believe government should take the lead in very many areas of life. Finally, there is the negative-passive personality (like Presidents Taft and Harding), who not only do not initiate but tend to withdraw from the political contest.

Now this is a useful way of looking at the interrelationships of presidential personality and public policy, but there are problems with the approach as well. At least four problems may be identified. First, the scheme may be politically biased: it tends to favor those who want a stronger (positive) governmental role (Democrats) as against those who want government to be less active (Republicans). Second, it runs the risk of engaging in pop psychology on the basis of incomplete information: none of us really knows for certain what forces shaped the personalities of Presidents Johnson and Nixon or precisely how their backgrounds influenced their decisions in the White House.

A third problem is that the four categories are too simple and do not allow for sufficient gradations and mixed types. We should be skeptical of any psychoanalytic scheme that seeks to stuff all personalities into four boxes using only two measures, since most persons (including our presidents) are much more complex than that. Where does one place John F. Kennedy or Jimmy Carter, for example, who had both positive and negative personality traits at the same time?

And that gets us to the fourth problem with this approach: scholars and others may well disagree about the category in which to place a person. For example, in the spring of 1988 students in my classes were asked to categorize the then presidential candidates in the light of Professor Barber's four boxes. The students were in considerable agreement in most cases. They considered Jesse Jackson, Richard Gephardt, and Joseph Biden as positive-active personalities; but that did not mean that they (or the voters in the primaries) favored these candidates for the presidency. Mario Cuomo, who chose not to run in 1988, was considered a positive-passive personality. Alexander Haig, Gary Hart, Robert Dole, and Michael Dukakis (all viewed as having chips on their shoulders), were considered negative-active personalities. But no one knew enough about Albert Gore's background to typecast him safely. And the students disagreed strongly about Bush: they agreed that he was passive but were divided as to whether he was passive-negative or passive-positive. Doubtless, their politics also had something to do with these disagreements.

Psychohistory and the study of presidential personality, background, and character are thus useful tools of analysis, but they are easily subject to abuse and must be employed with great care. There is utility in this approach but grave dangers as well that oblige us to maintain a healthy dose of skepticism.

DYNAMIC FACTORS

In recent decades, more and more power, including power in foreign affairs, has come to be concentrated in the hands of the president. Even more than previously, and even allowing for the resurgence of congressional power, the president has become *the* focal point of the American system. Television concentrates our attention on the president's every move, and summit meetings of heads of state as well as ceremonial occasions put the president constantly in the news spotlight. Our recent presidents have, in addition, engaged in a form of personal diplomacy that makes them their own secretaries of state. It is the president who often meets with Soviet or allied leaders, travels frequently abroad, and charts foreign policy strategy. In the process, he and his advisers become a kind of super state department, relegating the real State Department to the sidelines and sometimes making the secretary of state into an errand runner.

Presidents often look to score triumphs in the international terrain because the domestic problems—poverty, budget deficits, the economy—are so intractable, have little glamour, and often cannot be solved. In contrast, foreign policy offers the promise of vast media coverage in an exotic setting, with the president appearing statesmanlike as he meets with other heads of state in sumptuous and important-looking surroundings. What president could resist those possibilities when compared with the drudgery of yet another battle over welfare or the domestic budget? At the same time, as the United States since World War II has become more and more involved in the world, not just politically and strategically but now economically and financially as well, foreign policy matters have become increasingly important.

Yet, despite the increased importance and salience of foreign policy issues, our presidents tend to be woefully ill-prepared to deal with these complex foreign policy issues. Most of our presidential candidates, as we have seen, lack serious or extensive background in foreign policy. They have to learn on the job, a dangerous practice that helps explain the numerous foreign policy mistakes of recent years. Foreign policy has become increasingly important to our existence and survival as a nation, but the sad fact is that while television and other forces concentrate our attention on the presidency, as the major foreign policy player, that is the place usually least well-equipped to deal with foreign policy crises. Most foreign policy issues, we have said, are more or less routinely handled in the bureaucracy; only the biggest issues get elevated to the White House, where there tends to be the *least* expertise.

It is not just that our presidents are usually poorly informed and inexperienced in foreign policy issues, but so, often, are their principal advisers. The staffs as well as our recent presidents tend overwhelmingly to be domestically oriented. They serve as loyal, enthusiastic lieutenants to the candidate during the campaign; they are then rewarded with a high position in the White House; and they generally carry with them into these high positions the domestic preoccupations that are their specialties. If we look at the persons who were closest to President Carter in the campaign and in his White House years—Hamilton Jordan, Jody Powell, Mrs. Carter—none of them had any foreign policy experience whatsoever. Although Mrs. Carter had no official standing in the White House and no foreign affairs background, she had de facto cabinet status and the president sent her on several diplomatic missions. That was an insult to the other countries because of her lack of official standing; and when she went abroad, Mrs. Carter's method of preparation was to try to read the Bible in the local language—justifiable, perhaps, from a religious point of view but not a sufficient preparation for the art of diplomacy. Or, if we look at President Reagan's chief staff assistants—Edwin Meese, James Baker, and Michael Deaver during the first term, as well as Nancy Reagan; Donald Regan, Howard Baker, Kenneth Duberstein, and again Mrs. Reagan in the second—none of them had any foreign policy experience either. If it is true that, in the modern executive, we elect a staff as much as a president, then in our most recent elections we have not gotten the kind of foreign policy expertise that we sorely require. George Bush's foreign policy staff may be an exception to this pattern.

The situation often gets worse as we go down the staff ladder. Most of those chosen to serve at lower levels on the White House staff are selected because of their fierce and unquestioning loyalty to the president. Loyalty is usually valued more strongly than competence or expertise. Those who faithfully helped the candidate in his campaign, or carried his luggage, are rewarded for their services with a low-level White House job. But once in their jobs, they are often given more and more responsibilities, and then something important—and potentially dangerous—happens: the luggage carriers acquire power. They learn what the channels are, who has influence, what secretaries to work through, how the system works. Pretty soon, what were very low-level officials, reflecting their youthfulness and lack of experience, are exercising influence way beyond their competence— including in the area of foreign affairs. At upper levels of the White House staff, such power in the absence of very much knowledge or experience tends to result in capers like that of Colonel Oliver North in the Reagan administration; at lower levels, it produces great (often excessive) enthusiasm for the president's programs but not usually very sound or workable policies. Sometimes it produces the "dirty tricks" division of the White House. There are of course persons with foreign policy expertise on the president's staff, but often these persons are subordinated to the domestic or political affairs officials and their voices are only weakly heard.

In all these considerations, what emerges is a perpetual conflict between the political skills necessary to *become* president and the talents in foreign policy required to successfully *be* president. In the United States we tend to be strong on the former and weak on the latter—not only in terms of the skills and specialization of the staff but also in terms of the experience of the president himself. Our system prepares a candidate and his advisers to run and campaign for the presidency; but it does not usually bring to the surface those skills and people able to govern effectively— especially in the arena of foreign policy—once they have achieved the presidency. Both our presidents and their staffs tend to be woefully inexperienced and ill-prepared in foreign policy matters.

Moreover, the time frame in which a president can initiate major new policies is now woefully short. In the modern era, it is effectively limited to the first year of the president's term, to what is referred to as the "honeymoon" period. Only then, ordinarily, does the president have the popularity, the backing, the legitimacy conveyed by the election, and the freshness of a new administration to carry out his agenda. That is why President Reagan was so successful in his first year: he skillfully used his popularity, the media attention focused on him, and the newness of his ideas to get his program through Congress. He concentrated on a few issues—the economy, the defense buildup, restoring national strength—so as not to overload the congressional docket. His legislative accomplishments were impressive, comparable to those of Lyndon Johnson in 1965 and to Franklin Roosevelt during his "first hundred days." In contrast, Jimmy Carter did not take advantage of the opportunities afforded by his first year in office, managed to pass little significant legislation, and never again recovered the momentum to achieve a successful presidency.

But after the "window of opportunity" of that first year, a president's capacity to lead and dominate the system fades rapidly. The honeymoon ends; the window of opportunity closes. During a president's second year, the Congress is again preoccupied with its own reelection possibilities and unwilling to consider many new initiatives. By the third year, the newness of the president's agenda has worn off; in addition, it is usually the pattern that the president's party loses ground in the off-year election and, therefore, the coalition he had to get his program through during the first year begins to dissolve. By the fourth year, everyone (both in the Congress and in the White House) is again preoccupied with a new presidential election, and little can be expected to be accomplished. The wisdom of Washington, therefore, is that, if the president is not successful in getting his agenda through Congress during the first year, he is unlikely to be successful in later years.

THE POSTMODERN PRESIDENT

The difference between a modern and a postmodern president is that a postmodern president can no longer dominate the outside world the way an American president once could.[7] A postmodern president must not only be skillful in domestic politics, but he must be able to operate skillfully at the international level as well. If a postmodern president is not able to adapt and navigate in this international arena, then he is likely to fail at home as well as abroad. Even more than before, therefore, the skills needed to become president are not at all the skills needed to be president, especially in dealing with foreign affairs.

If Franklin Delano Roosevelt was the first modern president, then Jimmy Carter may be considered the first postmodern president. He was the first president to serve out a full term of office during a time of relative United States decline in the world, both economically and politically. By now we all know that the United States has lost its former position of dominance in the world, yet no other country has taken this position over and, among the world's powers, the United States is still ranked number one. But we have lost ground and our *relative* position in the world has declined. The United States is now much more *interdependent* with the rest of the world economically and politically, whereas before our position could be described as dominant. The postmodern president must learn to operate within this new framework of interdependence and make it work for us, rather than operate on a collision course with other countries of the world. Much as we might prefer to do that, the United States cannot go it alone in the world any more; and a skilled president will have to forge some new accommodations between our historic isolationism and this new interdependence.

The postmodern president must think how his policies will play not only in Peoria but also in Paris (the one in France, not in Illinois). No longer are economic and national security problems contained within national boundaries; because they are international, the United States has no choice but to cooperate as well as compete within the broader international system. To be successful in these new arenas, a postmodern president must not only maintain popular support at home but also be able to direct his policies to influence the international arena as well. Hence, a postmodern president must be able to do more than manipulate the power centers in Washington, D.C.; he must go international.

For good or ill, the standing of a postmodern president is as much influenced by international events as by domestic events. A postmodern president must be not just a national leader but a global one who is judged, perhaps preeminently, by his successes abroad. If the postmodern president cannot succeed on the global stage as well as the domestic, then he is likely to be judged a failure. Jimmy Carter's presidency came to grief on the shoals of his failed international policies—in Iran, in Central America, in dealing with the Soviet Union, and in his failure to begin adjusting the American economy to changed international economic conditions. Ronald Reagan was widely criticized for his Central America policies, and his economic policies have also been criticized strongly abroad (though remaining popular at home) because the United States is consuming far more than it produces and racking up enormous trade deficits. But the arms control agreement signed by Reagan and Soviet leader Mikhail Gorbachev is a positive example of world leadership by a postmodern president.

The postmodern president requires skills that most recent American presidents have lacked. Brilliance and eloquence are not required in a president—those abilities can often be found in the president's staff. But the presidency does require a person of honesty, firmness, pleasantness, sincerity, and level-headed common sense—precisely the skills needed today to run a moderate-sized company or a university. Along with these other traits, however, is now required some level of knowledge and experience in foreign affairs: living abroad for a time, studying other languages, serving with an agency (private or public) that does foreign affairs work, learning to empathize with another country or culture, even taking an introductory course in United States foreign policy. In this new interdependent era, those are also the skills that the head of a modern, multinational corporation requires. But few of our presidents, or our heads of companies, have had even these minimum-level skills.

Perhaps that is why both our foreign policy and our economy at the international level have not been overly successful in recent years. We have entered a postmodern or more interdependent era, but our leadership and political system are not yet attuned to thinking and operating in those terms. That is a very dangerous and potentially damaging situation for the United States to contemplate.

Notes

1. The analysis here and in succeeding paragraphs follows the discussion in James M. McCormick, *American Foreign Policy and American Values* (Itasca, Ill.: Peacock Publishers, 1985).
2. Aaron Wildawsky, "Two Presidencies," *Transaction* 3(December 1966).
3. The analysis here follows that of Frederick Hartmann and Robert L. Wendzel, *To Preserve the Republic* (New York: Macmillan, 1985).
4. Michael Shuman, "Dateline Main Street: Local Foreign Policies," *Foreign Policy* (Winter 1986):154–74.
5. Richard Neustadt, *Presidential Power* (New York: John Wiley & Sons, 1980).
6. James David Barber, *The Presidential Character,* 3rd ed. (Englewood Cliffs, N.J.: Prentice-Hall, 1985).
7. See the discussion in Richard Rose, *The Postmodern President: The White House Meets the World* (Chatham, N.J.: Chatham House Publishers, 1988).

Suggested Readings

Barber, James David. *The Presidential Character,* 3rd ed. Englewood Cliffs, N.J.: Prentice-Hall, 1985.

Cronin, Thomas. *The State of the Presidency,* 2nd ed. Boston: Little, Brown, 1980.

————, ed. *Rethinking the Presidency.* Boston: Little, Brown, 1982.

Destler, I.M. *Presidents, Bureaucrats, and Foreign Policy.* Princeton, N.J.: Princeton University Press, 1974.

Hunter, Robert E. *Presidential Control of Foreign Policy.* New York: Praeger, 1982.

Mueller, John. *War, Presidents, and Public Opinion.* New York: John Wiley & Sons, 1973.

Neustadt, Richard. *Presidential Power.* New York: John Wiley & Sons, 1980.

Reedy, George. *The Twilight of the Presidency.* New York: Mentor, 1970.

Rose, Richard. *The Postmodern President.* Chatham, N.J.: Chatham House Publishers, 1988.

Rossiter, Clinton. *The American Presidency.* New York: Harcourt, Brace, Jovanovich, 1960.

Schlesinger, Arthur M., Jr. *The Imperial President.* Boston: Houghton-Mifflin, 1973.

Wildavsky, Aaron (ed.). *Perspectives on the Presidency.* Boston: Little, Brown, 1975.

CHAPTER FOURTEEN

The National Security Council

✪
✪

The National Security Council (NSC) is an extension of the presidency. Located in the White House complex, the NSC consists of the president's own, personal, foreign affairs staff. The NSC is, hence, inseparable from the presidency and a reflection of it. A president can—and all recent presidents did so—change and shape it to suit his own plans and decision-making style. When we say, as we did in the previous chapter, that in choosing a modern-day president we are also voting for a staff, it is mainly the NSC staff of which we are speaking. Along with the presidency itself, the NSC lies at the narrowest end of our decision-making funnel; it is the innermost of the rings of concentric circles.

The National Security Council has become one of the key agencies —if not *the* key agency—in foreign policy-making. First, since it is located in the White House, presidents tend to rely on it more than they do on such farther away agencies as the State Department. Second, the president can appoint his own trusted advisers and loyalists to the NSC, again in contrast to the Department of State whose career foreign service officers are not always faithful to the elected president's program. The third reason the NSC has become such an important agency is that its organization is not elaborately detailed in the legislation that created it and, therefore, presidents can reorganize and restructure it to their liking in ways they cannot at State, DOD, or the CIA. Finally, we should say that professors like to write about the NSC and pay close attention to it because it is one of the few foreign policy agencies in Washington to which academics can hope, someday, to be appointed. The State Department, Defense, and so forth, are all career agencies that are attractive to work for in some ways but usually imply a lifetime commitment; the NSC, in contrast, often recruits academics with real expertise on an issue or area for positions that are shorter term, corresponding to the president's own tenure in office. A position on the NSC is, for an academic foreign policy specialist, about as high as one can go in the American system.

ORIGINS

The National Security Council came into being as a result of the National Security Act of 1947—that same monumental piece of legislation that created the Department of Defense, the Joint Chiefs of Staff, and the Central Intelligence Agency. The NSC was created as the cold war with the Soviet Union was heating up in Europe, when it was felt that American security and strategic policy needed to be better coordinated in the White House. The need for an NSC also grew out of the experience of World War II and the fact that during the war American military policy, diplomacy, and intelligence were not always coherent and needed better coordination.

There is a lot of confusion about the NSC and what it is, and we should get the terminology straight right at the beginning. Technically, the formal NSC consists only of the president, the vice-president, the secretary of state, the secretary of defense, and others whom the president may designate—usually that includes the director of the CIA, the ambassador to the United Nations, the chairman of the Joint Chiefs, and perhaps one or two others. While the NSC is thus a small, high-level, interagency decision-making group with specializations and a focus on national security, in actual practice the term *NSC* has come to mean the entire staff of the National Security Council. When people say they work for the NSC, therefore, they mean they work on the NSC staff, not that they are one of the legislatively designated members (cabinet level or above) of the NSC. The NSC has a director, called the national security advisor, who meets regularly with the president and who, by presidential designation, may be a member or sit in on meetings of the formal, interagency NSC. One other note here: the National Security Council should not be confused with the National Security Agency (NSA). While the NSC is located in the White House and provides foreign-policy advice to the president, the NSA is located at Fort Meade, halfway between Washington and Baltimore, and specializes in gathering information gleaned from worldwide radio bradcasts, telephone conversations, and diplomatic exchanges. Unfortunately for our clear understanding, both the National Security Agency and the director of the NSC, the national security adviser, use the same initials, NSA.

The National Security Council was originally created as a nonpolitical, nonpartisan, professional staff organization designed to coordinate foreign policy options for the president. As the legislation creating the NSC stated, its purpose was to "advise the president with respect to the integration of domestic, foreign, and military policies relating to national security." The NSC as originally conceived was thus to be an integrator and a coordinator, not an independent policymaker. Here was the problem: the president would get reams of advice, memos, and intelligence from the State Department, Defense, CIA, and other agencies. The volume of paper was becoming so immense that someone had to organize it, boil it down into digestible form, coordinate it, and present it to the president in terms of a clear set of policy options. None of the other agencies could do that because they often had a biased, bureaucratic interest in the outcome. Hence, the role of the NSC was to take all of this information from the several foreign policy agencies, integrate it, and put in a form that a too-busy president could deal with and make rational choices.

EARLY EXPERIENCES

President Harry S Truman was the first president to work under the newly created NSC machinery.[1] He viewed the NSC as chiefly an advisory agency, sat in on few of its meetings, and insisted that he himself would carry out the coordinating and synthesizing roles assigned to the NSC. Initially Truman himself implemented foreign policy through two very able secretaries of state, George Marshall and Dean Acheson, not through the NSC. This began to change with the beginning of the Korean war in 1951, however. From this point on, Truman attended *all* NSC meetings, increased its staff to twenty persons, and came to rely more and more on the NSC.

President Eisenhower, a former military general, viewed the NSC as basically a staff agency. He preferred a more formal and structured chain of command in the decision-making process, and he used the NSC accordingly. He wanted clear lines of authority and responsibility, with the NSC staff meeting and coordinating policy, arriving at a consensus, and then presenting its recommendations to the president for a final decision. Ike preferred not to get involved in the arguments over policy himself but to wait for the staff to complete all the work and *only then* to become involved. Robert Cutler, a Boston banker, was appointed to the post of Special Assistant to the President for National Security Affairs (head of the NSC staff); General Andrew Goodpaster also served as the president's staff aide. The size of the NSC rose to twenty-eight in 1955.

The Eisenhower system is generally considered a model of how the NSC ought to work. It remained nonpolitical, nor did the national security adviser seek to become a visible personality, a media star, or a rival to the secretary of state. The Eisenhower NSC strictly separated NSC planning from implementation, which was wisely left to other agencies. The NSC saw its role as not to make policy but to coordinate the analyses and recommendations coming to the president from other departments, and to present the options to the president neutrally and without bias. The Eisenhower NSC system was not without its problems, including the preparations of position papers that were sometimes obsolete by the time they were finished; recommendations to the president that were so watered down (Ike made a point of reading only one-page memos) that they suffered from oversimplification; and the fact that Eisenhower's secretary of state, John Foster Dulles, frequently bypassed the NSC and carried out his own foreign policy without coordinating it with other agencies. But having served extensively in Europe during the war, Ike was a diplomat as well as a soldier. He knew and understood foreign affairs, and his system of foreign policy decision making—with the NSC staff doing all the preparatory work and the president making the final decisions—worked quite smoothly and well.

POLITICIZING THE NSC

Under President Kennedy some major changes were introduced into the NSC. Kennedy distrusted the State Department and was also unhappy with the CIA because he felt it had led him astray in recommending the disastrous Bay of Pigs invasion of Cuba. He therefore preferred to rely on the NSC as his main foreign policy advisory agency. McGeorge Bundy, a Harvard dean and part of the Kennedy political entourage, was appointed as national security advisor. Bundy was a *political* adviser to the president as well as the person responsible for carrying out the NSC function of presenting options. In this way, the tasks of advising, coordinating, and also implementing policy out of the White House began to be merged.

In addition, because of the president's distrust of the State Department, the NSC doubled in size under Kennedy and became a miniature Department of State with staff persons appointed for every geographic area (Europe, Latin America, etc.) as well as functional issues (military affairs, strategic planning, and so forth). Every office and function performed at State were now repeated separately at the NSC. These changes served to diminish the power of the State Department and to vastly increase the concentration of foreign policy decision making in the White House. Kennedy came to rely more on the NSC for advice (including political advice) than on the regular foreign policy agencies; he also bypassed both State and the CIA by relying on friends, relatives, and a number of academics who had a political connection with the White House.

It must be said that, even with this politicization of the NSC, the merging of functions, and the bypassing of State, the NSC under Bundy functioned quite well. Bundy now became a spokesman for the president's foreign policies (unlikely his largely anonymous predecessors), but he was consistently careful to clear these statements beforehand with Secretary of State Dean Rusk. As the NSC became more activist and more politicized, its neutral, policy-coordinating functions diminished; but Bundy was careful to present the different viewpoints fairly to the president and to avoid a strictly partisan stance. Nor did Bundy engage in any power grabs or seek to embarrass and ignore the secretary of state. It is the consensus of foreign policy analysts that it was Kennedy who politicized the NSC, that Bundy handled these broader responsibilities well, and that the growing flaws in the system became apparent only later on.

It was under Lyndon Johnson that these growing defects in the NSC system became most visible. First, Johnson distrusted not just the State Department as his predecessor had done but also the NSC, which he viewed as staffed by "Kennedy men." So he bypassed the NSC, preferring to make decisions through what was called the "Tuesday Lunch Bunch," which consisted of Secretary of State Rusk, Secretary of Defense Robert McNamara, National Security Adviser Bundy (until 1966, then economic historian W. W. Rostow took over), the CIA director, the chairman of the Joint Chiefs of Staff, and the president's press secretary. The inclusion of the press secretary in this group guaranteed that the advice the president received would be considered, more than before, in the light of its political implications—another step in the politicization of national security policy. In addition, the members of the Tuesday Lunch Bunch all generally shared the same assumptions about United States policy (especially regarding Vietnam), were not always open to other points of view, and closed off the possibilities for alternative policy viewpoints.

While largely ignoring the NSC in practice, Johnson did reorganize it in ways that would become more important later on under Kissinger. Johnson created within the NSC a permanent Senior Interdepartmental Group (SIG) chaired by the undersecretary of state, which was supposed to include members from each of the several foreign policy agencies and to better coordinate policy among them. Below the SIG were a number of Interdepartmental Regional Groups (IRGs) chaired by the appropriate assistant secretaries of state, and again aimed at better coordination of policy among the several agencies by incorporating members of those agencies in the IRGs. The system was formally put in place, but it largely failed to operate under Johnson. The president, preoccupied with Vietnam and his own reelection possibilities for 1968, preferred his Lunch Bunch, and the NSC reforms were never implemented.

Not only did the NSC not play a major role under Johnson, it was reduced to near impotence. At the same time, the flaws in the system that had been introduced during the Kennedy administration but kept within bounds now became manifest. The NSC was more and more politicized, no longer presenting alternative policy options but simply reinforcing Johnson's already strongly held conclusions. His later NSC adviser, Rostow, was also more ideological than Bundy and may have committed the cardinal NSC sin of coloring the advice that the president received in accord with his own strongly felt views (although other sources deny that was the case). In any event, the NSC under Johnson went into a period of institutional decay and atrophy.

THE KISSINGER SYSTEM

With the election of Richard Nixon in 1968, the NSC was reorganized once more, and an entirely new "model" of the NSC came into existence. Nixon appointed Henry Kissinger, one of the country's preeminent academic foreign policy analysts, to the position of national security adviser. Kissinger proved to be an adept bureaucratic infighter who quickly learned the ways of Washington and how to operate there to maximum advantage. Kissinger saw himself as a lone ranger, operating (with Nixon who, despite the later debacle of Watergate, was also a shrewd foreign policy analyst) as a one-man show. Neither Nixon nor Kissinger had any use for the State Department, and they were agreed in wanting to concentrate virtually all foreign policy decision making in the White House. The Nixon-Kissinger team proved enormously effective, and they certainly changed the way American foreign policy was conducted.

We now have the virtually complete politicization of the NSC and the virtually complete eclipse of the State Department, then led by the hapless and ineffectual William P. Rogers. No longer was the NSC neutral or a mere coordinator; no longer did it even try to separate its synthesizing and integrating roles from its political and implementing ones. Every policy paper and recommendation now had to be filtered through Kissinger. No cabinet secretary had access to Nixon on any foreign policy issue without Kissinger also being in on the meeting. All memos from the separate departments had to be channeled through the NSC, where Kissinger would attach a cover letter containing his own interpretations and recommendations.

Kissinger also went public in a big way and in a style that no other NSC head ever had: he was a highly visible fixture on the Washington social circuit, he held press conferences and briefings, he spoke for the president, and he was the president's chief agent and implementer. Kissinger arranged the opening to China, conducted negotiations on the Middle East, worked out the arrangements for detente with the Soviet Union, and negotiated the end of the Vietnam war—all *implementing* as distinct from *coordinating* functions. There was no fragmentation of policy-making in this administration as Nixon and Kissinger kept everything to themselves, spoke with one voice, and conducted a strong, forceful, coherent foreign policy. For the first time, the NSC adviser became both more visible and more powerful than the secretary of state.

Kissinger also introduced broad structural changes within the NSC. He created seven main NSC subcommittees: the Senior Review Committee (SRG—Johnson's old SIG, a key policy-making body), the Undersecretaries Committee (USC), the National Security Council Intelligence Committee (NSCIC, which provided assistance to the several American intelligence agencies), the 40 Committee (which oversaw covert action), the Verification Panel (which maintained arms control), the Washington Special Action Group (WSAG, which handled crisis management), and the Defense Program Review Committee (DPRC, which kept an eye on the defense budget). *All* of these committees were chaired by Kissinger or his designated assistants—none by the State Department, as had been the system under Johnson.

To run the office and this growing activity, Kissinger brought into the NSC the ablest people he could find from all areas of the government, increased the size of the NSC by 50 percent, and made it into a prestigious agency—*the* center of American foreign policy-making, with Kissinger himself as the star. The NSC subcommittees and the Interdepartmental Groups (IGs, at the assistant secretary level) helped rationalize United States foreign policy and made it far more efficient, enabling the NSC to tap the views of the several departments and—in accord with its original mandate—to coordinate foreign policy and present options to the president for his decisions.

This system also had its flaws. By 1970-71, Nixon and Kissinger were conducting a two-man foreign policy, and the elaborate subcommittee system was more and more ignored. The State Department bitterly resented, in addition, that it was always being cut out of decision making. Furthermore, the fact that Kissinger had become something of a media star was beneficial to American foreign policy in some ways (it generated publicity for the issues), but the hype involved and the publicity became, for many people, too much. In addition, Kissinger himself, while a brilliant analyst and a tremendously stimulating intellect, was also a difficult taskmaster who not only wore out his associates but also got into some terrible public battles and court cases with some of them. The Nixon-Kissinger model was an innovative and effective one, providing probably the most creative period in American foreign policy since the 1940s; but it was really a one- (or two-) man show that was heavily dependent on Kissinger and likely could not survive him.

In the fall of 1973, Kissinger was named by Nixon to be secretary of state, replacing Rogers. He was now both national security adviser and secretary of state. At the NSC, Kissinger kept in place his old staff, which he continued to direct. He also now had the honored position of secretary of state, a position he controlled de facto even while he was at the NSC. Little changed under this new arrangement, since Nixon and Kissinger continued to run a two-man foreign policy. But in the meantime, the Nixon administration began to be caught up in the Watergate scandal, which eventually forced Nixon to resign, paralyzed the United States government (including its foreign policy), and cast a dark cloud over the earlier foreign policy accomplishments of the administration.

After Gerald Ford took over in 1974, not much changed at the NSC. Kissinger continued as secretary of state, despite rising hostility toward him on the part of both liberals and the conservative wing of the Republican Party, which did not like his policy of detente with the Soviet Union. Ford, like his predecessors, reorganized the subcommittee system of the NSC but did not change its fundamental structure. In November 1975, Ford appointed Brent Scowcroft as national security adviser, although Kissinger kept his other hat as secretary of state.

The brief Scowcroft era (1975–76) is sometimes seen as an attempt to return, after the flamboyant Kissinger period, to the neutral, coordination NSC model of the Eisenhower era. It was—and it wasn't. While Scowcroft, a general, was a quiet, efficient, self-effacing manager and coordinator, he was widely viewed as "Kissinger's man" at the NSC. Not only had he earlier served as Kissinger's NSC deputy, but Kissinger himself was still functioning as secretary of state, from which position he also kept a firm hand in at the NSC. So only in a very limited sense could we say that the Eisenhower model had been revived, for the dynamic Kissinger continued to be the dominant voice in foreign policy—including at the NSC. Later, the self-effacing Scowcroft was again chosen to lead the NSC by Bush.

POLICY FRAGMENTATION

Jimmy Carter (1977–81) sought to change the Kissinger system. Reacting against the Kissinger model, he wanted a national security adviser who would be more low key, providing coordination and advice but not operating as the chief policy architect and implementer as Kissinger had. Carter also intended to restore the prestige and power of the secretary of state and to make him the chief spokesman on foreign policy. Carter reduced the number of NSC committees, although the changes were largely on paper, with the NSC system continuing to function much as before. Moreover, like his predecessors, Carter sought at times to bypass the NSC and had regular Thursday working lunches with his secretaries of state and defense as well as his NSA, and also Friday morning planning sessions with the same group as well as Vice-President Walter Mondale.

Few of the changes introduced by Carter worked very well, and the result was the greatest fragmentation and lack of coordination of United States foreign policy-making since World War II—precisely what the NSC system had been designed to overcome in the first place. First, Zbigniew Brzezinski, Carter's national security adviser, was certainly not low key, nor was he content to play the role of a "mere" coordinator of policy. He was a rival of Kissinger from twenty years before at Harvard, and he wanted to be the same kind of highly visible and glamorous presence that Kissinger had been. Second, Secretary of State Cyrus Vance, who was supposed to be Carter's "main voice" on foreign policy, turned out to be diffident and so soft-spoken as to be almost inaudible—not what you want in a "main voice." Carter wanted to rely on Vance but he liked Brzezinski and came to rely on him more and more, as Carter's early romantic foreign policy positions gradually gave way to his adviser's *realpolitik*.

The third problem was the personality and character of Carter himself: idealistic, unable to delegate authority, unable or unwilling to build political coalitions for his policies, and unable to make clear to the public or even to his own advisers what it was that he wanted. Fourth, Carter had allowed his cabinet secretaries to pick their own assistant secretaries without coordinating these appointments through the White House, a process that resulted in some pretty far-out people coming into the adminstration, people who had strong ideological views, refused to subordinate their own ideas to those of the larger team, and did not know when to shut up. The result was that the administration all too often spoke with a cacophony of voices; the State Department was constantly at war with the NSC (or vice versa); no one knew what the policy was; the president could not clarify matters or enforce discipline; and United States policy began to come apart at the seams.

Ronald Reagan took office in 1981 determined to reassert strong leadership over foreign policy. He and his advisers in the 1980 campaign believed that Carter had been a weak and ineffectual leader, and they were determined to reverse the Carter policies. To accomplish these purposes they put forth an agenda that had three main goals—goals that by this time seem terribly familiar since each new administration has promised almost exactly the same things:

1. The administration would speak with one voice on foreign policy.
2. The secretary of state would be the chief foreign policy spokesman.
3. The NSC would return to the Eisenhower model.

But in practice, none of these goals worked out very well. The administration, to ensure a single voice on foreign policy, was very careful to recruit to the NSC staff only persons who were known to be loyal to the president's ideological agenda. While ideological consistency was achieved, that sometimes came at the cost of quality and pragmatism; and in terms of talent and ability, the Reagan NSC staff was thought to be the weakest in its history. As regards the second promise, the administration wanted the secretary of state to be its chief spokesman, but the person named, Alexander Haig, proved to be overly ambitious, preoccupied with his place and position, insecure, not very effective, and unable to get along with other administration personnel. The last criterion—a neutral, Eisenhower-like NSC adviser—did not work out either. The person named, Richard Allen, did not have sufficient intellectual stature, ran afoul of Nancy Reagan, failed to work well with the rest of the president's White House team, and was soon forced to resign. Allen had tried to manage the NSC on the Eisenhower model, but his position was relegated to such unimportance that he was not allowed to see Reagan unless Edwin Meese or another of the president's "troika" of advisers (Baker or Deaver) were also there. Nor was Reagan well informed on foreign policy issues as Eisenhower had been—the sine qua non for making the "Eisenhower model" work.

The system soon began falling apart. Haig resigned after a year and a half. Allen had also been forced out, replaced by Reagan's friend and political confidant, William Clark, who knew absolutely nothing about foreign affairs. The NSC, hence, became more politicized. Meanwhile, the more ideological supporters of the president, who were dominant in the early months, were gradually shunted aside in favor of career specialists and professionals—producing some epic battles between what was called Team A (ideologues) and Team B (pragmatists). At the same time Reagan, although holding deeply felt ideological beliefs, remained generally aloof and disengaged from the process. Reagan did not make clear decisions, and his own staff had little or no clear sense of where the president stood on many issues. Plus Reagan, like many of his predecessors, knew very little about foreign affairs. He had strong feelings and some good instincts, but he knew almost nothing about strategy, tactics, or conceptual design.

The result was that the NSC under Reagan represented the worst of all possible worlds. We can have either an NSC where the staff provides options and the president decides (the Eisenhower model) or one where the NSC under able leadership takes the lead (the Kissinger model). For the Eisenhower model to work, it requires not just a neutral NSC but a president who is engaged, knows foreign policy, and makes decisions—as Ike did. For the Kissinger model to work, it requires a very able NSC staff and a dynamic national security adviser (Kissinger) to bring it off. But Reagan neither had a talented NSC nor was the president himself clearheaded and well informed on foreign policy, as Truman, Eisenhower, and Nixon had been. The result was a new round of foreign policy incoherence and failure, grumbling, and even fights among the president's advisers, and a process of fragmentation that was worse than anything anyone had seen before—worse even than Carter's.

While Reagan's overall foreign policy accomplishments—the reestablishment of American military strength, restored national self-confidence, a strong economy, new agreements with the Soviet Union—were significant, his NSC system was not working very well. Eventually some order began to emerge out of this chaos. When George Shultz replaced Haig as secretary of state, the entire American foreign policymaking structure calmed down a little—although the intense rivalries between the Reagan ideologues and Shultz's State Department continued. The next two NSC advisers, Robert McFarlane and John Poindexter, both military officers and "technocrats," were faceless coordinators and admin-

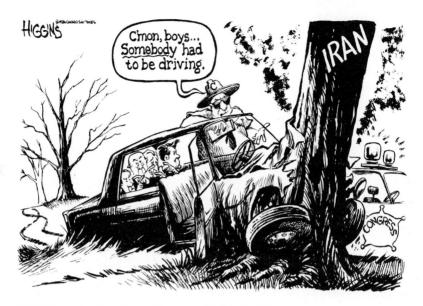

© 1986 Chicago Sun Times. Reprinted courtesy of Chicago Sun Times.

istrators in the mold of the Eisenhower system; but "coordination" in that context meant largely deferring to Shultz's State Department on policy matters—including the shoving aside of the last of the Allen-appointed Reagan stalwarts in favor of State Department personnel. That step meant that State Department foreign service officers now dominated not only in their own agency but also at the NSC, where their role often went beyond that of "neutral referee."

But McFarlane and Poindexter, in trying by some inappropriate means to circumvent the creeping paralysis and sclerosis of the American political gridlock, also went way beyond the coordination roles of the NSC, got involved in trying to implement policy, saw their careers in government ruined by their involvement in the Iran-Contra scandal, and were forced to leave the NSC. Frank Carlucci, a savvy bureaucrat with wide experience at the highest levels of the United States government, then took over, began to reform and restructure the NSC, and got the NSC out of action policies that properly belonged with other agencies. Carlucci soon was named secretary of defense and, at the NSC his deputy, General Colin Powell, became national security adviser. Under this team (unfortunately very late in Reagan's term), with Shultz at State, Carlucci at Defense, and Powell at the NSC, the system finally began functioning in the neutral, pragmatic, coherent way that was the designers' original intention. With Scowcroft back at the NSC, James Baker at State, and former congressman Richard Cheney at Defense, President Bush offered the promise of continuing on such a pragmatic course.

IMPROVING THE SYSTEM

What then does one make of the NSC system, this high-level agency at the pinnacle of American foreign policy-making? And can its performance be improved?

First, the quality of the staff needs to be upgraded. This is no place for amateurism or loyalty in lieu of competence. Too many low-level NSC staff are chosen on the basis of personal or political connections, in the absence of knowledge and experience. Often NSC personnel know little of the area to which they are assigned responsibility, do not know the language or culture, lack experience in the area, and similarly have little prior experience in American foreign policy-making. The result is numerous mistakes and some quite awful disasters. While political loyalty to the administration in power is important, surely it is possible to find persons in this vast country who are both politically loyal *and* competent. And while youthful vigor and brightness are valuable, experience and a solid background are also critical. Appointments to the NSC need to be better than they have been.

The second concluding comment concerns the NSC structure. Three models have been set forth: the neutral referee (Eisenhower) model, which works if the president is himself well-informed; the activist (Kissinger) model, which can work if the president is or is not well-informed as long as the NSC adviser is super-powerful; or the (early) Reagan system which combined a weak, neutral NSC with an uninformed, unengaged president. Every president has tried to tinker with the structure of the NSC. But, of course, in such a small (but highly influential) body as the NSC, it is not always the precise structure that is critical but rather the interpersonal relations between the president and his NSC team. Structure counts, as reflected in the more elaborate interagency committee system that the NSC has evolved over the years, but perhaps equally important is the chemistry between the individuals—chiefly the president and his national security adviser—involved.

As a result, third, there is no one single answer to the question of the proper structure of the NSC. The Eisenhower model can work in some circumstances and the Kissinger model in others, or there can be new hybrids of these two. Organizationally, we do not have a final solution to the issue of the best system to provide coherence and continuity to our foreign policy. It really does come down in considerable part to chemistry, interpersonal relations, and the personalities of the individuals involved. That is not a very satisfactory answer, but it does reflect the realities of the situation. It depends . . .

In the final analysis, the national security adviser has to be a neutral referee among the contending bureaucratic agencies in our foreign policy, and he has to be able to present these views fairly to the president. But the modern NSA also needs to have stature and knowledge of his own, to present his own staff-researched and duly considered recommendations to the president in ways that go beyond the neutral referee model. He also needs the skills to explain these policies to the media and the public, to conceptualize them within the broader context of overall American foreign policy, and to be a clever politician (in the best sense of that term) and bureaucrat who knows how to get things done in Washington—where the levers are and how to use them. Finally, he may need, given the foreign policy inexperience of most of our presidents, to educate the president to keep him from making mistakes and going off in wrong directions.

It is a daunting set of skills and tasks. Unfortunately, we have seldom in recent years found the set of political, intellectual, and bureaucratic talents—or the personalities—to make the system function effectively. President Bush's administration offered promise in these regards, but we shall simply have to wait and see how successful the Bush foreign policy system proves to be.

Notes

1. The discussion in this section follows the outline and history provided in Frederick Hartmann and Robert Wendzel, *To Preserve the Republic* (New York: Macmillan, 1985).

Suggested Readings

Bock, Joseph. *The White House Staff and the Security Assistant.* Westport, Conn.: Greenwood Press, 1987.

Brzezinski, Zbigniew. *Power and Principle.* New York: Farrar, Strauss & Giroux, 1983.

Destler, I. M. "National Security Advice to U.S. Presidents: Some Lessons from Thirty Years," *World Politics,* 29 (January 1977): 143–76.

————; Leslie H. Gelb; and Anthony Lake. *Our Own Worst Enemy: The Unmaking of American Foreign Policy.* New York: Simon & Schuster, 1984.

Henderson, Philip. "Organizing the Presidency for Effective Leadership: Lessons from the Eisenhower Years." *Presidential Studies Quarterly* 17 (Winter 1987).

Hess, Stephen. *Organizing the Presidency.* Washington, D.C.: Brookings Institution, 1976.

Kissinger, Henry. *White House Years.* Boston: Little, Brown, 1979.

Menges, Constantine. *Inside the National Security Council.* New York: Simon & Schuster, 1988.

Sorenson, Theodore. *Decision-making in the White House.* New York: Columbia University Press, 1963.

CHAPTER FIFTEEN

Conclusion

✹
✹

Over the years, and especially during and since Vietnam, the United States has become much more divided and fragmented over foreign policy issues than was the case before. Our two main political parties, the Congress and the White House, and pundits and individual citizens are frequently at loggerheads over Central America, southern Africa, and the proper course of United States-Soviet relations. The conflict has frequently been so intense that it produces paralysis, the inability to make or carry out any decisions at all, what people caught in hopeless traffic snarls call gridlock.

American foreign policy has become a veritable kaleidoscope of shifting political forces, groups, and interests—so many of them going in so many separate directions that one has difficulty keeping track of them all. Nor is it easy anymore for a president—any president—to weld a coherent, sensible foreign policy out of the myriad of actors and voices now participating in the foreign policy arena. The image that comes to mind is of numerous planets or even whole galaxies of interests and pressures out there in the universe that is American foreign policy, planets that are increasingly spinning out of orbit with little sense of gravity or attachment to a central core. The sheer numbers of these groups and their strongly felt views have served to paralyze our foreign policy in many instances and to render it all but unworkable.

The causes of this growing paralysis creeping in our foreign policy-making are many. The frustrating Vietnam war was certainly one major cause, sapping our self-confidence and provoking a heated debate every time the United States contemplated energetic action abroad. The perpetuation of divided government, with the Congress under the control of one party and the White House dominated by the other, was another major cause. Then, too, the parties themselves have become more divided and more ideological over foreign policy issues than ever before. Plain old incompetence and lack of knowledge in both the executive and the legislative branches have also been important factors in our foreign policy difficulties.

The rise of single-issue interest groups, and stronger assertiveness, including over foreign policy issues, on the part of ethnic and racial groups constitute another set of factors explaining our divisiveness and the shrillness of our debates. The media's insertion into the foreign policy arena, not just as neutral reporters of events abroad but as goads and (oftentimes) biased participants, has added another element of fragmentation. At the level of the general public we have lost our consensus over foreign policy issues, making it virtually impossible anymore to construct a bipartisan foreign policy. The bureaucratic politics, rivalries, and turf battles between the often-contending foreign policy agencies of the United States government add a further divisive factor. Mean and nasty debates on college and university campuses, competing think tanks organized along ideological lines, activist church groups intent on making political statements rather than saving souls—all these and other factors have added to the intensity and the partisanship of our debates, and to our foreign policy paralysis.

Power in the American political system is now more diffuse and divided than ever before. Power is not only more divided but it is also more elusive and difficult for even a president to mobilize. There are more players in the foreign policy "game" than ever before, including the general public and public opinion, which are similarly divided. America has lacked cohesion and a sense of common purpose in the last two decades. There is too much deadlock and not enough unity and working together. The gridlock and divisiveness that affects the public as well as our governmental institutions are causing our whole political system and decision making to be quasi-paralyzed and ineffective.

These comments imply that the roots of our divisions are deep and will not easily be removed or overcome. Such fissures will not be closed by the simple act of electing a new president, reforming the Congress, or tinkering with the bureaucratic machinery. Instead, the reason our foreign policy is quasi-paralyzed and often ineffective is because we ourselves, as a nation and as a people, are much more confused, uncertain, and divided than we used to be over foreign policy matters. We are unsure whether to act forcefully or with restraint in the Third World; how to deal with the changes in the Soviet Union and Eastern Europe; how to redefine our relationships with our now stronger and more independent allies; whether our foreign policy should necessarily be morally based (democracy and human rights) or be purely in defense of our national interests; and how to adjust to our changed, somewhat diminished economic situation in the world. Until we as a nation are agreed on some of these matters, we should not expect our political institutions, which, in a democracy, ultimately reflect the national will, to exhibit a unity that we ourselves lack. The reason our foreign policy is divided and fragmented is because we our-selves as a nation are often divided and fragmented. "The fault," as Shakespeare wrote in *Julius Caesar,* "is not in our stars, but in ourselves." So until, if ever, we reach a consensus nationally on foreign policy goals, we cannot expect our political institutions and leadership to be much more clearheaded and decisive than we ourselves are.

Even with paralysis and confusion all around, it is nothing short of remarkable that we still manage on many issues and in many areas to carry out an effective foreign policy. First, crises tend to force us to act decisively and to cut through all the barriers. When Lyndon Johnson sent the troops to the Dominican Republic in 1965 or when Reagan sent the fleet to the Persian Gulf, they did so without being encumbered by "bureaucratic politics" or other constraints. They simply acted. Only in hindsight did some question the wisdom of these actions, but that was after the fact of presidential action, not before. In genuine crises it is clear that the United States can and does act decisively. It may be, in fact, that the fragmentation and divisiveness of which we have spoken is in part a reflection of the luxury of not in recent decades having to face a severe national crisis. Crises like World War II tend to bring things into sharp focus very quickly; in contrast, divisiveness is often a product of peaceful and affluent times.

A second point to remember is that on many issues we are not deeply divided and do have an effective foreign policy. With regard to the People's Republic of China, for example, we have over the last two decades followed a shrewd, sensible policy that has generally enjoyed bipartisan support. The brutal suppression of the Chinese student protests in the summer of 1989 evoked consternation in the U.S. but is unlikely to result in basic policy changes toward China. Our relations with our NATO allies and with Canada, Australia, and Japan, despite some occasional flaps that in the normal course of things are to be expected, are generally good, sensible, and prudent. Relations with most of the larger countries of Africa, the Middle East, and South America are also quite decent and even maturing. Of course on some issues there will continue to be differences between Washington and Brasilia or Cairo regardless of who is in power in these capitals because as nations we have somewhat different interests. Such differences are, again, normal and to be expected, but they do not mean we have bad relations with very many of these countries. Even on Soviet relations there seems to be considerable agreement that we should con-tinue to deal with the Soviets from a position of strength while also seeking peace and agreements to reduce the threat of nuclear weapons, and that we should be hopeful but watchful and vigilant about the changes taking place there.

That leaves relatively few areas that are genuinely controversial and divisive. Southern Africa is one of these; Central America is another. With the 1988 agreement calling for both Cuba and South Africa to pull their military forces out of Angola, a part of the southern Africa problem is being resolved—but not the troubling issue of what to do about South Africa's apartheid regime. United States policy toward El Salvador and Nicaragua has also been divisive, although perhaps less so now than in the early-to-mid-1980s. In part these areas have been controversial because they relate to domestic concerns (human rights and racial prejudice), in part because the stakes are relatively low (as compared with Soviet, Middle East, NATO, or Japan relations), and in part because there are so few domestic costs (few South Africans, Nicaraguans, or El Salvadorans vote or have political clout in the United States) that politicians and others can afford to say extreme things about these countries that they would not dream of saying about more important or dangerous ones. Perhaps, then, our foreign policy divisiveness, fragmentation, and gridlock, limited as they are to certain issues and areas, are not so extensive or so severe as they sometimes are portrayed in the media.

A third consideration concerning the divisiveness issue is that not all such divisiveness and debate are bad. The fact is we *are* divided over what to do about Nicaragua, and that has been reflected in our domestic policy debate. Moreover, out of this debate, which is after all what democracy is all about, has often come a more effective and acceptable policy. For example on El Salvador, even though the debate in the early 1980s was often shrill, polarized, and exaggerated, out of that debate came a policy that was more sensible and prudent. There is no doubt that the efforts and opposition of the Congress, the press, the human rights groups, and others did help pull Reagan administration policy toward El Salvador back toward the center. Those same groups helped force the administration to move away from a predominantly military solution to Central America's manifest problems and toward a more defensible emphasis on economic aid, democracy, human rights, *as well as* the strategic considerations. What often seems chaotic and divisive may in fact be the normal workings of the democratic process.

But this suggestion can only carry us so far in our understanding. To the extent that the democratic process does in fact lead to better, saner policies, we can all applaud. In actuality, however, our divisiveness as a nation has gone beyond merely democratic give-and-take. It involves unprecedented nastiness and bitterness on some issues, guerrilla strategies practiced by some groups, efforts to subvert the president's policies by some elements and to destroy the opposition by others. It involves sneak attacks, massive leaks of secret documents, the politics of confrontation, lying, deceit, and so forth. These activities not only go beyond the pale but they serve to undermine democracy rather than strengthen it. It would be pleasant to conclude that all our divisions, fragmentation, polarization, and gridlock of recent years were just the workings of the democratic process; but unfortunately that is not the case. Democracy does work to improve our foreign policy, but what we in the United States have been practicing in recent years has often come closer to guerrilla theater rather than democracy.

The Bush administration began in 1989 with the hope that it could reduce the polarization and maybe even pursue a bipartisan foreign policy. Bush is an experienced person in foreign policy matters—more so than any recent president since Nixon. His cabinet and staff appointments consisted mostly of moderates and centrists, persons from the mainstreams and the center, from the Washington foreign policy establishment. They were experienced pragmatists, not ideologues. Moreover, Bush himself is not intensely ideological as his two predecessors were. His style is to look for workable solutions, not confrontation and polarization. And, despite the rancor and bitterness of the 1988 presidential election campaign, a spirit of working together was in the air. At least during the time between Bush's election and his actual inauguration as president, people seemed inclined to give him the benefit of the doubt. In this comparatively calm transition period before Bush's swearing in, people in Washington joked that it was like a modern marriage: the honeymoon came before the marriage—and may have been the only good part!

For Bush faced formidable obstacles. We need therefore to go beyond the good wishes that people expressed for Bush at the beginning and look at the hard realities. The hard realities are that Bush faces budgetary gridlock as well as foreign policy gridlock, with the result likely to be a possible financial crisis, conflict with the Congress over this, and a host of pressing economic dilemmas, both domestic and foreign. In addition, because of the mean spirit of the election campaign, a lot of Democratic knives are out for Bush, hoping to embarrass him early and pave the way for a Democratic victory in 1992. Bush's electoral margin was thin, he does not have deep or widespread public support, he lacks Reagan's charisma, and his electoral mandate is uncertain. Congress remains in the hands of the Democrats and the number of Democratic seats is larger than it was under Reagan. Most governorships and state houses are in the hands of the Democratic party—and all of these persons would love to have their party win the White House next time.

The hard reality is that success in governing is not a matter of goodwill but a function of the number of seats in Congress held by the president's party. When one party controls both the executive and legislative branches, the success rate for a president's legislative agenda is never below 75 percent. But when both houses of Congress are in the hands of the opposite party, as at present, a president's success rate is almost certain to be below 50 percent. Bush wants to proceed with his agenda, but the Democrats seem almost to be daring him to run the country without them. Hence the possibilities for more conflict and confrontation are strong. In addition, there are those other interest groups and lobbies out there, whose reactions to Bush are not of the same ugly, visceral sort sometimes exhibited toward Reagan, but who would like to "get" Bush nonetheless and undermine his presidency. This is not democratic politics but the politics of destruction. As Senate Democratic majority leader George Mitchell put it, "Divided government cannot work in a polarized society, one in which mistrust and deceit are widespread."

So what should we as citizens who want a decent and sensible foreign policy do? The answer is that there is not all that much we can do. We can seek to turn down the decibel rate of our political discourse somewhat, we can demand reasonable and prudent policies from our politicians, and we should remain skeptical and suspicious of special interest groups that have a private agenda that they are pursuing, a special ax to grind. We should be suspicious of the ideological and partisan posturing of the political parties, skeptical of what we see on television, skeptical of ideologues of all kinds, including those in office and those on college campuses. We need to elect solid, sensible people to public office and then be on guard to see that, once in office, they stay solid and sensible. And we can demand responsible foreign policy positions from our leaders, not policies designed merely to score political points or to gain partisan advantage. We should insist that these leaders build on the solid consensus that does exist in the country on most issues, even on such controversial matters as Central America where there is considerable agreement waiting to be pulled together into a coherent policy.

But when all is said and done, there remains little that we as individual citizens can do to change the system in its basic fundamentals. We cannot much change the way the Congress operates, or much affect the bureaucratic rivalries between the several departments, or change the way the State or Defense departments operate, or alter the way the media covers the news, or cut out partisan politics from our foreign policy discussions. Over the long term some of these things can be changed in modest ways, but not in the short term and certainly not all that much. The result is that we are pretty much left with working with and through the system we have which, despite all its faults, can be made to function effectively.

After all, the broader political process in America returned Jimmy Carter to the center from an early left-wing position, and that same political process returned Ronald Reagan to the center from a right-wing position. Moreover, in officials like Robert Strauss, Joseph Califano, George Shultz, James Baker, Brent Scowcroft, and many others, we have some very able people who understand electoral politics, know how to make the system work, how to weld compromises between the executive and legislative branches, how to deal with the media, how to play the bureaucratic politics game effectively, how to get things done. Such actions require talented people of enormous skill and learning, and with a love and flair for the process. But America is full of young, able, skillful, dedicated persons like that; let us hope that more of them emerge to staff our many needed foreign policy positions.

Suggested Readings

Burns, James McGregor. *The Deadlock of Democracy.* Englewood Cliffs, N.J.: Prentice Hall, 1967.

Destler, I. M.; Leslie H. Gelb; and Anthony Lake. *Our Own Worst Enemy: The Unmaking of American Foreign Policy.* New York: Simon & Schuster, 1984.

Wiarda, Howard J. *In Search of Policy: The United States and Latin America.* Washington, D.C.: The American Enterprise Institute for Public Policy Research, 1984.

———. *Finding Our Way? Toward Maturity in U.S.-Latin American Relations.* Washington, D.C.: American Enterprise Institute, 1987.

Index